MAPS AND PLANS

David Smith

MAPS AND PLANS

For the Local Historian and Collector

A guide to types of maps of the British Isles
produced before 1914 valuable to local and other historians
and mostly available to collectors

B.T. Batsford Ltd · London

© David Smith 1988
First published 1988

ISBN 0 7134 5191 2

Typeset by Servis Filmsetting Ltd, Manchester
and printed by
Anchor Brendon Ltd
Tiptree, Essex
for the publishers
B.T. Batsford Ltd
4 Fitzhardinge Street
London
W1H 0AH

For Chris, Dave, Gill, Hermione, Jason, John, Maureen, Mo, and Stuart.

'Before we present you the matters of fact, it is fit to offer to your view the Stage whereon they were acted, for as Geography without History seemeth a carkasse without motion, so History without Geography, wandreth as a Vagrant without a certaine habitation.'

Captain John Smith, 1624.

'To the antiquarians of the 25th century I hope the map will be useful as affording them an opportunity of determining the positions of many places in the County of which the devouring hand of time may not, perhaps, have left the last vestige remaining.'

Joseph Lindley & William Crosley: *Memoir of a Map of the County of Surrey, from a Survey Made in the Years 1789 and 1790* (1793)

'History is exceedingly difficult to follow without maps . . . and it may be whispered, geography untouched by human element is dull to an extraordinary degree, duller even than mapless history, and that, the Dodo said, was the driest thing that it knew.'

Sir Charles Close: *The Map of England* (1932)

Contents

List of Illustrations   9

Abbreviations   13

Preface   15

Introduction   17

1 Sources   25

2 Decoration   31

3 Parliamentary deposited plans and associated documents   35

4 Estate plans   36

5 Enclosure plans   50

6 Tithe plans   57

7 Regional maps   65

8 Drainage maps   69

9 County maps   72

10 Maps of county divisions   88

11 Military maps   91

12 Ordnance Survey maps   101

13 Transport and communications maps   112

14 Marine charts   135

15 Settlement plans   148

16 Specialized urban plans   178

17 Other parish plans   186

18 London and other ward plans   191

19 Industrial maps   194

20 Themes and thematic maps   197

Notes   211

Select bibliography   221

County bibliography   223

Index   227

List of Illustrations

 1 Enfield Chase: Gunton & Rolfe, 1658
 2 Bull's Cross Farm: Chapman, 1773
 3 Cheshire: Burdett, 1777
 4 River Aire: anon., *c.*1700
 5 Leeds: Cossins, 1725
 6 Surrey: Greenwood, 1829
 7 Kent: Symonson, 1596
 8 London: Morgan, 1681/2
 9 Chertsey Abbey: anon., n.d.
10 West Horndon: Walker, 1598
11 Weedon Pinckney: anon., 1593
12 Old-Byland: Saxton, 1598
13 Clandeboye estate: Raven, 1625/26
14 Currabee Parish: Manning, 1801–3
15 Warren Farm: Wright, 1829
16 Kilwinning: Ainslie, 1789
17 Long Lane Farm: Bowra, 1768
18 Manor of Hedingley: Dickinson, 1711
19 Pirbright Parish: Newland, 1805–7
20 'Fowlers': Adams, 1830 [*colour section*]
21 Manor of Lyons: Roe, 1801
22 Croydon allotments on common: Bainbridge, 1800
23 Harewood Common: Teal, 1801
24 Roecliffe: Potter, 1841
25 Tunstall: Tuke, 1788
26 Bexley tithe plan: Darbyshire & Sons, 1844
27 Croydon tithe plan: Roberts, 1847
28 Azerley tithe plan: Bradley & Son, 1839
29 Erith altered tithe apportionment plan: Ordnance Survey, 1906
30 Glasgow environs: Richardson, 1795
31 London environs: Rocque, 1746
32 Borough of Leeds: Lizars, 1834
33 Fens: Cox, 1720
34 Adlingfleet: Tate, 1764
35 Bedfordshire: Jefferys, *c.*1765
36 Kent: Andrews, Dury & Herbert, 1769 [*colour section*]

37 Devon: Donn, 1765

38 Somerset: Day & Masters, 1782

39 Somerset: Greenwood, 1822

40 Buckinghamshire: Bryant, 1825

41 Wisbech Hundred: anon., 1597

42 Knightlow Hundred: Beighton, 1729

43 Gosport: Desmaretz, 1751 [*colour section*]

44 Castle of Carrigfoile: Stafford, 1633

45 Fishguard Bay: Laurie & Whittle, 1797

46 Artillery Ground: anon., 1641

47 Armagh: Bartlett, *c.*1602

48 Plymouth Dock: Donn, 1765

49 Kent: Ordnance Survey, 1895

50 Kent: Ordnance Survey, 1895

51 Turnpikes between Leeds and Doncaster: Fowler, 1822

52 Hurst road diversion: anon., 1865

53 Road from Whitby to Durham: Ogilby, 1675

54 St Mary Cray: Cary, 1786

55 Erith tramways: Waterlow & Sons, 1903

56 Forth-Clyde canal: Laurie, *c.*1790

57 Thames-Dartford canal: Hubbard, 1835

58 Aire-Ouse canal: Jessop, 1774

59 Stockton-Darlington railway: Stephenson, 1822

60 Leeds-Selby railway: Walker, 1829

61 Bexleyheath railway: anon., 1893

62 Sidcup station: anon., 1902

63 Irish railways: Ordnance Survey, 1907

64 Cork harbour: Admiralty, 1891

65 Exmouth haven: anon., *c.*1536

66 Woolwich dockyard: Milton, 1753

67 Dublin harbour: Admiralty, 1891

68 Wooton-Underwood: Sargeint, 1649

69 Kingsbridge: anon., 1586

70 Chelmsford: Walker, 1591

71 Cambridge: Lyne, 1574

72 Dunwich: Agas, 1587

73 Cork: Speed, 1611

74 Norwich: Blomefield, 1746

75 Manchester & Salford: Green, 1794

76 Southampton: Ordnance Survey, 1851 [*colour section*]

77 Swansea: Gant, 1852

78 Warwick: Ordnance Survey, 1851

79 Chester: Ordnance Survey, 1884

80 Leeds: Ordnance Survey, 1890–91

81 Crayford: Goad, 1908

82 Edinburgh: Lizars, 1826

83 Chester: De Lavaux, 1745

84 Southampton: Mazell, 1771

 85 Inverness: Wood, 1821
 86 Oxford: Davis, 1797
 87 Leicester: Prior, 1804
 88 London: Greenwood, 1856
 89 Lenney Park Estate: Smith, 1874
 90 Clothworkers' Hall: Treswell, 1612
 91 Manchester Carriers Warehouses: Goad, 1900 [*colour section*]
 92 Palace of the Savoy: Virtue, 1816
 93 Leeds: Tayler, 1819
 94 Holly Hill House: Palmer, 1889
 95 Westheath House Estate: Cook & Hammond, 1907
 96 London: Cooke, 1802
 97 Parishes of Doonabrooke & Tannee: Farrand, 1655–57
 98 St Marylebone: Potter, *c.*1832
 99 Chelsea: Thompson, 1836
100 Walbrook & Dowgate Wards: Cole, 1755
101 Holbeck: Clarke, 1893
102 Collieries in Derbyshire & Nottinghamshire: Hutchinson, 1739
103 Surrey: Rocque, *c.*1768
104 London: Booth, 1889 [*colour section*]
105 Julius Caesar's Camp: Crawter, 1803
106 Leeds Race Ground: Fowler, 1823

Abbreviations

" : Inch(es)

' : Foot (feet)

m. : Mile(s)

1 inch = 2.54 centimetres
1 foot = 0.30 metres
1 yard = 0.91 metres
1 mile = 1.61 kilometres

Map scales

Representative Fraction	Inches to the mile / Miles to the inch	Centimetres to metres / Centimetres to kilometres
1:2500	25in. to 1 m.	1 cm: 25 m
1:10,000	$6\frac{1}{4}$in. to 1 m.	1 cm: 100 m
1:10,560	6in. to 1 m.	1 cm: 105.6 m
1:25,000	$2\frac{1}{2}$in. to 1 m.	1 cm: 250 m
1:50,000	$1\frac{1}{4}$in. to 1 m.	1 cm: 500 m
1:63,360	1in. to 1 m.	1 cm: 633.6 m
1:100,000	$1\frac{1}{2}$m. to 1 in.	1 cm: 1 km
1:126,720	2m. to 1 in.	1 cm: 1.26 km
1:150,000	$2\frac{1}{4}$m. to 1 in.	1 cm: 1.5 km
1:175,000	$2\frac{3}{4}$m. to 1 in.	1 cm: 1.75 km
1:200,000	$3\frac{1}{4}$m. to 1 in.	1 cm: 2 km
1:250,000	4m. to 1 in.	1 cm: 2.5 km
1:253,440	4m. to 1 in.	1 cm: 2.53 km
1:500,000	8m. to 1 in.	1 cm: 5 km
1:633,600	10m. to 1 in.	1 cm: 6.33 km
1:750,000	$11\frac{3}{4}$m. to 1 in.	1 cm: 7.5 km
1:1,000,000	$15\frac{3}{4}$m. to 1 in.	1 cm: 10 km

Preface

The value of maps in the reconstruction of past landscapes and as clues to earlier landscapes is self-evident.[1] Unfortunately, in general works on historical sources, particularly for local history, maps and their locations have usually been described only in generalized and obvious terms. There has been little celebration of the range of material available or discussion of its nature and uses. All too often the bulk of cartographic evidence has been ignored. However, no class of cartographic material should be dismissed as evidence. Never assume that national, regional, county, thematic, marine, military or other maps have no relevance, local or otherwise. Never assume that small-scale maps show less than large-scale. Study every map you can find. Hopefully this work will highlight available material: what it shows, its limitations, and how it has been or can be used.

Cartographic evidence is a treasury so far underused by historians – particularly local historians – despite acknowledgement of its importance. A good series of maps can record landscape changes over two or three hundred years – perhaps longer. Maps must, of course, be checked both for internal consistency and against other contemporary documents and maps. They are composite documents which must be examined, evaluated and appreciated in the context of their time. Cartographic accuracy is a relative term. Even the most unreliable map may contain that nugget of information which brings insight, clarification and understanding. Maps can reveal at a glance information only laboriously gathered elsewhere; they are rapidly interpreted and understood, and lighten subsequent study of weightier records. Those who need this guide will not be familiar with its scholarly foundations. Readers are directed to other studies which will enhance appreciation, interpretation, understanding and use of maps. Beyond this, historians must search out not only the maps themselves but also background information relevant to their studies.

Many historians will already be collectors of early maps and others will find the desire to collect growing as their knowledge and use of them increases. Obviously, many of the maps discussed here are unique items and certain classes of maps, such as Board of Health plans and the Ordnance Survey's manuscript drawings, are never offered for sale. However, in contrast, most of the types of maps described do appear in the collector's market, albeit somewhat infrequently and only at high cost in certain cases. Thus, this book is also of relevance to collectors and the opportunity must be taken to encourage historians to become collectors in order to, in turn, persuade dealers to broaden the range of maps and plans on offer and considered saleable. Already there are dealers who specialize in marine charts, Ordnance Survey publications, large-scale county maps and town plans, and other types of maps. Away from the mainstream themes of collecting there are fascinating opportunities for building collections of many of the map types considered here. Assiduous study of dealers' catalogues and stocks will reveal a remarkable variety of material on offer encompassing everything from duplicates of parliamentary deposited plans to mining plans, estate and enclosure plans, and almost every other type of map. The historian's responsibility for discovery and rescue must extend to the preservation of maps and plans which have not found their way into public archives, for who else is to care for them but the collector?

Acknowledgements

A number of publishers and researchers have kindly allowed material to be drawn from their publications. Thanks are due to: John Bartholomew & Son for *Bartholomew 150 years*; Eason & Son for *Irish Maps*; Ebury Press for *London in Maps*; Donald Hodson; Ralph Hyde; David Kingsley; and Surveyors Publications for F.M.L. Thompson's *Chartered Surveyors*. Special acknowledgement must be made of the help of: Dr John Andrews for his work on the cartography of Ireland, both published and unpublished; Dr Brian Harley for numerous works on British cartography and, in particular, for the framework provided by his booklet *Maps for the Local Historian* (1972); and Dr P.D.A. Harvey, not only for his published works but also for access to research not published at the time of writing. Many other sources are recorded only in bibliographies and notes in the hope that this is sufficient acknowledgement.

Numerous individuals and institutions, far too many to acknowledge separately, have provided information on their map holdings and access to them. My thanks to all in the hope that this book will stimulate greater interest in and use of their cartographic collections.

The illustrations have been brought together from many sources. Facsimiles have sometimes been illustrated in the hope that it will encourage more widespread production and copies of earlier maps have occasionally been used in order to point out their advantages and drawbacks. The following have generously allowed the reproduction of material: John Bartholomew & Son Ltd: 30, 82; Bexley Library Service: 7, 15, 17, 26, 29, 52, 55, 57, 61, 62, 89, 94, 95; John Booth: 45; British Library: 3 (K.9.2.2.TAB), 8 (Crace II 58), 31 (Maps C11c8), 35 (Maps 1335(19))), 37 (Maps 24e25), 38 (K.37.6.8.Tab.end), 39 (Maps C23b12), 40 (Maps C23a2), 43 (K.Top.XIV.23), 48 (Maps 24e25), 56 (Maps 24e17(1)), 71 (Maps C24a 27(3)), 85 (Maps C21e4), 86 (K.Top.XXXIV.7.(5 Tab.end)), 87 (Maps 3260(8)), 88 (Maps 3480 (145)), 96 (Crace 17/17), 99 (Maps 175.T.4 (2)), 103 (K.40.7.8.Tab.end); Buckinghamshire Archaeological Society: 68; Chas. E. Goad Ltd.: 81, 91; Chester City Record Office: 79, 83; Codrington Library, All Souls College, Oxford: 11 (Hovenden I: 12 (Weedon Pinkney)); Croydon Public Libraries: 22, 27; Earl of Eglinton & Winton and the Scottish Record Office: 16; Essex Record Office: 10, 70; Greenwich Library Service: 66; Earl of Harewood: 23; House of Lords Record Office: 59 (HLR, Deposited Plan, H.L., 1823, Stockton and Darlington Railway); Kent Archives Office: 20; Local History Library, Leeds City Libraries: 80, 93, 101; Leeds Library Service: 5, 18, 32, 51, 60, 106; Lincoln's Inn Library: 102 (Lincoln's Inn Tracts, M.P. 102, f.92); London Topographical Society: 46, 90, 104; Jason Musgrave: 6, 92; Council of Trustees of the National Library of Ireland: 47, Nos 14, 21, 44, 63, 73, 97 are reproduced in *Ireland from Maps* (1980); Neil Richardson Local History Publications: 75; Ordnance Survey: 49, 50; Public Record Office: 12; Public Record Office of Northern Ireland: 13 (T.870/2/50); 'Royal Oak', Pirbright: 19; Southampton City Record Office: 76, 84 (Reproduced in *Southampton Maps* '12 facsimile maps of different dates, showing the historical development of the City'); Swansea City Council: 77; Warwick Leadlay Gallery: 36; Warwickshire County Record Office: 78 (Reproduced in *The Town Maps of Warwick 1610–1851* – 'An Archive Teaching Unit prepared by the Warwick County Record Office', published by and obtainable from the County Museum, Warwick); West Yorkshire Archive Service, Leeds District Archives: 4 (TN/LA 5/3/7), 23 (HAR Map 14), 24 (ACC: 1599), 28 (RD/RT/14), 34 (TN/HC/D 8), 58; Westminster City Libraries: Archives and Local History Department, Marylebone Library: 98 (Reproduced by Westminster City Libraries in association with The St Marylebone Society); Trustees of the Wisbech and Fenland Museum: 41. My thanks to all concerned for permission to reproduce, and, in many cases, for much effort in supplying material. Particular thanks are due to B.L. Harrison of the West Yorkshire Archive Service and the staff of Bexley Local History Library.

The writer 'is not aware than any inaccuracies exist in it; but if unfortunately any such should have occurred in a work of such extent, from any of those trifling causes which frequently baffle the most acute and attentive surveys, he will be happy to avail himself of any communication to that effect, and to correct . . . as occasion may require.'[2] Any errors are, of course, entirely my own responsibility.

David Smith
Joydens Wood, November 1987

Introduction

Although maps are vital historical sources, they must be interpreted cautiously and carefully. Historians must appreciate limitations and assess accuracy before using map evidence. There is no standard procedure for assessing maps appropriate to all cases, but they should always be evaluated in a number of ways before drawing conclusions.

Maps must not be used in isolation. Related documents may explain why they were made and methods used, providing an assessment of accuracy and establishing what information is unique and what merely repeated from other sources. In many cases maps are only the graphic part of a larger survey, as with enclosure, estate, and tithe plans, and can only be interpreted satisfactorily in conjunction with accompanying books of reference, awards, schedules, and other documents. Similarly, marine charts need sailing directions to supplement evidence on navigable channels and landmarks. Unfortunately, all too often maps have been separated from associated documents, thus inhibiting their evaluation as historical evidence.

Historians usually know who made a map and when. However, sometimes it may need to be dated or a suspicious dating verified. Generally, dates given on maps should be distrusted and checked, whenever possible, from internal evidence. Many undated maps can in practice be roughly dated, often to within quite narrow limits. Physical characteristics of vellum, parchment, paper, ink and paint can be subjected to scientific testing in order to ascertain date, but these techniques are likely to be of little relevance for most historical studies. Watermarks and chainlines in paper can establish the earliest possible date of printing; however, paper was often stored for a considerable time before use. Supplementary detail, such as heraldry and dedications, and decorative embellishment, such as cartouche, compass indicator, border, and lettering, may aid dating and identification. Even method of drawing, use of particular signs and colours, and choice of decorative motif may point to the cartographer. Most useful are copyright notices, publication dates, and addresses given in imprints. However, publication dates can mislead due to the time lapsed since actual survey. Dates and addresses were frequently changed for a new issue or when plates passed from publisher to publisher, without any alteration of geographical content. Conversely, geographical detail might be updated without re-dating the map. The appearance or disappearance of topographical features can help date a map, or at least part of it, and date revisions when the exact date of change is known from independent evidence. In contrast, the latest production date cannot be inferred from what a map omits.

Maps were commonly copied, particularly in surveyor's office and military establishment and by later antiquarians, to provide additional reference copies, to insure against loss and as practice for apprentice draughtsmen. Copying introduced the danger of transcription error by careless draughtsmen; even the Ordnance Survey failed to produce facsimiles of Bodley's barony maps without error and omission. Unfortunately, the copier often signed and dated his copy, frequently without acknowledging source or date of original. Thus, an apparently reliable map bearing an unambiguous date may be merely a re-dated copy of an earlier version. Similar difficulties occur when reduced versions of large-scale maps were produced.

Given date and authorship, the map's validity as a representation of landscape at a specific date must be assessed. Historians rarely require mathematically exact locational information and, therefore, can avoid the complexities of scale, projection, orientation, and distortion – simply checking these against modern maps for comparison. Scale can vary within a map and may be computed in

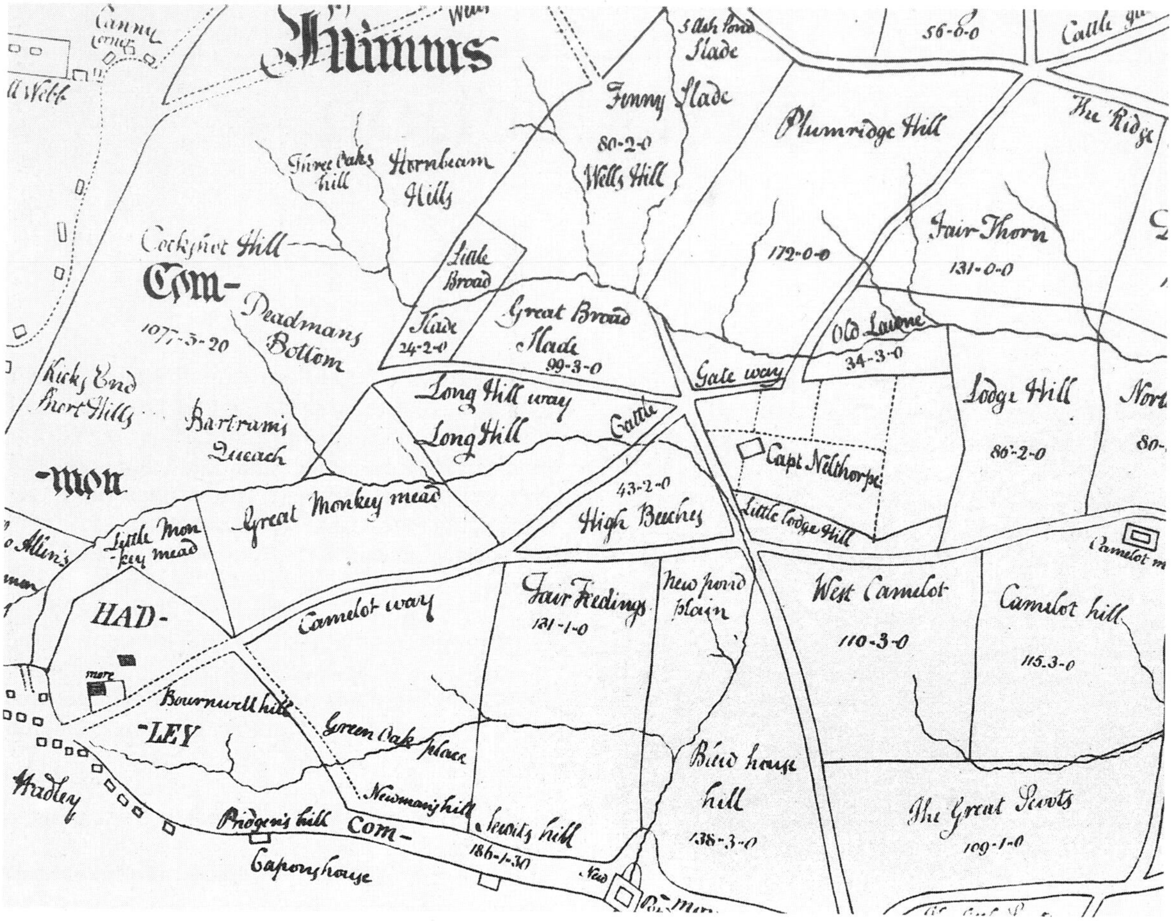
Fenny Slade
80-2-0
Wells Hill
Plumridge Hill
56-6-0
Three Oaks hill
Hornbeam Hills
Cockpit Hill
Com-
Deadmans Bottom
1077-3-20
Little Broad
Slade 24-2-0
Great Broad Slade
99-3-0
172-0-0
Fair Thorn
131-0-0
Old Lawne
34-3-0
Gate way
Lodge Hill
86-2-0
Kicks End
Short Hills
Bartrams Queach
Long Hill way
Long Hill
Cattle
Capt Nelthorpe
-mon
43-2-0
High Beeches
Little Lodge Hill
Great Monkey mead
Little Mon-key mead
HAD-
Camelot way
Fair Feedings
131-1-0
New pond plain
West Camelot
110-3-0
Camelot hill
115.3-0
Bournwell hill
-LEY
Green Oak place
Newmans hill
Bird house hill
138-3-0
The Great Sewets
109-1-0
Hadley
Pridgens hill
Com-
Sewits hill
186-1-30
Caponshouse

1. Maps were frequently copied. The evidence of copies must be interpreted carefully, because errors could frequently arise during transcription. A manuscript map of Enfield Chase 'on a thick parchment, with rollers' was copied for Ford's *History of Enfield* (1873). However, Ford's copy is not a true facsimile since there are some differences in detail. Maps of Royal Chases, such as Enfield Chase, East Greenwich and Bushey Park, were drawn, particularly during the seventeenth century, illustrating the progressive diminution of the private hunting grounds of the Tudors and Stuarts.

'FACSIMILE TRACING from The original in the Bodleian Library OF "ENFIELD CHASE as now divided between the Commonwealth & Commons By Nich. Gunton & Edm Rolfe. 1658" (Edward Ford, July 1874.).' (Detail)

obsolete or confusing measures, particularly when local land measures were used in estate surveying.[1] Most maps are distorted to some degree in comparison with modern counterparts due to crude technique, faulty compilation, or shrinkage and warping of paper. Historians will not need sophisticated cartometric tests because inaccuracy in a map's mathematical framework does not usually reduce the value of topographical content. History generally has wide tolerances as to what is acceptable in terms of accuracy, and the geodetic inadequacies of early maps must not obscure their value as contemporary documents.

Nevertheless, topographical content must be assessed for completeness and reliability, remembering, of course, that neatness and artistic design do not necessarily denote accuracy and that the crudest plans are not necessarily the least valuable. The purpose of the map often determined levels of accuracy within it. Tithe and enclosure plans, for example, were designed to be cadastral records with legal authority, whilst, in contrast, maps accompanying sixteenth-century legal disputes were drawn merely to clarify simple geographical relationships. Inevitably, map-makers exercised

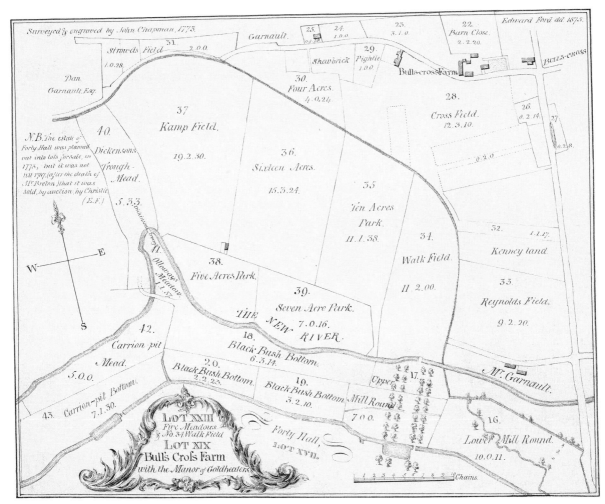

2. Ford also copied a property plan of 1773 by John Chapman, adding the information that the 'estate of Forty Hall was planned out into lots for sale, in 1773 – but it was not till 1787, (after the death of M.ʳ Breton,) that it was sold, by auction, by Christie. (E.F.).' Copies are frequently the only cartographic evidence available when the originals cannot be traced.

'LOT XXIII Five Meadows & No. 34. Walk Field LOT XIX Bull's Cross Farm with the Manor of Goldheaters.' 'Surveyed & engraved by John Chapman, 1773. Edward Ford del. 1875.'

choice, pre-selecting categories of information to be shown, omitting some features and over-emphasizing others according to end function.[2] Being aware of what a map omits is as important as treating its evidence suspiciously, although this is difficult when the purpose of the survey is unclear.

Content and accuracy were partly determined by the author's personality and intentions. Although cartographers generally failed to explain their work, it is clear that most expressed subjective preferences, either consciously or unconsciously, in the landscape portrayed. How conscientiously, and to what extent, did map-makers observe and record features outside their interest and purpose? Even after they began to use conventional signs generally, intention is still not clear. Varying signs could be used to depict the same feature, or, conversely, the same sign might represent different features even on a single map. Similarly, terminology could be inconsistent. Thus, comparisons may be difficult or impossible. Often cartographers had several intentions but only the dominant one is clear because motives are hidden by format or convention. Maps not only portrayed the real world but embodied concepts about its nature in their symbolism, evoking place as well as recording

3. Confusion concerning the meaning of conventional signs frequently hinders the interpretation of cartographic evidence. Often no key to signs was provided, perhaps because contemporaries would have readily understood their meaning. In such cases meaning can be deduced only by studying the map in its historical context. Even when signs are explained, it is not always clear what cartographers meant. For instance, the asterisk sign for watermills may represent a single wheel, or a single building with more than one wheel, or a complex of buildings with several independent wheels. It is difficult to distinguish active watermills from those whose names survived after they had ceased work, particularly as the appropriate conventional sign was not always used for working mills. Similarly, it is not always possible to identify waterwheels that had been temporarily or permanently replaced by a steam engine. Map-makers did not always take account of the often frequent changes in name and function of particular mills. It is not at all easy to identify a watermill with a similar site shown on a later map or on the ground today, particularly where several mills occupied a short stretch of water. Although Burdett missed some watermills, he did mark 156 in Cheshire and some are known only from his map.

'. . . . Survey of the County Palatine of Chester . . . P.P. Burdett,' 1777. (Detail)

topography. Hence, they illuminate not only the map-maker's perceptions and feelings but also the attitudes and intellectual background of the age and locality in which they were made. The map-maker's primary concerns were usually to satisfy the demands of employers, patrons, subscribers or customers and to ensure financial success and continued livelihood; thus, the expectations of purchasers and users became a potent force in determining the nature of maps. Considerations of profit and business survival kept many maps in publication long after their landscapes had disappeared. Hence, inaccuracy in a map may well be explained by the intentions, perceptions and motives of a map-maker who knew full well that his map was inaccurate, incomplete or out-of-date.

The complex stages by which information was first gathered and then processed to produce a map also determined reliability. Reconstruction of methods of survey, drafting and engraving aids understanding of the finished article – and may indicate the reliability of its landscape. Surveying methods imposed limits on the degree of accuracy that could be attained. Accounts of surveying methods in prefatory remarks, professional papers, contemporary textbooks, and in specifications and instructions for survey assist evaluation, facilitating assessment of technical proficiency and theoretical limitations at a particular date.[3] However, often little evidence exists concerning the training, competence or integrity of those who tried to follow specifications and instructions and regarding the extent to which they could put theory into practice, or, indeed, to which practice preceded theory. The most impartial and incontrovertible evidence of method – the surveyor's actual field notebooks and sketches – rarely survive, although valuable fair copies have more often avoided destruction. A surveyor's contemporary comments concerning progress or conditions of survey are informative. A few surveyors readily acknowledged the limitations and inadequacies of their work. Generally, though, memoirs, prospectuses, catalogues and advertisements are not scientific records, being aimed simply at securing a wider market through self-promotion and self-praise.

Quality and accuracy of survey obviously depended on instrument reliability and survey method. In a sense all maps and, particularly, charts record past landscapes because there was inevitably a time gap between field survey and finished map. Some surveys, especially of large areas such as counties, lasted years, and a few took decades, with the result that landscapes of different dates can appear on a single map.

The high cost of field survey enticed map-makers to glean information from existing sources, usually without acknowledgement. Material was refashioned into an apparently new map, as, for example, when Blaeu's seventeenth-century maps of Scotland were derived mainly from Pont's sixteenth-century manuscripts.[4] Maps might incorporate materials of different date and dubious reliability, making them composite documents whose component parts must be compared with other material to reveal possible sources. How much data has been derived from genuine field work; how much from other sources; how much from cursory examination; and how much from oral testimony?

A map's draughtsman might make critical decisions about reduction, scale and principles of generalization. His interpretation could exclude or correct data; thus, some drafts may show information not found on the finished map. Transcription errors were highly likely in drafting, as indeed they were whenever maps were copied, engraved, or lithographed, and surviving manuscript versions of a particular map may differ slightly. Mistakes were particularly likely when the engraver was cutting plates in an unfamiliar language, making some maps notorious for spelling errors. Engraved plates could be revised and corrected at any time by simple re-engraving, usually without noting date of alteration, and publication history must be traced carefully through its variants. Later data, particularly transport information, was often added to outdated landscapes on ancient plates. Wear or damage and any accompanying text may indicate at what stage of a plate's life the actual impression being studied was made. Multi-sheet maps subject to regular revision were frequently made up of sheets revised to different dates without any note of revision dates. Conversely, features long disappeared from the landscape could live on in the map despite revision and re-dating. Particular difficulties occur where 'improvement' information was superimposed on to a base map showing an earlier townscape. Even careless hand colouring could introduce error into a map.[5]

Too often historians judge maps less critically than other documents. Contemporary views of a map or a map-maker's work provide perspective and evaluation. The general state of cartography was assessed by John Green[6] and others; and numerous individual maps and map-makers were judged by well-informed contemporaries such as Pepys and Gough.[7] Specific criticisms are found in letters; in newspapers and periodicals like the *Gentleman's Magazine*; and in the Society of Arts's minutes. However, beware of criticism aimed merely for commercial advantage by rivals.

Other contemporary maps aid interpretation and should be studied as a matter of course in order to indentify inaccuracy, assess reliability and reveal change. Confidence in a map's reliability is increased when it displays the proven characteristics of a larger family of maps. Very early maps, in particular, may be understood only through reference to others. Comparison can place a map within a clearly identifiable group with particular known characteristics.

Map evidence must be interpreted with the greatest care, both qualitatively and especially quantitatively. Maps must be judged on their own merits – mere existence is no guarantee of value. Understanding and evaluation require knowledge of a cartographer's purpose and motives in making the map; his information sources; his production methods; the meaning of his signs and symbolism; and the time taken to survey and turn survey data into finished map. Different stratas of accuracy within the map must be identified and assessed. The realistic historian will not expect too much and will not judge early maps by modern standards. However, whilst understanding of limitations tempers evaluation, maps must not be dismissed and too often their evidence has been rejected or damned too quickly. Maps are occasionally the sole authority for a particular fact; are commonly a primary information source, and are generally useful supplements to other sources. However imperfect maps may be, they depict geographical facts of location and extent more precisely than written documents and the crudest map may well supply the evidence sought. Provided historians recognize that the answers a map offers are only as good as the questions asked of it, maps will provide a bonanza of information for the study of history, particularly local history.

Select Bibliography:
Dating & Identification

(Bibliographies to later chapters may also aid identification)

AKERS, B., 'History of watermarks' (*Map Collector*, 6; 1979) (*continued*)

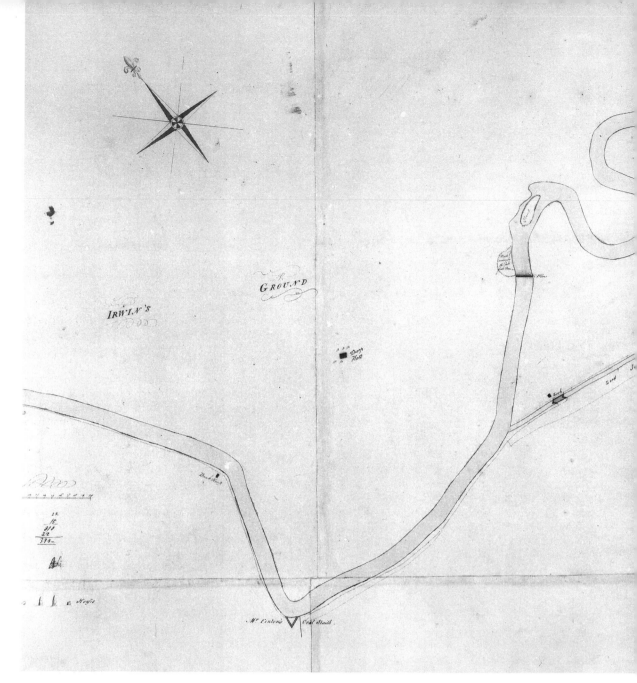

4. Even the simplest and crudest of maps may contain information not found elsewhere. The plan of Crier's Cut, cutting off a meandering section of the River Aire, locates the position of locks, a pond and a bridge on the Cut; the 'Crier Cut Ale House'; a dam, an area washed away by the fall from the dam, a paper mill, 'Mr. Fenton's Coal Staith', and Bank House on the river; and 'Glass Houses' and Thorp Hall in the neighbouring area.

'The River Aire, Crier's Cut, etc., from Woodlesford Lock near Woodlesford to a place called The Breaks near Hunslet.' *c*.1770 (Detail)

CHURCHILL, W.A., *Watermarks in Paper in Holland, England, France . . . in the XVII and XVIII centuries* (1935)

EDEN, P. (ed.), *Dictionary of Land Surveyors and Local Cartographers in Great Britain and Ireland, 1550–1850.* Pt. 1 (1975), Pt. 2 (1976), Pt. 3 (1976), Supplement (1979)

HANNAS, L., *The English Jigsaw Puzzle, 1760–1890* (1972)

HEAWOOD, E., 'The use of watermarks in dating old maps and documents' (*Geog. Journ.*, 63; 1924). Reproduced in full in R. Lister: *How to Identify Old Maps and Globes* (1965)

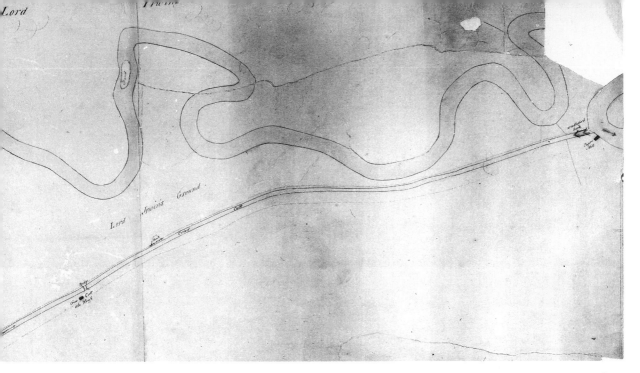

HEAWOOD, E., 'Paper used in England after 1600' (*Trans.Biblio.Soc.*; 1930–31)

HEAWOOD, E., *Watermarks, mainly of the 17th and 18th centuries* (1950)

HODSON, D., 'Dating county maps through mapsellers' advertisements' (*Map Collector*, 26; 1984)

NORTON, J.E., *Guide to National and Provincial Directories* (1950)

PLOMER, H.R., *A Dictionary of Booksellers and Printers*, [1641–1775], (3 vols.; 1907–32)

SKELTON, R.A., 'The dating of engraved maps and atlases' in *Decorative Printed Maps of the 15th to 18th Centuries* (1952; new edn., 1965)

TYACKE, S., 'Map-sellers and the London map trade c. 1650–1710' in H. Wallis & S. Tyacke (eds.): *My Head is a Map* (1973)

TYACKE, S., *London Map-Sellers 1660–1720* (1978)

TOOLEY, R.V., *Dictionary of Mapmakers* (1979)

TOOLEY, R.V., *Dictionary of Mapmakers Supplement* (1985)

Select Bibliography: Accuracy & Interpretation

BLAKEMORE, M.J., & HARLEY, J.B., 'Concepts in the history of cartography' (*Cartographica*, 17, 4; 1980)

CARR, A.P., 'Cartographic record and historical accuracy' (*Geography*, 47; 1962)

COSGROVE, D. & DANIELS, S.J. (eds), *The Iconography of Landscape* (1987)

HARLEY, J.B., 'The evaluation of early maps: towards a methodology' (*Imago Mundi*, 22; 1968)

HARLEY, J.B., 'Ancient maps: waiting to be read' (*Geog. Mag.*, 53; 1981)

HARLEY, J.B., 'Meaning and ambiguity in Tudor cartography; in S. Tyacke (ed.): *English Map-Making 1500–1650* (1983)

HARLEY, J.B., *The Map as Ideology* (Forthcoming)

KOEMAN, C., 'Levels of historical evidence in early maps' (*Imago Mundi*, 22; 1968)

MORGAN, V., 'The cartographic image of "the country" in early modern England' (*Trans. Roy. Hist. Soc.*, 5, 26; 1979). See also: MORGAN, V., 'The lasting image of the Elizabethan era' (*Geog. Mag.*, 52; 1980)

MURPHY, J., 'Measures of map accuracy assessment and some early Ulster maps' (*Irish Geog.*, 11; 1978)

NORTH, F.J., *Maps, their History and Uses, with special reference to Wales* (1933)

RAVENHILL, W., & GILG, A., 'The accuracy of early maps? Towards a computer aided method' (*Cart.Journ.*, 11; 1974)

RICHESON, A.W., *English Land Measuring to 1800: Instruments and Practice* (1966)

SKELTON, R.A., *Looking at an Early Map* (Univ. Kansas Libs; 1965)

STONE, J.C., & GEMMELL, A.M.D., 'An experiment in the comparative analysis of distortion on historical maps' (*Cart.Journ.*, 14; 1977)

TAYLOR, E.G.R., *The Mathematical Practitioners of Tudor and Stuart England* (1954)

TAYLOR, E.G.R., *The Mathematical Practitioners of Hanoverian England 1714–1840* (1966)

1

Sources

Much has been written detailing sources of cartographic material for historians. However, information is often soon outdated as collections are transferred and consolidated. The British Library, for example, recently purchased the map collection of the Royal United Services Institution and some two thousand manuscript fire-insurance plans and letter books produced and previously held by the Goad firm; the Church Commissioners' maps are on indefinite loan to record offices and libraries; the British Railways Board's records have been transferred to the Public Record Offices; and the National Coal Board's plans have been deposited in county record offices. Growing interest in local history has generated an archival revolution, vastly increasing numbers of local record offices, archives, local history libraries, and museums, each with rapidly improving systems of listing and indexing records. Energetic archivists, curators and librarians are building increasingly comprehensive local cartographic collections at remarkable speed by rescuing maps and plans from a morass of other documentary material; by acquiring estate and family records either permanently or on loan; by purchasing material; and by acquiring facsimiles of maps held elsewhere, particularly in private custody. Maps and associated documents, previously separated in an earlier age of misguided archival practice, are also being re-united. Archives, libraries, museums and record offices are continually acquiring both individual maps and collections which alter any description of cartographic resources. In such changing circumstances it would be misleading and counter-productive to direct historians to specific repositories, for they may then be the only sources consulted. Relevant maps may be found in many different places and institutions. Local historians must search ever wider for maps; beginning with obvious local sources and moving on, if necessary, to collections held by national

institutions and libraries. No list of cartographic sources can ever be exhaustive and imagination and energy must be used to locate relevant maps.

Any search for cartographic evidence should begin at the local history library, archives or museum, as this will be the most accessible source, able usually to offer specialized knowledge and experience of local material. Even if the repository does not hold relevant maps, more often than not its staff can guide historians to them. Local collections are often surprisingly rich in un-researched material. It is not unusual to find estate plans by nationally-known map-makers dating from the seventeenth and eighteenth centuries. Bexley Local History Library, for example, contains, amongst an interesting collection of eighteenth-century plans, Burdett's survey of Brampton Place (1768) in facsimile and Eyre's original plan of 'Lamaby House' (1761). Similarly, Chesterfield Public Library contains railway plans in its Stephenson collection, and Barrow Library holds important local mining and railway maps. As yet there is no national guide to this wealth of material, but ultimately it should appear in a union catalogue.

Although the older records of many smaller boroughs and towns are increasingly deposited in county record offices, many other towns have actively developed their own local map collections. Generally, the more ancient a city, the more complex its cartographic records; and the more extensive its municipal landholdings, the more property plans it will possess. The archives of cathedral cities, in particular, may contain valuable information on church property and estates, such as the plans concerning the sale of land for the Royal Military Canal held in the Cathedral Archives at Canterbury Record Office. Outstanding amongst town cartographic records is the Fairbank collection 'of several thousand maps and plans, accumulated by a local family of surveyors' (*c*.1740–1840) held in Sheffield Central Library.[1] The Greater London Record Office and Historic Library holds 'archival maps' which 'range from parish maps to estate maps taking in on the way marginal plans on deeds and related documents of parts of parishes and estates', including the district surveyors' monthly returns which provide unique information on development, 'improvement', building and alteration. The collections of libraries, such as Leeds Central Library, Manchester Public Library and the Linenhall Library, Belfast, are important by any standards. Whilst most town archives will inevitably be more modest, they nevertheless contain much exciting material. Wigan Record Office, for instance, contains surveys of the Douglas Navigation 1720–72; Birmingham Reference Library holds plans of the Birmingham Canal; and Lincoln Archives Office contains voluminous records of Commissioners of Sewers from the seventeenth century and of Drainage Commissioners from the eighteenth century.

Records of public-utility undertakings, improvement commissions and Boards of Health are amongst the most neglected of local cartographic resources. Plans prepared for local government – such as those concerning water supply and sewerage – are found not only in local collections but also, still, in the possession of relevant departments. Hopefully they will increasingly be found in local archives – such as the Swansea City Record Office, which holds the City's Board of Health plans as well as many local industrial plans. However, it may be necessary to seek plans elsewhere; for instance, part of Terbutt's Board of Health plan of St Michael's Hamlet (1856) is held in the Private Streetworks Section of Liverpool Corporation's City Engineer's Department.

County record offices have built important collections by adding semi-official and private archives to official records. Recently, national collections have increasingly left the acquisition of local maps to local archives, although, of course, they still purchase outstanding examples of early estate plans and large-scale works by nationally significant cartographers. Maps previously dispersed in country houses; in the offices of estate agents, solicitors, and businesses; and elsewhere, are steadily being united, creating collections of surprising variety and significance. Tyne and Wear County Council Archives Department, for instance, contains records of the River Wear Commission from 1719 and the Tyne Improvement Commission from 1850; Cambridgeshire Record Office holds records of 15 internal drainage boards dating from 1646; Northumberland Record Office has an extensive collection of mining plans dating from the eighteenth century, plus records of mining engineers and agents from the seventeenth century; Glamorgan County Record Office contains plans of the important Dowlais Works from *c*.1750 and the Neath Abbey Iron Company from 1792. Oxfordshire County Record Office, for example, typically holds 'many hundreds of maps ranging from early printed maps to estate maps, railway, canal and turnpike maps, enclosure maps, tithe maps, maps forming part of sale catalogues to small maps drawn in the margins of deeds . . . the record office's map index . . . runs to about 3,000 cards; with about 500 further cards which relate to 2 uncatalogued but listed collections . . . early printed maps date from the late 16th century . . . these early maps are small scale maps of the county, the earliest estate map is of Harpsden . . . dated 1586 . . . by John Blagrave.'

If maps are not found locally, archives further afield must be consulted. Obvious national sources are the map collections of the British Library[2] and the national libraries of Ireland, Scotland, and Wales. Cartographic records are found not only in map departments but also in those relating to official publications, manuscripts, personal papers, and so on.[3] Equally important are the national record offices. The Public Record Office, for example, contains 'a very large accumulation of maps amounting probably to several hundred thousand, which are public records . . . transferred to the Office by . . . courts or government departments (or their successors) where they originated or accrued . . . either as separate map classes or within volumes and files attached to relevant papers.'[4] 'Maps and plans . . . fall into three main categories: maps that have been extracted from volumes and files and given separate references; maps in classes consisting solely of maps; and maps in classes of correspondence and papers, occasionally as single pieces but more usually in volumes and files whose description in the class list will not, as a rule, reveal the presence of a map.' The Scottish Record Office's large plan collection consists mainly of sheriff court plans, relating particularly to railways and other nineteenth-century public utilities, and the Register House plans which form a general series drawn from various sources, notably from Court of Session records, records of Scottish-based government departments, and the older records of the sheriff courts.[5] Similarly, the Public

Record Office of Northern Ireland holds manuscript town plans prepared for the Valuation Office and 'almost always the only maps surviving for a particular area prior to 1830'. Deposited plans, enclosure awards, and so on, are held by the House of Lords Record Office: 'Some three million documents are preserved . . . archives of the House of Commons as well as . . . the House of Lords, together with certain other groups of records . . . accumulated within the Palace of Westminster.'

University libraries, such as the Bodleian Library, Oxford, and Cambridge University Library, often hold valuable collections. Aberdeen University Library, for example, contains the O'Dell collection of railway maps; and University College, Bangor, holds important documents relating to Lewis Morris's hydrographic activities. The acquisition of the Clinker and Garnett Collections and the Transport Trust Library has made Brunel University a premier centre for the study of railway history. Amongst collections in Trinity College Library, Dublin, are Carew's Elizabethan Irish maps containing plans of fortified places in Munster and Ulster and of new English towns in Ireland; maps of Trinity College estates throughout Ireland and of other estates; Vallancey's military surveys in southern Ireland; maps of Church of Ireland dioceses; maps of the Incorporated Society for Promoting Protestant Schools in Ireland; and maps and surveys relating to properties of the archbishop of Dublin. Other educational institutions may hold useful local maps; the Fellows' Library of Winchester College, for instance, contains local Ordnance and Geological Survey maps as well as 'a very fine collection of early maps and atlases of a more general nature'.

Many landowning institutions are important sources. All Souls College, Oxford, for instance, possesses four portfolios of unsurpassed Elizabethan estate plans of its properties, and St Bartholomew's Hospital holds farm maps dating from the early seventeenth century. Similar, if less spectacular, sources survive in other ancient institutions such as the Church, the City Guilds and the Livery Companies. Property and estate plans may remain in private hands or deposited with the family solicitor, particulary when referring to a trust; other property plans may be found in records of building societies, freehold land societies, and estate agents – if they still exist. Archives held at Arundel Castle, for example, include several hundred plans of the Duke of Norfolk's estates in Sheffield, which, with the Fairbank Collection,

make Sheffield one of the best mapped towns of the late eighteenth century. Other bodies such as the Royal Geographical Society[6] and the Royal Irish Academy hold important material, and even local historical and archaeological societies may possess small but unique collections. The content of such collections is often surprising; Shakespeare's Birthplace Trust, for instance, holds local railway plans and Buckinghamshire Archaeological Society possesses a manuscript plan (1649) of the old village of Wootton Underwood.

Besides general collections, both local and national, there are some specialized sources. Whilst all local libraries hold Ordnance sheets, it is certain that holdings will be incomplete; even national and major university libraries have only partial collections and it may be necessary to consult the Ordnance Survey's own records, although those at Southampton suffered badly during World War II. The Ordnance Office in Dublin, for example, holds the manuscript copies of the Irish town plans. Similarly, major collections of marine charts and hydrographic surveys are scattered, with no single institution having a complete holding. The chief repositories are the National Maritime Museum, Greenwich, and the Hydrographic Department, Taunton, which contains 'the products, in both Home Waters and overseas, of the diligence of numerous 19th century Royal Navy surveyors' in some 146,000 manuscripts and 500,000 printed documents.[7] For mining plans, 'maps and plans inherited by the National Coal Board . . . have been deposited in County Record Offices', and Scottish records are housed in the Scottish Record Office; 'other plans of mining activities are housed in seven Mines Record Offices located in coalfield areas.' The North of England Institute of Mining and Mechanical Engineers holds geological and mining maps of Northumberland and Durham. Similarly, the Post Office Archives holds postal maps. The National Army Museum contains military maps although most refer to 'battles, fortifications and lines of march in foreign parts'.

Although most archives are open to historians it is essential that times of opening and eligibility for access are always checked. It is wise to make an appointment to view maps and to ensure that relevant material has not been transferred elsewhere. Some institutions obviously have a policy of limited access; the Hydrographic Department, for example, 'being part of the M.O.D, is not normally open to members of the public. . . . However, a limited number of visitors engaged on . . . research are permitted, subject to certain restrictions, to consult documents.' Many private institutions, educational bodies, firms and families guard their cartographic treasures jealously, and much energy may be spent obtaining access. Whilst most archivists, librarians and curators do their utmost to help researchers, a few do try to deter or divert enquiry. Historians must develop patience and cunning amongst other research skills if all relevant material is to be traced and consulted.

Bibliographies and lists, both published and unpublished, are a valuable aid. Carto-bibliographies have been published of some counties and towns and for others lists have appeared in local archaeological, record or historical society journals. The best listings note libraries where copies of maps are found. However, many bibliographies fail to show that all copies of a printed map are not necessarily identical; as many copies as possible should, therefore, be compared. Upcott's *Bibliographical Account of the Principal Works relating to English Topography* (1818) is the only reasonably systematic guide to engraved maps in topographies, but it is far from comprehensive and maps are difficult to identify amidst the mass of illustration entries.[8]

Many local archives, libraries, museums and record offices have produced easily-digestible lists of enclosure and tithe maps, public schemes and other official plans, and private estate maps. *Local Maps of Derbyshire to 1770*, for example, contains notes on 439 maps in 379 entries, with 23 additional copies. There are many excellent guides to the nature and location of records and it is unnecessary here to expand on the problems of locating maps within archives. Increasingly, lists of all maps held within a particular area, including those held privately, are being compiled; Belfast Central Library, the Linenhall Library, and the Public Record Office of Northern Ireland, for example, have produced a union list of Belfast maps, and Angus District Museums has listed 65 maps of the Angus area in museums at Arbroath, Brechin, Forfar and Montrose. The Manorial and Tithe Documents Registers – maintained by the Royal Commission on Historical Manuscripts – specifically indexes out tithe and manor maps but no other map types are systematically recorded in indexes, although many collections noted in the subject index include estate maps. A catalogue of maps before *c.*1650 in county record offices is due for publication by the Association of County Archivists, and a guide to maps of the British Isles *c.*1150–1900 is under preparation for the Royal

Historical Society. Catalogues issued for exhibitions often contain details of maps displayed. The *Directory of U.K. Map Collections* offers a simple reference guide to many collections; it covers the five copyright libraries and 139 other collections, indicating major interests. However, it is not comprehensive. All major collections should be catalogued, with maps usually appearing under both maker's name and area covered. Often, cross-referencing is not perfect and all likely entries should be checked. Some 60,000 individual plans, for instance, have been listed so far in the Register House plan collection at the Scottish Record Office. Many maps held by the Public Record Office are described in its published catalogue, with others described in the supplementary card catalogue and in typescript lists of certain record classes consisting entirely of maps and plans. However, at the Public Record Office, as at many other repositories, 'innumerable maps remain undiscovered among files and volumes of papers and correspondence; there is no means of reference to such material.' The National Library of Scotland houses a central index to large-scale manuscript plans of Scotland, which will eventually record all such plans in the union catalogue, whatever their location.[9] Other listings may be available; a carto-bibliography of London parish surveys, for example, currently being compiled[10], is available for reference at the Guildhall Library.

Relevant maps are to be found anywhere and everywhere. Whilst historians will find many in easily accessible local collections, they must be prepared often to go beyond the obvious and search out material from every conceivable source. It is even worthwhile monitoring map-sellers' catalogues and, particularly, letting local dealers know of specific interests. It is certain that a vast number of important maps remain unrecorded and forgotten. If they are to be rescued, researched, and recorded, historians must be active, energetic and imaginative in their investigations. Two examples will suffice to illustrate significant cartographic material that has only very recently come to light. Inspired detection located a Board of Health plan of Croydon, unknown to the local history library, the British Library or the Ordnance Survey, in two metal drums at Addington Hills Water Works[11]; and the cataloguing of previously unstudied archives at Kirklees Hall, prior to its sale, revealed an unrecorded map which suggests that the world's first iron bridge was constructed across the lake in its grounds rather than as always thought across the Severn at Coalbrookdale.

To list and recommend just a few particular sources might constrict notions of what may be available and would risk diverting historians away from the very sources which they must identify if our cartographic heritage is to be fully discovered and preserved.

Select Bibliography

ADAMS, I.H., *Descriptive List of Plans [in the] Scottish Record Office* (3 vols.; 1966; 1970; 1974)

Bedfordshire County Record Office, *Catalogue of Maps in the Bedfordshire County Muniments* (1930)

Birmingham Public Libraries Reference Department, *Catalogue of the Birmingham Collection* (1918)

BONAR, LAW, A., *Three Hundred Years of Irish Printed Maps* (1972)

BOND, M.F., *Guide to the Records of Parliament* (1971)

British Cartographic Society, *A Directory of U.K. Map Collections* (2nd edn.; 1985)

British Museum, *Catalogue of Maps, Prints, Drawings, etc. forming the Geographical and Topographical Collection attached to the Library of King George the Third* (1829)

British Museum, *Catalogue of the Manuscript Maps, Charts and Plans, and of the Topographical Drawings in the British Museum* (1844; 1962)

British Museum, *Catalogue of Printed Maps, Charts and Plans [to 1964]*, (15 vols.; 1967)

British Library, *Catalogue of Printed Maps, Charts and Plans. Ten Year Supplement. 1965–1974* (1978)

British Library, *Catalogue of Additions to the Manuscripts 1951–1955* (1982)

Brunel University Library, *Railway Maps from the Garnett, Clinker and Transport Trust Collections*, Catalogue of the exhibition (1986)

Bury St Edmunds & West Suffolk Record Office, *Handlist of Surveyors' Work in West Suffolk, to 1850* (1961)

CASH, C.G., 'Manuscript maps by Pont, the Gordons, and Adair, in the Advocates' Library, Edinburgh' (*Scot. Geog. Mag.*, 23; 1907)

COBB, H.S., 'Sources for economic history amongst the Parliamentary records in the House of Lords Record Office' (*Econ. Hist. Rev.*, 2, 19; 1966)

Crosby Central Library, *Local Maps & Documents in the Local History Library* (1972)

CUBBON, A.M., *Early Maps of the Isle of Man: A Guide to the Collection in the Manx Museum* (Manx Museum & National Trust; 1967)

DICKINS, K.W., *A Catalogue of Manuscript Maps in the custody of the Sussex Archaeological Society* (1981)

DICKINSON, P.G.M., *Maps in the County Record Office, Huntingdon* (1968)

Dunfermline District Libraries, *A Guide to Local Maps & Plans held in Dunfermline Central Library's Local History Collection.*

DUNLOP, R., 'Sixteenth-century maps of Ireland' (*Eng. Hist. Rev.*, 20; 1905)

Edinburgh University Library, *The Development of Mapping in Scotland. Exhibition of Maps and Atlases in Edinburgh University Library* (1973–4)

EMMISON, F.G., *Archives and Local History* (1966)

EMMISON, F.G., & GRAY, I., *County Records* (1948)

Essex Record Office, *Catalogue of Maps in the Essex Record Office 1566–1855* [and supplements] (1947–68)

FERGUSON, P., *Irish Map History. A Select Bibliography of Secondary Works, 1850–1983, on the History of Cartography in Ireland* (1983)

FORDHAM, SIR H.G., *Hand-List of Catalogues and Works of Reference relating to Carto-Bibliography and Kindred Subjects for Great Britain and Ireland 1720 to 1927* (1928)

FORDHAM, SIR H.G., *Studies in Carto-Bibliography British and French and in the Bibliography of Itineraries and Road-Books* (1914; reprinted 1969)

FREEMAN, M.J., & LONGBOTHAM, J., *The Fordham Collection: A Catalogue* (Hist. Geog. Research Ser., 5; 1981)

FULLER, G., *Catalogue of the Maps and Plans accumulated by the late William Figg of Lewes, Land Surveyor. Published by George Fuller, successor of the late Mr Figg* (1870)

GALE, L., *Catalogue of pre-1900 non-Ordnance Survey Maps and Plans held in the Mitchell Library* (1983)

HARDIMAN, J., 'A catalogue of maps, charts and plans, relating to Ireland, preserved among the manuscripts in the library of Trinity College, Dublin, with preliminary observations. (*Trans. Roy. Irish Acad.*, 14; 1821–25)

HARLEY, J.B., *Maps for the Local Historian. A Guide to the British Sources* (1972)

HARVEY, P.D.A., & SKELTON, R.A., 'Local maps and plans before 1500; (*Journ. Soc. Archivists*, 3; 1969)

HARVEY, P.D.A., & SKELTON, R.A., (eds.), *Local Maps and Plans from Medieval England* (1986)

Hastings Museum, *Catalogue of Maps and Plans in the Exhibition of Local Maps* (1936)

HAYES, R. (ed.), *Manuscript Sources for the Study of Irish Civilization* (11 vols.; 1965). Supplement (3 vols.; 1979)

HENDERSON, T., *Shetland Maps & Charts*. Descriptive catalogue of an exhibition in the Picture Gallery of Zetland County Museum. (Zetland County Lib.; n.d.)

Historical Manuscripts Commission, *Record Repositories in Great Britain* (1964)

HODGKISS, A.G., & TATHAM, A.F., *Keyguide to Information Sources in Cartography* (1986)

JESSOP, N.R., & NUDDS, C.J., *Guide to Collections in Dublin Libraries, Printed Books to 1850 and Special Collections* (1982)

JONES, P.E., & SMITH, R., *A Guide to the Records in the Corporation of London Records Office and the Guildhall Library Muniment Room* (1951)

LESLIE, K.C., & McCANN, T.J., *Local History in West Sussex. A Guide to Sources* (2nd.edn.; 1975)

McMARTIN, J.S., *An Exhibition of Maps of Dunbar, East Lothian and Scotland in Dunbar Burgh Library, Castellau House* (Dunbar Town Council; 1971)

Middlesex Standing Joint Committe, *Middlesex in Maps and Surveys. Catalogue of Exhibition of Manuscript Plans and Estate Surveys 15th to 19th Century chiefly from the County Record Office* (1957)

MITCHELL, SIR A., & CASH, C.G., 'A contribution to the bibliography of Scottish topography' (*Scot. Hist. Soc. Pub.*, 2, 15; 1917)

MOORE, J.N., *The Mapping of Scotland. A Guide to the Literature of Scottish Cartography prior to the Ordnance Survey* (*O'Dell Memorial Monograph*, 15; 1983). See 'Exhibitions' and other sections for exhibition catalogues not noted in this select bibliography.

National Maritime Museum, *Catalogue of the Library.* Vol. 3 (2 pt.) *Atlases & Cartography* (1971)

National Register of Archives & Berkshire County Council, *Catalogue of Exhibition, Art Gallery, Town Hall, Reading* (1951)

Newcastle University Library, *A Catalogue of an Exhibition of Old Maps of North-East England, 1600–1865* (*Library Publications Extra Ser.*, 8; 1967)

NICHOLS, H., *Local Maps of Derbyshire to 1770* (Derbyshire Library Service; 1980)

NOLAN, W., *Sources for Local Studies* (1977)

O'NEILL, T.P., *Sources of Irish Local History* (1958)

Ordnance Survey, *Catalogue of Photographs of Old Cadastral and other Plans of Great Britain* (1935)

OWEN, D.M., 'The records of the established church in England, excluding parish records' (*Brit. Rec. Assoc.*, 1; 1970)

Public Record Office, *Maps and Plans in the Public Record Office. Vol. 1. British Isles, c.1410–1860* (H.M.S.O.; 1967)

Public Record Office of Ireland, *Reports of the Deputy Keeper of the Records 1–59* (H.M.S.O.; 1869–1964)

Public Record Office of Northern Ireland, *Reports of the Deputy Keeper of the Records* (H.M.S.O.; 1925–   )

Public Record Office of Northern Ireland, *How to Use the Record Office*, nos. 11–18. *Maps, Plans and Surveys* (1972)

Public Record Office of Northern Ireland,
Maps and Plans c.1600–c.1830 Co. Antrim (n.d.)

Maps and Plans c.1600–c.1830 Co. Armagh (n.d.)

Maps and Plans c.1600–c.1830 Co. Down (n.d.)

Maps and Plans c.1600–c.1830 Co. Fermanagh (n.d.)

Maps and Plans c.1600–c.1830 Co. Londonderry (n.d.)

Maps and Plans c.1600–c.1830 Co. Tyrone (n.d.)

REDSTONE, L.J., & STEER, F.W., *Local Records* (1953)

Royal Institution of Chartered Surveyors & Leeds City Libraries, *Surveyors and Map Makers. Catalogue of an Exhibition . . .* (1955)

Royal Scottish Geographical Society, *The Early Maps of Scotland.* Vol. 2. (1983)

SHIRLEY, E.P., 'Catalogue of maps and plans relating to Ireland in Her Majesty's State Paper Office, Whitehall, London, 1567–1609' (*Ulster Journ. Arch.* 3; 1855)

SKELTON, R.A., 'The royal map collections of England' (*Imago Mundi*, 13; 1956)

SKELTON, R.A., & SUMMERSON, J., *A Description of Maps and Architectural Drawings in the Collection made by William Cecil, first Baron Burghley, now at Hatfield House* (1971)

STEER, F.W., *A Catalogue of Sussex Estate Maps, West Sussex Inclosure Maps, West Sussex Deposited Plans, Miscellaneous and Printed Sussex Maps* (*Sussex Rec. Soc.*, 66; 1968)

STONE, J.C., 'The cartographic treasures of Aberdeen University Library' (*Map Collector*, 36; 1986)

TATE, W.E., *The Parish Chest* (1960)

University of London, *University of London Guide to Geography and Map Collections* (1985)

WALNE, P., *A Catalogue of Manuscript Maps in Hertfordshire Record Office* (1969)

WARREN, K.F., 'Introduction to the map resources of the British Museum' (*Prof. Geographer*, 17; 1965)

WEST, J., *Village Records* (1962)

WHITAKER, H., *The Harold Whitaker Collection of County Atlases, Road Books and Maps presented to the University of Leeds. A Catalogue* (1947)

WOOD, H., *A Guide to Records deposited in the Public Record Office of Ireland* (H.M.S.O.; 1919)

WOOD, P.H., *Descriptive Catalogue of Topographical Maps and Plans of Lands in and adjoining the old Parish of East Grinstead, Sussex from 1597 to 1900* (1964)

2

Decoration

Map decoration is sometimes of considerable documentary as well as decorative value, with landscape and activity portrayed in cartouche and vignette and potential customers flattered by representation of houses and heraldry. Cartouches decorating title, scale, inscriptions and dedications are generally simple abstract designs, but sometimes, particularly on eighteenth-century maps, they portray economic and cultural life, generally

5. Map decoration often provides valuable architectural information concerning buildings which have been demolished or much altered by now. On either side of Cossins's plan of Leeds are 15 sketches of the principal residences of the town, noting owner and address, and one of the Moot Hall.

'A New & Exact PLAN of the Town of LEEDES, Survey'd by John Cossins.' 1725.

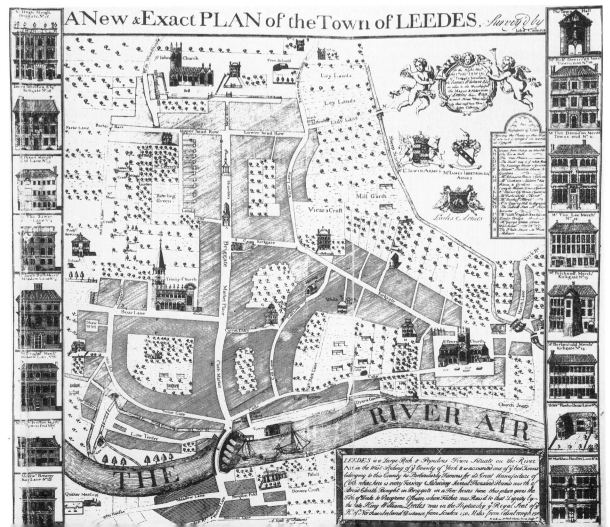

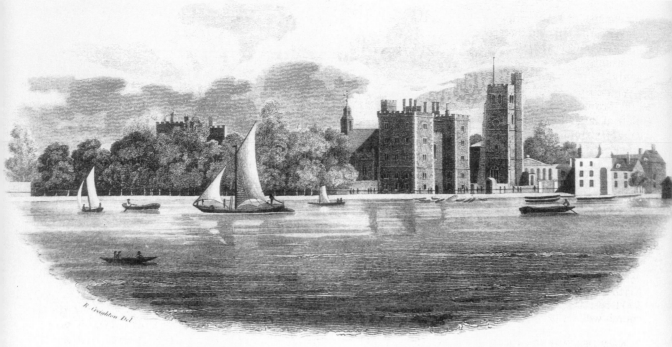

LAMBETH PALACE & CHURCH.

6. Although vignettes were added to maps to make them more attractive to potential purchasers, they may offer valuable information on contemporary life. The well-known topographical draughtsman R. Creighton produced a vignette of 'Lambeth Palace & Church' to adorn Greenwood's Surrey, which provides a valuable picture of London's river traffic of the day. At left centre the vignette shows a swim-headed barge, with its large outboard rudder and a gaff sail, which would usually carry hay, straw, or fruit. This is apparently unique evidence of the use of this type of rig on the Thames for the London river barge commonly had a square, or later a sprit, sail.

'MAP of the COUNTY of SURREY. from an Actual Survey made in the Years 1822 & 1823, By C. & I. Greenwood ... 1829.' (Detail)

in an imaginary rural scene epitomizing local activities and emphasizing occupations and products. Although many cartouches have little or no connection with the actual landscape of the day, some do offer valuable visual records of agricultural and industrial practices and equipment and of other aspects of contemporary life, such as the use of coracles on the Severn pictured on Rocque's Shropshire (1752). Illustration of survey-ors at work can be particularly valuable in clarifying current technique.

Finance by subscription encouraged emphasis of landownership. Map-makers attracted patrons by naming them on maps and depicting their lands and country seats in detail. They also featured their coats-of-arms, sometimes in an intricate frame, providing a useful reference to ownership of houses shown on the map.

Vignettes were used in estate plans and sale prospectuses to portray mansions and other important buildings as, for example, on Ainslie's Eglinton estate plans (1790). Similarly, town plans were embellished with vignettes of buildings and 'improvements', often in an elaborate border. Millerd's Bristol (1671), for example, is surrounded by views portraying architectural subjects not recorded elsewhere and since demolished or altered. As the true ground plan emerged from the mid seventeenth century, pictorial representation on the map itself was increasingly replaced by vignettes of buildings in blank areas and borders, and even on additional sheets sold with the map. The Barnsdale Toll Bar, for instance, was sketched for Fowler's turnpike plan of the Leeds area (1822); and Greenwood added vignettes 'from the pencils of distinguished artists' to his maps. Whilst vignettes decorating nineteenth-century maps by such as Moule, Pigot and Greenwood usually portray well known buildings within an idyllic landscape, they can on occasion depict much more and warrant careful study.

Vignettes also portray rural life. Minute, carefully-drawn, accurate vignettes on Aberdeen's plan of lands at Castlehill, for example, illustrate salmon fishing with seine-nets; use of the spoke-wheeled dung-cart at that date; and, most importantly, use of the 'Old Scotch Plough' of which many disparaging descriptions but no examples have survived.[1] Similarly, Home's Assynt survey (1774) depicts various ploughs and cottages.[2]

---

7. Symonson's Kent portrays each church accurately in tiny engravings distinguishing churches with spires, with towers, and so on. For example, it clearly depicts North Cray's towered church which was pulled down in 1851 because it was too small and replaced by a new church with a shingled spire.

'A NEW DESCRIPTION OF KENT . . . . with the parish Churches . . . . By the travayle of Phil: Symonson of Rochester gent 1596.' (Detail)

From *c.*1630 local life was also portrayed within the map by pictures of farming and other activities, probably designed to distinguish between arable and pasture and high roads and lanes. Johnson's plan of the Manor of South Mimms (1726), for example, shows processes of hay-making. This pictorial method was used most effectively in town plans. The 'copperplate' map of London (*c.*1553–59), for instance, depicts archery practice in Finsbury Fields; and Braun & Hogenberg's London (1572) illustrates the bull- and bear-baiting rings of Bankside and the laundresses in Moorfields.[3] Pictorial representation of buildings is at its simplest a stereotyped elevation and at its most complex a perspective bird's-eye view showing more than one elevation. From the beginning, cartographers pictured actual buildings, as on the map of Methwold Warren (*c.*1427), providing evidence of considerable architectural and archaeological value. Rogers's map (1541) of fortifications on the River Hull shows the town in bird's-eye view, probably drawn from life; and variations in Pont's sketches of houses and castles suggest individual representation. In Ireland, Raven distinguished gables, windows, and chimneys on cabins and houses; and Bartlett portrayed many lesser houses.[4] Agas's Oxford (1578–88) provides the earliest known view of Oxford Castle; and Dugdale's Warwickshire hundreds (1656) show churches with towers, spires, and bellcotes, and even distinguish roof pitch for nave and chancel. Building representation in block plan virtually eliminated portrayal in elevation or perspective on the map face, except when it was used as a novelty, as, for example, on Todd's Luton (1853), with its 'Elevations of the Principal Buildings WAREHOUSES, &c.', and Bacon's 'Monumental Map' of London (*c.*1900–1905).

Profile or perspective building views indicate character and general appearance, often even distinguishing roofing materials and window glass. The more important the building, the more accurate the representation. Interpretation of architectural detail, however, must always take account of artist's licence, as can be seen in differing versions of the same building on duplicate copies of the 'Down Survey'. Nevertheless, maps may provide a unique record of the architecture of church, manor house, mansion, inn, courthouse, exchange, town hall, almshouse, school, library, barn – or any other type of building.

Maps portray many other features pictorially, such as the crosses and cairns marking boundaries.

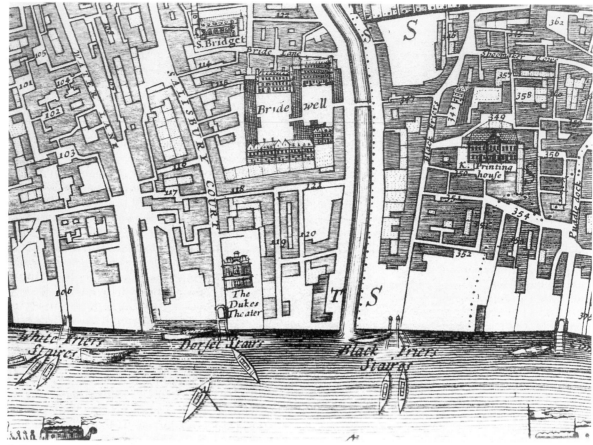

8. Decoration within a map may provide useful evidence of the nature of buildings and contemporary life. William Morgan's London is the most decorative British town plan ever produced with a mass of decoration, vignettes, dedications, explanatory and reference panels, scale cartouche, and a magnificent prospect surrounding and all but engulfing the actual survey. Morgan was one of the last map-makers to insert successfully large numbers of ornamental engravings on to the face of his map, not only to make the map more decorative, but also to offer recognizable views of prominent buildings in elevation. The pictorial representation of the ubiquitous light skiffs on the Thames emphasizes the importance of individual ferry services along and across the river from the numerous 'staires' or access points, such as 'White Friers Staires', which are located by concentrations of boats.

'LONDON &.c. ACTUALLY SURVEY'D by W.ᵐ Morgan his Ma.ᵗⁱᵉˢ Cosmog.ʳ 1681/2.' (Detail)

Even the attractive ships which sail the waters of early maps often faithfully depict craft likely to be encountered off various coasts. Waghenaer's herring fleets off East Anglia and Packe's 'Folkestone Fishery for whitings, mackerel, herrings etc.', for example, reveal a diversity of local craft and their activities. Poker's map of Romney Marsh (1617) depicts practically every kind of sea-vessel then in use in the area. Conversely, study of ships on Southampton's first map, which certainly originated before 1656, exposes extensive repainting, rendering the map almost worthless as evidence of the town's history.

Select Bibliography

LYNAM, E., *The Map-Maker's Art* (1953)
SKELTON, R.A., 'Decoration and design in maps before 1700' (*Graphis*, 7; 1951)

3

Parliamentary deposited plans and associated documents

Beginning in 1793 Parliament progressively required deposition of large-scale plans with proposals firstly for canal, river, and navigation bills, and then for highway and turnpike bills; railway bills; local authority improvement bills; bills dealing with construction of harbours, docks, ports, piers, quays, tunnels, archways, bridges and ferries; bills relating to drainage and supply of water, gas and electricity; and some other types of private bill. In 1795 it was ordered that these plans should be at a minimum scale of $\frac{1}{2}$ inch to the mile, and in 1813 this was increased to 1 inch to the mile for some classes of plan. Generally scales vary between 2 and 24 inches to the mile, but for some classes minimum scale was increased to 4 inches to the mile with provision for enlarged drawings of buildings at up to 44 inches to the mile.

Early deposited plans are in manuscript, but these were quickly superseded by printed copies. Many plans are hand coloured or drawn in coloured inks. Sections through proposed works, recording ground level in relation to the work's height or depth, have normally been deposited with plans or are shown on the plans themselves. As satisfactory large-scale Ordnance sheets became available, increasingly proposals were simply superimposed on Survey plans. Proposals investigated by House of Commons' committee were often altered. Amendments were recorded on a second set of plans for submission to the House of Lords. The chairman of the investigating Commons' committee signed each amended plan, initialling on it any agreed alterations. Minutes of evidence, petitions, and so on, presented in committee proceedings and on appeal to the Lords sometimes contain valuable maps and plans, as, for example, those presented in opposition to the Liverpool–Manchester Railway. Sometimes several sets of plans – each with further modifications – had to be deposited before opposition was overcome and approval attained. Care should be taken to ensure that plans show a scheme's final version and that it was not subject to any amending acts. Plans illustrating an intention to build are no proof of building and, although surrounding topography is faithfully portrayed, it is often the case that the scheme was never actually constructed.

The most important document accompanying deposited plans is the Book of Reference containing details of all owners, lessees, and occupiers of land affected by a scheme. Books were required to accompany plans of proposed canals from 1793, of railways and tramways from 1803, and of turnpikes from 1813; the requirement becoming general in 1838. Each land parcel is numbered to correspond with the plan and general descriptions of each property are given. Lessees' names were always noted from 1838 and may have been recorded earlier. Additionally, from 1794, proposals were accompanied by Consents' Lists of owners and occupiers of property to be compulsorily purchased, showing whether each individual consented to, dissented from, or was neutral concerning the Bill. Lessees were added from 1836, although in practice they had often been included earlier. 'Demolition statements' (or 'working class statements' or 'rehousing statements') were required from 1853 detailing number, description, and situation of houses to be compulsorily acquired when 30 or more working-class houses were to be demolished in any one parish or place. The statement, specifying numbers to be displaced and provisions for rehousing, was frequently accompanied by detailed plans. From 1899 statements were required where more than 30 people in any area were to be displaced. However, few – if any – of these statements are anything like accurate, being neither exact estimates of proposed demolitions nor reliable records of actual clearances. Total displacement was usually larger than stated due to the unrecorded volume of small demolitions, and there were many acts which had no statements.

4

Estate plans

Medieval land surveying meant valuation in a written survey derived from existing written documents, oral testimony, walking the boundaries and viewing the landmarks. Thus, estates were defined in imprecise and potentially disputable terms. There was little actual measurement. Primitive plans were needed only in complicated cases of enclosure, consolidation, or dispute.[1] A plan was prepared c.1300 to illustrate cow-pasture boundaries disputed in the Fens; a diagrammatic plan (c.1300) detailed ownership of meadowland for Fineshead Priory; a crude plan (c.1376) defined Sherwood Forest's boundaries; and marshland at Cliffe at Hoo was mapped also in the fourteenth century. However, these crude sketches seem to be merely *aides mémoires* to written surveys. In the fifteenth century, knowledge of map-drawing increased – although scale could vary within the map and exaggerated perspective drawing was emphasized. But there was still no mathematical survey. Primitive monastic estate plans were drawn to show, for example, Minster Manor, owned by St Augustine's Abbey, c.1414 and Chertsey Abbey's rich lands in the mid or late fifteenth century.[2] Only two medieval local plans are known amongst rough draft and estate surveys, respectively relating to open-field strips at Shouldham (1440–41) and small fields at Tanworth-in-Arden (c.1500).[3]

In the early sixteenth century, improvement was slow, with – for example – the crude and crowded plan of Elford (1508), showing disputed meadowland, being little better than earlier plans. Technical advance was, perhaps, pioneered by the Duchy of Lancaster which increasingly used ever better large-scale local plans in legal disputes from c.1520. Disputed common pasture, for instance, was mapped for the Duchy's Chamber c.1528.[4]

Apparently mapping became part of estate surveying quite suddenly in the late 1570s. Israel Ames or Amyce illustrated surveys in Essex with maps in 1576 and 1579.[5] Precise, detailed estate maps quickly became essential supplements to written surveys, although they did not always cover the whole manor. Agas's West Lexham (1575) and Treswell's Holdenby (1580) seem to have first presented the full details of estate survey in graphic form. Increasingly, plans were carefully and accurately drawn from measured survey to a consistent scale. The works of Agas, Treswell, Clerke, Blagrave, Walker and Langdon in the 1580s and '90s provide the fullest, most detailed, and exact portrayal of Tudor landscape and its medieval antecedants. Henceforth, the practise of attaching plans to written descriptions became widespread, encouraged by the growing complexity of landholding and agrarian advance.[6] Although estate plans were primarily private records of ownership or occupation, delineating everything from a single farm to a large estate's entire, complex, scattered lands,[7] they increasingly entered the public domain as legal evidence concerning matters of trespass, disputed boundaries and contested wills. Plans were prepared for actual litigation or in anticipation of it as the land market became more fluid following the dissolution of the monasteries; a plan-view of Ashbourne (1547), for instance, illustrated a dispute over enclosure and common land.[8]

From the Crown downwards, landowners commissioned property plans to ensure effective rent fixing and collection, thus spreading knowledge of improved practice and standardizing style as a surprisingly large band of land surveyors travelled the country in their service. Apart from Hombrestone's surveys of confiscated lands and possessions in Wales and Cornwall, surveys of Crown lands were initiated only from 1604 by a poverty-stricken James I. A comprehensive survey of Crown woodlands began in 1607. Land confiscation under the Commonwealth ended the

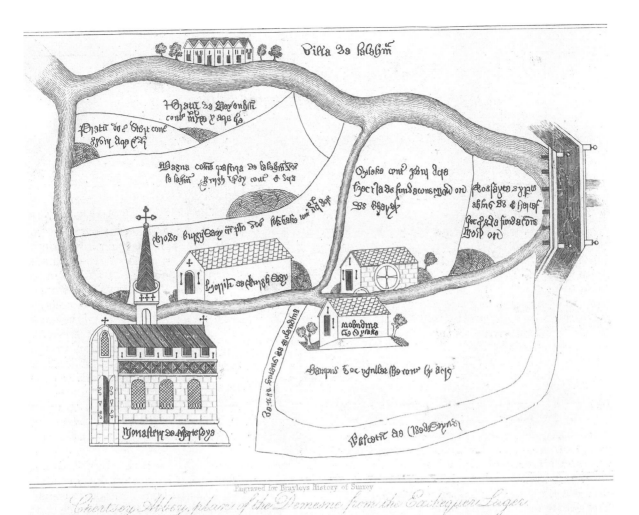

Engraved for Brayleys History of Surrey

Chertsey Abbey, plans of the Demesne from the Exchequer Leiger

9. The much-copied plan of the demesne lands of the Benedictine Abbey of Chertsey, originally drawn in the mid or late fifteenth century, shows fields, roads and streams in plan and buildings and woods in elevation. Despite the lack of scale and regard for distance or proportion, the plan effectively displays the extent and importance of the Abbey's estate. Each field is named, its size given in acres, and its usage specified. At the top the Thames flows past the town of Laleham, which is fringed with willows. The Abbey barn and two mills are shown, as are osier beds in the meadows.

'Chertsey Abbey, plan of the Demesne from the Exchequer Leiger.' Copied from the original plan for Edward Brayley's *A Topograpical History of Surrey* (1841).

work of the Crown Surveyors abruptly. Although Parliament surveyed forfeited land prior to sale, many estates were not mapped and few plans have survived. Maps were commissioned by Oxford and Cambridge Colleges, the Duchies of Cornwall and Lancaster, the hospitals, the great noble families, and large landowners like the Coke family.[9] The Duchy of Lancaster, for instance, had over 60 local plans drawn before 1603, the earliest being a diagrammatic representation of the herbages and towns of the Royal Forest of the Peak. In the monastic tradition, the Church carefully protected its lands against lay encroachment and legal challenge through regularly updated glebe terriers which from 1571 recorded the lands of each rectory and vicarage.

Familiar figures produced some of the finest Tudor estate surveys. Symonson, as Expenditor,

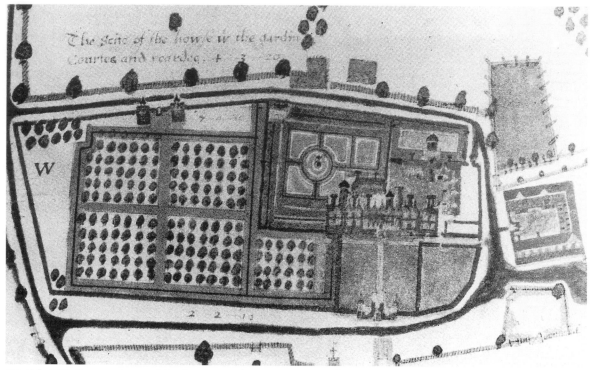

The scite of the howse w the gardin Courtes and reardos. 4 - 3 - 20.

W

10. John Walker, senior and junior, were the most notable of early Essex surveyors producing fine maps exhibiting great skill in execution and a wealth of detailed information. Walker senior mapped Sir John Petre's properties in East and West Horndon in 1598, providing a detailed picture of a Tudor manor house and its gardens which no longer exist. The only other known representation of Old Thorndon Hall appears on a print of c.1669.

The Manor of West Horndon. John Walker, 1598. (Detail)

Superintendent, and Surveyor of the Bridge and Bridge estates at Rochester in 1592–98, produced at least four manuscript maps of estates belonging to the Rochester Bridge Wardens. Norden surveyed ex-monastic estates in Northamptonshire 1588–90 and Orford and Sudbourne[10] in 1601; c.1604 he surveyed Crown estates in Cornwall; c.1606 he surveyed for Sir John Spencer in Sussex and Hertfordshire; and in 1607 he presented a magnificent book of plans of Windsor to James I. Norden's son John, with whom he jointly held the Surveyorship of the Duchy of Cornwall, mapped the Manor of Laleham (1623).[11] Another father and son surveying-duo was that of Christopher and Robert Saxton. Although Christopher worked

mainly in his native Yorkshire, during 1587–c.1608 he surveyed throughout England for employers such as St Thomas's Hospital, the Savile family, and the Earl of Northumberland.[12] Many Saxton surveys were commissioned for disputes and litigation; the Crown, for instance, employed him to arbitrate on its behalf, as did various courts to map lands, watercourses, and boundaries in question.[13] From 1601 Christopher was assisted by Robert, who surveyed estates in Yorkshire until c.1621, mapping – for example – Tanshelf (1611), for the Duchy of Lancaster, and Manningham (1613). Other surveyors, such as Brasier and Pierse, worked in several areas, but most localized their activities, as did the John Walkers in Essex[14] and the William Figgs, both fathers and sons, in Sussex, and Boycot in Kent.

Irish estate maps apparently date from the redistribution of properties forfeited following English suppression when surveyors, including Francis Jobson, were employed to measure and map newly confiscated areas of Munster for the plantation of 1586–89. However, only two large-scale maps survive, showing subdivisions of Sir Walter Raleigh's seignories. Following official survey, some estates were divided into tenant farms but only the tenement map (1598) of Raleigh's Mogeely estate survives. Some engineers and map-

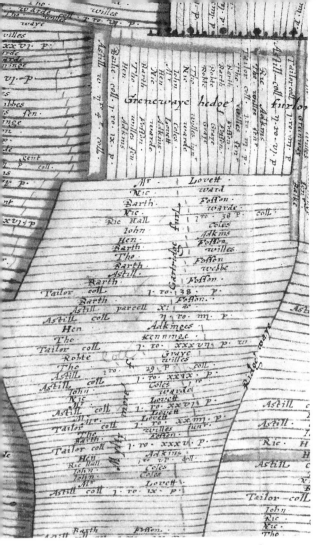

11. Estate plans were a far more effective and accurate method of representing the disposition of an estate than the traditional verbose written description. Plans were prepared to record land ownership rather than use but in so doing they portrayed a topography probably unchanged for several centuries. When land ownership in an open-field village was divided between two or more manors, it was essential to know which strips in the open fields went with which manor. Warden Hovenden of All Souls College, Oxford, commissioned plans of the College's land holdings, showing the strips owned by manors in the College's possession. The north-west of the parish of Weston and Weedon was mapped in 1593 at about 15″ : 1m. recording the College's lands in 'redd letters' and naming the occupants of each strip with area noted for College properties.

'The description certain tenementes in Weston in the parishe of Weedon Pinckney in the Countye of North'ton togeather with certeine landes thereto adioyninge lieinge on the South weste parte thereof and extending unto the river or brooke that deuideth Helmesden from Weedon made in September 1593.' (Detail)

12. Many early estate plans were by-products of litigation. In July 1598 Christopher Saxton was commissioned to draw a map of Old Byland on the North Yorkshire Moors to be used as evidence in a boundary dispute before the Court of Exchequer between Sir Edward Wotton and Sir William Bellasis, who owned lands at Old Byland and the neighbouring parish of Murton respectively. This elaborate map shows in detail trees, woods, field-names, buildings, sheep-cotes, tumuli, earth banks, gates, roads, and tracks. Each boundary claimed by the parties is shown, together with all the boundary stones mentioned in the depositions to the Court.

'A plat of the pishe of Old Bylande wherein all the Inclosed groūdes are colored wᵗʰ red, The comōns are coloured wyth yelowe, The Defendants bounder betwixt Oldbyland and Morton, is drawen with a grene lyne; and the confines left white. Made by Christofer Saxton. Anᵒ: Dm: 1598.' (Detail)

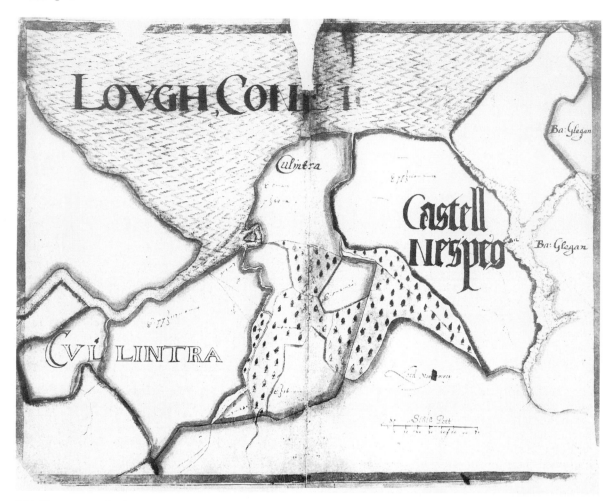

13. The maps of Thomas Raven provide the most valuable cartographic evidence about the plantations in Ulster in James I's reign. After producing surveys for the Londoners who settled Ulster and Sir Thomas Phillips, Raven was engaged in 1625 by Lord Clandeboye to map his estate in the north of County Down, producing a portfolio of fine maps.

Untitled. From a collection of maps of the Clandeboye (Bangor) estate in County Down by Thomas Raven, 1625–26, held by Bangor Borough Council.

makers who accompanied forces sent to quell the Earl of Tyrone's rebellion (1598–1603) stayed on to produce plantation surveys in Ulster and elsewhere. Most gifted was Thomas Raven, who helped prepare the rather sketchy official maps used by the Ulster plantation commissioners. By the 1620s he was surveying privately for the City of London, Sir Philip Perceval and other landowners, depicting not only the castles and churches found on almost every Irish map but much else besides.[15] The foundations of a permanent Irish land-surveying profession were laid through increasing demand from British proprietors for tenement boundary surveys.

Lack of money and surveying talent in Ireland created a distinctive outline 'plantation' survey showing only name, acreage, and boundaries of forfeited land, usually at 6 inches to the mile. From the Elizabethan settlement of Munster, the style continued in Strafford's Connaught survey (1636–40), in Petty's 'Down Survey' (1655–56), and in surveys for the Williamite trustees of forfeited estates (1700–3). Despite covering large areas, these official 'plantation' surveys mapped only small units, being, thus, essentially surveys of estates. 'Plantation' surveys, whether official or private, are usually disappointingly uninformative, although perhaps reflecting the emptiness of the landscape itself, with only tenement acreage always reliable. They represent relief boldly but primitively. Land use and fences (except tenement boundaries and 'improvements') are rarely shown. Buildings appear only in conventionalized profile or perspective view. The typical 'Down Survey' map, for example, covers a block of townlands at either 40 or 80 Irish perches to the inch, showing townland boundaries; profitable and unprofitable land; arable, meadow, bog, wood, mountain, and types of pasture, with acreage figures for each; and other features depending on the surveyor's initiative and energy. Petty's areas are, however, rarely correct, being usually deficient by about 11.5 per cent. Generally, traversing round property borders with chain and circumferentor left a bare interior with only the most obvious detail of roads, houses and fields recorded. 'Plantation' style survived until the early nineteenth century with its outdated signs and stiff, geometrical decoration. In Ireland, land surveyors seldom had to map complex strip patterns in a pre-enclosure open-field landscape.

Agrarian change in the seventeenth century created an insistent demand for estate maps. William Senior, for example, and others mapped estates in many counties for the Earl of Devon (1609–28), the Earl of Newcastle (1629–40), and other 'improving' landowners. Typical is a plan of Wymondham (1652), which shows every building in the village, all roads and lanes, and each field with its name, acreage, and use. From 1700 improved instruments and techniques, introduced partly by immigrant map-makers such as Rocque and his pupil and brother-in-law Scalé, increased accuracy. Presentation and decoration became more sophisticated. Generally, a healthy living developed for the country land surveyor, particularly in mapping the formal gardens and landscaped parks of Georgian England. Rocque, for example, mapped many gardens and country residences such as Wanstead, Wrest Park, Hampton Court and Richmond Palace in the 1730s and '40's; and Isaac Taylor advertised that 'Estates are Survey'd & Mapped in a very Accurate & Neat manner at ye usual Prices.' Forty-six per cent of all eighteenth-century manuscript maps in the Bedfordshire Record Office were prepared for estate management for individual owners or to divide estates on inheritance or sale. The best work, such as Richardson's glorious Royal Manor of Richmond (1771) and Rhodes's Kensington (1776), is outstanding. Yeakell & Gardner, apparently the period's only salaried surveyors, created perhaps the finest contemporary plans for the Duke of

Richmond *c.*1765, delineating his Goodwood estates in manuscript at 20 inches to the mile and in engraved cut-outs at 6 and 2 inches to the mile (thus eliminating the cost of hand copying). This format seems unique for the period. The 6-inch map is the first printed delineation of an extensive area at such a large scale in English cartography.

Rocque and Scalé founded a 'French' school of estate surveying in Ireland which flourished until the 1820s through an unbroken chain of apprenticeships and partnerships.[16] Its style, characterized by elegant marginal decoration,[17] was

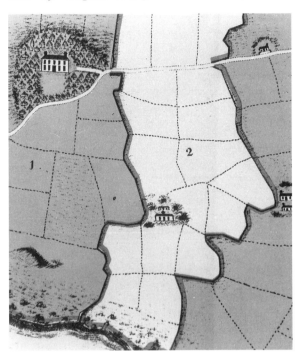

14. Many Irish land surveyors remained uninfluenced by the 'French' school of estate mapping, whose technical mastery and creative artistry was perhaps inappropriate to large estates consisting mainly of unproductive land. Manning's maps of Arthur Shuldam's estates covered 10,000 acres, 75 per cent of which was classified as mountain and bog. Despite his technical competance, Manning's reckoning of the acreage for Currabee was some 60 acres short. The houses are probably realistic enough representations but many were omitted. The field boundaries cannot represent those existing in the first years of the nineteenth century and it is possible that the pattern shown is Manning's suggestion for a more rational system of field enclosure.

' A MAP of CURRABEE Parish of Dreenagh Barony of Carbery and County of Cork.' Richard Manning, 1801–3. (Detail)

The Warren Farm.
— As now Arranged. —

<u>The Buildings</u>, consist of a brick and tile Farm House; a board and thatch Barn with 2 Bays, and boarded Threshing Floor, a brick board and thatch Stable with Hay Loft over; also a board and thatch Straw House with Cattle Sheds on Posts. —

The Contents and Yearly Value of the Land are as follow.

— Warren Farm —

Refer.ce	Names of the Fields.	Quantity. A	R	P	Price per Acre	Annual Value. £	S.	D.
1	Broomy Field	7	1	21	Oats ... 20/	7	7	7.
2	Farther Seven Acres	7	2	1	Wheat 26/	9	15	1.
3	Twenty-one Acres	21	2	22	Broom & Pasture 8/	8	13	1.
4	Eleven Acres	11	1	30	Wheat & potatoes 25/	14	5	11.
5	The Five Acres	5	1	12	Oats ... 30/	7	19	9
9	River Field	8	3	25	Pasture 32/	14	5	"
10	Long Eleven Acres	9	1	38	Oats ... 20/	9	9	9.
11	Brakey Field	8	2	27	Rye Barley and Oats 16/	6	18	8.
12	Heath Field	7	3	9	Wheat 28/	10	18	6.
13	Buildings Yards and Orchard	"	3	25	Gratis	"	"	"
14	Wood	"	2	36	Wood 6/	"	4	4
15	Garden and House	1	"	"	Garden 2/	"	"	"
	Carried over	90	3	6.	£.	91	17	8

15. A surveyor's field note books, if they have survived, can provide information which was not included on the finished plan. Usually these books are working documents used to record measurements, angles, compass directions, and so on. Additionally they may record field names, ditches, fences, footpaths, roads, buildings, names of adjacent owners, etc. On occasion the working drawings were converted into a book of carefully prepared plans of small sections of the estate which complemented the large-scale plan, providing additional detail.

'Survey and Valuation of The Bexley, Erith and Plumstead and Romney Marsh Estates, in The County of Kent. belonging to Francis Dashwood Esq.r, By H.C. Wright 1829.' (Detail)

inaugurated in eight volumes of plans produced by Rocque for Lord Kildare (1755–60). The fuller countryside portrayed resulted partly from improvement and enclosure and partly from greater attention to detail. 'French'-style maps show buildings and relief in plan, with colour differentiating materials, and distinguish land use by colour, sign and ornament, depicting landscape more completely than has since been attempted in Ireland.[18] Sample checks suggest Rocque's plans to be comprehensive and accurate. Rocque's and Scalé's works, particularly for the Dukes of Leinster and Devonshire respectively, created standards and a style which were followed in the less well embellished plans of native map-makers. Earlier outline surveys are not necessarily inferior in content to the more impressive 'French' plans, and, certainly, Scalé thought well enough of the earlier style to develop two 'editions' of his plans, with one emphasizing the townland boundary and restricting interior detail to durable features rather than changing land use. Although 'French' style continued until *c.*1830, its essence was greatly diluted and, inevitably, a simpler, less decorative form became fully established, omitting relief and not differentiating arable from grass.

Plan production accompanied the spread of agricultural improvement. In Wales, for example, only a very few large estates were surveyed before 1760, including estates in Anglesey mapped by Lewis Morris 1724–29. However, towards the end of the century, growing awareness of the value of surveys in estate management stimulated production. Of 135 volumes of plans held by the National Library of Wales, only 12 predate 1760, whilst 64 were produced in 1760–99. Although scale and accuracy of Welsh plans varies greatly, broad land-use categories are occasionally represented. Generally, Welsh property boundaries were surveyed with some accuracy, eradicating the uncertainty of centuries.[19]

There was little need for plans before the arrival of agricultural improvement in Scotland. Crude large-scale sketches began to appear only in the early eighteenth century. Increased demand highlighted the dearth of local land surveyors. Initially, landowners had to import English surveyors such as Laud and Winter, but a native surveying school soon emerged.[20] In 1720–1810 the Scottish countryside was remodelled, erasing the old runrig and infield-outfield systems and replacing them with the new geometrical commercial farming. Although pre-improvement survey was unusual, it was often necessary to map existing land tenure to create the new landscape, and many Scottish estates had farms mapped both before and after consolidation and enclosure. Winter, for instance, recorded runrig lands mainly in the 1750s in areas as far apart as Midlothian and Inverness, delineating each rig with its acreage and tenant's name.

The estates of Jacobite supporters were forfeited following the collapse of the 1745 rebellion and most were sold. However, the 13 largest Highland estates were retained and annexed to the Crown in order to stimulate progress and eradicate sources of discontent and disaffection. Commissioners were appointed in 1755 to manage and improve these 'annexed estates', with express power to have lands surveyed and plans prepared. Until 1784 a wealth of plans were commissioned of remote Highland areas which otherwise could not have supported

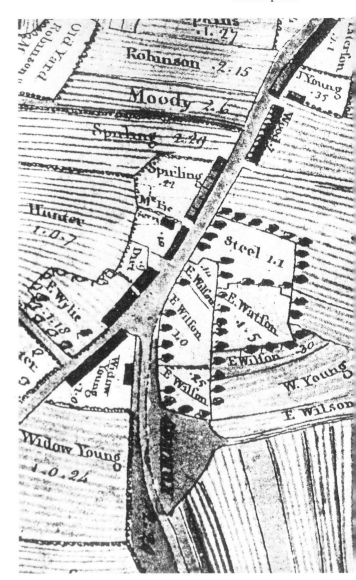

16. The runrig system was established to ensure a wide and fair distribution of land amongst the co-tenants of farms. Land holdings were re-allocated periodically in this form of co-operative husbandry. However, by the seventeenth century, possessions were almost invariably frozen in a pattern of fixed tenure of considerable inconvenience. Estate plans had to be drawn on a scale large enough to show holdings that frequently amounted to fractions of an acre, giving exact acreages. The most detailed plans, such as Ainslie's pre-enclosure plan of part of the Barony of Kilwinning, show each named arable field with its individual rigs, noting acreages and names of possessors.

The runrigs of Corshill, parish of Kilwinning, Ayrshire. John Ainslie, 1789. (Detail)

such work. Skilled resident surveyors, such as May[21], mapped the Forfeited Estates dividing runrig lands and laying out villages for disbanded soldiers. At the same time they also worked for local proprietors; May, for example, produced plans for Grant of Grant.

As Forfeited Estate work declined, these talented and experienced surveyors were snapped up by landowners fevered with improvement to map and manage estates and lay out model villages such as Ballater and Tomintoul. May's assistant Milne, for instance, surveyed for the Earl of Fife and the Duke of Gordon. Towards the end of the century, a new type of competent, professional surveyor emerged in Scotland mapping great estates and interpreting their potential. Foremost and most prolific was Ainslie, who produced numerous plans during 1770–1828, notably of the Eglinton estate in Ayrshire. However, after 1770 surveying opportunities declined and Milne and others were forced to seek employment further south.

Plan production in England and Wales was encouraged by continuing high agricultural investment. Additionally, plans accompanied property sale, lease, valuation and arbitration in an increasingly fluid land market in which estate land was taken for development. And plans continued to illustrate litigation. Although plan decoration was declining, it experienced a final flourish in Thomas Horner's 'panoramic chorometry' which attempted to portray 'picturesque' aspects of an estate, notably in specimen plans of Clerkenwell and Kingston-upon-Thames and in maps of estates in the Vale of Neath.[22] Towards the mid nineteenth century, particulary after *c.*1850, the character of plans was altered by the increasing large-scale coverage of the Tithe and Ordnance Surveys and by the development of lithography which could produce cheap, accurate, multiple copies avoiding the pitfalls and delays of hand copying. More plans were produced but in plainer style. It was simpler and cheaper to derive plans from large-scale Ordnance maps rather than from actual survey, and increasingly common just to superimpose extra information on to Survey sheets or to cut out the estate from the Ordnance map and paste it on a blank sheet to create a traditional-looking plan with additional data added in manuscript. The pattern in Scotland was much the same, with plan production reflecting agricultural demand until the availability of large-scale Ordnance maps sent the land-surveying profession into rapid decline in the 1840s.[23] Henceforth, very few manuscripts

were drawn and Ordnance sheets were simply marked up to create plans.

The Ordnance's impact on estate mapping was first felt in Ireland. It was quickly recognized that property maps could be obtained more cheaply by enlarging 6-inch sheets by pantograph, usually to 20 statute perches to the inch, than by private survey. A ready market was satisfied in the mid-century by the many firms of lithographic printers and law stationers, and particularly by the Dublin

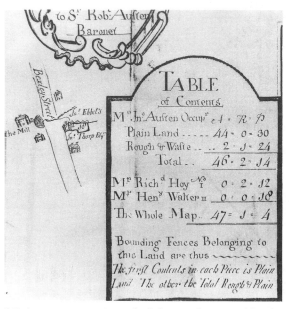

17. A summary terrier, schedule, or reference table was frequently added to farm plans detailing in tabular form the numbered or lettered fields with their acreages, the rough and waste, names, tenants, holdings, land use, the terms on which the land was held, comments about the holding, and so on, to supplement information shown cartographically. Field acreages are sometimes given in two parts, representing the area which could be ploughed or mown and the rough scrub around the edges of the field. Some plans even have tables of the number of trees to be found in each field. Often a small part of the estate or neighbouring area is portrayed separately at a larger scale, ranging from highly detailed and accurate insets to the crudest of 'thumb-nail' sketches, such as that of properties in High Street, Bexley. Sometimes an owner or tenant might use the plan to sketch in ideas and schemes for improvement or to note proposals for next year's crops. Surveys which have been heavily used in estate offices may be covered with decades of revision, up-dating and annotation.

'Long Lane Farm. Lying in the Parish of Bexley in the County of Kent. Belonging to S.r Rob.t Austen Baronet.' John Bowra, 1768. (Detail)

booksellers Hodges & Smith. Irish land surveyors openly offered to check local details of Ordnance maps and to add further information according to instructions. McArthur, for instance, advertised that 'Where economy is an object of importance, a complete Survey may be had, from inserting on the Ordnance Maps the Mearings, Ec. of each Farm.'

---

18. Dickinson's plan of the Earl of Cardigan's lands near Leeds names fields, lists tenants with a key to their fields, and details ownership of surrounding lands. An accompanying 'Field Book' details 'the Quantity, Quality, and Yearly Value, of all the particulars in every respective Farm'.

'A MAP of all ye Lands belonging to ye Right Hon:ble GEORGE Earl of CARDIGAN in his MANNOR of HEDINGLEY, KIRKSTALL, AND BURLEY, near Leeds, in ye WEST-RIDING of the County of YORK. Surveyed By, Joseph Dickinson, 1711.'

After 1849 many more enlargements were made for the Incumbered Estates Court (later known as the Landed Estates Court and the Land Judges' Court) which regulated the flood of land transactions following the great Famine. Although the Court made a grant towards survey and lithography, most maps were still copied or enlarged from Ordnance sheets, but so many were deemed unsatisfactory that from 1859 the Ordnance produced special maps for the Court, by replotting at larger scales from its 6-inch field books, to ensure more accurate calculation of parcel areas. This became compulsory in 1862. Ordnance mapping was extended in 1872 to land transfers handled by the Church Temporalities Commission and in 1888 the Survey was empowered to make similar maps of land undergoing tenant purchase through the Irish Land Commission. Thus, by 1890 the Ordnance had made property maps in multiple copies

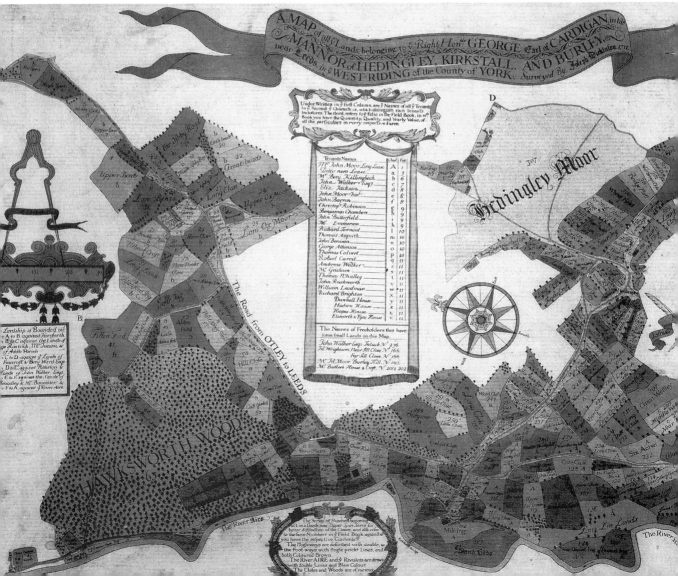

covering some 14 per cent of Ireland, usually at the 6-inch scale but with more intricate landscapes at 25 inches to the mile.

'Estate' plans range from small garden plots, through individual farms, to the scattered holdings of massive estates; perhaps covering a whole parish, or most of it, or even several parishes, or isolated land parcels scattered amongst parishes. Estates possess plans ranging from a single anonymous manuscript map to a grand series of finely bound volumes, intended for the landowner's library, documenting thousands of acres, perhaps in a sequence covering centuries. Seale, Sherrard & Browning's 1777 survey of Madden's estates, for example, is subdivided into 70 townland maps and nine bog areas, varying in size from 19 acres to a mountain stretch of 500 acres.[24] Dispersed holdings usually appear on separate plans, but Burton ingeniously portrayed the position, size and orientation of each scattered field on one piece of vellum (1636) without reference to the surrounding countryside. Details of tenants, holdings, fields and acreages appear either in a summary terrier on the map or in an accompanying book of reference. Plan scales usually range from 10–40 inches to the mile but there are larger and smaller; a survey of Kennington, for example, contains 27 plans ranging in scale from 30–60 feet to the inch showing such minute detail as cesspits at the bottoms of gardens.[25] At worst, 'estate' plans may be nothing more than crude working documents, but at best they offer the historian a microscopic view of landscape; Williams, for example, even recorded individual species of trees. However, most plans lack much detail, for they were designed as functional documents to indicate generally only an owner's lands, boundaries and buildings, and responsibility for upkeep. Together, estate plans present an almost complete inventory of rural landscape, although Irish plans produced before the later eighteenth century are sparse in detail. Every conceivable feature is recorded somewhere by exuberant colour and varied, unstandardized signs and shading, very often with great artistic beauty. Details of enclosure or 'improvement' schemes have frequently been superimposed on plans of the existing, or even an earlier landscape; Milne's 1770s' plan of the Strathbogie estates, for instance, has new field and farm boundaries added dated 1822.

Plans were frequently drawn from memory rather than survey. Rough diagrammatic sketches, for example, accompanying Archer's Tanworth estate survey *c.*1500, appear to record holding distribution from memory because neither shape nor direction is accurate.[26] Since many plans were produced to facilitate land sale and to solve boundary disputes, their information was generally carefully considered and is precise. However, so variable was surveying technique and skill that even plans drawn from actual survey can differ dramatically in accuracy. Nevertheless, no matter how crude the survey and how inaccurate the result, the estate plan may be the best cartographic source available; Norden's estate map of Orford and Sudbourne, for instance, has been judged 'the most reliable old map of the district extant' despite its inaccuracies.[27]

Landscape change, such as that of the Upchurch Marshes in the sixteenth century,[28] can be reconstructed from the detail of estate plans. They have been most widely used to study field systems and settlement patterns, since they offer the most reliable portrayals of enclosure and field and settlement layout.[29] Pre-enclosure estate plans, such as that of Strixton (1583), may show the complex layout of strips in open fields[30] and the nature of old roads and hamlets prior to improvement.[31] (However, such plans may not present a complete picture of the medieval landscape due to changes such as the contraction of the ploughed area and the establishment of closes left as permanent pasture.) Plans, for instance, emphasize the excessive fragmentation of Scottish possessions that almost inevitably occurred when a farm became overloaded with tenants during runrig.[32] Plans document the landscape on the eve of enclosure, as in Merioneth in the 1790s,[33] and in transition as the agrarian revolution took hold – as in central Ayrshire from the 1760s.[34] They can establish the rate of enclosure and the extent of remaining open-fields, as at Hooton Pagnell in

19. 'All the Land coloured green is either Meadow or Pasture. The red dotted line athwart the two inclosures N° 362 and N° 363 shews where anciently was a hedge the Land on the North side of which is freehold and belongs to the Manor of Cowshott. The Land &c Numbered with red belongs to M.r Halsey, the others Numbered with black belongs to the different Tenants.'

'A MAP of the Manor and Parish of PIRBRIGHT in the County of Surrey which includes the Manor of Cowshott A Manor within the said Manor of Pirbright – The Demaines of Henry Halsey Esq.' 'Surveyed by W. Newland in 1805, 1806, and 1807.'

A MAP of the Manor and Parish of PIRBRIGHT in the County of Surrey which includes the Manor of Cowshott, A Manor within the said Manor of Pirbright — The Demaines of Henry Halsey &c. Surveyed by W. Newland in 1805, 1806 and 1807

Yorkshire,[35] and may highlight the contrasting landscapes resulting from varying degrees of enterprise, often in close proximity; Saxton's plans of Spofforth (1606/8), for instance, reveal the intensive exploitation of the Earl of Northumberland's estates.[36] Enclosure can be dated from estate plans, as in Kent where plans reveal that the county was largely unaffected by it in the sixteenth and eighteenth centuries. Kent plans also unveil the county's agrarian peculiarities and expose patterns of land-holding, establishing their relationship with physical conditions.[37] Generally, details of current land use and improvement schemes identify usage, crops, livestock, woodland, and so on, and may also suggest land capability.[38] Plans of the Welsh highlands during the Napoleonic Wars, for example, reveal a farming region concentrating on animal husbandry with a little arable.[39] In contrast, plans may give no indication of farmland use as in the case of most of those of Bromley, Beckenham and Penge produced after *c*.1750.[40] Plans also record the disparking of former medieval parks; the removal of houses and fields and the diversion of roads and paths to create and enlarge landscaped parks; and their eventual submergence under the tide of suburban growth.

Estate plans portray ownership, tenancy and settlement patterns, often recording minor place-names lost by the time of the Ordnance's large-scale survey, as does Roberts's map of properties in Llaniden parish (1756). Reid's plan of North Uist (1799) provides a vivid visual impression of the runrig patterns of settlement and population and of the planned landscape which replaced them;[41] and plans of estates drawn in preparation for Highland clearance expose the crowding and low living standards of a population about to be removed in order to extend sheep farming.[42]

Many thousands of estate plans are recorded and more are continually coming to light. However, coverage is patchy. Some areas are well covered over time: the Bute and Dunraven collections in the National Library of Wales, for example, contain nearly three hundred estate plans dating from 1767, mainly relating to Glamorgan; and the Gogerddan collection contains 160 maps from 1737 of mid and north Cardigan. In Kent 187 estate maps produced before 1700 have been located, portraying landholdings in 117 out of about four hundred parishes.[43] Some areas were comprehensively covered at particular periods by energetic local surveyors. Their plans facilitate meaningful regional studies, allowing generalization about the unmapped residue, as in the study of pre-1700 land-holding patterns in Kent. Aram, for example, produced 76 maps in Monmouthshire (1763–94), Couling 118 maps in South Wales generally (1790–1815), and Minshull 85 maps in north-east Denbigh, west Flint, and south Monmouthshire (1766–1803).

Estates, particularly those remaining in the same hands for a long period, may be recorded on a sequence of plans produced over decades, if not centuries. Plans are particularly useful in sequence when prepared on similar instructions and/or by

---

21. Roe's manuscript map of the Manor of Lyons concentrates on land parcels, giving the name, acreage and boundaries. Adjoining lands are named; main roads are marked; and a few houses are shown, usually in relief, although the 'old house and offices' are delineated in ground plan. The colouring of the demesne and the leaving of the outlying townlands uncoloured emphasizes the importance given to the mansion and park within the estate by the map-maker.

'A Map OF The MANOR of LYONS, the Estate of The R.t Honble Lord Baron Cloncurry. Surveyed in 1801, by John Roe.' (Detail)

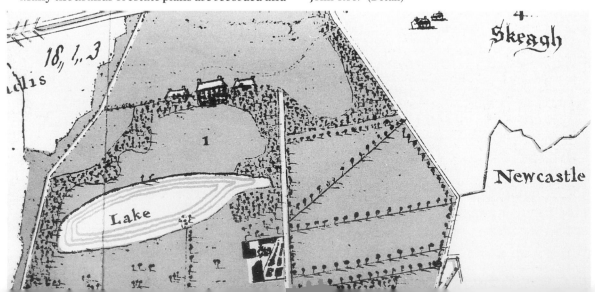

the same surveyor.[44] However, since plans relate only to holdings under particular ownership, possibly scattered over several parishes or even several counties, they give little idea of conditions in areas separating the various parts of an estate. Unfortunately, though, all too often the continuity of estate records has been disrupted by land-ownership changes.

Select Bibliography

AALEN, F.H.A., & HUNTER, R.J., 'The estate maps of Trinity College' (*Hermathena*, 98; 1964)

AALEN, F.H.A., & HUNTER, R.J., 'Two early seventeenth century maps of Donegal', (*Journ. Roy. Soc. Antiquaries Ireland*, 94; 1964)

ADAMS, I.H., 'Scottish large-scale plans: their value for studying the evolution of the Scottish rural landscape' in *Early Maps as Historical Evidence* (Papers given at the Conference on the History of Cartography held at the Royal Geographical Soc.; 1967)

ADAMS, I.H., *The Mapping of a Scottish Estate* (Univ. Edin. Dept. Educ. Studies; 1971)

ADAMS, I.H., 'Sources for Scottish local history – estate plans' (*Local Historian*, 12; 1976)

ADAMS, I.H., 'Two maps of Kindrogan and their land surveyor, William Panton, M.A.' (*Report, Scot. Field Studs. Assoc.*; 1977)

ANDREWS, J.H., 'Geography and government in Elizabethan Ireland', in N. Stephens & R. Glasscock (eds): *Irish Geographical Studies presented to E. Estyn Evans* (Inst. Irish Studs.; 1970)

ANDREWS, J.H., 'Henry Pratt, surveyor of Kerry estates' (*Journ. Kerry Arch. Hist. Soc.*, 13; 1980)

Buckinghamshire Record Society: *Handlist of Buckinghamshire Estate Maps* (1963)

Buckinghamshire Record Society: *Buckinghamshire Estate Maps* (1964)

BYRNE, M.J., 'Old Kerry maps' (*Kerry Arch. Mag.*, 3; 1914–16)

COBBE, H., 'Four manuscript maps recently acquired by the British Museum' (*Journ. Soc. Archivists*, 4; 1973)

EDEN, P., 'Land surveyors in Norfolk, 1550–1850: the estate surveyors' (*Norfolk Arch.*, 35; 1973)

EDEN, P., 'Three Elizabethan estate surveyors: Peter Kempe, Thomas Clerke and Thomas Langdon' in S. Tyacke (ed.): *English Map-Making 1500–1650* (1983)

FAIRHURST, H., 'An old estate plan of Auchindrain, Mid-Argyll' (*Scot. Studs.*, 12; 1968)

FREY, J., 'A catalogue of the eighteenth and early nineteenth century estate maps in the Antrim estate office, Glenarm, co. Antrim' (*Ulster Journ. Arch.*, 3, 16; 1953)

GREEN, E.R.R., 'A catalogue of the estate maps, etc., in the Downshire Office, Hillsborough, county Down' (*Ulster Journ. Arch.*, 3, 12; 1949)

HANLY, J., 'Oldcastle and Loughcrew, 1778' (*Ríocht na Midhe*, 3,3; 1965)

HORNER, A.A., 'Carton, co. Kildare; a case study of the making of an Irish demesne' (*Irish Georg. Soc. Quart. Bull.*, 18; 1975)

HORNER, A.A., 'New maps of co. Kildare interest in the National Library of Ireland' (*Kildare Arch. Soc. Journ.*, 15, 5; 1975–76)

HULL, F., *Catalogue of Estate Maps 1590–1840 in the Kent County Archives Office* (Kent County Council; 1973)

IRVINE, J., 'A map of Glenarm, 1779' (*The Glynns*, 9; 1981)

LOCKHART, D.G., 'The land surveyor in Northern Ireland before the coming of the Ordnance Survey *circa* 1840' (*Irish Geog.*, 11; 1978)

LONGFIELD, A.K., 'A co. Sligo estate map of 1768' (*Irish Georg. Soc. Quart. Bull.*, 20; 1977)

LOVE, H.W., 'A seventeenth century map of Dromiskin, county Louth' (*Louth Arch. Soc. Journ.*, 15; 1964)

McCOURT, D., 'The maps of the Brownlow estate and the study of the rural landscape in north Armagh' (*Ulster Journ. Arch.*, 3, 20; 1957)

MOODY, T.W., *The Londonderry Plantation, 1609–41. The City of London and the Plantation in Ulster* (1939)

O'SULLIVAN, H., 'Two eighteenth century maps of the Clanbrassil Estate, Dundalk' (*Louth Arch. Soc. Journ.*, 15; 1963)

PHILLIPS, A.D.M., 'William Fowler's seventeenth-century maps and surveys' (*Cart. Journ.*, 17; 1980)

PHILLIPS, A.D.M., 'William Fowler's Staffordshire maps', (*Trans. S. Staffs. Arch. Soc.*, 25; 1981)

RAVENHILL, W., 'The mapping of Great Haseley and Latchford: an episode in the surveying career of Joel Gascoyne' (*Cart. Journ.*, 10; 1973)

RAVENHILL, W., 'The plottes of Morden Mylles, Cuttell (Cotehele)' (*Devon Cornwall Notes Queries*, 35, 5; 1984)

SIMMS, J.G., *The Williamite Confiscation in Ireland, 1690–1703* (1956)

SMITH, B.S., 'The business archives of estate agents' (*Journ. Soc. Archivists*, 3; 1967)

SMITH, B.S., 'The Dougharty family of Worcester, estate surveyors and mapmakers, 1700–60. Catalogue of maps and plans by the Dougharty family' (*Worcs. Hist. Soc. Miscellany*, 11, 5; 1967)

STEER, F.W., *A Catalogue of Sussex Estate Maps and Tithe Award Maps* (Sussex Rec. Soc., 61; 1962)

STEER, F.W., *A Catalogue of Sussex Estate Maps, West Sussex Inclosure Maps, West Sussex Deposited Plans, Miscellaneous and Printed Sussex Maps* (Sussex Rec. Soc., 66; 1968)

STORRIE, M.C., 'A note on William Bald's plan of Ardnamurchan and Sunart, 1807' (*Scot. Studs.*, 5; 1961)

THIRD, B.M.W., 'Longniddry in transition (1778–1798)' (*Trans. E. Lothian Antiq. Field Naturalist's Soc.*, 6; 1955)

THIRD, B.M.W., 'The significance of Scottish estate plans and associated documents. Some local examples' (*Scot. Studs.*, 1; 1957)

5
Enclosure plans

Enclosure brought additional land into cultivation by dividing common land and rearranging existing cultivated strips to eliminate communal open fields; thus creating enclosed fields and consolidated holdings. It was a response to increased agricultural demand, taking place gradually over a long period but with three main periods of accelerated change in the thirteenth, sixteenth, and eighteenth/nineteenth centuries.

Much early enclosure was a matter of voluntary assent or arbitrary action, proceeding steadily and remorselessly, and causing little excitement, interest or indignation. Private agreement required neither surveyor nor map. Apart from estate plans recording agreements, the few maps of private enclosures known are rarely more than rough sketches; those, for example, prepared to disafforest the Royal Forest of the Peak (1635–40) for enclosed grazing land are sketches designed simply to grade and divide waste and common.[1]

Inevitably, land reorganization sometimes gave rise to agitation and complaint over titles, rights and areas involved. Prudent enclosers enshrined agreements in the official records of manorial courts, vestries, and Courts of Chancery or Exchequeur. Disputes were brought before the courts. Both occasioned map production. Maps were prepared, for example, as evidence c.1675 in appeals by commoners to the Duchy of Lancaster Court concerning disafforestation of the Peak, but they are a poor topographical record, being concerned only with areas, boundaries, access to water, land quality and equal division.

Parliamentary acts were rarely petitioned for early enclosures, although they were sometimes obtained for division of common and waste, and for marsh drainage and enclosure. As enclosure accelerated in the later eighteenth century, larger landowners increasingly sought the sanction of a sympathetic Parliament to override opposition and push through enclosure by private act which was thought safer and faster than private agreement. Before 1760 there were just 225 enclosure acts covering at most 400,000 acres, mainly in Warwickshire, Northamptonshire and Gloucestershire and in the vast wastes of Yorkshire. However, in the next 40 years 1479 enclosure acts dealt with nearly $2\frac{1}{2}$ million acres of open fields and more than 500 acts enclosed 750,000 acres of waste; and in George III's reign (1760–1820) alone more than 3000 private enclosure acts were passed. Commissioners were usually appointed to inspect proposed enclosures and arrange compensation. In many parts of central England they virtually planned a new landscape of regular fields, roads and drains. Their land division was embodied in an award which was usually accompanied by a map, particularly after c.1770. Measured plans of lands to be enclosed and of land parcels belonging to various properties were prepared, although some acts allowed use of existing maps for division. Surveys and valuations were produced by such as William Fairbank who built up extensive enclosure practices. Objections raised at the reading of an award necessitated new hearings, surveys, and a general re-allotment; in the Nevin enclosure, for instance, the Crown and others objected to allotments made on their behalf in 1814 and new plans had to be drawn up.[2]

Enclosure was hastened by war shortages and population growth and redistribution. In Wales, for example, one of the least affected areas during the French Wars, acts (1793–1815) authorized enclosure of about one-eighth of the common and waste – over 200,000 acres.[3] As ever more marginal land came into cultivation, demand increased for a general act to simplify and cheapen enclosure. General enclosure acts of 1801, 1836 and 1845 initially standardized a simpler and cheaper procedure; then allowed enclosure by

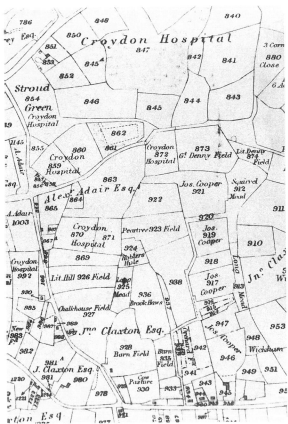

22. 'A PLAN OF THE PARISH OF CROYDON IN THE COUNTY OF SURREY Shewing the allotments in the Common and Common fields as divided by Act of Parliament in the Year 1800 by Tho. Bainbridge.' (Detail)

consent of a majority of landowners without a private bill; and then established a permanent commission able to enclose whenever necessary without Parliamentary sanction – except for certain categories of land covered in single general acts passed annually. The 1845 Act allowed use of tithe plans but only about one-sixth of these were sufficiently accurate for enclosure and many areas were resurveyed. More than a thousand acts dealt with over $1\frac{1}{2}$ million acres of open fields in 1800–44, and after the 1845 Act another 164 awards cleared up nearly 200,000 more acres of the remaining open fields. During the nineteenth century another 1300 acts and awards covered $1\frac{1}{4}$ million acres of waste.

Enclosure acts usually directed that one copy of the award and accompanying map should be deposited either in one of the central courts of justice at Westminster or with the Clerk of the Peace for the county; and another copy with the parish incumbent and churchwardens. Alternatively or additionally copies were enrolled in a specified court of record. However, directions given in the acts for deposition and enrolment were frequently disregarded and not carried out. Increasingly both sets of plans are now held by county record offices. The Public Record Office has a notable collection, particularly relating to Crown estates. All too often the map accompanying the award has been lost; Leicestershire County Record Office, for example, possesses official copies of 102 awards but only 20 maps. Commissioners' records sometimes contain surveys and field books, valuations made prior to redistribution, early estate maps investigated and assessed by enclosure surveyors, and so on.

Since Scottish enclosure was the by-product of 'improvement' by independent landlords rather than Parliamentary legislation, it was mapped by estate plans rather than special enclosure plans prepared for Parliamentary application. Acts of the Scottish Parliament for runrig consolidation (1695) and commonty division (1695) created compelling legal reasons for the production of large-scale plans connected with enclosure. The Court of Session appointed commissioners to supervise commonty division. Surveyors such as Mercer and Oman were appointed to map commonty boundaries and land quality, with freedom to extend their terms of reference. The Court divided nearly half a million acres of commonty in 1720–1850, providing a remarkable record of landscape during this period of change in the hundreds of commonty plans that have survived.

Although divisions of commons by private or local arrangement in Ireland dated from the mid seventeenth century, enclosure by Parliamentary act was introduced only in 1800 for Dromiskin, followed in 1803 by Garristown. Without general legislation, all enclosures were by individual act; the few enacted by 1820 relating mainly to County Dublin. Again, maps were to be prepared if there was no existing survey of sufficient accuracy or authenticity. Although extinction of the rundale system was the nearest thing in Ireland to enclosure of open-field strips elsewhere, no pre-Famine maps exist showing individual plots with measurements, names and details of owner or tenant. The earliest true rundale map seems to be Brassington's survey (1850), showing intermixed holdings of Crown lands at Boughill subject to official investigation at the time of the Famine.

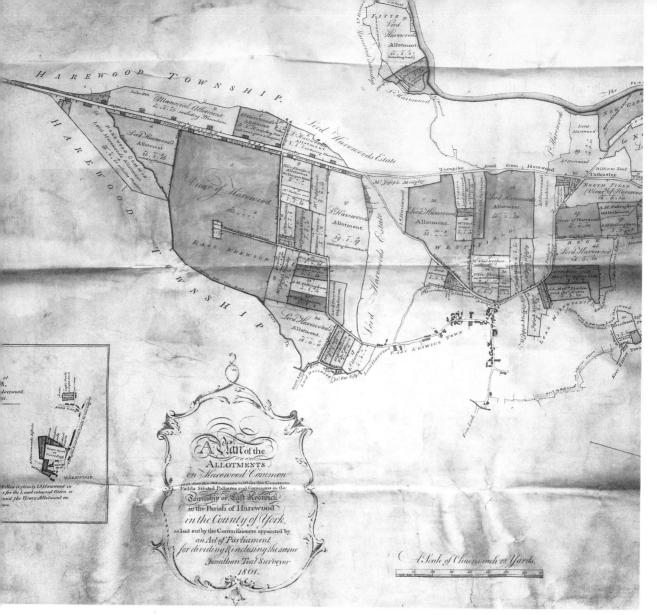

'A Plan of the ALLOTMENTS on Harewood Common and also the Allotments within the Common Fields Stinted Pastures and Commons in the Township or East Keswick in the Parish of Harewood in the County of York, as laid out by the Commissioners appointed by an Act of Parliament for dividing & inclosing the same Jonathan Teal Surveyor 1801.'

23. Enclosure plans frequently give valuable information other than the reference numbers, owner's names and acreages for each plot. Teal's plan names some fields, marks old enclosures, and notes land exchanges and donations. An inset plan shows 'the Land at Harewood, exchanged by Ld Harewood and the Vicar'.

'A Plan of the ALLOTMENTS on Harewood Common and also the Allotments within the Common Fields Stinted Pastures and Commons in the Township OF East Keswick in the Parish of Harewood in the County of York, as laid out by the Commissioners appointed by an Act of Parliament for dividing and inclosing the same Jonathan Teal Surveyor 1801'. (Detail)

Before open-field strips (often up to 4–5000 within a single parish) could be re-assigned, it was sometimes essential to delineate the existing landscape in detail, particularly ownership and area, as Jalland did for Nottingham (1819). These so-called draft enclosure plans became more common after 1830. Commissioners sometimes superimposed their proposals on this medieval countryside showing new fields, hedges and roads; thus plans can illuminate the planning process and illustrate how completely enclosure reconstructed the landscape, as at Barton (1840). Similarly, boundaries of former commons, open fields and earlier enclosures may be depicted on the enclosure plan.

Most enclosure maps show, at a large scale, commissioners' proposals for new land allotments and the new landscape of straightened roads and regular boundaries, with small towns or villages often inset at larger scales. All items mentioned in the written award are identified on the plan; obviously, sub-divisions made later do not appear and for areas such as Huggate in the Yorkshire Wolds, the plan shows only the skeletal framework of the modern field pattern.[4] Commissioners not only straightened existing roads but also laid out new highways, making their plans important sources for the history of roads and tracks.

Enclosure maps may cover a whole parish in areas, such as the Midland Plain, Lincolnshire, and East Anglia, where open fields had lasted almost intact; but elsewhere, where only remnants of an open-field system survived from previous enclosure, the area shown will be small. Similarly, enclosure maps of small commons, strips of waste alongside the highway, or the village green, usually did not warrant careful survey; a simple sketch showing adjoining lands affected by the enclosure being generally sufficient to illustrate the proposal. Sometimes, enclosure of large tracts of waste produced an outline map of thousands of acres of more-or-less featureless moor or heath, divided into regular blocks ready for new ownership; plans of the northern Pennines, for example, show new farmlands being carved out of moorland and occupied by farmer/miner families in a period when Parliamentary enclosure coincided with mining expansion.[5] Maps produced for private enclosure acts vary enormously in scale, style, and quality ranging from a barely adequate sketch of the terms of the award to a pair of carefully surveyed maps showing the area before enclosure and after the new apportionment. After the 1845 Act the Commission enforced more uniformity, although still employing local surveyors. For effective use, particularly in landscape reconstruction, plans must be studied in conjunction with written awards which specify commissioners' decisions about various topographical, economic and tenurial matters, detailing amongst other things, field names and boundaries, land use, the extent of glebe lands, roads and footpaths, and endowments of local schools and charities.

Obviously, enclosure plans show the new land units resulting from the award, particularly the apportionment of common land with details of ownership and acreages. Conversely, they also record existing farmlands unaffected by enclosure, establishing location and naming owners; thus presenting a full picture of post-enclosure owner-

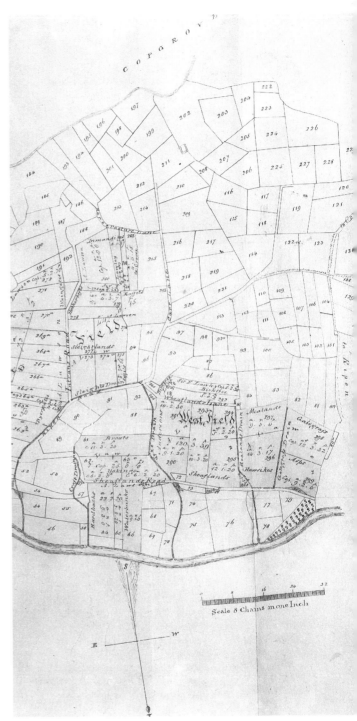

24. Plan of enclosures at Roecliffe at 1″ : 8 chains with open fields coloured pink and 'Exchanges' green.

'Plan of Roecliffe in the County of York.' Joshua Potter, 1841. (Detail)

53

ship. However, allotments created by commissioners were not necessarily immutable and sometimes land plots were sold very quickly afterwards. Furthermore, the terms of the award were not always followed strictly and new boundaries shown on maps sometimes never actually existed on the ground. Enclosure plans illuminate types of land tenure prevalent in different districts and in many parishes serve as the ultimate title deeds to a great part of the land, both that belonging to ordinary proprietors and that allotted to rectors, vicars, and lay impropriators in lieu of tithe and glebe. Lands forming endowments are delineated and allotments of land for public purposes, such as those to the parish highways' surveyor for use as gravel pits, are specified. Plans are also the final authority on the course and breadth of highways; the existence of footpaths, bridleways and rights of way; and to the courses, breadths and liability for cleansing of most surface drains. Even ownership of hedges and other boundaries may be noted.

Enclosure plans normally distinguish old enclosures from those established by the act, locating the actual extent of waste or common at enclosure, and recording the amount of illegal enclosure thereon. In Wales, for example, plans demonstrate two stages in the gradual disappearance of commons in the Arwystli region at the beginning of the nineteenth century, with only broken remnants left in low fertile areas where most common land had already been appropriated but only piecemeal encroachment in high, infertile areas where large expanses of common survived untouched.[6] For one area of the region, for instance, old enclosures, common waste and illegal encroachment can be reconstructed from the map and award of an upland moor enclosure (1826). Plans may also explain absence of encroachment; for example, plans of farms in Llanaber, Llanbedr, Llanddwywe, and Llanenddwyn not only illuminate the local agricultural system but also indicate reasons for the lack of encroachment on to common by owners and tenants adjoining it. The depiction of ancient enclosures and other pre-enclosure features sometimes facilitates location of the open-field pattern; indeed, enclosure plans may well be the only cartographic evidence of the open-field pattern.[7]

Town development owes much to enclosure patterns which established the lines of field boundaries and trackways determining urban expansion. Building in towns such as Leicester and Stamford was confined to the central town core by the late survival of open fields with their complicated

rights. The enclosure award immediately created a pattern for streets and building; when the open fields were finally enclosed around Nottingham, for example, in 1845, compact blocks were promptly developed by their owners without the slightest reference to neighbouring allotments or owners.[8]

Tithe payments were usually extinguished on Parliamentary enclosure by allotting land to the parson and other receivers of tithe. Where enclosure was most extensive, most tithes were already commuted by the early nineteenth century and tithe surveys were not needed, making enclosure plans the best information source on tithe in those areas. In England and Wales some 2230 enclosure acts passed before 1835 provided for abolition of tithe payment in kind, replacing it with land allotments to the tithe-owner, or annual money payments, or a combination of both. Limits of land allotted or of lands charged with a money payment are generally delineated on the enclosure map.

Enclosure information is found on many general topographical maps. As early as 1405–8 a map of the pasture of Inclesmore displayed enclosures. Adair's county maps have been employed as a source on early enclosure[9], as have Ogilby's road maps whose distinction of fenced by 'double Black Lines' and unfenced roads by 'Prick'd Lines' has been used to estimate distribution of enclosed and open or waste land in Restoration England.[10] Couchman's reduction (1849) of Richardson, King & Driver's map of the New Forest, produced for the Select Committee on Woods and Works, shows 'Portions enclosed . . . for the growth of Navy timber'. Enclosure is most comprehensively recorded on those 25-inch Ordnance plans where every land parcel is delineated with a reference number referring to an *Area Book* detailing area, land use, and so on.

Enclosure acts related to lands in roughly five thousand ancient parishes in England. Parts of at least several hundred Welsh parishes must also have been affected. Altogether after 1760 over 5100 enclosure acts plus enclosure under general acts covered over $6\frac{1}{2}$ million acres in England alone.

---

25. Plan of the lordship or manor of Tunstall in Holderness in East Yorkshire 'Engraved for Dade's History & Antiquities of Holderness'. 'The shaded Lands are ancient Inclosures, the rest new Inclosures.'

'A PLAN of the LORDSHIP of TUNSTALL. Surveyed in the Year 1777 By R. Atkinsen of Leaven Reduced in 1788 by J. Tuke of York.'

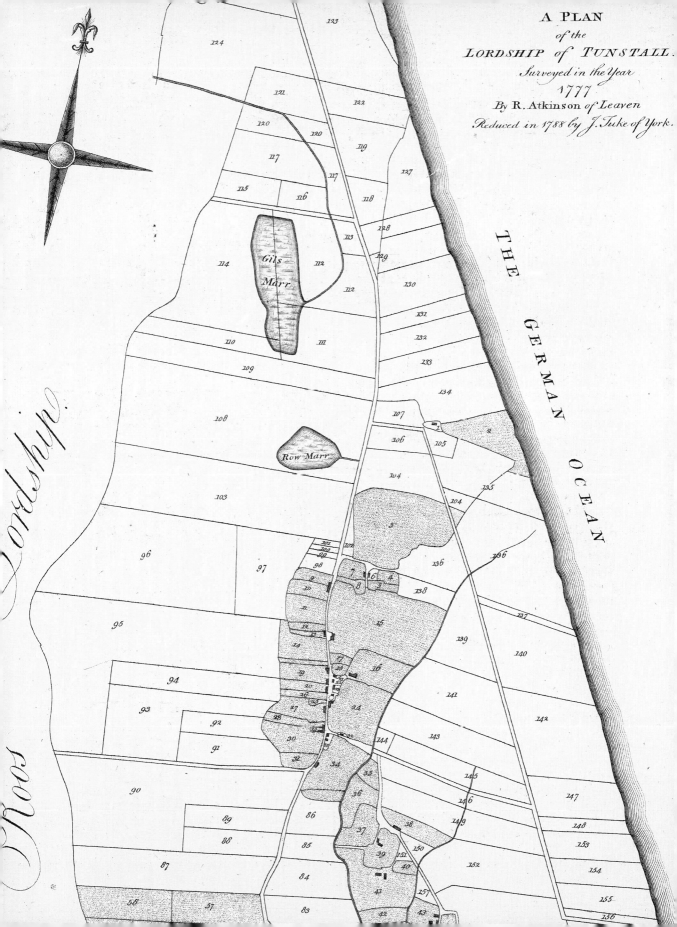

A PLAN
of the
LORDSHIP of TUNSTALL.
Surveyed in the Year
1777
By R. Atkinson of Leaven
Reduced in 1788 by J. Tuke of York.

THE GERMAN OCEAN

Lordship.

Roos.

Gils Marr

Row Marr

However, map coverage is inevitably patchy both in terms of time and area, with enclosure being completed faster in some areas than in others. For example, 35 per cent of eighteenth-century manuscript maps in the Bedfordshire Record Office are enclosure maps, but for 1760–80 only 24 per cent are concerned with enclosures whilst for 1790–1815 60 per cent are enclosure maps. A great number of counties possess no enclosure awards relating to open fields, although they do usually have awards and maps dealing with common and waste, as in Devon where awards were made in 1802–74. Enclosure in areas such as Kent and Essex was by arbitrary and informal reclamation direct from forest and moor, without passing through the open-field stage at all. In highland areas generally the small proportion of arable cultivated in common in the middle ages had been mostly privately enclosed before Parliamentary enclosure, so that very few maps are concerned with open fields. Extensive upland commons and wastes, however, remained unenclosed until well into the nineteenth century. Many individual parishes have no enclosure maps, perhaps because the parish, or a sizeable part of it, was enclosed by private agreement without any mapping; perhaps because it was never enclosed at all; or perhaps because commissioners used an existing estate map rather than drawing a new plan.

Despite the patchiness of coverage, enclosure awards and maps are some of the most reliable and easily accessible of local records. Map and award had to be compared line by line and verified on oath by the surveyor. However, they are very variable in what they show, ranging from detailed maps of whole parishes to outline sketches showing nothing more than property boundaries. They span a long time period, often even among adjacent parishes, and their information, particularly on land use, is frequently disappointing.

Select Bibliography

Bedford County Records Committee, *Catalogue of Enclosure Awards, Supplementary Catalogue of Maps and List of Awards upon Tithe, in the Bedfordshire County Muniments* (1939)

EDEN, P., 'Land surveyors in Norfolk, 1550–1850: the surveyors of land inclosure' (*Norfolk Arch.*, 36; 1975)

EMMISON, F.G., *Catalogue of Maps in Essex Record Office; First Supplement* (1952)

FOWLER, G.H., *Four Pre-Enclosure Village Maps* (Beds. Hist. Rec. Soc.; 1936)

Huntingdon County Record Office, *List of Inclosure Awards & Plans* (1971)

Lancashire Record Office, *Handlist of Lancs. Enclosure Acts and Awards* (1946)

LEWARNE, J.G.W., 'A cartographical survey of the area.XII: Fetcham enclosure award, 1813' (*Proc. Leatherhead Dist. Local Hist. Soc.*, 3; 1967)

Northamptonshire County Council, *The County of Northampton and County Council Handbook for 1955–6* (1955)

Oxfordshire County Record Office, *A Handlist of Inclosure Acts and Awards relating to the County of Oxford* (1963)

RUSSEL, R.C., 'Parliamentary enclosure and the documents for its study' in A. Rogers & T. Rowley (eds): *Landscapes and Documents* (1974)

STEER, F.W., *A Catalogue of Sussex Estate Maps, West Sussex Inclosure Maps, West Sussex Deposited Plans, Miscellaneous and Printed Sussex Maps* (*Sussex Rec. Soc.*, 66; 1968)

TATE, W.E., 'Enclosure awards and acts' (*History*, 51; 1966)

TATE, W.E., *A Domesday of English Enclosure Acts*. Edited with an introduction by M.E. Turner (1978)

WALNE, P., *A Catalogue of Inclosure Maps in the Berkshire Record Office* (1954)

6
Tithe plans

Basically, tithe was a tenth of the produce of land and stock paid by landholders for the maintenance of the clergy and other church purposes. Tithes were paid in kind from medieval times. From the Reformation tithe assessment and collection had become increasingly varied. When ecclesiastical land was sold, the right to tithe passed into lay hands, increasing existing dissatisfaction over payment even to the Church. Payment in kind became increasingly inconvenient and impractical, involving assessment, collection, storage and disposal of tithe goods. Hence, in many parishes tithes were commuted into simpler cash rent payments by mutual agreement or were removed altogether during enclosure. An agreement to alter the method of paying tithes had to be accompanied by a full valuation of them with a schedule of titheable plots and, usually, a large-scale plan. Early tithe maps, such as that of Ashtead (1638), are scarce. Later pre-1836 maps, such as that of Hatfield (1824), are commoner, being generally as comprehensive and detailed as the later Parliamentary tithe surveys.

Despite efforts to commute tithes, by 1836 they were still payable in about two-thirds of parishes in England and Wales. Tithes had always been resented and payment obstructed, but the problem intensified as agrarian change progressed. In order to regularize the situation and partly to satisfy opponents of both tithe and wealthy Church, the Tithe Commutation Act (1836) was passed, providing for the abolition of tithes in kind throughout England and Wales. Adjustable rent-charges apportioned on each land plot were substituted, being settled either by voluntary agreements made before October 1838, subject to confirmation by the new Tithe Commission, or by compulsory award of the Commissioners. Existing corn-rents were left unaffected. In voluntary agreement, a valuer apportioned the agreed rent-charge on the basis either of a new map or of existing maps of any scale and accuracy, provided that three-quarters of landowners by value agreed to them. In practice most parishes left the difficult task of apportioning payments to the Commissioners appointed under the Act.

In order to apportion rent-charges on to individual properties, all parish titheable lands had to be valued and an award made distributing the rent-charge in proportion to values. A map had to be drawn up 'which shall indicate such properties with sufficient accuracy to enable parties to identify the lands which are respectively subject to the several amounts of rent-charge'. The Tithe Commissioners had to approve award, apportionment and map, all of which then became matters of official record and evidence. The Tithe Commission was established in London and assistant commissioners operated the Act in the parishes by convening public meetings, commissioning surveys, and drawing up provisional apportionments to be confirmed by the Commission.

The passing of the Act marked the beginning of a year of controversy over the nature of the maps required for commutation and over the possibility of combining tithe surveys with a general cadastral survey. Dawson's specification and instructions for a survey of 'rigid accuracy' using only the 'great mass of existing Plans and Surveys . . . with proper precautions' brought howls of protest from landowners at the potential expense of surveys.[1] The Act was amended in 1837 to allow apportionment confirmation without map certification, so that the Commissioners could accept maps as being those referred to in an apportionment without being satisfied of their accuracy. However, without the Commissioners' seal as well as signature, maps would not be 'evidence of the quantities and boundaries of the lands referred to'. The Commissioners sealed maps considered to be 'first class',

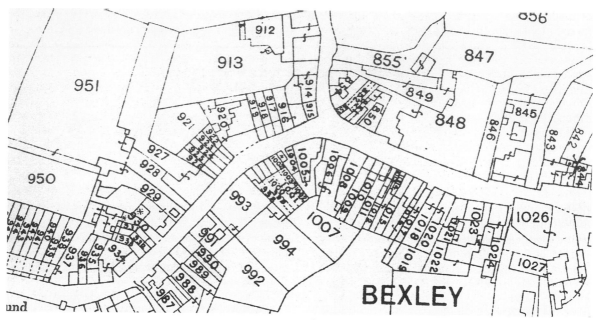

26. 'PLAN OF THE PARISH OF BEXLEY KENT Surveyed in 1838 & 9 by G. Darbyshire & Sons. BROMPTON Scale 3 Chains to 1 inch (Sd.) F. O. Martin April. 15/44.' (Detail)

showing that they were satisfied with the reliability of the purpose-designed tithe map. Although they still retained their full powers to refuse to confirm an apportionment accompanied by a map considered wholly unsatisfactory, in practice maps adopted by landowners were only rejected in very exceptional circumstances. A new survey made to Dawson's standards was required only in parishes where no previous map existed and where apportionment was compulsory. The Commissioners continued to try to persuade landowners to commission first class, accurate plans at 26.66 inches to the mile, constructed according to a system of internal triangulation; and as an added inducement the Tithe Act (1842) empowered the Poor Law Commissioners to pay any proportion they saw fit of the cost of making or providing a map for tithe commutation, provided that it received the Commissioners' seal.

In the event, apparently only some nineteen hundred maps, about a sixth of the tithe surveys, were sealed as 'first class', although there appears to be no extant listing of sealed maps. These are generally highly accurate since they were legal documents for proof of title, being subject to public scrutiny and challenge. Reports to the Commissioners, minutes of local enquiries, and correspon-

dence in tithe files testify to the thoroughness of survey and the vigilance of both tithe-payers and tithe-owners in correcting error. However, there seems no common factor by which a 'first class' map may be recognized. Most, but not all, were drawn at the recommended scale of 3 chains to the inch; some were apparently constructed by triangulation but not all triangulated maps were sealed; and Dawson's recommended conventional signs were seldom adopted. The same map-maker may have produced both sealed and unsealed maps. The Commissioners did not check maps on the ground or make spot surveys themselves. Mistakes were only pointed out when the map was deposited in the parish prior to confirmation. 'First class' maps may not, therefore, be as reliable in all cases as always supposed. Unsealed maps are a mixture of sub-standard original surveys, copies of earlier maps, and compilations pieced together from existing maps of different dates, perhaps with a few modern details filled in by guesswork. Thus, an unsealed map may be anything from one marginally failing to satisfy the Commissioners to a notoriously inaccurate hybrid. Many are little more than a topographical sketch of no cadastral value, showing only boundaries of tithe areas and positions of buildings. However, unsealed maps were considered good enough to be used by the Ordnance Survey as a source for parish boundaries for its 25-inch plans. Tithe-free land within a tithe district was particularly prone to inaccuracy because it was pointless to pay for accurate mapping of land benefitting neither landholder nor tithe-owner. Contemporary estate maps are only of limited value in testing tithe-plan accuracy because most were either consulted or copied by tithe surveyors, or alternatively were copied themselves from the tithe map. Some were even drawn by the same surveyor. The end result is a patchwork of tithe surveys without uniform scale or accuracy.

The essential purpose of tithe surveys was to measure accurately the acreage of each land parcel and record its observed state of cultivation. Surveyors tended to treat matters of no concern to the Commissioners superficially; rights of way, for example, were seldom delineated precisely and unambiguously. Scales and styles vary, although there is sufficient uniformity to allow comparison. Some 75 per cent of the maps are at 3, 4 or 6 chains to the inch (26.6, 20, and 13.3 inches to the mile), although scales can vary from 1–12 chains. Boundaries of tithe areas are always shown, usually corresponding with fields but in some cases constituting whole farms. Some land uses are recorded on the map but others appear only in the schedules. Boundaries of enclosed fields are usually shown by continuous lines and unenclosed by dotted. Occasionally hedges, fences and gates are marked. Dotted lines may also represent property divisions, separating holdings in open field or common meadow showing furlongs and strips; or may indicate divisions between different land usage in a field under single ownership. Fields are named, but often unreliably from local pronunciation. Courses of streams, canals, ditches and drains are usually marked, as are lakes, ponds, roads and footpaths. Gardens, orchards, closes, heaths, greens, and commons are shown and usually named. Many tithe maps distinguish between coniferous and deciduous woodland by tree signs, and between dwellings and other buildings by colouring red and grey respectively. A few maps are fully coloured to distinguish titheable land or various properties or farms or sometimes to indicate land use. Some tithe maps, particularly the uncoloured, such as those of Ashford, Azerley, and Laxton are so faded in places that they are barely legible. Individual mills are often distinguished, sometimes in elevation, as are churches. Individual industrial sites and mines are marked with functions noted, sometimes providing their only cartographic record. Tithe maps document early medieval parish boundaries and islands of tithe-free former monastic land and manorial waste.

27. 'PLAN of the Parish of CROYDON, IN THE COUNTY OF SURREY. 1847. Surveyed & Valued for the Tithe Commutation by W. ROBERTS. 68, Chancery Lane.' '9 Chains to an Inch.' (Detail)

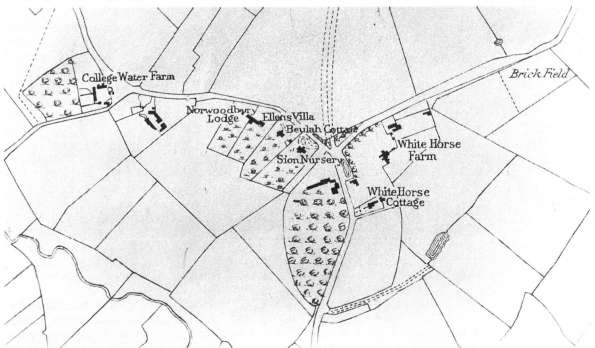

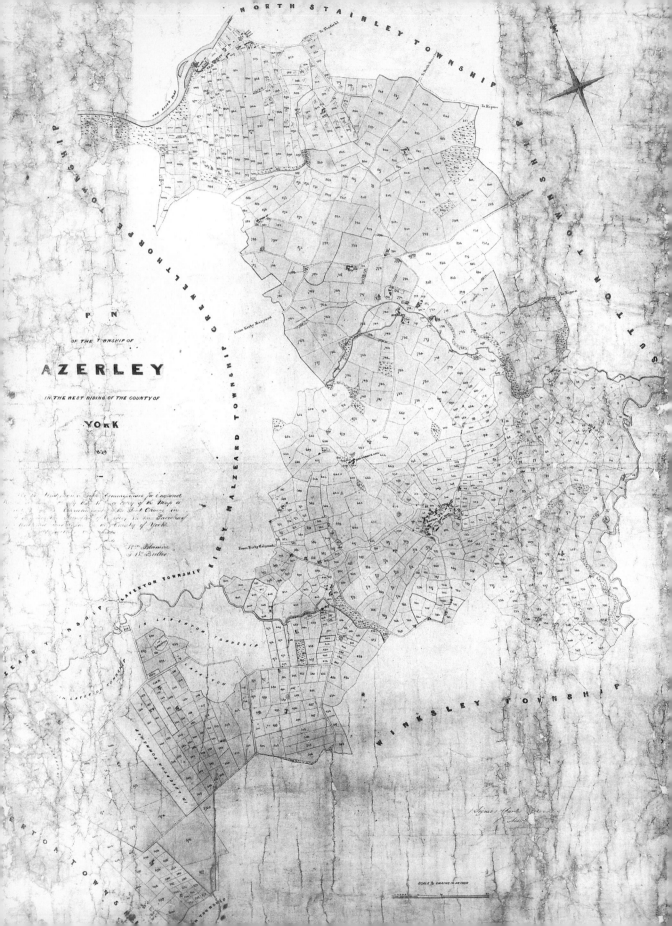

NORTH STAINLEY TOWNSHIP

GRE WELTHORPE TOWNSHIP

SUTTON TOWNSHIP

KIRBY MALZEARD TOWNSHIP

WINKSLEY TOWNSHIP

LAVERTON TOWNSHIP

P N

OF THE TOWNSHIP OF

AZERLEY

IN THE WEST RIDING OF THE COUNTY OF

YORK

Other details obviously depend on locality. Generally, however, tithe maps rarely contain many place-names and offer a rather flat, featureless picture of settlement and landscape.

For many nucleated villages, such as Llanblethian, the tithe plan is the first to identify individual buildings. In urban areas, insets often show built-up zones at larger scales. Towns were also sometimes surveyed separately by the Tithe Commissioners who, for example, mapped Leeds in 1847. For some towns, tithe awards are extremely detailed with the schedule listing contents of each plot. In contrast, town centres are frequently blank with just a single parcel number, often because the core of a medieval borough was tithe free. However, the carefully delineated surrounding fields and estates, which provided building land throughout the ensuing years, may hold the key to later urban development.

Plan size is partly proportional to that of the parish, ranging from one to over one hundred square feet and being anything from 1–14 feet wide with corresponding length, some unrolling to 24 feet or more. Generally, tithe maps – prepared by local surveyors and supervised by assistant commissioners – are clear, detailed and functional. However, there are often minor differences between manuscript maps submitted to the Commissioners and those retained by the parish due to transcription error in copying. In order to reduce dangerous hand copying, some tithe maps were lithographed by Standidge & Co. for official records.

The accompanying apportionment schedule lists owners, occupiers, land use and tithe rent-charge for each land parcel, allowing information to be plotted on the map using the reference numbers matching parcel to written description. Plans and written apportionments were designed to be used together and only together do they offer an exhaustive local inventory. Unfortunately, since apportionment and map usually differ considerably in size, they have often been separated in the interests of preservation and storage, causing in some cases loss of the map. Apportionment and map have tended to remain combined only for smaller tithe

districts. Together they offer a large-scale cross-section of the parish in the year of the award. Maps were sometimes completed well in advance of the final agreement to the apportionment. Hence, map and schedule may disagree concerning landownership and tenancy because information was collected at different times. Properties shown and numbered may not appear in the award, probably because they belonged to the tithe-owner, as with the significant gaps in the Christchurch award. Tithe files contain details of survey and sometimes information about cropping, rotations and so on. At least three copies of the tithe documents were prepared: one for the Tithe Redemption Commission (the complete set now transferred to the Public Record Office and currently being microfilmed); one for the Diocesan records (many now transferred to local record offices, or, in Wales to the National Library of Wales); and one for the parish incumbent (many now transferred to local record offices but many others remain *in situ*, hidden away and forgotten). Additional private copies were frequently made. Unfortunately, although the Public Record Office holds a comprehensive collection, many of the larger maps are split into several sections; the altered apportionment maps rarely follow the original tithe map in chronological sequence; and numbering is often illogical.

Occasionally, reduced explanatory maps of apportionments were produced. In 1853, for example, Roberts published a map of Hammersmith as a guide to the apportionment, providing a detailed picture of the area just before urbanization.

The 1836 Act placed an additional 'extraordinary charge' on hop-grounds and market gardens. This was removed by the Extraordinary Tithe Redemption Act (1886), which was in effect a further process of commutation, creating another set of tithe documents consisting of a Certificate of Capital Value and related map for some 500 districts in 16 counties. Maps, however, were simply prepared on 6-inch Ordnance sheets and mainly cover larger areas than the original tithe plans.

Most tithe maps were made in 1836–41, with the rest mainly by 1851. By 1886 some 11,800 apportionments had been made under the 1836 Act, with only a handful of parishes still paying tithes in kind because commutation was impracticable.

Apportionment sometimes had to be altered and

28. Many tithe maps have barely survived to the present day, being now in very poor condition.

'PLAN OF THE TOWNSHIP OF AZERLEY IN THE WEST RIDING OF THE COUNTY OF YORK 1839.' Surveyed by J. Bradley & Son of Richmond at 1″ : 8 chains.

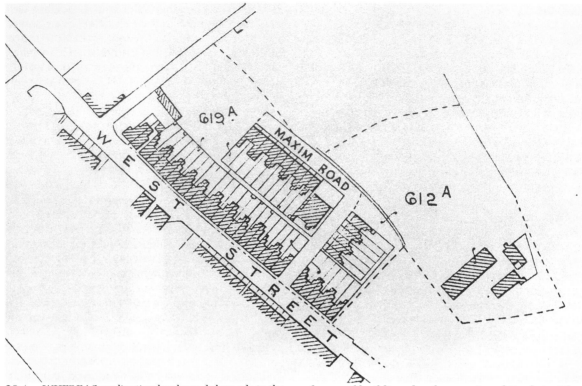

29. '. . . WHEREAS application has been duly made to the Board of Agriculture and Fisheries to alter the apportionment of the said Rentcharges. Now the Board . . . DO HEREBY ALTER the apportionment . . . in the manner and proportions mentioned in the Second Schedule hereof . . . 22-9-1906.'

'ALTERED APPORTIONMENT PARISH OF ERITH COUNTY OF KENT $\frac{1}{2500}$. PRINTED AT THE ORDNANCE SURVEY OFFICE, SOUTHAMPTON, FROM A TRACING MADE AT THE BOARD OF AGRICULTURE.' (Detail)

new maps made to take account of changes such as railway or suburban development or general urbanization. Some parishes may have one or more altered apportionments, each with a map, relating to areas ranging from the whole parish to just a few acres. In some counties, such as Cambridgeshire, tithe apportionments were made before enclosure and, consequently, had to be altered on later enclosure; Totternhoe, for example, was re-surveyed on enclosure in 1892. However, documents relating to alteration were often prepared some years after ownership change and in a great many cases changes were not in practice followed by any altered apportionment. The chief value of maps accompanying altered apportionments is as evidence of building development and its date. They may illustrate significant states of urban development and some striking examples of Victorian town-planning are to be found. Maps also sometimes accompanied certificates of redemption of tithe rent-charge.

Tithe documents are invaluable because their information is so readily available for so many parishes at about the same date. They are the most frequently consulted cartographic source.[2] They give detailed data about each piece of real property, providing a remarkable record of names of landowners and occupiers and of fields belonging to them. They have been used extensively in the reconstruction of rural conditions, determining what land was occupied by owners and what by tenants. Tithe awards allow location of land parcels recorded otherwise only in rentals, leases and tithe deeds – and may be the key to identifying ownership or occupation. They provide a record of estates at a time when many had reached their greatest extent, showing how much titheable land belonged to estates of various sizes and how much was owned by Church, university or railway company.

Tithe plans reveal the extent of land remaining unenclosed, showing where it was situated and who owned it, sometimes, as at Crimscote, delineating thousands of scattered open-field strips. Generally, open-field location can be roughly assessed and the topographical results of early private enclosure traced. They record fields, both enclosed and unenclosed, in every variety of size and shape, and facilitate reconstruction of changes in both field and farm boundaries. Farms are delineated in all parts of the country, illuminating every type of holding from fragmented open-field tenements to compact units, situated in the middle of their own fields or attached to villages or hamlets. Agriculture is depicted at a critical stage on the eve of its 'Golden Age' with land use differentiated, allowing the distinction of arable from grass and productive from unproductive for individual farms. Tithe surveys of the north-west of the East Riding, for instance, offer the only information bearing on the land use of the area as a whole, showing that it was a patchwork of arable and grass fields with the former generally outnumbering the latter in the 1840s. Tithe plans have been employed to construct land utilization maps of certain parishes in south-west London *c.*1840.[3] Tithe documents have been judged of inestimable value to the understanding of mid-nineteenth-century agriculture[4], and have been widely exploited in historical sections of the County Reports of the Land Utilization Survey of Britain to reconstruct past land usage.[5]

Tithe plans record parish boundaries before major changes took place. They show how much land was occupied by commons, greens, heaths, highways, and so on; and are the first detailed parish maps to show the impact of industrial and railway development. In urban areas, they are essential for tracing property and for study of suburban growth; comparison with later maps can show, for example, the infilling of medieval burgage plots behind main street frontage, creating slum 'courts' and 'yards'. Tithe maps, obviously, have many other potential uses; that of Orford parish, for example, aiding reconstruction of the physical history of Orford Spit.

Many counties in England and Wales are almost completely covered by tithe surveys; the major exceptions being those, such as the Midland counties, which had commuted tithes on enclosure. Thus coverage of tithe maps in Devon, Cornwall, Kent, and Shropshire is almost one hundred per cent, but in Northampton, Leicester, Bedford and Huntingdon it may be as low as a quarter or a third of the parishes. Roughly 79 per cent of England and Wales in all is covered by tithe surveys but the uneven spread inevitably dilutes their value. However, their uniformity and comprehensiveness are surpassed only by the Land Utilization Survey of the 1930s. The coverage offered by estate plans is much more limited and patchy. The tithe map may well be the earliest complete survey of a parish and possibly the only one before the 1870s.

In Ireland tithes aroused as much dissatisfaction as elsewhere, partly because so few Irishmen adhered to the established Church and partly because of irregularities of collection. Assessment of titheable acreage led to production of some maps in the 1650s, notably of the baronies of Counties Antrim and Dublin, and of single baronies in Queen's County and Wexford. Despite being in typical 'Down Survey' style, these maps are significant in showing more detail, including names, outlines, and areas of unforfeited townlands. Controversy in the 1780s led to an act of 1793 giving a seven-year exemption from tithe on all land reclaimed from waste. Applications for exemption had to be accompanied by a survey verified on oath by two surveyors representing proprietor or occupier and parish incumbent respectively. From 1823 tithe commissioners were empowered to conduct their own surveys or to use any existing plans or surveys of sufficient authenticity and accuracy. However, no instructions were given concerning choice of surveyors or assessment of accuracy and authenticity in earlier surveys. Hence, procedure in Ireland was quite unlike that adopted in England and little cartographic material of value was produced. Generally, only a few farms in any district were surveyed afresh, either because they had recently been reclaimed from waste and not yet mapped, or because no existing maps were forthcoming. A variety of maps are found with tithe applotments, including glebe terriers, general locational diagrams, and old estate maps, but the commonest are what might be called 'certificate maps' which were prepared to illustrate certificates of agreement to pay the tithe composition for a specified portion of a parish. Although 'certificate maps' were designed to show only location of lands and not quality and quantity, they range greatly from bare generalized outlines to careful, detailed, accurately surveyed maps with correct scale and orientation.

Select Bibliography

Bedford County Records Committee, *Catalogue of Enclosure Awards, Supplementary Catalogue of Maps and List of Awards upon Tithe, in the Bedfordshire County Muniments* (1939)

BEECH, G., 'Tithe maps' (*Map Collector*, 33; 1985)

Cumbria Archives Department, *Cumberland Tithe Awards* (1978)

HOOKE, J., & PERRY, R.A., 'The planimetric accuracy of tithe maps' (*Cart. Journ.*, 13; 1976)

KAIN, R.J.P., 'The tithe commutation surveys' (*Archaeologia Cantiana*, 89; 1974)

KAIN, R.J.P., 'Tithe surveys and landownership' (*Hist. Geog.*, 1; 1975)

KAIN, R.J.P., 'The tithe files of mid-nineteenth century England and Wales' in M. Reed (ed.): *Discovering Past Landscapes* (1984)

KAIN, R.J.P., & PRINCE, H.C., *The Tithe Surveys of England and Wales* (1985)

List & Index Society, Vol. 68: *Inland Revenue Tithe Maps and Apportionments*, pt. 1 Bedford to Northumberland, (1971); Vol. 83, pt. 2 Nottingham to Yorkshire [and] Wales, (1972)

MUNBY, L.M., 'Tithe apportionments and maps' (*History*, 54; 1969)

PRINCE, H.C., 'The records of the Tithe Redemption Commission' (*Journ. Soc. Archivists*, 1; 1956)

PRINCE, H.C., 'The tithe surveys of the mid-nineteenth century' (*Agric. Hist. Rev.*, 7; 1959)

STEER, F.W., *A Catalogue of Sussex Estate Maps and Tithe Award Maps* (*Sussex Rec. Soc.*, 61; 1962)

7
Regional maps

National or regional maps should not be disregarded because of their small scale. The fourteenth-century 'Gough' map of Great Britain, for example, depicts the medieval road system[1]; Lythe's map of southern and central Ireland (*c*.1571) bears numerous notes on harbours, coastal features, woods, pasture, land quality, and fisheries; and Beaufort's Ireland (1792) is a comprehensive treatment of parochial geography based on his own travels and a wide range of local and regional surveys by reputable cartographers.[2] National maps may provide valuable evidence of particular features. Both Mercator's large map (1564) and Saxton's general map (1583), for instance, help to establish the shape of Spurn Head at those dates.

Many regions, particularly drainage areas, were mapped as separate entities and regional studies were frequently accompanied by maps; Lewis's account of the New Forest (1811), for instance, was illustrated by a map by Charles Smith. Victorian interest in scenic beauty stimulated mapmakers to produce popular maps of the Lake District, Killarney's lakes, and other enticing areas, and there was an enormous increase in the publication of guide-books containing regional maps.

The major islands of the British Isles, particularly Jersey and the Isle of Wight, were mapped a

---

30. Comparison of Richardson's map of Glasgow and environs with that by Ross produced 22 years earlier shows the town's rapid expansion into the surrounding countryside. Estates and villages such as Anderston, Cowcaddens, and St Rollocks would soon be swallowed by the growing town. References to estates and their proprietors appear in the margin.

'MAP of the Town of Glasgow & COUNTRY Seven miles round, FROM ACTUAL SURVEY. By Tho: Richardson Landsurveyor Glasgow.' 1795. (Detail)

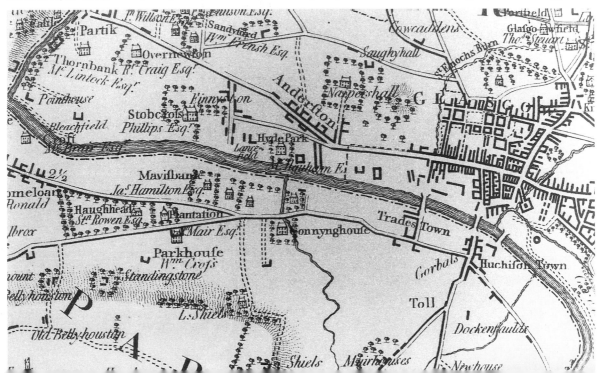

number of times at large scales during the period 1750–1850 when large-scale county maps were popular and produced in numbers. Some were mapped at larger scales for strategic reasons on behalf of the Board of Ordnance from the late eighteenth century.

Environs maps became more important as towns grew beyond the confines of the restricted town plan to cover areas not shown in sufficient up-to-date detail by county or other maps. In 1891 the Ordnance Survey's Director-General noted that because London had doubled in area since the first detailed Ordnance survey, some districts had altered so much that re-survey rather than revision was essential; and in 1881 the London School Board judged Stanford's London 'practically useless' because of suburban development since publication. The dense detail of environs maps reveals the town's surrounding landscape, documenting, for example, nurseries flanking main roads and industrial premises and hamlets destined to be swallowed by urban growth, such as those shown on Richardson's Glasgow environs (1795). Knight's Dublin environs (*c.*1852), at about $\frac{3}{4}$ inch to a mile, records features not found on either the 6- or 1-inch Ordnance sheets, and Cruchley's maps of London's environs, at $\frac{1}{2}$ or $\frac{3}{4}$ inch to the mile, are in some respects clearer than the Ordnance 1-inch maps. Cartographers of environs pandered to potential customers by emphasizing their houses and parks, and made turnpike information a vital

---

31. Rocque's map of the environs of London on 16 sheets shows in great detail the land use and villages of the outlying rural areas of Middlesex and Surrey, which were soon to be absorbed and are now very much districts of inner London. Heath, ploughland, orchards, pasture and so on are differentiated by conventional signs and varied stippling.

'An Exact Survey of the CITY'S of LONDON WESTMINSTER yᵉ Borough of SOUTᴴWARK and the COUNTRY NEAR TEN MILES ROUND BEGUN IN 1741 & ENDED IN 1745 BY JOHN Rocque LAND SURVEYOR & ENGRAU'D BY RICHARD PARR.' 1746. (Detail)

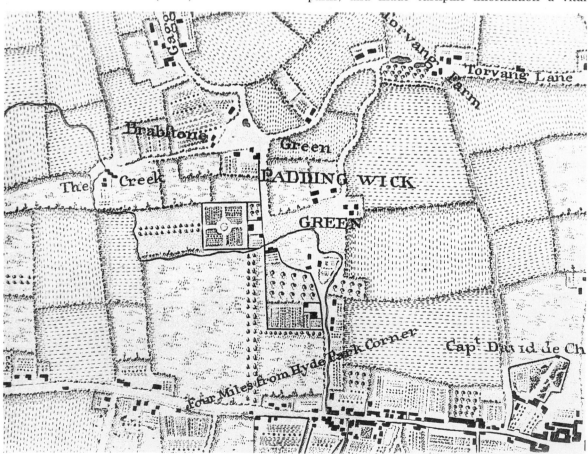

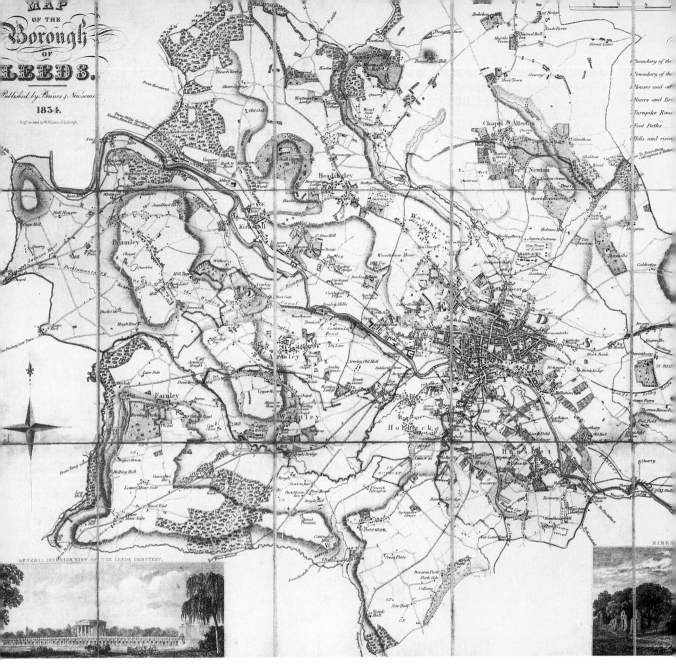

ingredient since most buyers were travellers. Some recorded surrounding land use; Pride & Luckombe's map of country 10 miles round Reading (1790) indicates open pasture, and Laurie's map of the Edinburgh area (1766) marks field boundaries, although these fail to agree with contemporary estate plans. The most celebrated and comprehensive environs maps were prepared by Rocque, whose 16-sheet map of 10 miles round London (1746), for example, documents a host of features in fascinating and elaborate detail, including '. . . Lanes . . . Paths . . . Walls, Pales, Hedges

32. The town and environs' maps which appeared in commercial directories are often vital links in the cartographic history of a commercial centre. Those in directories published by Edward Baines are amongst the best of the genre. His map of the whole borough of Leeds seems to have been inspired by Robert Kearsley Dawson's administrative map of 1832, but the Leeds township is drawn more accurately and the map is generally more detailed, showing industrial works, collieries, parks, mills and quarries, and naming farms and inns.

'MAP OF THE Borough OF LEEDS.' Published in Baines's *General and Commercial Directory of Leeds* (1834).

Non-Ordnance large-scale printed topographical maps of British Islands not issued in atlases 1693–1850 ($\geqslant \frac{3}{4}''$: 1m.)

First Issue	Scale		
1693	$1\frac{1}{4}'':c.1$m.	Orkney Islands	Wallace
1694	$\frac{3}{4}'':1$m.	Jersey	T. Lempriere
c.1698	$2\frac{3}{8}'':1$m.	St Kilda	Martin
1751	$1''$:$1\frac{1}{4}$m.	Islay	S. McDougal
1756	$1''$:$c.1$m.	Channel Islands	Le Rouge
1757	$1\frac{1}{4}'':c.1$m.	Guernsey, Sark, Herm	Le Chevalier de Beaurain
1764	$2\frac{1}{4}'':1$m.	St Kilda	Macaulay
1769	$2''$:1m.	Isle of Wight	Andrews
1781	$1''$:1m.	Isle of Wight	Haywood
1782	$1\frac{1}{2}'':1$m.	Jersey	Anon.
1786	$1\frac{1}{2}'':1$m.	Jersey	C. Lempriere
1787	$6''$:1m.	Guernsey	Gardner
1789	$1''$:1m.	Isle of Man	Fannin
1795	$1''$:1m.	Isle of Wight	Albin
1795	$6''$:1m.	Jersey	Gardner & Cubitt
c.1797	$1\frac{1}{2}'':1$m.	Anglesey	Morris [now lost or never completed]
1799	$1\frac{1}{2}'':1$m.	Jersey	Stead
1799	$5''$:1m.	North Uist	Reid
1805	$2\frac{1}{4}'':1$m.	Benbecula	Bald
1805	$2''$:$c.1$m.	South Uist	Bald
1806	$\frac{3}{4}'':1$m.	Isle of Wight	Baker
1807	$1''$:1m.	Orkney & Shetland Islands	Arrowsmith
1809	$2''$:1m.	Lewis	Chapman
1812	$1''$:1m.	Isle of Wight	Clarke
1814	$1\frac{1}{2}'':1$m.	Guernsey	Wilson
1816	$\frac{3}{4}'':c.1$m.	Channel Islands	Gray
1816	$1''$:$c.3$m.	Guernsey, Sark, Herm, Jethou	Gray
1817	$1\frac{1}{2}'':1$m.	Jersey	Plees
1818	$1''$:1m.	Isle of Wight	Foquett
1821	$1\frac{1}{4}'':1$m.	Jersey	White
1825	$1''$:$c.1$m.	Jersey	Laurie
1826	$1''$:1m.	Isle of Man	Drinkwater
1831	$1''$:$c.1$m.	Guernsey, Sark, Herm	Laurie
1832	$2\frac{1}{4}'':1$m.	Guernsey	Goodwin
1833	$2\frac{1}{2}'':c.1$m.	Alderney	Wyld
1836	$1\frac{1}{2}'':c.1$m.	Jersey	Wyld
c.1838	$1''$:1m.	Isle of Wight	Walker
1844	$1''$:1m.	Isle of Wight	Nichols
1844	$1''$:1m.	Isle of Wight	Wyld
1848	$4''$:1m.	Guernsey	P. MacDougall
1849	$4''$:1m.	Jersey	Godfray
c.1850	$2\frac{1}{4}'':c.1$m.	Jersey	Le Feuvre

. . . Ferries . . . Ponds . . . Gardens, &c.'. However, even environs maps of such high repute can be misleading; at least eight editions of Rocque's map had been published by 1769 and, although there had been some revision and up-dating, much of it was out-of-date by the later issues. Environs maps also appeared in town histories such as Enfield's of Liverpool (1773) and Jenkins's of Exeter (1806). Those featured in commercial directories are frequently particularly useful to the historian, recording successive developments in areas surrounding commercial centres. Environs maps were also sometimes divided to create small sectional atlases, as Cary did with his map of 15 miles round London, which appeared on 50 small sheets (1786).

Select Bibliography

ANDREWS, J.H., 'An early map of Inishowen' (*Long Room*, 7; 1973)

Ashmolean Museum, *Notes on an Exhibition of Maps Illustrating the Historical Development of Wychwood Forest and North Oxfordshire* (1968)

BEVERIDGE, E., 'Maps of West Fife' in *A Bibliography of Works Relating to Dunfermline and the West of Fife including Publications of Writers connected with the District* (1901)

BEVERIDGE, E., 'Ancient maps of North Uist, and descriptions recorded by early travellers in that island' in *North Uist; Its Archaeology and Topography* (1911)

CUBBON, A.M., 'The Isle of Man on maps of the sixteenth century' (*Proc. Isle of Man Nat. Hist. Antiq. Soc.*, 5, 4; 1955)

DIXON, F.E., 'Taylor's map of the environs of Dublin' (*Dublin Hist. Rec.*, 10; 1948)

LETT, REV. H.W., 'Maps of the mountains of Mourne' (*Ulster Journ. Arch.*, 2, 8; 1902)

O'KEEFFE, P., 'A map of Beare and Bantry' (*Journ. Cork Arch. Hist. Soc.*, 63; 1958)

PALMER, M., *Maps of the Isles of Scilly* (*Map Colls. Circle*, 3; 1963)

Public Record Office of Northern Ireland, *General Maps of Ireland and Ulster c.1538–c.1830* (n.d.)

QUIXLEY, R.C.E., *Antique Maps of Cornwall and the Isles of Scilly* (1966)

SHEPPARD, T., 'East Yorkshire history in plan and chart' (*Trans. E. Riding Antiq. Soc.*, 19; 1912)

TURLEY, R.V., 'Printed county maps of the Isle of Wight, 1590–1870: a check-list and guide for students (and collectors)' (*Proc. Hants. Field Club Arch. Soc.*, 31; 1976)

WARREN, J.P., *Evolution of the Map of Guernsey* (La Société Guernesiase; n.d.)

8

Drainage maps

From 1531 until the nineteenth century, Commissions of Sewers could be established wherever necessary to protect land against flooding, to drain marsh, to supervise mill-streams and bridges, and to ensure free passage of water in streams and sewers. They were never bodies designed or able to deal with navigation. Each commission controlled a 'level' and frequently ordered maps of the area which are found in their records deposited in record offices.[1] The records of the London Commissioners of Sewers are particularly full.[2] Plans may detail river and sea walls, marshes, areas liable to sea flooding, sluices, mills, roads and field names. Maps of 'levels' around London, for example, which might have been flooded beyond reclamation except at enormous expense if commissioners had

not drained them, record the metropolis's expansion over the south Essex marshes during industrialization.

Preoccupation with flooding and drainage gen-

33. Thomas Cox published a very accurate reduction of Sir Jonas Moore's great 16-sheet map of the Fens (1684) in *Magna Britannia et Hibernia, Antiqua et Nova* (1720). The waterways are still shown in great detail but the coat-of-arms, supporters and crest of the original have been omitted.

'A MAP of the GREAT LEVELL of the FENNS Extending into y[e] Countyes of Norfolk, Suffolke, Northampton, Lincoln Cambridge, Huntingdon and the Isle of Ely Surveyed by S[r] Jonas Moor.' 1720. (Detail)

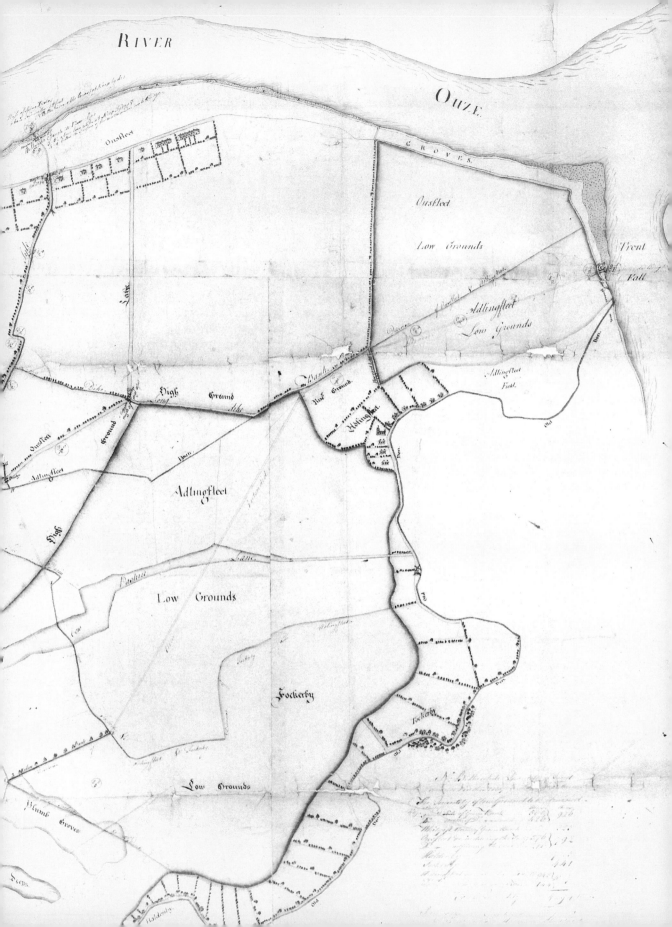

RIVER

OUZE

Ousfleet

GROVES

Ousfleet

Low Grounds

Trent

Fall

Adlingsfleet

Low Grounds

Adlingfleet
Field

High   Ground

Ousfleet

Adlingfleet

Adlingfleet

Low Ground

Adlingfleet

High

Adlingfleet

Low Grounds

Adlingfleet

Fockerby

Fockerby

Low Grounds

Plumb Groves

Deeps

Haldenby

erated maps delineating extent of flooding and location of breached banks; a map of Dagenham Breach, for example, shows the effects of a sea-wall collapse during an exceptionally high tide in 1707[3], and inundation of marshland caused by a break in the Fens Middle Level Drain was mapped in 1862[4]. Maps were used to compare the pre-flood situation with subsequent damage; Badeslade, for instance, drew the Denver Sluices on the Ouse before and after their destruction by high tides in 1723.

Proposals to Parliament for drainage schemes or embankment construction had to be accompanied by large-scale plans from the early nineteenth century. Generally, drainage proposals and projects were usually well mapped. Drainage of Scottish marshland, for example, in areas such as the Upper Forth valley in the early nineteenth century, was recorded in detail. In Ireland large-scale maps were commissioned in 1809 to examine the potential of the principal peat bogs for drainage and reclamation from the best of the grand jury surveyors who incidentally provided information on settlement, place-names, and industry.

Many regional maps cover drainage areas, although frequently not confining themselves to drainage information. Poker's Romney Marsh (1617), for example, shows 'Highwayes, Lanes, Parish Churches, Dwelling Houses & Cottages within the said several Levels.'[5] The best mapped regional drainage area in England is the Fens. Burghley's collection contains a map prepared c.1590 by John Hexham as evidence in disputes over drainage schemes between Peterborough and Wisbech. William Hayward seems to have con-

ducted the first general survey of the Great Level in 1604. The first published map (1632), by Henricus Hondius, shows pre-drainage conditions, bringing out the contrast between peat and silt areas. Henceforth, the Fens were mapped many times, particularly in numerous books on their 'imbanking and drayning', history, geology, fisheries, and navigation, providing a comprehensive record of development and reclamation.[6] Moore's much-copied map (1684), for example, records the waterways in very great detail[7]; and Baker's Cambridge and the Isle of Ely (1821) offers a useful survey of windmill pumps just before the introduction of steam-engines, and its second edition (1830) gives much evidence of draining and reclamation north of Ely.

Large-scale topographical maps of the Fens *c.*1630–1829 ($\geq \frac{1}{2}$″:1m)

First Issue	Scale		
*c.*1630	$\frac{1}{2}$″:1m.	Hondius	
*c.*1654	$\frac{1}{2}$″:1m.	Moore	
1662	Various	Dugdale	
1684	2″:1m.	Moore	
1723	$\frac{2}{3}$″:1m.	Stukeley	
1727	1″:1m.	Hayward/	
		Smyth	[manuscript]
1767	1″:1m.	Jefferys	
1789	$\frac{3}{4}$″:1m.	Cole	
1800	$\frac{2}{3}$″:1m.	Arrowsmith	[Lincoln Fens]
1821	1″:1m.	Baker	[Cambridgeshire & Isle of Ely]
1829	$\frac{2}{3}$″:1m.	Wells	

34. A reference table details the areas of low ground to be drained and manuscript additions note the levels of tides.

'PLAN from an Actual Survey describing the LOW Grounds of Adlingfleet, Eastoft, Whitgift, Ousefleet, Haldenby & Fockerby. by CHA. TATE, Surveyor with a Scheme for Draining the same by JOHN SMEATON Engineer.' 1764. (Detail)

9
County maps

Until the emergence of the Ordnance Survey the county was the basic unit of regional British mapping. Most counties are represented on numerous maps, in many variant states, published sometimes individually but more often in county atlases. This enduring format originated in Saxton's atlas (1579), which served as a model for the map trade.[1] Over the next three hundred years several hundred county atlases were published as its direct descendents.[2] As in all small-scale county maps, Saxton's evidence is limited and questionable; his Lancashire woodland, for example, ignores wooded areas reliably recorded elsewhere. Nevertheless his maps offer a good general picture of Elizabeth's counties; indicating relative town size through their settlement classification, approximate woodland areas, and Tudor place-name pronunciation.[3] More specifically, his Yorkshire, for example, is the earliest to show unambiguously Spurn Head's bulbous tip. Other innovatory contemporaries were Norden and Smith, but arguably the finest Elizabethan county map is Symonson's exceptionally detailed Kent (1596) at nearly 2 miles to the inch.[4]

In Scotland, Pont[5] followed Saxton by attempting a national survey in 1583–1601, probably before 1596, covering much of the country.[6] The 35 manuscript maps credited to Pont in the National Library of Scotland form a unique cartographic record of Scotland's late-sixteenth-century human landscape: 'portraying all that was essential in the landscape of his day . . . a most reliable basis for the detailed analysis of rural change since his epoch.'[7] However, it seems that maps directly derived from Pont's manuscripts by Blaeu represent only about 70 per cent of the then existing settlement. Although Pont crowded his manuscripts with farm and township names, he missed townships concealed in minor valleys and, undoubtedly, omitted many cottages to avoid over-

crowding. On occasion it has proved impossible to identify Pont's settlements, as, for example, in the case of 26 on his map (c.1590) of the Buchan District. Pont's techniques were relatively crude, but his landscape representation is remarkably faithful and useful, despite its deficiencies and omissions.[8]

The surveys of Saxton, Smith and Norden were copied by later map-makers, notably Speed whose atlas (1611) was in turn plagiarized. Hence, they remained the basis of county maps until superseded by larger-scale surveys anything up to 250 years later. Although derived from earlier surveys, Speed's maps were innovatory in introducing inset town plans and hundred names and boundaries taken from Parliamentary Rolls and Sheriff Books.[9] Not only were Tudor maps plagiarized throughout the seventeenth century, notably by the Dutch, but the original maps themselves were reprinted, sometimes with roads or inset town plans added to modernize them.[10] The few new county surveys produced in the late seventeenth century – Ogilby's Middlesex (1677) and Essex (1678), and Seller's Hertfordshire (1676), Kent (1680), and Middlesex (1680) – brought no general improvement in content or quality.

In Ireland, as early as 1587, Jobson had mapped Limerick, followed by Cork, Monaghan,[11] and Connaught (now lost), but comprehensive coverage awaited Cromwell's reconquest. In 1655–56 William Petty conducted a cadastral survey of lands forfeited by evicted owners which he always envisaged as a broader topographical survey.[12] His 'admeasurement down' (or 'Down Survey'), supplemented by other survey material mainly from 1636–40 and 1656–59, formed the basis of *Hiberniae Delineatio* (1685), the first printed atlas of Ireland, whose county maps show barony boundaries and other detail from the larger-scale surveys.[13] However, apparently Petty's survey did not extend much beyond the forfeited lands, as detail is scarce in areas where Cromwellian plantations did not take place.[14] After Petty's work, Irish counties were rather neglected until the mid eighteenth century, although Oliver Sloane did map County Down (1739) in manuscript at 1 inch to the Irish mile. In 1750 County Dublin by Stokes was published, followed by Kildare by Noble & Keenan (1752),[15] and by Armagh and Dublin by Rocque, both in 1760. Rocque's Dublin was good enough to survive unchallenged for over 60 years, but Armagh was criticized to such an extent that the grand jury decided to replace it in the 1770s. The McCreas' manuscript replacement is now lost. At about this time the Irish local government authorities, the grand juries, became interested in county mapping. Juries commissioned maps of a few counties in the 1750s and '60s, but only a handful reached completion and survive, notably Oliver Sloane's Queen's County (*c*.1763), Neville's Wicklow (1760), and Wren's Louth (1766); the latter two following Rocque's style. Mooney's King's County and Meath probably by John Sloane, for example, are known to have been made but are now lost. By the end of the 1760s county maps had been either announced, drawn or actually published for 11 prosperous counties in Dublin's hinterland.

Gascoyne's Cornwall, published on 14 sheets *c*.1700 at 1 inch to 1 mile, heralded a revolution in county map-making.[16] It established new standards of accuracy, trying to place the county at its correct latitude as well as satisfactorily recording topography. Wood's Shropshire (*c*.1710), Williams's Denbeigh & Flint (*c*.1720), Budgen's Sussex (1724), Beighton's Warwickshire (*c*.1728), Senex's Surrey (1729), and Gordon's Bedfordshire (1736) soon followed. Williams still depicted relief crudely and generalized the road system, but did attempt to plot and name all notable settlements and houses, and even revealed the earthworks of Offa's and Watt's Dykes. Beighton's Warwickshire is outstanding, being soundly based on trigonometrical survey and illustrating on the map the triangular framework used. Warwickshire's economic and cultural life is portrayed by various signs, and place-names far exceed those on any previous publication. However, a survey as technically advanced as Beighton's was exceptional. Many large-scale county map-makers merely up-dated Saxton and Speed; Gordon's Bedfordshire, for example, gives disappointingly little topographical information despite being more precise than earlier

maps, and Richard Gough, the antiquarian, thought little of Budgen's Sussex. To be fair, with all its failings Budgen's map was a great improvement, being based on painstaking research and some original fieldwork, and showing much information not previously published, particularly concerning the iron industry. Improving standards are exemplified by Martyn's re-mapping of Cornwall (*c*.1748), which conscientiously examined every cove and headland and minutely surveyed every road and lane. Large-scale county maps produced by Rocque;[17] Jefferys;[18] and Andrews, Dury & Herbert in the 1760s and '70s confirmed new levels of accuracy, exhibiting a multitude of detail found previously only in manuscript estate plans. Jefferys refused to skimp costs or employ second-rate surveyors to such an extent that his commitment to quality contributed towards his bankruptcy.[19]

The Royal Society of Arts' decision to award prizes for 'an accurate Survey of any County upon the Scale of one Inch to a Mile', first announced in 1759, reinforced the mapping of county units.[20] This stimulus combined with the growing demand for maps to foster a re-mapping of practically every English and many Scottish counties from 1750.[21] In Wales, Evans mapped the 'Six Counties of North-Wales' (1795), but only Glamorgan (1799) and Cardigan (1803) were covered, respectively by George Yates and Joseph Singer, in the south before the coming of Greenwood and the Ordnance Survey. In 1759–1808, 13 maps successfully claimed the prize, the first being Donn's Devon (1765).[22] Other awards were made to Armstrong; Burdett;[23] Prior;[24] Day & Masters; Hodskinson;[25] William Yates;[26] Cary; Yeakell & Gardner; Davis; Evans; and Baugh.[27] Some surveyors, notably Armstrong, William Yates, and Burdett covered several counties at large scales.[28] Yates's Warwickshire (1793), for instance, represented the first important advance for the county since Beighton's map, showing: street layout in settlements; distribution of mining and industrial activity; turnpikes and toll bars; and precisely portrayed vegetation.

Many maps did not win the award or were never submitted for it. Reasons for rejection, such as Taylor's faulty Dorset orthography, should not obscure the quality of large-scale county maps of

35. (*Over*) 'THE COUNTY OF BEDFORD, SURVEYED Anno MDCCLXV, and Engraved by THOMAS JEFFERYS Geographer to His MAJESTY.' *c*.1765. (Detail)

Selby Esq.r

Wavendon

N

Newport Road

45

White Hart

Aspley Mills

Radwell Pitt

Wendon Hill

Crawley Moors

44

11

Coach & Horses

Fullers Earth Pitt

Mill How

Totte

Crawley

Brook

Afple Guife

Husbor Crawl

I

Hogsty End

43

12

Pigs Park

The Grange

Crawley dean Gate

Fullers Earth Pitt

Birchmoore House

Ever Green Plant.s

K

Bow Brickhill

Brick kilns

13

Birchmoor Green

Keepers Lodge

43

WOBURN the PA Farm

Wavendon Heath

Durant Gate

Old Toll House

Horsemore Farm

WOBURN

13

C

Shire Oak

Charle Wood

Lodge Gate

Wob

42

the Cold Bath

Watling Street

Nares Lane

14

Vicote Grange

Cold Harbour

Borders Lodge

Great Lodge

Turnpike

41

U

Apefield Farm

Shire Ash

5

15

M

A

41 Miles from London

Potf grave

Sand House

Kings Wood

16

40

B

Reach

Battlefdon

LII

o

MILLBROOK

The Plain

WARREN

The Hospital

WARREN Grange Corner

Flying Horse

Watch House

Grange House

Bickrings Park

Doe little Mill Rev.d Mr Reynolds

9 How Green

Frog Hall

FLITWICK COMMON

Dennel End

Segenhoe Mad.m Potter

Hampton Corner

Brick Kiln

Stepingley Pinkerton

Ridgemont Church End

Park House

Flitwick

Fisher Esq.

Leg House

Warren House

Waks End Hunts Green

Warren House

Higher Berry End

Kingseys H

Warren House

Lower Berry End

New England

Tattle End

Sheldons Farm

Westoning

Water End

Hill End

Froxfield

Tyrells End

Witts End

Lower Rads End

Thrixoe

Brook End

Higher Rads End

Reddall Esq Church End

Eversholt

Willaume Esq

Tingrith

Westoning Wood End

Cranfield Bridge

Potters End Green

Harlington Wood End

Astre D.D.

S H E A D

Long Lane House

Red Hill

Arthur Jennings Esq

Millton Bryant

Stair Green

TUDDINGTON

Nobbins Green

Johnson Esq

Hairn

P A R K

Earl Strafferd Manor House

13

14

Old Park

Mill

39

TUDDINGTON 15

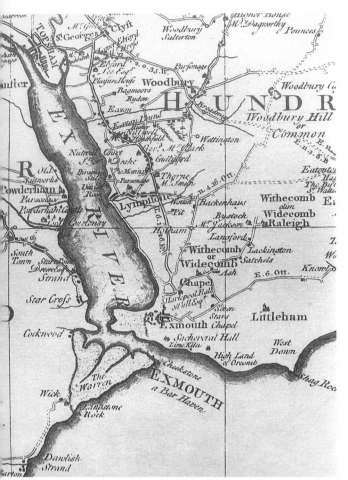

37. Donn's Devon emphasizes roads and settlement. Although many cottages off the roads are marked, some have been omitted and the map does not give a complete picture of settlement. Within the county boundary 656 gentlemen's 'Seats or Noted Houses' are represented by miniature elevations of the building, usually naming the house and owner. However, this method of representation consumes too much space and perhaps overemphasizes the country house as a form of settlement. The delineation of towns in plan is often the earliest record of the shape, size and street pattern of Devon's larger villages and towns. Donn adopted an elaborate system of road classification based on the importance of the road in terms of quality and the presence or absence of hedges. Although he did not show all the minor roads, he plotted more than any previous map-maker. The map gives little information about agriculture, but much emerges indirectly about the state of industry, with mills, salt works, lime kilns, quarries, and mines located.

'A MAP of the COUNTY of DEVON, with the CITY & COUNTY of Exeter. Delineated from an actual Survey, by BENJAMIN DONN. Engraved by Thos, Jefferys, Geographer to His MAJESTY.' 1765. (Detail)

38. Day & Masters recorded the Somerset landscape after the disappearance of the open arable fields, but at a time when there were still vast areas of common grazing on the high ground. The state of enclosure can be reconstructed from the careful delineation of enclosed and open roads which indicates the spread of road improvements away from the major routes. It is surprising that so little attention was paid to the layout of ornamental parks, since it was customary to flatter potential customers by naming them and depicting their estates in detail.

'COUNTY OF SOMERSET SURVEYED BY DAY AND MASTERS . . .' 1782. (Detail)

the period. At best, the work of Chapman and other talented contemporaries all-but equals the quality of the Ordnance's early work.[29] Particularly from the mid-century, large-scale county maps were derived from carefully measured baselines and properly executed triangulations. Burdett's Cheshire survey (1777), for example, provided the first comprehensive data for a new map since Saxton. The resultant map is a primary topographical record for the late eighteenth century, showing traditional features in greater detail than before and adding new ones such as land use, industrial activity, and transport facilities. Burdett's record of some 150 Cheshire watermills is a valuable commentary on their importance as a contemporary power source.[30] Similarly, Baugh's Shropshire (1808) distinguishes wind and water mills, forges, glasshouses, lime works, and coal pits. Some maps have valuable inset town plans at larger scales, such as Donn's insets of Exeter, Plymouth, and Plymouth Dock and Stoke Town. For many counties large-scale maps produced in the decades after 1750 warrant judgement equal to that passed on Yeakell & Gardner's Sussex (1778–83): 'the first real map of the county, faithfully rendering every detail visible on the ground'.[31]

Adair surveyed the Lothians in the early 1680s.[32] His manuscripts were engraved c.1735 to produce three maps at scales of $1\frac{1}{4}$–$1\frac{1}{2}$ inches to the mile but these were already 60 years out-of-date on publication, being inaccurate and lacking detail. Elphinstone claimed to correct Adair's mistakes on his map (1744) at 2 miles to the inch. In the same period, Edgar surveyed Peebles (1741) and Ross mapped Renfrew (c.1754). However, reliable Scottish county surveys were pioneered only when Laurie mapped Midlothian (1763), producing an accurate, detailed delineation of its road network. Nevertheless, he still generalized plantations and recorded heights inaccurately. In the 1770s there was widespread cartographic activity in lowland Scotland where large-scale county maps were produced by Ross; Andrew Armstrong;[33] Stobie; Garden; and Ainslie. Garden, for example, meticulously mapped enclosures, plantations and roads in Kincardine (1776). Unusually, even his field boundaries appear to be accurate. In the early nineteenth century, Forrest precisely recorded the extent of woodland and moss in Lanark. Although his map (1816) fails to show all farms, note accurate heights, and define the extent of arable and pasture, it does illuminate the extent and distribution of enclosure, farmland, coal workings, ironworks, mills and quarries.

In 1774 the grand juries were empowered to help finance map production, usually at 1 or 2 inches to the Irish mile. Within the next 50 years most Irish counties were mapped, although not all maps were published and some were exhibited only twice a year at the assizes. The maps are superficially similar in clearly and attractively representing physical features, roads, principal buildings and administrative divisions using customary early-nineteenth-century conventional signs. The earlier maps tend to be less accurate, being surveyed by men experienced only in estate surveying who probably pieced their maps together from separate road traverses by circumferentor and perambulator rather than chain and theodolite. Later maps, prepared with superior instruments and to higher standards, are generally more accurate with Duncan's Dublin (1821) outstanding. Bald's Mayo (1830) is in a class of its own, being drawn at 5 inches to the Irish mile, with impeccable accuracy based on triangulation.[34] Nevertheless, it proved useless for townland valuation. In contrast, Cahill's Queen's County (1805) was considered to be an indifferent survey; Williamson represented relief imperfectly in Down (1810); Gill's Wexford (1811) was judged very incorrect; and McCrea's Tyrone (published with additions by Knox in 1815) was dismissed as being a compilation of old surveys.[35] In 1780–1815 the three firms of Bath, the McCrea family and Williamson supplied a total of 13 grand juries. The later period of county map production came to be dominated by nationally-known engineers rather than local land surveyors, notably by William Larkin who surveyed nearly a dozen counties and published six county maps in 1808–19. What may be regarded as Ireland's first modern county map was published at 2 inches to the mile of Louth (1777) by the road surveyors Taylor & Skinner. George Taylor's brother Alexander mapped Kildare (1783) to equally high standards.[36]

Opportunities for more accurate large-scale county map production grew in the early nineteenth century with increased demand and publication of the Ordnance's trigonometrical data. Price's Hereford (1817) initiated a second re-survey of the counties of Great Britain which was carried through mainly in the 1820s and '30s in the ambitious schemes of Greenwood and Bryant, increasingly reflecting the style, content and standards of the ever more influential Ordnance Survey.

Greenwood's projected national series was all

Taunton area map

Staplegrove · Norton Fitzwarren · Fair Water · Silk Water · Br. Ford · Tuckings Mill · Barr House · Upcott · Bishops Hull · Gibralter · North Town · Yard Ho. · Castle · Priory · Soho · Linton Fm · Maidenbrook Farm · Bath Pool Inn · TAUNTON · Black Brge · Layord · H 20 N · Wheadon · Neale · Morgrave Farm · Belmont Villa · Mount Yebett · Galmington · Wilton · Barracks · Hobway Green · Hoyd · Rumord · Scengrove · Sherford · Pool Fm · Halfway House · Fullands · Jiffigham Comytrowe · Battle · Cutlass Farm · Cotlake Barn · Shoreditch · Castle Hill · Chillys · Trull · Orchard · Broughton

Newport Pagnel area map

New Quarry Hall · Quarry Hall · Sherrington Mill Land · Bridge House · Lathbury · Sherrington Bri · T.B. · Kickells Fm · Bury Field · Miles to Bedford · Woad Ho. · Newport Field Fm · NEWPORT PAGNEL · Brew Ho. · Tickford Abbey · Tickford End · Linford Bridge · Beggars · New B. · Cottage · Newport Canal · Wharf · Bridge · Nursery Garden · Public Ho. · Caldecot Mill

39. 'MAP OF the County of SOMERSET, from Actual Survey made in the Years 1820 & 1821 by C. & I. Greenwood.' 1822. (Detail)

but successful with 35 counties mapped to a very high standard (1817–34), mainly at 1 inch to the mile. Four Scottish counties and London were also mapped, but Greenwood failed to cover six English counties and the three south-eastern most Welsh counties. Data was checked against earlier maps and other publications, but incorporation of estate plans of unknown quality into his maps undermined reliability. Competition between Greenwood, his rivals and the Ordnance Survey often necessitated hurried preparation and signs of haste are apparent. Small streams are missing; industrial sites generalized; and fields and woodlands remote from roads poorly represented. Greenwood's chief rival, Bryant, published similar maps of 12 counties and the East Riding, usually at 1½ miles to the inch. His maps of Buckingham, Hereford, Hertford, Norfolk and Oxford seem to have dissuaded Greenwood from surveying those counties. Only Cambridge of English counties was not covered by either map-maker. Generally, Bryant's maps give more place-names and show more minor roads, tracks and detail outside the county than Greenwood's. Besides these two failed national schemes, many counties were mapped individually at large scales by such as Ellis, Price, and Swire & Hutchings during this period.

Large-scale county maps were frequently re-issued by later publishers, often many years after original publication. Sometimes they were updated, as in the 1775 re-issue of Jefferys's 20-sheet Yorkshire on which 'the numerous Errors of . . . former Editions are remedied, . . . made correct to the present Year, upwards of 500 Additions and Improvements having been inserted.' Mostly, however, revision only updated the most obvious features; Jefferys's Buckinghamshire, for instance, was re-issued with only names of country-house owners altered.

At best, large-scale county maps are highly informative. Stobie's Roxburgh, for example, surveyed in 1770 and apparently compiled from his own surveys without copying earlier work, shows some 17 per cent more settlements than the 'Military Survey', thus probably indicating those abandoned in the intervening 20 years. However,

40. 'Map of the County of BUCKINGHAM From actual Survey.' Andrew Bryant, 1825. (Detail)

copying of earlier maps, as when Lindley & Crosley plagiarized Rocque's Surrey[37], incorporation of untrustworthy estate surveys, and other doubtful practices generally impair their reliability. Land use and other features could well change during long surveys, explaining such anomalies as the sharp and unlikely break in cultivated land where two sheets meet on Rocque's Berkshire.[38] Reliability is also affected by shortcomings in survey method, and many – particularly earlier – maps show technical defects such as the inexact orientation of Rocque's Surrey and the distortion and underestimated distances of Hodskinson's Suffolk. Large-scale county maps produced before the attempts of Greenwood and Bryant to construct a national survey are the uncoordinated products of a variety of private practitioners at various scales, in differing styles, with different conventions. They do not join comfortably together. At worst, they are mere enlargements of the simplest existing maps showing only the most basic information.

Most of the British Isles was mapped by county at large scales within a relatively short period. English counties are covered by at least one such map, generally several, often at widely separated dates; Cheshire, for example, was surveyed in just 12 years by Greenwood (1819), Swire & Hutchings (1830), and Bryant (1831), with the Ordnance Survey following in 1833–43. There is at least one map for most Scottish and Irish and some Welsh counties. They provide the only comprehensive cartographic source for landscape change. Despite inherent problems of accuracy and reliability, they have been used for distributional analysis of land use, parks, industrial sites, communications and so on – and are of paramount importance as sources for regional studies.

Smaller-scale county maps in books and atlases were derived from large-scale county maps until this role was usurped by the Ordnance Survey. Although generally their derivative nature renders them of little value to the historian, there are exceptions, usually produced at larger scales than average. Bowen & Kitchin's *Large English Atlas* (1760) was the first systematic attempt to cover England and Wales in a uniform way on fairly large scales. However, despite elaborate detail and decoration, topographical content is disappointing and the copious historical notes which fill every available space are merely an amalgam of fanciful ideas and current description culled from other sources. This atlas enjoyed a long life, being issued almost into the next century, with only imprints and plate-numbers changed. Altered reductions of its maps appeared as the *Royal English Atlas*.[39] Thomson published Scotland's finest county atlas (1832) with maps derived, wherever possible, from existing county maps although it was necessary to commission new surveys for some counties. Names of surveyors and others attesting map accuracy are noted. However, despite being the most complete and detailed source prior to the Ordnance Survey for many Scottish counties, Thomson's maps sometimes omit settlements reliably recorded by other maps. The rival *New English Atlases* of Cary (1809) and Smith (1804) contain edited and standardized maps derived from late-eighteenth-century surveys; and Greenwood reduced and simplified his large-scale maps for an accurate, attractive county atlas published in an attempt to avert financial collapse.

County maps in histories and topographies usually have the added advantage of an accompanying text providing extra information on what is shown and often an insight into sources and techniques, allowing some assessment of quality. Despite a scale usually of only some 4 miles to the inch, these maps, generally folded in as frontispieces, were often the most useful and advanced surveys to date; Coltman's Monmouthshire, for instance, in Coxe's *Historical Tour in Monmouthshire* (1801), was an improvement on Snell's disappointing 1-inch map (1785).

Norden made the first attempt to produce a series of county histories with new, improved maps. His *Speculum Britanniae* failed through lack of response and finance, but during his lifetime histories of Middlesex (1593) and Hertfordshire (1598) were published; others appeared after his death; and yet other maps survived in manuscript.[40] Later schemes also foundered; Plot, for instance, issued only Oxfordshire (1677) and Staffordshire (1686), with their highly decorative maps, in a projected series of county natural histories. In contrast, popular individual histories could appear over the years in new editions with more up-to-date maps. The second edition of Hutchins's *History and Antiquities* of Dorset (1796–1815) replaced Bayly's original map (1774) with a new one by Robert Rowe; and Dugdale's *Warwickshire* substituted Beighton's advanced map in its second edition (1730). Several works may cover one county, providing a chronological sequence of maps; Hertfordshire, for example, was not only mapped by Norden but also in Chauncey's *Historical Antiqui-*

ties (1700), Salmon's *History* (1728), and Clutterbuck's *History Antiquities* (1815).

County maps in a chronological sequence can be weighted as evidence according to comprehensiveness, locational accuracy, plagiarism or originality. Sequences allow the reconstruction of landscape change. They have been used, for instance, to analyse changes in quantity and pattern of upland cultivation and settlement in the Lammermuir Hills and Stow Uplands 1600–1860.[41] Only 14 of 29 printed and three manuscript county maps of the area extant were found to provide a more or less complete, accurate and original basis for landscape study, recreating a pattern of settlement abandonment, confirmed by field evidence, in which some 24 per cent of all settlements in the study area were deserted *c*.1596–1860. A similar study of the topographical contents of 550 maps of Yorkshire, starting with Saxton's map of 1577 and ending in 1877, showed that only 150 contain at least one item not previously recorded; these frequently date from 1837–57 when railways were extensively introduced.[42] Of the 150 maps, only 60 were found to provide any significant new topographic information that 'at worst was not definitely wrong and at best was clearly the result of new material being added'. Only a handful of maps were judged outstanding for accuracy, content, and reliability, being clearly based on some form of field survey: notably, the county maps of Saxton, Warburton (1720), Jefferys (1770–1), Tuke (1786), and Greenwood (1817–8); Dickinson's South Yorkshire (1750) and Bryant's East Riding (1829); Ogilby's road maps; and the Ordnance Survey 'Old Series' and 6-inch maps of Yorkshire (1848–57).

National coverage of county maps at successive dates provides a control and a framework of comprehensive information on quantity and location, into which more fragmentary, specific topographical sources may be fitted, thus partly avoiding the dangers of making generalizations based on specific evidence. County map sequences facilitate approximate dating of landscape change and reconstruction of spatial patterns of development. Providing those based on original survey are studied, rather than their plagiarized relations, a fairly complete record of several landscape features will emerge.

Select Bibliography

ANDREWS, J.H., 'Proposals for eighteenth century maps of co. Kildare' (*Kildare Arch. Soc. Journ.*, 16; 1980)

BAGLEY, J.J., 'County maps and town plans' in *Historical Interpretation 2: Sources of English History 1540 to the Present Day* (1971)

CHAMBERS, B., 'M.J. Armstrong in Norfolk: the progress of an eighteenth century county survey' (*Geog. Journ.*, 130; 1964)

CHUBB, T., *The Printed Maps in the Atlases of Great Britain and Ireland* (1927; 1966; 1974; 1977)

FORDHAM, SIR. H.G., *Notes on the Cartography of the Counties of England and Wales* (1908; reprinted in *Studies in Carto-Bibliography*; 1914 & 1969)

HEAWOOD, E., Introduction to *English County Maps in the Collection of the Royal Geographical Society* (1932)

HODSON, D., *County Atlases of the British Isles Published after 1703*, Vol. 1. Atlases published 1704 to 1742 and their subsequent editions, (1984)

LAXTON, P., 'The geodetic and topographical evaluation of English county maps 1740–1840' (*Cart. Journ.*, 13; 1976)

LEE, R.J., *English County Maps: the Identification, Cataloguing and Physical Care of a Collection* (Library Assoc. Pamphlet; 1955)

MARGARY, H., Publishes facsimiles of large-scale county maps from Lympne Castle, Kent.

MOORE, J.N., 'Early printed county maps of Scotland in Glasgow University Library' (*College Courant*, 73; 1984)

RODGER, E.M., *The Large-Scale County Maps of the British Isles, 1596–1850: A Union List* (2nd edn., 1972)

SKELTON, R.A., *County Atlases of the British Isles 1579–1703* (1970)

TOOLEY, R.V., 'Large scale English county maps and plans of cities not printed in atlases' (*Map Collector*, in parts from 1978)

WALTERS, G., 'Themes in the large-scale mapping of Wales in the eighteenth century' (*Cart. Journ.*, 5; 1968)

Large-scale printed topographical county maps of the British Isles not issued in atlases 1700–1800 ($>\frac{1}{2}$″:1m.; excluding re-issues and reductions). [N.B. A few other surveys were not completed or are known to have been proposed but have never been traced]

First Issue	Scale	ENGLAND		First Issue	Scale	WALES	
1700	1″ :1m.	Cornwall	Gascoyne				
c.1710	$\frac{3}{4}$″ :1m.	Shropshire	Wood				
1715	$\frac{3}{4}$″ :1m.	Oxfordshire	Overton				
				c.1720	1″ :1m.	Denbigh & Flint	Williams
1724	$\frac{2}{3}$″ :1m.	Middx., Herts., Essex	Warburton				
	$\frac{3}{4}$″ :1m.	Sussex	Budgen				
1727–28	1″ :1m.	Warwickshire	Beighton				
1729	1″ :1m.	Surrey	Senex				
1731	$1\frac{1}{2}$″:1m.	Huntingdonshire	Gordon				
	$\frac{2}{3}$″ :1m.	Norfolk	Goddard & Chase				
1736	1″ :1m.	Bedfordshire	Gordon				
	1″ :1m.	Suffolk	Kirby				
1739	$\frac{2}{3}$″ :1m.	Norfolk	Foster				
1740	$\frac{2}{3}$″ :1m.	Norfolk	Goddard & Goodman				
1747	$\frac{2}{3}$″ :1m.	Staffordshire	Jefferys				
c.1748	1″ :1m.	Cornwall	Martyn				
c.1749	$\frac{2}{3}$″ :1m.	Hertfordshire	Warburton				
1749	1″ :1m.	Middlesex	Warburton				
1750	1″ :1m.	Yorkshire (South)	Dickinson				
1752	1″ :1m.	Shropshire	Rocque				
1754	1″ :1m.	Herefordshire	Taylor				
	2″ :1m.	Middlesex	Rocque				
1759	1″ :1m.	Hampshire	Taylor				
1761	2″ :1m.	Berkshire	Rocque				
c.1765	2″ :1m.	Bedfordshire	Jefferys				
1765	1″ :1m.	Devon	Donn				
	1″ :1m.	Dorset	Taylor				
1765–69	2″ :1m.	Surrey	Botley				
1766	1″ :1m.	Hertfordshire	Andrews & Dury				
1767	1″ :1m.	Derbyshire	Burdett				
	1″ :1m.	Oxfordshire	Jefferys				
c.1768	2″ :1m.	Surrey	Rocque				
1768	1″ :1m.	Durham	A. Armstrong				
	2″ :1m.	Huntingdonshire	Jefferys				
1769	2″ :1m.	Kent	Andrews, Dury, Herbert				
	1″ :1m.	Northumberland	A.&M. Armstrong				
1770	1″ :1m.	Buckinghamshire	Jefferys				
	1″ :1m.	Westmorland	Jefferys				
1771	1″ :1m.	Yorkshire	Jefferys				
1772	1″ :1m.	Worcestershire	Taylor				
1773	2″ :1m.	Wiltshire	Andrews & Dury				
1774	1″ :1m.	Cumberland	Donald				
1775	1″ :1m.	Staffordshire	W. Yates				

First Issue	Scale	SCOTLAND		First Issue	Scale	IRELAND	
*c.*1735	$1\frac{1}{4}$″:1m.	Midlothian	Adair				
1736	1″ :1m.	East Lothian	Adair				
*c.*1737	$1\frac{1}{2}$″:1m.	West Lothian	Adair				
1741	1″ :1m.	Peebleshire	Edgar				
1745	$1\frac{1}{4}$″:1m.	Lothians	Adair				
				1750	$\frac{3}{4}$″ :1m.	Dublin	Stokes
				1752	1″ :1m.	Kildare	Noble & Keenan
1754	1″ :1m.	Renfrewshire	Ross				
				1755	1″ :1m.	Down	Kennedy
				1760	$1\frac{1}{2}$″:1m.	Armagh	Rocque
					2″ :1m.	Dublin	Rocque
					$\frac{3}{4}$″ :1m.	Wicklow	J. Neville
1763	$1\frac{1}{2}$″:1m.	Midlothian	Laurie	*c.*1763	1″ :1m.	Queen's	Sloane
				1766	$1\frac{3}{4}$″:1m.	Louth	Wren
1770	1″ :1m.	Roxburghshire	M. Stobie				
1771	1″ :1m.	Berwickshire	A.&M. Armstrong				
1773	1″ :1m.	Lanarkshire	Ross				
	1″ :1m.	Lothians	A.&M. Armstrong				
	1″ :1m.	Selkirkshire	Ainslie				
1775?	1″ :1m.	Ayrshire	A. Armstrong				
1775	1″ :1m.	Fife & Kinross	Ainslie				
	1″ :1m.	Peebleshire	M.J. Armstrong				

First Issue	Scale		ENGLAND	First Issue	Scale		WALES	
1776	1″ :1m.	Nottinghamshire	Chapman					
c.1777	1″ :1m.	Cheshire	Burdett					
1777	2″ :1m.	Essex	Chapman & André					
1777	1″ :1m.	Gloucestershire	Taylor					
1779	1″ :1m.	Leicestershire	Prior					
	1″ :1m.	Lincolnshire	A. Armstrong					
	1″ :1m.	Northamptonshire	Eyre & Jefferys					
1780	1″ :1m.	Rutland	A. Armstrong					
1782	1″ :1m.	Somerset	Day & Masters					
1783	1″ :1m.	Suffolk	Hodskinson					
	2″ :1m.	Sussex (South)	Yeakell & Gardner					
1785	1″ :1m.	Monmouthshire	Snell					
	$\frac{3}{4}$″ :1m.	Surrey	Cary					
1786	1″ :1m.	Lancashire	W. Yates					
	1″ :1m.	Middlesex	Cary					
1791	1″ :1m.	Hampshire	Milne					
c.1792	1″ :1m.	Surrey	Lindley & Crosley					
1793	1″ :1m.	Warwickshire	W. Yates					
1795	1″ :1m.	Sussex	Gream	1795	$\frac{3}{4}$″ :1m.	North Wales [Anglesey, Flintshire, Denbighshire, Caernarvonshire, Merionethshire, Montgomeryshire]	Evans	
1797	1″ :1m.	Norfolk	Donald & Milne					
	2″ :1m.	Oxfordshire	Davis					
1798	$\frac{3}{4}$″ :1m.	Middlesex	Stockdale					
				1799	1″ :1m.	Glamorgan	G. Yates	

Large-scale printed topographical county maps of the British Isles published separately 1801–1851 ($>\frac{1}{2}$″:1m.; excluding re-issues and reductions)

First Issue	Scale		ENGLAND	First Issue	Scale		WALES	
1801	1″ :1m.	Kent	Mudge					
				1803	1″ :1m.	Cardigan	Singer	
1808	1″ :1m.	Shropshire	Baugh					
1817	1″ :1m.	Herefordshire	Price					
1817–18	$\frac{3}{4}$″ :1m.	Yorkshire	Greenwood					
1818	1″ :1m.	Lancashire	Greenwood					
1819	1″ :1m.	Cheshire	Greenwood					
	2″ :1m.	Middlesex	Greenwood					

First Issue	Scale	SCOTLAND	First Issue	Scale	IRELAND
1776	1" :1m.	Kincardineshire			Garden
c.1777	1" :1m.	Dunbartonshire			Ross
1777	¾" :1m.	Stirlingshire	1777	1½":1m. Louth	Edgar (Surv.c.1743) / G. Taylor & Skinner
1782	1" :1m.	Wigtownshire	1782	1¼":1m. Antrim	Ainslie / Lendrick
1783	1" :1m.	Perthshire & Clackmannon	1783	1½":1m. Kildare	J. Stobie / A. Taylor
			1787	1¼":1m. Clare	Pelham
			1789	3" :1m. Carlow	P.&R. Butler
			1793	1¼":1m. Monaghan	W. McCrea
1794	1" :1m.	Angus			Ainslie
1797	1" :1m.	Berwickshire			Blackadder
	1" :1m.	Kirkcudbrightshire			Ainslie
			1798	1" :1m. Carlow	Allen
				¾" :1m. Wicklow	A. Neville
1800	2" :1m.	Renfrewshire			Ainslie

First Issue	Scale	SCOTLAND	First Issue	Scale	IRELAND
			1801	1" :1m. Donegal	W. McCrea
1802	1" :1m.	East Lothian			Forrest
c.1804	1" :1m.	Dumfriesshire			Crawford
			1805	1½":1m. Queen's	Cahill
			1808	1½":1m. Westmeath	Larkin
			1810	1¼":1m. Down	Williamson
			1811	1" :1m. Cork	Bath
				1" :1m. Wexford	Gill
1812	1½":1m.	Midlothian			J. Knox
			1814	1½":1m. Londonderry	Sampson
				1½":1m. Longford	Edgeworth
			1815	1" :1m. Tyrone	W. McCrea & G. Knox
1816	1½":1m.	Lanarkshire			Forrest
1817	1½":1m.	Stirlingshire	1817	2" :1m. Meath	Grassom / Larkin
1818	1½":1m.	West Lothian	1818	1½":1m. Waterford	Forrest / Larkin
			1819	1½":1m. Galway	Larkin
				2" :1m. Leitrim	Larkin
				1½":1m. Sligo	Larkin

First Issue	Scale	ENGLAND		First Issue	Scale	WALES	
1820	1″ :1m.	Durham	Greenwood				
	1″ :1m.	Northumberland	Fryer				
	1″ :1m.	Staffordshire	Greenwood				
	1″ :1m.	Wiltshire	Greenwood				
1821	1″ :1m.	Cambridgeshire	Baker				
	1″ :1m.	Kent	Greenwood				
1822	1½″:1m.	Hertfordshire	Bryant				
	1″ :1m.	Somerset	Greenwood				
	1″ :1m.	Warwickshire	Greenwood				
	1″ :1m.	Worcestershire	Greenwood				
1823	1″ :1m.	Cumberland	Greenwood				
	1″ :1m.	Surrey	Greenwood				
	1½″:1m.	Surrey	Bryant				
1824	1″ :1m.	Berkshire	Greenwood				
	1″ :1m.	Gloucestershire	Greenwood				
	1½″:1m.	Gloucestershire	Bryant				
	1″ :1m.	Huntingdonshire	Ellis				
	1½″:1m.	Oxfordshire	Bryant				
	1″ :1m.	Westmorland	Greenwood				
1825	1½″:1m.	Buckinghamshire	Bryant				
	1″ :1m.	Derbyshire	Greenwood				
	1″ :1m.	Essex	Greenwood				
	1″ :1m.	Nottinghamshire	Ellis				
	1″ :1m.	Suffolk	Greenwood				
	1″ :1m.	Sussex	Greenwood				
1826	1″ :1m.	Bedfordshire	Greenwood				
	1½″:1m.	Bedfordshire	Bryant				
	1″ :1m.	Dorset	Greenwood				
	1½″:1m.	Dorset	Outhett				
	1″ :1m.	Hampshire	Greenwood				
	1″ :1m.	Leicestershire	Greenwood				
	1¼″:1m.	Norfolk	Bryant				
	1″ :1m.	Northamptonshire	Greenwood				
	1″ :1m.	Nottinghamshire	Greenwood				
	1″ :1m.	Rutland	Greenwood				
	1¼″:1m.	Suffolk	Bryant				
1827	1″ :1m.	Cornwall	Greenwood	1827	1″ :1m.	Pembrokeshire	Campbell
	1″ :1m.	Devon	Greenwood				
	1½″:1m.	Northamptonshire	Bryant				
	1″ :1m.	Shropshire	Greenwood				
1828	1″ :1m.	Lincolnshire	Bryant	1828	¾″ :1m.	Glamorgan, Brecon, Radnor	Greenwood
	1″ :1m.	Northumberland	Greenwood				
	1¼″:1m.	Westmorland	Hodgson				
1829	1″ :1m.	Yorkshire (East Riding)	Bryant				
1830	¾″ :1m.	Cheshire	Swire & Hutchings				
	¾″ :1m.	Lancashire	Hennet				
	1″ :1m.	Lincolnshire	Greenwood				
	1″ :1m.	Monmouthshire	Greenwood				
1831	1¼″:1m.	Cheshire	Bryant				
	1″ :1m.	Huntingdonshire	Greenwood				
1832	¾″ :1m.	Staffordshire	Phillips & Hutchings				
1835	1½″:1m.	Herefordshire	Bryant				
	2¼″:1m.	Nottinghamshire	Sanderson				
1836	1″ :1m.	Derbyshire	Sanderson				
c.1839	¾″ :1m.	Durham	Hobson				

First Issue	Scale	SCOTLAND		First Issue	Scale	IRELAND	
				1821	$2\frac{1}{4}''$:1m.	Dublin	Duncan
1822	$1''$:1m.	Aberdeenshire, Banff, Kincardine	Robertson				
				1824	$1''$:1m.	Carlow	Allen
1825	$1''$:1m.	East Lothian	Sharp, Greenwood, Fowler	1825	$\frac{2}{3}''$:1m.	Limerick	Coffey
					$\frac{2}{3}''$:1m.	Roscommon	Edgeworth & Griffith
1826	$1''$:1m.	Berwickshire	Sharp, Greenwood, Fowler				
1828	$1''$:1m.	Fife & Kinross	Sharp, Greenwood, Fowler				
	$1''$:1m.	Midlothian	Sharp, Greenwood, Fowler				
				1830	$1\frac{1}{2}''$:1m.	Mayo	Bald
1833	$1''$:1m.	Sutherland	Burnett & Scott	1834	$1''$:1m.	Wicklow	Allen
1840	$\frac{2}{3}''$:1m.	Roxburghshire	Tennant				
1848	$2''$:1m.	Clackmannanshire	Morison				
1851	$1\frac{3}{4}''$:1m.	Selkirkshire	Mitchell				

10

Maps of county divisions

County sub-divisions were sometimes mapped. Moses Glover, for example, delineated Isleworth Hundred (1635) at 20 inches to the mile, showing types of soil and land use and naming fields. Usually maps of individual hundreds illustrated county histories and topographies. Nine manuscript hundred maps were prepared to accompany Norden's description of Cornwall, eventually published in 1728, but were apparently never engraved and printed.[1] However, the manuscript maps survive, recording, in particular, ownership details of gentlemen's houses. Morant's *History and Antiquities* of Essex (1768) contains eight maps of grouped hundreds at 2 miles to the inch. Hasted's *History and Topographical Survey* of Kent (1778–99) has 34 maps of grouped hundreds, at approximately 2 inches to the mile.[2] These maps appear to derive their basic topography from Andrews, Dury & Herbert's large-scale map (1768), but much additional detail has been included from Hasted's personal local knowledge and from information supplied by his correspondents. Warwickshire's four hundreds were mapped twice for editions of Dugdale's *Antiquities*: firstly in 1656 showing more place-names and parks than earlier small-scale maps; and secondly by Beighton in 1730, deriving data from his county survey (1722–25).

In Ireland, small-scale barony maps were produced in the 1560s and '70s. In Ulster, Bodley directed a survey in 1609 as a preliminary to British colonization, producing the earliest set of Irish townland surveys surviving in cartographic form.[3] Twenty-eight manuscript barony maps survive, covering Fermanagh, Tyrone, Cavan and Armagh, drawn mostly at roughly $1\frac{1}{4}$ inches to the mile, although there is considerable scale variation due to systematic underestimation of mountain and bog. Colour vividly depicts a close and complex mesh of individually-named territorial divisions within a landscape of hills, lakes, rivers, bogs, and woods, with churches, castles, and other military strongpoints. However, patchy topographic representation suggests that Bodley's surveyors did not visit all the country mapped. Other barony maps surviving from contemporary surveys cover Longford. Parts of King's County are delineated in a collection of *c.*1628, which includes several maps of the new town of Banagher and its environs.

During his 'Down Survey' Petty compiled two sets of detailed topographical barony maps which were never engraved.[4] Most are at 1.6 inches to the mile, but about a quarter are at 0.8 inches to the mile and a few at 3.2 inches; all were considered too small by the Irish Parliament to be an adequate boundary record. The only complete set in existence was taken by French privateers and now resides in the *Bibliothèque Nationale*. It comprises 214 baronies covering all Ireland except Roscommon, Galway, and parts of Clare and Mayo which were not covered in the 'Down Survey'.

---

41. A map of Wisbech Hundred was prepared in 1597 by copying an earlier map, probably of *c.*1450, which is now untraceable. The 1597 copy was in turn copied by Thomas Watts in 1657 and the Ordnance Survey redrew this facsimile from Watts's original manuscript map. Revisions were probably made at each stage of copying; the two peasants dressed in Elizabethan costume must have been introduced to the original map at a later stage. The main purpose of the map was to define the boundaries of the Hundred and to show the extent of the Lordship of Thorney to eliminate confusion and dispute over the exact route of the boundaries. The map shows the town of Wisbech, with Wisbech Castle at its centre, and the settlement of the surrounding area represented by churches, manor houses and windmills, with each building in true representation.

'Descriptio omnium metarum et bundarum pro Hundreda de Wisebech.' 1597

LE WASH

et salsus Mariscus

Gedney

Sutton beate Marie

Tyd beate Marie

Tyd brigge

Sutton sti Jacobi

Tyd sti Epidij

ij Anno g dni 1340 cum capta fui[?]
rgareta [?] ac ceu de tonste et
B marisci XXiiij Jurati dixerunt
to acre & extendit in latitudine
uncupat le oldehea, [?] borea et
singer Thorney est le Southea et le
coud Lincolne et Cautebriet
ongitudine A Marisio de wisebeche
e ver occident phoria le latere dele
riple

Langregge

Leelegates

OLNE

de quatuor Goates

Rackenillowe Rowe

Newton hall et M. anerium de Larsinges

Newton

Fossatum maris ac etiam de Newton

Fossatum maris de wrasfort

Salsus Mariscus de warflot

Capella maris

PARS COMITATVS

Drana de la Goate in Comitat

Fossatum maris de Leueringtons et wisbeedt

Fossatum maris

Clowes Crosse

Manerium de Fytton modo

Extra de Buckworth [?] henrici

Manerium de Richmond modo Henrici Sebroillat

West W

Leuerington Parson droue

Le High fenne dike

Trokenholde

Park

Leuerington

Morshoe

Vetera Exuera et Com. Ge Twisbech

Wilbech Moorroe

Eastfelds

Comitatus Cantabrigie

Wal

Elm

Manerium Barton modo Regine

Wissieche beate Marie

Pons de

Wylebech sti Petri

Anno prudecimo regni Regis
Richardi secundi Aunsque
Dni 1387. Juuenis quidam
Jokes nomine filius Nicholai
Costdis de Trokenholde in
aqua de Southhea nauigans
nauiculam suam in ante
dirigens, Submersus est.
ob quam causam Daurbus
Kentofte Corronator Regis
in Com Cantabrigie excedit
exarcinacione. Itaq; missi
sicut officiam debit sub
forma fidelite executus est
ribi salis ante duo riportet
qd mariscus de wijbech[?]
in Com Cantabr et in Lincoln

Le High fenne dike

CANTABRIGIÆ

Manerium de white hall modo f. verardi Buckworth

The Fouste [?] Keckes milt

PARS COMITATVS

Guyhyrne

Magna Ripha demisrebeck

Beggedale

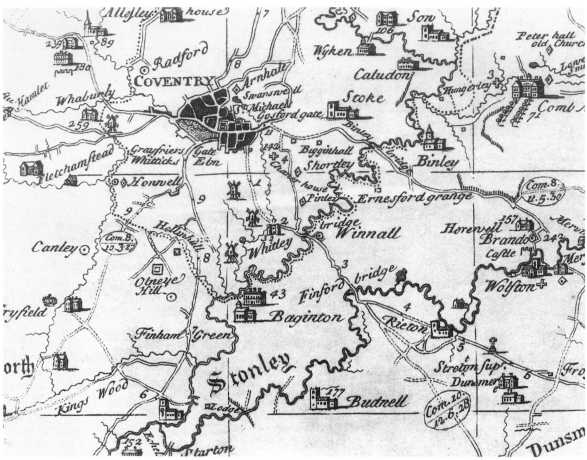

They show: parish divisions, which are further subdivided into denominations; hills; rivers; roads; and some settlement items such as castles and churches. Facsimiles of the Paris set were published by the Irish Ordnance Survey (1908).

42. For the 1730 edition of Sir William Dugdale's *Antiquities of Warwickshire*, the multi-talented Henry Beighton prepared sophisticated surveys of the four hundreds to replace the simple maps engraved by Robert Vaughan for the edition of 1656. The 1765 edition included both sets of maps. Beighton's map distinguishes a wealth of features. The locations of ten minerals are identified and the frequency of 'Depopulated Places' reflects the higher level of depopulation in Knightlow compared with the other three Warwickshire hundreds.

'A Map of KNIGHTLOW-HUNDRED. Reduced from an Actual Survey, made in the Year 1725; by Henry Beighton Fellow of the Royal Society 1729.' (Detail)

11
Military maps

Military maps provided the topographical information necessary for troop movement and subsistence, and for both offensive and defensive tactics. They record both the everyday business of armed forces and response to military and political situations, usually in manuscript since their information was not for wide dissemination. Only from the early nineteenth century, when they could be lithographed in limited numbers very quickly and cheaply from its own press, did the Quartermaster General's Office produce military maps in multiple copies for official use, starting with a map of Bantry Bay (1808) where Napoleon's forces were expected to land. Suggested defensive works may be recorded on parchment overlays loosely attached to topographical base maps, as they were to Popinjay's Portsmouth (c.1584), when threat of Spanish attack made strengthening of the town's fortifications urgently necessary. Proposals were also added by manuscript annotations, as on a Portsmouth map of 1545.[1] It is not always clear whether what is shown actually existed at the time or was merely proposed and there is no guarantee that suggested schemes were actually constructed.

The most strategically significant areas, such as main invasion targets, were mapped in detail many times. For many a remarkably full cartographic record exists from the mid sixteenth century. Detailed, large-scale fortification plans characterize the records of towns such as Berwick, Dover, Hull and Plymouth. Over 350 large-scale maps, mostly concerned with fortifications and defence, were prepared, for example, of the Portsmouth area before 1801, 22 of them in the seventeenth century; making Portsmouth one of the best mapped towns of its size anywhere in the world. Plymouth and Portsmouth were so strategically important that permanent Board of Ordnance drawing offices were established to prepare fortification plans.

Official surveys, accumulated by military authorities, governments, statesmen and royalty, have mainly remained in official or personal archives due to their once-sensitive nature. Most notable is the 'military' collection relating to defence and internal security assembled by Lord Burghley.[2] Its Irish surveys date from the 1560s. Maps cover the Scottish borders, including eight plans of Berwick alone; a manuscript map (1590) of the Annandale/Liddesdale area, for example, records castles and tower houses with owners named.[3] Cecil's pre-occupation with the Spanish invasion threat from the 1580s is reflected in some 40–50 maps related to Channel defences. In contrast to such unique manuscript maps, popular maps were later mass-produced by commercial publishers like Laurie & Whittle for individual sale or inclusion in histories and periodicals to satisfy interest in campaigns, military installations and manoeuvres. Bonnie Prince Charlie's march south, for instance, was mapped for the *Gentleman's Magazine*.

During Henry VIII's reign engineers and hydrographers, such as da Treviso and Rotz, were brought to England to superintend or advise on fortification work. Some drew plans; von Haschenperg, for example, in charge of royal works at Carlisle 1541–43, prepared three plans which survive of its castles and walls.[4] Knowledge of the latest designs and of use of maps drawn to precise scale in planning them spread from foreign military engineers, particularly the Italians, to an emergent native breed pioneered by Rogers[5] and Lee who became the foremost English designers of Tudor fortifications.[6] However, plans up to c.1685 make clear England's dependence on foreign-born engineers. From the sixteenth century most large-scale military plans produced for central government were drawn by military surveyors and draughtsmen employed by the Ordnance authorities, although on occasion private map-makers were apparently used as well.[7]

Military engineers played a crucial role in developing accurate scale-maps and introducing new surveying techniques into sixteenth-century England. Plan production was an integral part of military engineering and architecture. Engineers in the royal service stationed permanently at strategic points might produce sequences of plans over time, as did Popinjay who was at Portsmouth for over 25 years. Others prepared plans as they moved from one critical point to another, as did Ivye who worked at Portsmouth and in the Channel Islands and Ireland, or when they were assigned to a local command to plan and build temporary defences, fortifications, or siege works during military campaigns, as in the invasions of Scotland of 1547 and 1560.

Since the essence of Tudor warfare lay in attack and defence of fortified places, the military surveyor's primary concern was with fortification. For islands so close to Europe this usually meant harbour fortification against sea attack. The earliest maps record strongpoints along coasts most likely to be invaded. Henry VIII's foreign policy demanded systematic fortification of southern English coasts and the Scottish border. As part of the general programme of strengthening Portsmouth's defences, Popinjay made surveys which formed the basis of subsequent charts. At Hull, Rogers, Surveyor of Works from 1537, prepared maps of the area *c.*1541 and, in mapping new fortifications, produced the first detailed maps of the Humber, gaining a considerable reputation as a 'plat' maker.[8] In bird's-eye views of fortifications hydrographic information was only of secondary importance. Lee's chart of Orwell Haven (1533–4), for example, is really a defensive plan showing projected fortresses, as is a contemporary anonymous chart of Falmouth Haven. Works at Berwick-upon-Tweed (1558–64) were recorded by Lee and Johnson, and at Dover by Digges (1581), as tension between Spain and England continued – demanding continuous vigilance. The early warning system of beacons in Kent was mapped *c.*1596 for Lambarde's *Perambulation* of the county. The pacific policies of the penny-pinching Stuarts brought decline to fortification-plan production in the early seventeenth century, despite Civil and Dutch Wars. An undesignated plan of a pentagonal Cromwellian fort in Huntingdon County Record Office is thought to be Horsey Hill Fort. Thomas Phillips, Crown engineer, mapped fortresses in the Channel Islands in the late 1680s for James II. The

Ordnance Office continued to be active, producing, for example, plans of the Tower of London recording not only fortress layout but also neighbouring streets.[9] A plan of *c.*1682 is the earliest topographical record of property disposition within the Tower showing numerous lodgings, inns, coach-houses and stables which were converted into garrison accommodation within the next few years. The Jacobite rebellion threatened northern England (1745), forcing an urgent assessment of fortifications at towns such as Carlisle which might be subjected to siege. De Lavaux, for example, mapped Chester castle (1745), showing gun emplacements, to illustrate his unadopted scheme for an additional surrounding cordon of flankers and outworks. Fortification plans, such as Roy's '. . . Design for Fortifying Portsmouth Dock' (1770), accompanied official reports throughout the eighteenth century. Military installations, such as arsenals, powder magazines, batteries, and 'gun wharfes', were constantly mapped, particularly by the Board of Ordnance which surveyed most of its sites.

An important part of the engineer's job on active service was to plan and map fortifications. Robert Lythe, apparently a military engineer and fortifications expert, produced maps during the Elizabethan pacification of Ireland. He probably drew large-scale plans of Newry castle (*c.*1568), and certainly mapped Carrickfergus and Sidney's proposed fortifications there (1567).[10] The English habitually drew plans of places they attacked or fortified, as at Castlemilk (1547).[11] Bartlett or Barthelet documented Mountjoy's campaigns against O'Neill (1600–3), mapping fortifications

---

44. 'The Castle of Carrigfoile' was first captured in 1580 when it was mapped and a ground plan sent to Queen Elizabeth. In July 1600 Sir George Carew again found the castle in hostile hands and it was possibly re-mapped from memory by someone who had been present at the attack of 1580 in preparation for another assault. Carew was a noted collector of Irish historical materials which were used by Sir Thomas Stafford (probably Carew's illegitimate son) to compile an account of the Irish rebellion and Carew's campaigns in Munster (1600–3). The account in *Pacata Hibernia* (1633 – 'Pacified Ireland') was illustrated by a map-view based on an earlier map.

'The Castle of Carrigfoile in kerry, And a description how the Cannon was planted when itt was battred and wonne by S.[r] will. Pelham Lo: Justice of Ireland, on Palme Sunday in A° 1580.'

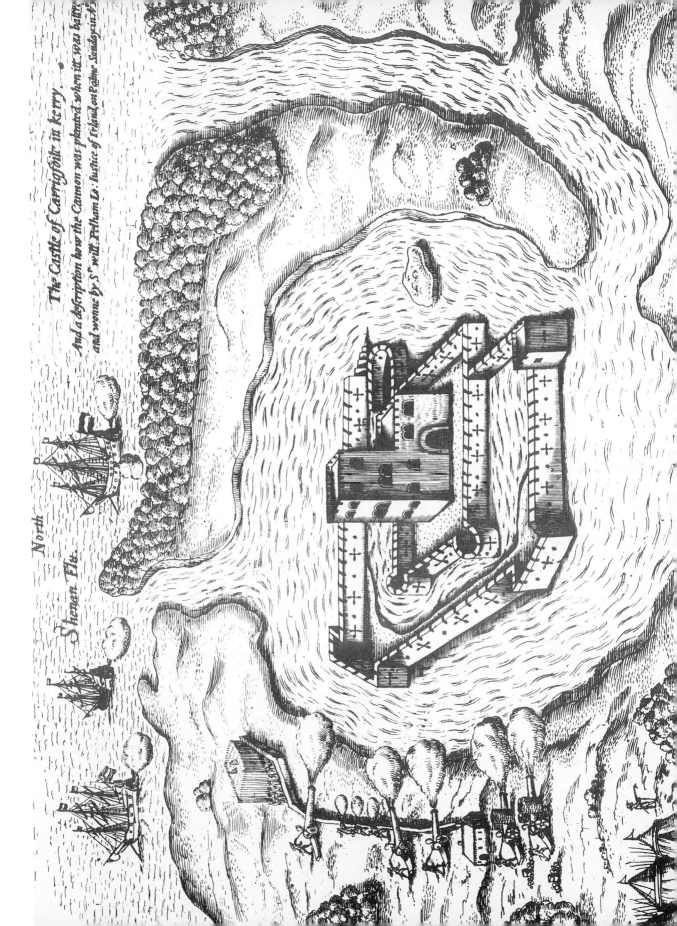

North

Shenan Flu.

The Castle of Carrigfoile in Kerry.

And a description how the Cannon was planted when itt was batter
and wonne by S.r will: Pelham L.d Iustice of Ireland on Palme Sunday 1579

such as that at Mount Norris (1601/2) with details of house types as well as defences.[12] In Ireland, the most accurate and comprehensive fortification plans were surveyed by Phillips (1685). Pacification of the Scottish Highlands after the '45 generated plans for improving barracks and building new fortifications at Fort William, Fort George, Fort Augustus, and elsewhere. Roy probably produced the plan of Braemar Castle (1748), showing improvements necessary for conversion to military barracks. He also mapped the principal Irish harbours (1765), although this work was in no sense original.

Plans of military engagements, sieges, and other tactical situations, and bird's-eye views of battle scenes have been produced since Tudor days, not only to record actual events but also to facilitate future strategic planning. Early battle plans, such as that of the Battle of Aghrim (1691) in Ireland, are valuable sources for military history. By combining picture-map and picture-story, they illustrate, for example, the nature of moveable protection, as well as providing much incidental information on the contemporary landscape.

A view (1514), with added notes on offshore anchoring conditions, records the French attack on Brighton,[13] and the earliest, fairly authentic contemporary picture-plan (1544) of a Scottish town shows Hertford's attack on Edinburgh. A later plan showing Drury's siege of Edinburgh Castle (1573) appeared in Holinshed's *Chronicles*. At least seven maps illustrate military actions following the Spanish landing at Kinsale (1601), including one 'somewhat roughly performed' by Boazio for Cecil from a plan by 'a gentleman not long since coming

45. Laurie & Whittle's plan of Fishguard Bay records the landing of a French force at Goodwick beach. The plan uses letters to identify the landing place and the positions taken by the French and British forces, amongst other locations. Colours identify the various British forces and 'dotted Lines denote the march of the Enemy down to Goodwick Sands, where they piled their Arms, and surrendered themselves Prisoners.'

'A PLAN of FISHGUARD BAY, near which the French Landed 1200 Men 22d Feb.y 1797 & Surrender'd Prisoners to Lord Cawdor on the 24th' Laurie & Whittle, 1797. (Detail)

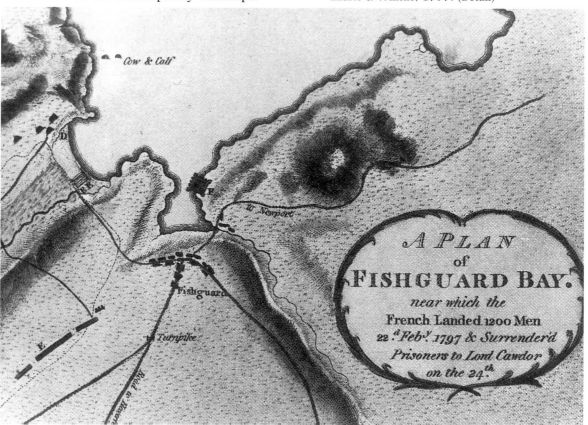

from the siege'; the 'gentleman' probably being Paul Ivye, the engineer.[14] Although written documentation of the landing is extensive, not all the issues raised by the maps have yet been worked out. A contemporary picture-map showing dispositions of Spanish, English and Irish troops offers valuable information on costume, armour, weapons, flags, troop formations, and the Munster landscape of the day. Attempts to develop rapidly-deployable marching formations able to withstand sudden attack are illustrated in a map (1599) of a successful Irish attack on the marching English in Wicklow. Maps of actions fought on the move are particularly helpful in fixing sites when location is uncertain. Carew's Munster campaigns 1600–3 are illustrated by battle views in Stafford's *Pacata Hibernia* (1633). Other contemporary maps show actions elsewhere in Ireland. Military map-makers documenting engagements they were involved in are largely unknown. John Thomas, for example, who signed himself simply as a soldier, illustrated the battle to cross the Erne (1593) and the siege of Enniskillen castle (1594); and officers present drew plans of the battles of Prestonpans (1745) and Falkirk (1746).

The true plan replaced view or picture-map in battle plans after the sixteenth century. Preston, for example, was mapped showing 'the batteries and barricades of the Rebels and the attacks of the King's Forces, commanded by General Willis, 1715'; a plan shows 'the attack and defence of Belfast by the Volunteers on the 20th July 1781'; and a plan of Fishguard Bay details the defeat of a French landing (1797).

Similar maps portray riots. Bowles overprinted his 'Reduced New Pocket Plan' of London to show defences against the Gordon Riots (1780), marking troop disposition, patrol routes, and encampments. Maps accompanied official reports on civil disturbance; the Ordnance Survey, for instance, illustrated the Belfast riots (1864), and the *Report of the Belfast Riot Commissioners* (1886) mapped the city's troublesome religious divisions.

Troop deployment was ideally suited to cartographic representation. In 1642, for example, Hollar engraved a detailed plan of Ormonde's forces in Ireland. Sir Harry Calvert, the Adjutant-General, annotated Rocque's London environs (1769) with troop and artillery dispositions to be adopted if Napoleon invaded. The names and locations of clans were added in manuscript to a map of Scotland (1731), with notes on the number of men they could muster. Roy often included his own

hand-drawn maps in reports (1765–81) on strategy and defensive troop deployments, and the Ordnance Survey sometimes supplied the army with 'manouvre' maps such as that of the Curragh of Kildare (1895). Troop quartering is illustrated by maps of barracks and encampments, both permanent and temporary. A plan (1639) of Charles I's camp on the Tweed, attributed to Hollar, distinguishes regiments by different colours; another (1639) illustrates the 'severall formes how King Charles his army enquartered in the Feilds being past New Castle on the March towards Scotland.' Another from the same campaign 'shewes the disposition of a single regiment of Infantry . . . according to the present dissiplyne', illustrating 'in what manner the hutts of the Souldiers in generall of every perticular Company are ordered, and how ye officers doe take their Roome, As ailso ye places for the Sutlers wch doe attend ye same.' A camp plan (1797) of the 29th Regiment of Foot even differentiates various types of tents. Mostyn Armstrong, when an 'Ensign in the Militia', mapped a militia encampment 'near Aldborough' (1779). Plans also illustrate review grounds such as that of the Belfast Volunteer review ground (1783), and of actual parades and reviews on sea as well as land; Loggan, for instance, published an 'Exact Plan of His Majesties Camp on Honslow-Heath, with a View of the Army as 'twas drawn up the 3d of July last' (1687). Plans of settlements created for discharged soldiers were also drawn.

Some of the earliest portrayals of English towns, including some of the very earliest English true plans made at a consistent and explicit scale, were produced in response to Spanish invasion threats in the 1530s and '40s. The mapping of fortified towns remained a major concern of military engineeers; Cecil, for example, commissioned Dromeslawer to map Hartlepool (1585) because of its strategic importance as a supply point for rebellious northern earls. Similarly, the earliest large-scale views of Scottish towns resulted from Hertford's invasions in 1544, 1545 and 1547. A military report on the West March and Liddesdale (1563–66) was illustrated by several large-scale plans of castles and towns. Bartlett produced important maps of Ulster's fortified towns, including the ruined Armagh; and in 1685 Phillips mapped other fortified towns including Dublin and Athlone.[15] Town mapping for defensive purposes continued in the following centuries, with Aberdeen, for example, being mapped for this reason in 1746.

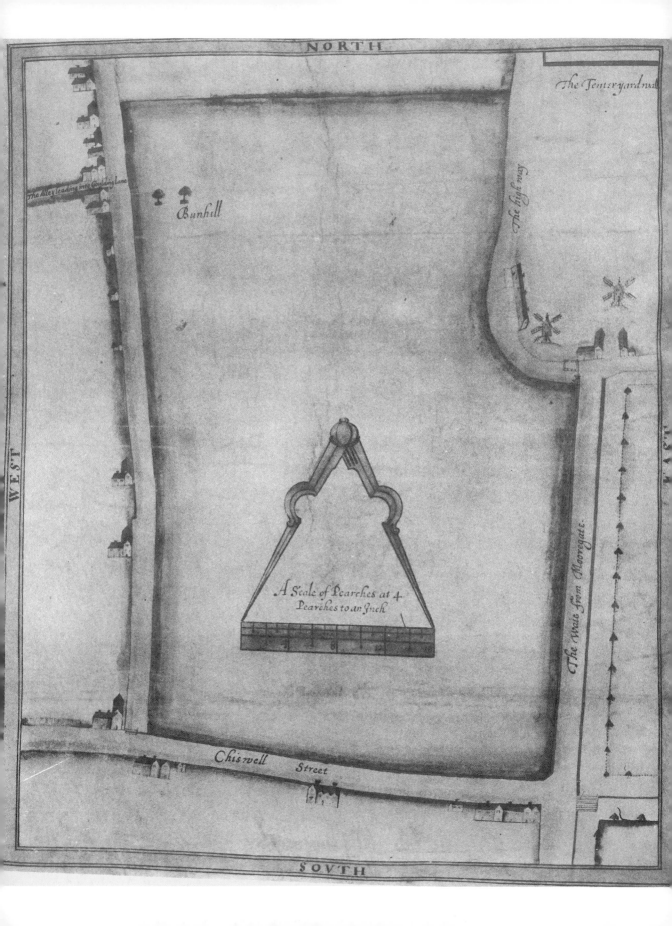

NORTH

WEST

EAST

SOVTH

The Tenter yard wall

The high way

The Alley leading into Goulding lane

Bunhill

The Waie from Mooregate

A Scale of Pearches at 4
Pearches to an Jnch

Chiswell Street

46. The Honourable Artillery Company received permission in 1641 to use the Artillery Garden or Ground for the practice of archery and artillery and the exercise of the Company. The manuscript plan accompanying the lease defines the area to be enclosed as an exercise area and for the construction of an armoury and other related buildings. Colours indicate boundaries. Ogilby & Morgan's London (*c.*1676) shows four regiments of pikemen and musketeers in battle array exercising on 'The New Artillery Garden.'

Untitled plan of the Artillery Ground. 1641.

---

47. The English subjugation of Ulster from 1593 was recorded on a series of at least 18 maps by Richard Bartlett, an English map-maker employed by the Irish Lord Deputy and almost certainly killed while surveying in Donegal in 1603. Armagh had suffered greatly in the warfare of 1551–1602 and was in ruins when mapped by Bartlett. It is possible to identify all the ecclesiastical buildings shown and valuable evidence of house types and fortifications is given. The enclosures and heaps of stones in the foreground seem to represent the town.

Armagh. Richard Bartlett, *c.*1602. (Detail)

Many general topographical maps were produced for specifically military purposes to show the countryside, with its fortified towns, through which armies might have to move. Military map-makers emphasized relief, drainage and vegetation cover, since terrain was vital to troop movement. Property boundaries were commonly disregarded because they could be crossed easily. Even in Tudor times, when attention focused on fortification, military topograpical surveying was beginning to emerge. Maps of military works were extended to show the countryside around, placing fortifications in their local context; one of Johnson's Berwick plans, for example, shows country for some 10 miles inland at a smaller scale than the town. Occasionally military engineers even produced maps not centred on fortifications. Bullock, for instance, mapped various alignments of the English/Scottish border north of Carlisle (1552). The Northern Rising (1569–70) demanded military communications maps. Probably the most important early topographical maps by military surveyors are those of Ireland made during cam-

paigns or on threat of invasion, since so little had been adequately mapped there before.

Ireland was mapped piecemeal in response to successive military and political developments. The need to garrison and colonize the newly-pacified and little-known Ulster in 1567 demanded regional topographical maps. Lythe was commissioned to map the area but instead produced maps of central and southern Ireland, recording not only towns and fortifications but also regions such as the rebellious Earl of Thomond's territory. A map of the lands of the White Knight and the Knight of the Valley (1571) cannot now be traced. Lythe's mapping of Leinster (1568–70) and Munster (1567–70) surpassed all earlier work in accuracy and comprehensiveness, particularly in the regions of his maritime surveys. Spanish invasion threat along the southern Irish coast caused Jobson to map Cork in the late 1580s; and Connaught was recorded by Browne (1590).[16] Ulster was extensively mapped during the Nine Years' War (1593–1603) by Bartlett, who produced at least 18 maps, including eight of extended areas which accurately picture the pre-plantation landscape. They are the finest extant group of maps of Gaelic Ulster.

Ireland was surveyed by military surveyors in the ensuing centuries. 'Captain Tho. Philips, Second Engineer of England', for instance, mapped Limerick (1691); and from 1776 Vallancey constructed bold, impressionistic military surveys of hills, roads and settlements in strategically important areas.[17] These were later worked up into an enormous hand-drawn map of the whole country.[18] Information collected in Vallancey's surveys of military outposts is summarized in a map of Ireland published in 1793. Maps of strategically important districts illustrated military reports such as those of General Dundas (1802) and Colonel Twiss (1803).

In Scotland, military engineers prepared topographical maps for General Wade's work on roads and forts 1725–35. The greatest cartographic activity followed the Jacobite Rebellion, inaugurating the earliest phase of modern mapping in Scotland. Maps of country between Aberdeen and Inverness were prepared for the Duke of Cumberland on his march to Culloden in April 1746. Watson and Roy organized the 'Military Survey' (1747–55) to map the lie of the land in the Highlands and parts of the Lowlands for military purposes at 1000 yards to the inch.[19] Although Roy judged the map just a 'sketch', and there was nothing technically exceptional in survey method,

the military precision of its preparation and its large scale, completeness, and relative uniformity make it a very useful historical source, depicting the pre-enclosure rural landscape on the eve of rapid agricultural change. The 'Military Survey' map, held by the British Library, is highly comprehensive, missing few settlements, and accurately locating land-use distribution. It is considered a faithful record of contemporary landscape and has been used to map distributions of some land-use types.[20] However, building layout in rural nucleations is stylized and sample checks of numbers of buildings depicted show no obvious pattern of correspondence with numbers of households contained in contemporary poll books.[21] Discrepancies in settlement spellings often make recognition difficult and, in the Highlands particularly, spellings are phonetic – confirming the presence of Lowlanders in the survey team. Many un-named settlements cannot be identified with any degree of certainty. Settlements are sometimes represented inaccurately; Rosehearty, for instance, shows no buildings at all despite having held a burgh charter for 70 years, and several settlements are located on the wrong side of streams. Field boundaries in the Lothians and other areas where new farming methods had been introduced are untrustworthy. The original plan of the south, which was never made into a fair copy, may be less accurate and less comprehensive than the fair copy of the north, which was altered and possibly resurveyed during preparation. The southern surveys exhibit inconsistencies of style and draughtsmanship and were hurriedly prepared as surveyors were transferred to more urgent work further south. Nevertheless, despite its inaccuracies and the suspect quality of its information, the 'Military Survey' represents the single most valuable landscape record of eighteenth-century Scotland.

From 1755 Roy reconnoitred coasts threatened by French invasion, mapping the north Kent coast and proposed defences at Milford Haven in 1756. Increasing awareness of vulnerability to invasion led Roy to propose a national survey to provide a 'good Military Plan or Map of the whole Country.'[22] The Board of Ordnance's sporadic surveys of military installations during the eighteenth century developed into an increasingly distinctive style of Ordnance cartography. Its topographical mapping of wider areas for defensive planning laid the foundations of a national survey, particularly the large-scale surveys of southern coastal regions threatened by Napoleon at the end of the century. Surveys were made piecemeal for short term military objectives, not for publication: 6-inch maps of the Plymouth region were derived from Gardner's survey (1784–86); Jersey (1787) and Guernsey (1787–88) were surveyed at the same scale; Kent (1789–1801), the Hampshire coastlands (1797–1810), the north Thames' shore (1798–1805), the Exeter area (1801–4) and to the west of Gardner's plan (1804–5) were surveyed at 3 inches to the mile; and the Isle of Wight was mapped at 6 inches to the mile (1793–1810). Areas of special military importance were surveyed from 1794, on scales of as much as 20 inches to the mile. These early Board of Ordnance large-scale maps, prepared by a military organization to a military specification, created a style which influenced content and character of the 1-inch maps. Early 'Old Series' sheets are clearly maps made in wartime, showing many signs of their original defensive purpose and the military training of their surveyors. On occasion, military information was removed from Ordnance sheets for reasons of national security, as, for example, when forts,

magazines and martello towers disappeared from the Irish 6-inch maps in the late 1870s.

The end of the French Wars did not remove fear of invasion. From the late 1850s the Ordnance anticipated acceptance of the 25-inch scale by surveying militarily important areas at that scale. Possible war with Napoleon III in the early 1860s demanded further fortification of ports and arsenals and production of military surveys of some 672,500 acres in strategic areas, mainly at the 25-inch scale but sometimes at 10.56 feet to the mile.

---

48. The inset plan of Plymouth Dock, at about $13\frac{1}{2}$":1m., on Donn's large-scale map of Devon, represents the dockyard in such detail that even the recently constructed dry docks and other installations appear clearly, as do the Gun Wharf and the military headquarters. It is remarkable that a map produced during such a period of international tension, which in fact caused the extension of the dockyard, should make public so much military information.

'A PLAN of STOKE TOWN, and PLYMOUTH DOCK.' Benjamin Donn, 1765. (Detail)

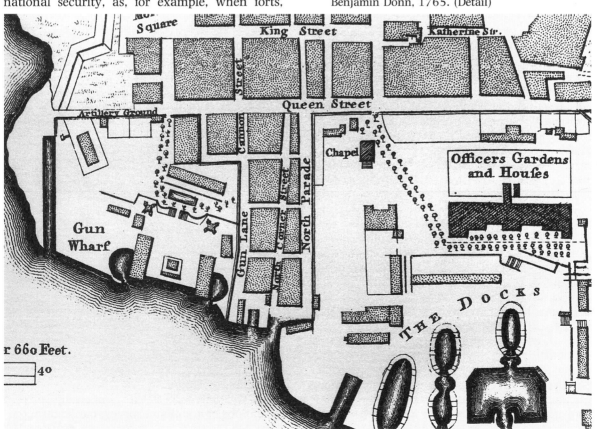

Official military topographical surveying expanded markedly only from the mid eighteenth century. Previously, privately-produced maps had generally been considered satisfactory for regional military planning. An early proof copy of Saxton's atlas with added manuscript regional maps, now known as the 'Burghley-Saxton' atlas, was used to plan deployment and arming of the militia and coastal defence improvement. Cecil copiously annotated Saxton's printed maps with details of defence and internal security, making them sometimes a geographical index to the government's friends and enemies or an instrument for Catholic suppression.[23] Demand for topographical maps during the Civil War caused maps by such as Saxton and Speed to be reprinted in numbers, despite being hopelessly out-of-date. Speed's maps were stitched together in stout vellum covers to form operational map folios. Jenner's road-book (1643) could have had little practical value for troops on the move since its 'thumb-nail' maps show no roads. Neither could his publication of Hollar's reduction of Saxton's wall-map (1583) of England and Wales – which also has no roads. This so-called 'Quarter-master's Map' (1644), was 'Vseful for all Comanders for Quarteringe of Souldiers, & all sorts of Persons, that would be informed, where the Armies be'.[24] When re-issued by Rocque (1752) an added colophon asserted falsely that it was made 'by Oliver Cromwell's order for the use of his Armies'. Despite the implications for national security in the disturbed times of the later eighteenth century, large-scale county mapmakers could display a wealth of military information. Donn, for example, portrayed Plymouth's defences in insets on his Devon in surprising detail for a map prepared for general publication.

Military maps and plans often provide unique detail of the nature of fortifications. Popinjay's plan of Portsmouth old town (*c*.1584), for example, even shows pictorially the defensive chain across the harbour entrance. Many fortifications were shortlived. Often military plans are the one and only historical source placing them in their environment. The military surveyor's specialized ideas of relevance naturally determined and restricted map content, reducing the wider historical value of much of his work. General topographical information was subsidiary to the main purpose of his map. Nevertheless, it is still a valuable record. A map of Sheppey, for instance, drawn *c*.1572 by 'IM', basically to depict the fort at Swaleness and

shipping access, delineates Lord Cheney's lands and differentiates individual farms. Although the 1545 Portsmouth map was prepared essentially to record fortifications, it also shows street and house layout. Roy's military map (1765) of south-eastern England documents Roman antiquities, Roman roads, names of 'Stations' and the location 'of the most memorable Battles.'

For military purposes any map, no matter how imperfect, was better than no map at all. Hence, this genre displays a greater variety of technique and style than other maps, ranging from bird's-eye views to instrumental surveys and measured ground plans drawn to a uniform scale. Sometimes different techniques of representation are found together in the same drawing. From the sixteenth century, military requirements were crucial in spreading map usage and for some areas almost every map produced was drawn for a military or naval purpose.

Select Bibliography

GOWEN, M., 'A bibliography of contemporary plans of late sixteenth and seventeenth century artillery fortifications in Ireland' (*Irish Sword*, 14; 1981)

HODSON, Y., 'The military influence on the official mapping of Britain in the eighteenth century' (*Int. Map Colls. Soc. Journ.*, 27; 1987)

INGLIS, H.R.G., 'The Wade maps and other additions to the Society's collection' (*Scot. Geog. Mag.*, 39; 1923)

JONES, F.M., 'The plan of the Golden Fort at Smerwick, county Kerry, 1580' (*Irish Sword*, 2; 1954–56)

JOHNSON, D.N., 'A contemporary plan of the siege of Caher Castle, 1599, and some additional remarks' (*Irish Sword*, 12; 1975–76)

KERRIGAN, P.M., 'A military map of Ireland of the late 1790's' (*Irish Sword*, 12; 1975–76)

KERRIGAN, P.M., 'Charles Fort, Kinsale, County Cork '(*Irish Sword*, 13; 1977–79)

MacIVOR, I., 'The Elizabethan fortifications of Berwick-upon-Tweed' (Antiquaries' Journ., 14; 1965)

PAKENHAM-WALSH, W.P., 'Capt Sir Josias Bodley, Director General of Fortifications in Ireland, 1612–17' (*Royal Engineers Journ.*, 8; 1908)

PAKENHAM-WALSH, W.P., 'Capts Sir Thomas Rotheram, Knt., and Nicholas Pinnar, Directors General of Fortifications in Ireland, 1617–44' (*Royal Engineers Journ.*, 10; 1909)

SHIRLEY, E.P., 'Notes on a plan of Carrickfergus, county Antrim, around the time of Elizabeth I' (*Ulster Journ. Arch.*, 4; 1855)

STEPHEN, J.S., 'Our 18th century plans and maps' (*Aberdeen Univ. Rev.*, 24; 1937)

12
Ordnance Survey maps

The most complex of cartographic sources, the Ordnance Survey, is the best documented in terms of its organizational history and techniques, and in the description of its maps. Ordnance maps are the basic guide to changing British landscape from the beginning of the nineteenth century, showing its state at a number of successive dates at different scales. In addition to their obvious local uses, they offer a national coverage which contributes to wider historical studies. However, use and interpretation is fraught with problems which can only be analysed for each individual case. To generalize and lay down detailed rules of interpretation would create too many dangers. There is much Ordnance material other than the regular published series: maps were published individually; prepared for internal use; supplied to other government departments and agencies; accompanied reports; and were drawn up during preparation of survey data for publication. Additionally, much written material appeared in memoirs, field-name books, and other internal records. Such material may well contain information which is not found on the Survey's published maps.

The original Ordnance series was published at 1 inch to the mile. However, widening demands forced the national survey to produce an increasingly sophisticated range of maps at different scales and levels of detail. As early as 1824, it was decided to survey Ireland at 6 inches to the mile, to provide a basis for fairer land taxation. Industrial development and expansion of towns and communications in the mid nineteenth century created an insistent demand for larger-scale maps. The Irish survey was so successful that the 6-inch scale was adopted in Great Britain in 1840, to map the remainder of northern England and Scotland not yet covered by the 1-inch, with subsequent 1-inch maps reduced from this larger scale. After a long controversy over the Survey's most suitable basic scale, a scale of 25

inches to the mile was initiated in 1854. Thus, after 1824 the British Isles were progressively covered by large-scale maps produced by the Ordnance Survey with, eventually, all cultivated areas covered at the 25-inch scale and uncultivated areas of waste and mountain at 6 inches to the mile.

The long trail from survey to publication was scattered with all kinds of useful diagrams, drawings, and documents. In particular, for some of the 'Old Series' 1-inch and most of the Irish 6-inch maps, the manuscript fair drawings, constructed from field surveyors' data, have survived. These drawings were traced with great care and skill to produce the printed map. Often they contain information which does not appear on the printed map, especially minor place-names in general and land-use detail on the 1-inch map in particular. Between drawing fair plan and publishing engraved map, material was edited and tidied to standardize it. Place-names were frequently corrected, standardized, and abbreviated, perhaps by an engraver trying to save space; and other names, particularly of farms and minor roads, were added. Details of buildings, roads and other features were often inserted during engraving, thus providing a time bracket for their appearance in the landscape between drawing of fair plan and engraving of plate. Prehistoric earthworks and archaeological sites were also frequently introduced. At the 1-inch scale, where space was at a premium, revision usually meant omission of data such as turnpike mileages, trigonometrical points, and identifications thought likely to become obsolete. Even at the 6-inch scale much was omitted in the cause of uniformity or economy, or because of doubtful accuracy, particularly concerning antiquities.

Field surveys for 'Old Series' sheets 1–90 covering England and Wales south of the Hull-Preston line were carried out mainly at 2 inches to the mile.

Strategically important areas in southern England, such as the Isle of Wight, were surveyed at 3 and 6 inches to the mile. Subsequently, 1-inch maps were reduced from the surveys at 6 and 25 inches to the mile. These unpublished preliminary drawings are preserved in the British Library with many ancillary drawings and sketches. They are the only sources giving date of topographical field survey, which often antedated publication by anything from 10–20 years. Considerable variation of style, colouring, and sign-usage indicates that the drawings are essentially the personal productions of individual surveyors. They must, therefore, be interpreted with care.

Colour, shading and conventional signs differentiate land use, but sometimes virtually all detail is obscured by heavy hill-shading. Since there is no key to the drawings, it must be assumed that their signs mean the same as those on the later maps. Even so it is not known how field surveyors defined categories of land use and whether they all defined each category the same. Field boundaries are certainly diagrammatic in some cases and the Survey recognized that its sketched boundaries were not good enough for publication and omitted them from the printed 1-inch maps. The drawings of Wales, for example, are less detailed than farm plans, adding little to the information derived from them, although confirming the absence of common and accessibility of most farms to main roads. Nevertheless, despite inadequacies, the 'Old Series' fair drawings can provide valuable information not available elsewhere; in Wales, for instance, they disclose a previously unsuspected dense settlement scatter over whole areas.

The fair plans for the Irish 6-inch maps (1825–42) are arranged by parishes, with small parishes combined on a single sheet and large divided on several sheets. They show water features, roads, named townlands with boundaries, altitudes of trigonometrical points, spot heights, antiquities and some land use. Short pen strokes show unmapped fences where they crossed the line of the chain or joined roads, streams and townland boundaries. Buildings appear in sufficient detail for sizes and shapes to be differentiated, sometimes coloured probably to distinguish construction materials. Many rural houses were removed from the printed maps at the proof stage because their isolated position was thought to make them look like dirt specks. Each plan is signed and dated. A few include larger-scale insets of areas of special interest for clarity.

Publication of the 'Old Series' represented the appearance of maps more accurate and more detailed than almost any before. However, interpretation is hindered by the lack of explanation of signs used. Sheets 1–90 should be regarded as the least accurate Ordnance maps, despite their superiority over most other contemporary material. After 1840, 1-inch maps were reduced from the 6-inch surveys; these later sheets are generally considered to be more accurate. The wide time-span of production of all Ordnance series makes comparison between different localities difficult and dangerous, particularly when they are far apart. The 1-inch maps show houses and garden plots around dwellings in rural areas with remarkable clarity; but gardens disappeared on the later northern sheets. Most farmsteads are named and generally many more place-names are given than on other contemporary maps. Some minor streams and many small landscape features such as copses, paddocks and ponds appear on printed maps for the first time. Turnpike and secondary roads, (with an indication of whether they were fenced or unfenced), tracks, footpaths and canals are more precisely delineated than on contemporary large-scale county maps. Windmills are marked, but not watermills; as are churches and chapels, and occasional named public houses and hotels. Settlements are distinguished by different lettering. Street layout is shown with buildings and villages marked in solid black and in built-up urban areas by shading.

The first 'Old Series' printings quickly became out-of-date. However, demand soon exhausted existing stocks. Before reprinting, copper plates were corrected and amended, particularly in respect of railways. Revised sheets were not described as a new edition and publication date was not altered; consequently, there may be many different versions of individual 'Old Series' sheets, depending on how many times a sheet was revised. The actual printing date must be deduced from features such as town extent and the presence of particular railways with all the dangers that that involves. In 1820 the field survey was reorganized to ensure greater accuracy. The immediate result was a substantial revision both of field plans in preparation, beginning in Lincolnshire and covering approximately 25,000 square miles in the Midlands during the 1820s and early '30s, and of maps published by *c*.1820. Since the southern sheets were less accurate than the northern, which were reduced from larger-scale surveys, it was decided to prepare new maps of the southern block from new large-scale surveys. The 'New Series' was constructed on somewhat different sheet lines with new numbering running from north to south. The more recently surveyed northern counties required less revision than those further south, surveyed much longer ago at smaller scales. The date of original survey on 'New Series' sheets 1–73 was not altered, but re-surveyed sheets to the south were freshly dated with the new field survey date. Survey and publication were much faster than for the 'Old Series', with the area south of the Hull–Preston line re-surveyed in 20 years as compared to 45 for the original survey. Further revision may well have occurred in the intervening period between survey and publication. Variant formats printed in colours or with relief hachured and shaded appeared after the black-and-white outline contoured version, often embodying minor corrections and adding railways. Minor revisions were dated by either amending publication date or adding notes such as 'Railways inserted to . . .' or 'Parish boundaries corrected to . . .' in the margin.

The 'Third Edition' appeared in four versions of the standard sheet, including 'fully coloured' and a Large Sheet Series, all bearing date of survey.

The 1-inch maps of both Scotland and Ireland were from the beginning reduced from surveys for the 6-inch maps. The separateness of the Irish Survey and the difference in landscape gave the Irish 1-inch a different appearance to Ordnance maps of other regions. Names and boundaries of counties, baronies and parishes are prominently marked but townlands are omitted, despite being shown on some early sheets. Transport networks are delineated in detail but rural settlement is treated selectively. Churches, chapels, constabulary barracks, schools, workhouses and land use are comprehensively represented as on the 6-inch maps. The Irish 1-inch can be remarkably detailed without overcrowding; in Dublin, for example, street-width variation is clearly visible, as are individual monuments. In 1852–58 rapid surveys of some new roads, public buildings, and other features were conducted specially for inclusion on the 1-inch map, which may, therefore, contain more or different information from the 6-inch. Local corrections and additions, particularly of railways, were made irregularly, and in 1889–95 some areas were more fully revised to match the latest 6-inch maps, with new imprints noting revision.

Larger-scale Ordnance maps do not necessarily offer more or clearer information than the 1-inch. On occasion 1-inch maps show information not found at other scales, although as a general rule many minor features are missing. They are ideal for delineating street layout and parish boundary alignment. Comparative studies of consecutive editions and issues of the 1-inch series reveal evolving landscape change which may not be as apparent at larger scales.

The earliest printed Ordnance maps at 6 inches to the mile were of Ireland, where the larger scale was deemed necessary for property valuation and tax-liability assessment. The resulting austerely beautiful maps cover the country in 1906 sheets, each delineating 24 square miles. Exact acreages of parishes, baronies and townlands are specified to the nearest statute perch on the maps and their indexes, and the various boundaries are very clearly shown. The series' worst flaw was the lack of fences on the northern sheets, particularly as it became clearer that valuation would have to be based on tenements and not townlands; consequently, the addition of fences to the northern sheets was authorized in 1844. Up to 1896 new railways were engraved as soon as possible after opening, but it proved impossible to treat roads the same. Municipal boundaries were inserted in 1868 and very occasionally antiquities were added to the original maps. A few small areas were more extensively revised on the original sheets.

Irish 6-inch maps were revised in two ways. In 'card revision' obsolete detail was cancelled on the printed sheet and additions were penned in. However, for areas where original field survey had been inaccurate, as in Derry, Tyrone, Antrim, Down and Armagh, a complete resurvey was necessary, producing maps sometimes perceptibly different from the originals. Townlands had to be created and named where land had been reclaimed, and there was much alteration of place-names and addition of features such as antiquities. Compared with the first edition, the revised maps have fewer descriptions, such as fort, quarry and spring, and more place-names. In 1887 it was decided to resurvey most of Ireland at the 25-inch scale and thenceforth most 6-inch sheets were prepared by reduction from the larger-scale sheets, greatly curtailing revision of existing 6-inch sheets. The Valuation Office added its reference numbers to 6-inch sheets. It used them for an annual manuscript revision of property boundaries, marking individual tenement boundaries in colour and adding new properties, even new streets. Irish 6-inch maps

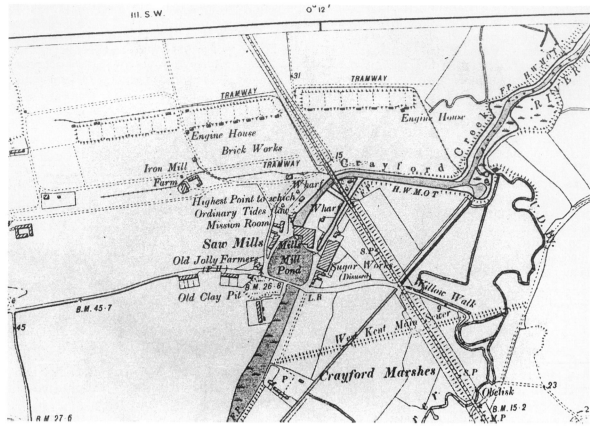

49. 'SECOND EDITION, 1898. KENT. SHEET IX.N.W. Heliozincographed from $\frac{1}{2500}$ Plans and Published at the Ordnance Survey Office, Southampton. Surveyed in 1862–64. Revised in 1895.' Scale: 6":1m. (Detail)

were regarded as so reliable that engineers readily testified that they were perfectly satisfactory for railway planning and preparation of deposited plans. Later, they were used to reconstruct ancient Irish settlement patterns.[1]

The success of the 6-inch scale in Ireland led to adoption elsewhere. Only narrow streets which were widened in order to insert legible names are not in exact plan. Six-inch maps clearly distinguish woodland and common and, in contrast with tithe maps, show a wealth of place-names and landscape detail. Small towns developing suburbs and industry around a medieval core are particularly well illustrated at this scale. In urban areas, streets are named, as are many industrial establishments. A 6-inch sheet has the advantage over a 25-inch in that it will cover a whole parish, giving an overall record of development, extent of land-use features, and so on. The 25-inch survey did not cover

'Highland and other partially cultivated and thinly peopled districts', confining itself to 'populous, mineral, and cultivated districts'. Hence, for upland areas 6-inch maps are the largest scale of Ordnance coverage. For many studies, the 6-inch scale provides adequate information and its sheets are easier to handle. Only minor detail is missing in comparison with the 25-inch scale; land parcels have no reference numbers or acreages; dense building is blocked rather than shown as individual properties; some boundaries are absent in towns where they would be illegible; and railways are portrayed conventionally rather than in plan.

The later 6-inch maps were reduced photographically from the 25-inch plans surveyed from the 1850s. For the first time, a series of printed maps covered most of the country at a scale equivalent to the estate survey. In fact, the Ordnance's 25-inch maps came to be used as a base for estate plans prepared by superimposing information on to the Survey's topographical maps. The 25-inch maps show landscape in the greatest detail, accurately delineating virtually all significant man-made features, often for the first time on

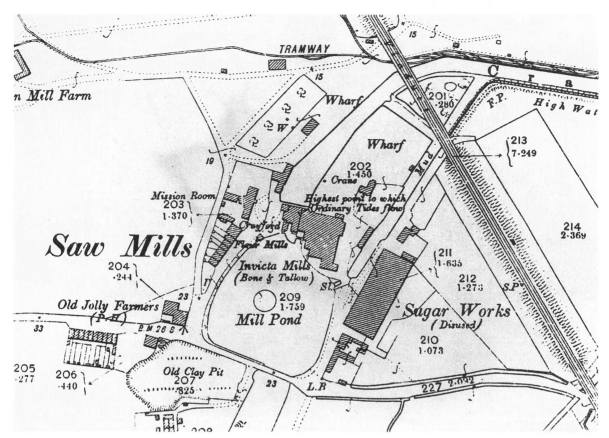

50. 'SECOND EDITION 1897. KENT. SHEET IX.2. Photo-zincographed and Published at the Ordnance Survey Office, Southampton, 1897. Surveyed in 1862–63–64. Revised in 1895.' Scale: 25":1m. (Detail)

any map. Until 1872, maps were produced as parish plans with areas outside the parish boundary left blank, but, henceforth, topographical detail was completed to the sheet edges – an arrangement not ideally suited to a cadastral map because edges may cut through land parcels. Since 25-inch plans are primarily cadastral there is little relief depiction, apart from spot heights and some slope drawing.

On 25-inch plans non-cultivated land is distinguished by 10 different signs for classes of woodland, marsh, and rough pasture. Boundaries of fields, smallholdings, gardens and other land parcels are shown, with serial numbers referring to the Area Book/Book of Reference for all but small private house-plots. Acreages were printed beneath reference numbers on the map after the Books were discontinued. 'The main consideration in numbering plans is to give separate numbers to

any space the area of which may be considered of use to the public, providing there is room for stamping the number and area without overcrowding the plan.' The exact shape and area of each enclosure, with hedges, fences, or stone walls, is truly represented in plan, and field boundaries are shown accurately, with fields named until 1888. Sometimes plans show the remaining strips and other vestiges of open fields and record common meadows. Quarries; sand, gravel and clay pits; numerous industrial plants; and many watermills are marked. Industrial activity is indicated. Transport facilities are treated in detail with every road marked; turnpike named; canal shown with locks, bridges, and towpaths; and railway delineated to scale width at the standard gauge with sidings, stations and sheds. In settlements, many of them named on maps for the first time, streets are drawn at correct widths and buildings are shown in exact plan with gardens and outhouses; even the interior design of large buildings is delineated. All administrative boundaries, both civil and ecclesiastical, are recorded; antiquities are marked; and the whole panoply of the cultural landscape is laid out in the depiction of churches, chapels, schools, hotels, public houses, post offices, and so on.

The 25-inch Ordnance plans constitute a display of the man-made landscape of almost unlimited use for the study of localities rather than regions, as they were, for example, for Middlesex.[2] Certainly for individual features, such as ironworks, colliery, or railway station, this scale of representation is indispensible.

The 'Second Edition' has buildings shaded diagonally and vegetation signs 'stamped' to repeat the design. Fields have been renumbered and acreages added. Apart from these small stylistic changes, it is marginally less detailed than the 'First'. Detail selection was criticized, particularly on the grounds that minute details were not primarily cadastral and were mapped simply to improve appearance. Depiction of railway lines, level crossings, turntables and sidings, gravel walks in gardens, and interiors of public buildings in detailed and exact plan was thought unnecessary. Hence, minor detail was progressively simplified and content reduced in an effort to cut expenditure. Fieldnames were omitted after 1888; interiors of public buildings, individual trees in hedgerows, gates in fields, paths and flower beds, and bay windows were discontinued in 1892; and from 1895 'unimportant detail was no longer shown.'[3] Generally, the 25-inch revision cycle was inadequate.

The newly-formed Inland Revenue Land Valuation Department required very large-scale plans for a general rating revaluation. Many plans were produced in 1911 at 50 inches to the mile, but these are simply mechanical enlargements of the then 25-inch sheets with no additional detail. These enlarged sheets were put on general sale. Similarly, land valuation and registration requirements necessitated plan enlargement to the 50-inch scale for local authorities and private individuals by special request.

In Ireland, County Dublin was initially published by parishes on the English pattern, but in 1887 continuous coverage to sheet margins was adopted and Books of Reference were discontinued, causing acreages to be marked on the maps. Irish 25-inch plans are much the same as those elsewhere and were subjected to the same process of simplification, with, for example, use of initial letters showing exact position of townland boundaries discontinued in 1899.

In addition to its series of topographical maps, the Ordnance Survey produced numerous individual maps useful to the historian; part of the Belfast town index, for example, was used to show the route of a provocative funeral procession. Particulary valuable are facsimiles of early maps, such as Symonson's Kent, the Jacobean escheated counties maps of Ireland, and the 'Down Survey' barony maps, the originals of which may be inaccessible or have since disappeared.

Land registration had been cartographically recorded since 1862 by the Land Registry using whatever map sources were available, particularly the 25-inch Ordnance plans and the tithe maps but also enclosure and estate plans. However, even after Ordnance Survey base maps became generally available, this proved unsatisfactory. Consequently, from 1898 the Registry's own Map Department conducted special surveys to revise Ordnance maps which were out-of-date. From 1903 land registration maps of the London area became available to the public as the 'Land Registry Series'. This developed in to the Registry's 'General Map', which from 1907 was prepared in sections consisting of extracts or printed copies of Ordnance maps revised to date by its own surveyors. The Ordnance, however, considered the map Department's work to lack accuracy and detail, whilst the Registry, in return, criticized the inadequacy of relevant detail on Survey maps.

Undoubtedly Ordnance maps and plans are amongst the most accurate available, an accuracy often attained by the penal incentive of lost pay. However, particularly at its smaller scales, the Ordnance, like other map-makers, was forced to select the features it would show. Often only a generalized partial distribution is given, especially where features cluster closely together. Ordnance surveyors were as fallible as others and their errors and mistaken interpretations can appear on the printed maps, as, for example, when the tumbled earthworks of deserted villages or medieval fishpond systems have been erroneously interpreted and marked as a *Moat*.

Dates of survey, revision and publication of Ordnance sheets are obviously of crucial importance, but, unfortunately, there can be no easy guide to dating. Date information given in sheet margins is sometimes confusing and dates are often not easily determined. Although dates of original survey and publication are usually readily available, this is not so with minor revisions not constituting a new edition. Sheets were often issued bearing original dates after revision, and there is virtually no way of determining when a particular revision was made. Only close comparison of sheets reveals the extent of correction and addition. Even the Ordnance itself admitted that it was extremely difficult to trace when and why changes were made. Sheets were often trimmed and mounted, removing dated imprints altogether. The problems of dating Ordnance maps have been discussed in detailed studies which should be consulted when precise dating is a matter of significance.[4]

Historians are faced by a large number of Ordnance sheets at different scales. The best guide to these is, where extant, the *Catalogue of Maps and other Publications of the Ordnance Survey* which was published from December 1862 in separate volumes for England and Wales, Scotland, and Ireland. Monthly lists were issued and full catalogues in certain years. Full annual catalogues appeared from 1888 until 1920, and the last was issued in 1924. The student who successfully negotiates the potential difficulties is faced with a treasure trove of cartographic information. Ordnance maps have already contributed to disciplines such as archaeology and place-name studies. They have been used to recreate the historical geography of a rural parish,[5] amongst many other areas. They undoubtedly have very much more to offer.

Select Bibliography

ANDREWS, J.H., 'Medium and message in early six-inch Irish Ordnance maps: the case of Dublin city' (*Irish Geog.* 6; 1973)

ANDREWS, J.H., *History in the Ordnance Maps. An Introduction for Irish Readers* (1974)

ANDREWS, J.H., *A Paper Landscape: The Ordnance Survey in Nineteenth-Century Ireland* (1975)

CLOSE, SIR C., *The Early Years of the Ordnance Survey* (1926. New edn., 1969; introduction by J.B. Harley).

HARLEY, J.B., 'Error and revision in early Ordnance Survey maps' (*Cart. Journ.*, 5; 1968)

HARLEY, J.B. (ed.), *Reprint of the First Edition of the One-Inch Ordnance Survey of England and Wales* (97 sheets with accompanying notes; 1969–71)

HARLEY, J.B., 'Place-names on the early Ordnance Survey maps of England and Wales' (*Cart. Journ.*, 8; 1971)

HARLEY J.B., MANTERFIELD, J.B. & B.A.D., & O'DONOGHUE, (later HODSON), Y., Introductions to *The Old Series Ordnance Survey Maps of England and Wales* (1976–to be published in 10 volumes)

HARLEY, J.B., & PHILLIPS, C.W., *The Historian's Guide to Ordnance Survey Maps* (Nat. Coun. Soc. Serv; 1964)

HUGHES, T.J., 'The six inch to the mile Ordnance Survey townland map' (*Journ. Assoc. Geog. Teachers Ireland*, 1; 1964)

JOHNSTON, D.A., *Ordnance Survey Maps of the United Kingdom–A Description of their Scales, Characteristics etc.* (1902)

MADDEN, P.G., 'The Ordnance Survey of Ireland' (*Irish Sword*, 5; 1962)

OLIVER, R.R., 'The Ordnance Survey in Lancashire in the 1840s' (*Sheetlines*, 8; 1983)

Ordnance Survey, *A Description of the Ordnance Survey Large Scale Maps* (1954) [for the 25-inch maps]

Ordnance Survey, *A Description of the Ordnance Survey Medium Scale Maps* (1955) [for the 6-inch maps]

SEYMOUR, W.A. (ed.), *A History of the Ordnance Survey* (1981)

SKELTON, R.A., 'The origins of the Ordnance Survey of Great Britain' (*Geog. Journ.*, 128; 1962)

WILLIS, J.C.T., *An Outline of the History and Revision of 25-inch Ordnance Survey Plans* (H.M.S.O.; 1932)

WINTERBOTHAM, H. ST J.L., 'The small scale maps of the Ordnance Survey' (*Geog. Journ.*, 79; 1932)

Ordnance Survey 1″:1m.(1:63,360)

ENGLAND & WALES

Format   'Old Series': Sheets 1–90: mainly full sheets of 29/36 × 23/24″, but some maps were also published in quarter-sheets. Sheets 91–110: although full sheets were still the basis of the numbering system, the maps were issued in quarter-sheets, i.e. 18 × 12″. Kent, Essex, Surrey and Sussex were first issued in small bound folios, one for each county. The sheets first appeared without hachuring due to delay in making hill sketches. 'New Series': Sheets 91–110: as above. Full-sheet numbering was abandoned in 1872 when existing quarter-sheets were withdrawn and re-issued as Sheets 1–73 of the 'New Series' (comprising 360 sheets, each 18 × 12″), available either in outline with contours or with hachured hills.

Survey   Triangulation of the country started in 1792 and the topographical survey began in Kent in 1795. The topographical survey extended quickly from south-east England into Devon and Cornwall. From 1840, 1″ maps were simply reduced from the 6″ survey which had started in northern England and Scotland; and from 1853 they derived their survey material from the 25″ survey which began in Durham. The 'Old Series' is the only set of Ordnance 1″ maps which does not carry date of topographical survey.

    The 'New Series' started with the beginning of the 6″ survey north of the Hull-Preston line in 1840, and was completed 1842–69. The 6″ survey was extended south of the Hull-Preston line in 1872 and completed in 1893. The survey for the 'Third Edition' of the 1″ maps began in 1901. From the 'New Series,' the date of field survey was printed on the sheet.

Publication   Although the 'Mudge' map of Kent, published by Faden, appeared in 1801, the 'Old Series' proper with Kent re-engraved was published 1805–73. Maps covered the country south roughly of an Essex–Pembrokeshire line by 1820 and south of a Hull–Preston line by 1844. The publication date noted below the map was not changed throughout the issue period despite revisions and later printings. 'New Series': Sheets 91–110, with hachured hills, derived from the 6″ surveys of the northern counties, were published 1847–69, for mainland England and Wales, with the outline map of the Isle of Man appearing in 1873 and the hill version in 1874. No 'Old Series' map of the Scilly Isles was published; the 'New Series' sheets in outline were published in 1892 and with hills in 1900. Sheets 1–90, covering the country south of the Hull–Preston line, were derived from the 6″ survey conducted 1872–93. Publication was completed, after revision, before 1899. Date of publication appears below the map, varying between 1–29 years after the finish of survey, but usually less than 10 years later. The 1″ sheets were published as an outline contoured map in black-and-white. However, the national revision of the 1890s produced the following variant forms: (i) Coloured (roads–sienna, woods–green, contours–red), (ii) Relief hachured and shaded in black, (iii) Relief hachured and shaded in brown.

Revisions   'Old Series': Some maps, particularly those covering the southern coast, were completely re-engraved in the 1830s and '40s, but generally revisions were made as needed by amending plates. Consequently, the faster the urban and economic development of an area, the greater and more frequent were revisions. Delineation of railways, in particular, tended to be kept up-to-date. Apparently the 'New Series' was fully revised 1893–98. Revision and re-publication dates are usually noted in the lower margin but it is quite possible that other un-noted revisions were also made at other times. The second national revision of the 'New Series' was surveyed 1901–12 to produce the 'Third Edition', published 1903–13. Sheet lines and numbers are identical to earlier issues of the 'New Series'. Later sheets often have corrections or addition of railways made after the main revision but prior to publication, and these are always dated in the bottom margins. The 'Third Edition' was also published in a Large Sheet Series, by amalgamating the smaller sheets, of 152 sheets of varying size, though mainly at 18 × 27″. The survey for the 'Fourth Edition' took place 1913–23, and the maps were published 1918–26.

SCOTLAND	IRELAND
131 sheets, 24 × 18″, numbered independently from the English series, running from south to north. Topographical detail of England was not included on maps extending over the border. Available either in outline with contours or with hachured hills.	Originally designed as 59 large sheets, 36 × 24″, but issued in quarter-sheets of 18 × 12″. Re-numbered in 1858 as a single consecutive series of 205 quarter-sheets. Contoured or un-contoured versions were produced for 17 of the first 1″ sheets; and 204 of the quarter-sheets were available with or without hachured relief.
The 'First Edition' of the 1″ map was derived initially from the 1843–55 6″ surveys and 1854–95 from the 25″ surveys.	Derived from the 'First Edition' 6″ maps surveyed 1829–42 (published 1835–46) with roads and other major features revised from special surveys rapidly carried out 1852–58. Antrim, Donegal, Fermanagh, Londonderry, and Tyrone were derived from the 'Second Edition' 6″ maps surveyed 1845–59 (published 1851–62).
Published 1856–87. Revisions in 1894–95 produced a 'Second Edition', published in 1896–97. Forms of publication similar to 'England & Wales'.	The 'outline' edition was published 1856–62, and the 'hill' edition 1855–95. Revisions in 1898–1901 produced the 'Second Edition' which became available in four variant formats: (i)Uncoloured and unhachured, (ii)Hachures in brown, (iii)Urban and rural districts in red, (iv)Coloured in black, blue, green, brown and sienna. Publication dates were noted for the 'hill' edition but did not become common on the 'outline' edition until the 1880s.
Revisions in 1894–95 produced the 'Second Edition', published in 1896–7. The revising survey for the 'Third Edition' on the same sheet lines was carried out 1901–10, and the series was published 1902–13.	Armagh, Down and Monaghan were revised from the 'Second Edition' 6″ maps in 1867–68. Dublin, Louth and Meath, and parts of Armagh, Carlow, Cavan, Down, Kildare, Leitrim, Longford, Monaghan, Offaly, Westmeath, Wexford and Wicklow were revised from the 'Second Edition' 6″ maps in 1889–95. The first general revision took place 1898–1901. Other revisions, particularly of roads and other major features, were made at irregular intervals. The second revision, conducted 1908–13, did not cover the whole of the country, being mainly confined to areas roughly north of a line from Fermanagh to Down and south of Clare to Wicklow, and even then not all the area revised was actually published.

Ordnance Survey 6":1m.(1:10,560)

Format   Most sheets published before *c*.1881 were engraved on copper and issued as large sheets of $36 \times 24''$, but subsequently they were produced by direct photographic reduction from the 25" scale and were issued usually only as quarter-sheets of $18 \times 12''$ (except for a few areas in Lancashire and Yorkshire). Obviously counties are covered by varying numbers of sheets according to area: eg. Hertfordshire (published 1872–84)–42 full-sheets, Northamptonshire (1883–86)–63 full-sheets, Gloucestershire (1883–88)–241 quarter-sheets, Norfolk (1883–88)–363 quarter-sheets, Warwickshire (1883–89)–210 quarter-sheets. In all some 15,000 quarter-sheets for the whole of Great Britain. Sheet lines are organised on either a county basis or in groups of counties, and within the county the maps are numbered in Roman figures with the quarter-sheets distinguished by the letters N.W., N.E., S.W., and S.E. Since many of the county series were constructed on different surveying meridians, chosen to minimise distortion from the projection, the county series are to some extent independent and there is no exact correspondence between counties. Topographical detail on some sheets extends beyond county boundary to the margin and on others (sometimes corresponding sheets) it stops short at the county boundary. However, neighbouring counties are shown in full detail to the sheet border on most sheets produced by photozincography after *c*.1882. From 1862 an index diagram showing the constituent 25" sheets was included on most 6" sheets.

Survey and Lancashire and Yorkshire were surveyed at the 6" scale 1840–54. However, the decision was taken to adopt the 25"
Publication scale, starting in County Durham in 1854, and, henceforth, from 1856 the 6" maps were produced by reduction from the 25", bearing the same date of survey but often published a little later. The 'First Edition' was completed 1888–93 by the re-survey of Lancashire and Yorkshire, and was published in both contoured and non-contoured forms. Publication date appears in lower margin.

Revisions   Revisions were approved in 1882 and re-survey work began in the London, Surrey and Middlesex areas in 1891. The revision was completed in Yorkshire in 1914. Sheets note revision dates; are designated as the 'SECOND EDITION'; and were printed by photozincography from the new maps drawn for the 'second edition' of the 25" series. In 1882 it was accepted that revision of the series was to take place every 20 years and a new edition published, with the aim that no sheet would be more than 20 years old and the average age of a sheet 10 years. Survey began in 1904 but was drastically interrupted by World War I and this periodic system of revision became impractical.

Ordnance Survey ≈ 25":1m.(I:2,500)

Format   Standard sheet size of $38 \times 25\frac{1}{3}''$ with 'FIRST EDITION' printed in the top margin. Cheshire, Cumberland, Denbighshire, Durham, Flint, Glamorgan, Hampshire, Middlesex, Monmouth, Northumberland, Pembroke, Westmorland and the Isle of Man, and parts of Essex and Surrey were issued as parish maps with areas outside the parish boundary left blank. After 1873, topographical detail was extended to the map edge but the sheets were still published as a county series and, therefore, detail does not extend beyond the county boundary. Obviously counties are covered by varying numbers of sheets according to area (a I:2500 sheet covers an area of $1\frac{1}{2}$ sq.mls.): eg. Hertfordshire (published 1867–82) – 518 sheets, Warwickshire (1884–90) – 718, Northamptonshire (1886–87) – 755. In all, some 51,000 sheets for the whole of Great Britain.

Survey and The 25" survey commenced in County Durham in 1854 and had covered the four northern counties by 1865. In
Publication anticipation of the extension of the 25" survey (authorised in 1862) areas of military importance were surveyed at 25" during the 1850s; but the extension proper took place from 1862, initially concentrating on the metropolitan counties, mineral districts, and areas prepared to contribute two-thirds of the costs in order to gain priority. The 'First Edition' was completed 1888–93 by the survey of Lancashire and Yorkshire. The 25" survey did not cover mountain, waste and un-cultivated areas. Most maps note survey date below the map and publication date above it. Most 'First Edition' sheets were sold either uncoloured or, on request, hand coloured, usually with water blue, metalled roads brown, and buildings red; and changes in local government boundaries sometimes generated special printings.

Revisions   Revisions were approved in 1882 and re-survey work began in the London, Surrey and Middlesex areas in 1891. The revision was completed in Yorkshire in 1914. From 1882, the Ordnance aimed to revise the 25" surveys every 20 years, so that the average age of a sheet would be no more than 10 years, and it maintained this schedule until World War 1. Sheets note revision dates. The new maps were printed by photozincography from a completely new set of drawings, not from those used for the first series, and full topographical detail was extended to the map frame. The second revision, based on surveys started in 1904, was initially designated as the 'Third Edition', but it was never completed. Selective but continuous revision of urban areas was adopted in 1922.

SCOTLAND	IRELAND

Similar to 'England & Wales.'

Published not as one national map but as 32 county maps, on sheets 36 × 24″ which, apart from some divided parishes and desmenes, leave areas outside the county boundary blank. Since there were differences in the meridians of the projections used, the county maps do not fit exactly together. As the engravers could not cope with the extra 6″ work generated by the 25″ survey, most Irish 6″ sheets were prepared by photographic reduction from the 25″ scale from *c*.1887, particularly from 1898, thus extending topographical detail to the sheet border. Sheet coverage varies between 25–153 per county.

The 6″ survey began in Wigtown in 1843, but ceased in 1855 after covering Edinburgh, Fife, Haddington, Kinross, Kirkcudbright, Wigtown, and the Island of Lewis. Following the pattern adopted in England & Wales, surveys were undertaken from 1854 at the 25″ scale, except for 'un-cultivated areas', and were completed in 1878. The six counties of lowland Scotland and the Island of Lewis, which had been surveyed originally at the 6″ scale, were re-surveyed at the 25″ scale 1892–95. (Publication details similar to 'England & Wales').

The 6″ survey was carried out 1829–43, with publication beginning in Antrim and Londonderry. Irish imprints do not specify publication date but simply note dates of survey and engraving; however, publication was usually within two or three years of the finish of survey and had been completed by 1846. No contours or latitude and longitude markings (although these were sometimes added to plates after the first issue).

The 6″ maps were revised from the 25″ re-surveys 1892–1905. The 20-year revision cycle could not be maintained due to World War 1. Stirling, Dunbarton, Fife, Linlithgow, Edinburgh, Haddington, Berwick, Peebles, Lanark, Renfrew, Ayr, Kirkcudbright and Wigtown were revised again 1905–20. Selective revision of urban areas began in 1922.

Antrim, Armagh, Carlow, Cavan, Donegal, Down, Dublin, Fermanagh, Kildare, Laoighis, Leitrim, Londonderry, Longford, Louth, Meath, Monaghan, Offaly, Sligo, Tyrone, Wicklow, Westmeath and part of Roscommon were revised at the 6″ scale 1845–91, particularly to incorporate fences onto the new maps because of their importance for land valuation. Slower survey progress due to reduced staff caused the revised sheets to be published separately when prepared, rather than as a complete county. The decision in 1887 to re-survey at the 25″ scale caused most further revisions to be made by photographic reduction. However, since the 25″ survey excluded mountain, moorland and sparsely-populated areas, 6″ maps covering these areas were revised by 'card revision'. Other revisions, particularly of railways, were made at irregular intervals.

SCOTLAND	IRELAND

Similar to 'England & Wales'.

Similar to 'England & Wales'. County Dublin was published by parishes, but by 1887 the system of completing topographical detail to sheet border had been substituted. Each sheet is identified not only by county name, but also by Roman numerals indicating the corresponding 6″ sheet and by Arabic numbers defining its position within that sheet. The whole 25″ series was printed by zincography.

Surveys were undertaken from 1854 at the 25″ scale except for 'un-cultivated areas' and were completed for all but Edinburgh, Fife, Haddington, Kinross, Kirkcudbright, Wigtown, and the Island of Lewis by 1878. The six counties of lowland Scotland and Lewis were surveyed at 25″ 1892–95. (Publication details similar to 'England & Wales').

County Dublin was surveyed at the 25″ scale 1863–67, but the rest of the large-scale was not authorised until 1887, and was surveyed 1888–1913, starting mainly in the western counties of Clare, Cork, Galway, Kerry, and Mayo. Mountain, moorland and sparsely-populated areas were not surveyed at 25″; however, the interpretation was rather liberal in that several closely-settled areas, including the Aran Islands, were not covered.

Revision of the 25″ survey started in 1892 and was completed in 1905. (See 'England & Wales' for objectives, etc.) The 20-year revision cycle could not be maintained due to World War 1. Stirling, Dunbarton, Fife, Linlithgow, Edinburgh, Haddington, Berwick, Peebles, Lanark, Renfrew, Ayr, Kirkcudbright and Wigtown were revised again 1905–20. Selective revision of urban areas began in 1922.

The 25″ survey was not revised until 1906–24, but even then revision proceeded irregularly and some areas remained unrevised.

13
Transport and Communications maps

Transport information has always been an important feature of maps. As early as *c*.1250, for example, Paris's Great Britain emphasized the commercially important river system and focal points of road and river traffic.[1] General representation of transport and communications illuminates routes and facilities of the time, aiding the study of transportation, travel and trade. For specific studies, specialist maps and plans concentrate only on line of route, detailed engineering features, facilities for travellers and the network of particular communications.

Maps not only planned a project and its route, but also stimulated interest and support; facilitated the raising of capital; reassured anxious shareholders; and advertised facilities on offer. For every proposal presented in a printed prospectus, objections and counter-proposals were voiced in opposing pamphlets and broadsheets. Most importantly, all but very minor transport constructions required Parliamentary assent in the passing of a private act.

Although the first transport bill was deposited at the House of Lords in 1504, only from 1784 were plans of land that might be compulsorily purchased required to accompany applications for canal, navigation or river bills involving new works or variations of existing undertakings. A minimum scale of $\frac{1}{2}$ inch to the mile was ordered in 1795. In 1803 railways and tramroads were brought under the legislation. From 1813 plans were required of tunnels, archways, bridges, ferries and for new roads and lengthy deviations. In 1836 railway plans at a minimum of 4 inches to the mile had to include enlarged portions for built-up areas at 1 inch to 400 feet, sections of the works, and small-scale maps of the project. Sections had to be drawn at the plan's horizontal scale and to a vertical scale of not less than 1 inch to one hundred feet. From

1838 duplicate railway plans had to be deposited with the Clerk of the Peace for every county or county borough cut by the project. In practice, duplicate plans had often been deposited earlier and were also deposited with parish authorities and other local bodies. Consequently, railway plans are found in Quarter Session and parish records, and in the sheriff court records in Scotland, as well as amongst company and trust records, and in family papers. Other deposited Parliamentary transport plans cover tramways, and trolley vehicle and omnibus provision.

Deposited plans were intended to demonstrate the effect of transport proposals on land ownership. Hence, they are generally strip maps showing projected routes with land anything between a hundred yards and several miles on each side. Land parcels are numbered, allowing identification in a Book of Reference, giving information on usage which illuminates anticipated agricultural traffic. Transport plans, thus, provide valuable evidence on tenure, ownership, field-names, buildings, footpaths, land use and industrial development. Some even show unenclosed strips in open fields. Large-scale urban railway plans may be the only record of the swathes of property demolished to construct lines and stations.

With the increasing availability of the 6- and 25-inch Ordnance sheets it became customary to prepare deposited plans by superimposing proposed routes in manuscript on the Survey's topographical detail. Because Ordnance sheets were so extensively used for planning Irish railways, independent railway surveys are virtually unknown in that country.

Many proposals were withdrawn or rejected by Parliament, or were defeated by the high initial cost of securing an act. Nevertheless, plans of unfulfilled projects do faithfully record topographical detail;

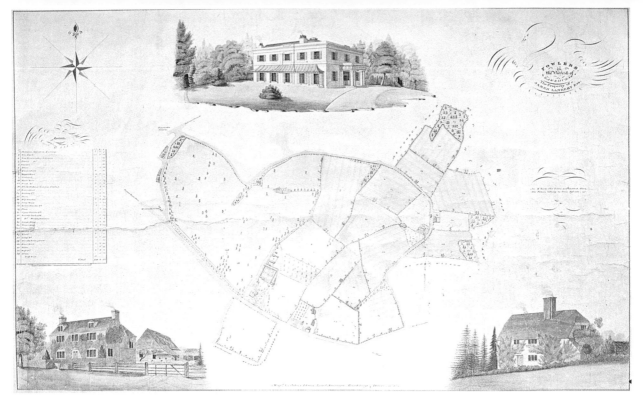

20. (*above*) Adams's plan of 'Fowlers' shows the layout of the gardens and includes perspective drawings of the mansion, 'Philpotts' and 'Duvals'. Fields are named, as are adjacent landowners; 'Where the lines are dotted thus .... the Fences belong to this Estate.' Barretts Green and the Queens Head Inn are located.

'FOWLERS in the Parish of HAWKHURST. The Property of JAMES LAMBERT Esq.' 'Map.ᵈ by John Adams, Land Surveyor, Hawkhurst & Dover, 1830.'

36. (*below*) 'A TOPOGRAPHICAL-MAP, of the County OF Kent, in Twenty five Sheets, on a SCALE of two INCHES to a MILE, from an ACTUAL SURVEY, in which are Expressed all the ROADS, LANES, CHURCHES, TOWNS, VILLAGES, Noblemen and Gentlemens SEATS, Roman Roads, Hills, Rivers, Woods, Cottages & everything Remarkable in the COUNTY; TOGETHER with the Division of the LATHES & their Subdivision into HUNDREDS, By Jn.º Andrews, And.ʷ Dury, & W.ᵐ Herbert.' 1769. (Detail)

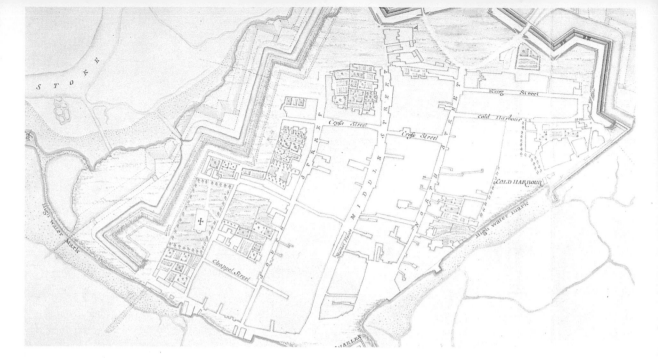

43. (*above*) Desmaretz mapped the existing defences of Gosport, showing proposed improvements by pecked lines and yellow colouring. A completely newly-designed Fort James was proposed on Burrow Island. The two proposed ravelins, each carrying a road into the town, were not constructed and Fort James was not rebuilt.

'PLAN of the TOWN of GOSPORT with the new FORTIFICATIONS begun in the Year 1748, shewing in Yellow the proposed Works not Compleated.' 'by I. P. Desmaretz 1751.' (Detail)

76. (*left*) The Southampton Improvement Commissioners engaged the Ordnance Survey to map the whole of the then Borough of Southampton at 5':1m. (1:1056). The resulting plan is very detailed, showing the town shortly after the construction of the docks and the railway in 1840, in a volume of 33 sheets. It may be used for the study of the town from the late Middle Ages since there were comparatively few rebuildings and extensions in the town between 1500 and 1800.

'PLAN OF THE Borough OF SOUTHAMPTON SURVEYED IN 1845-6. BY SERJEANT W. CAMPBELL and a Detachment of ROYAL SAPPERS and MINERS UNDER THE COMMAND OF CAPTAIN W. YOLLAND, R.E.' (Detail)

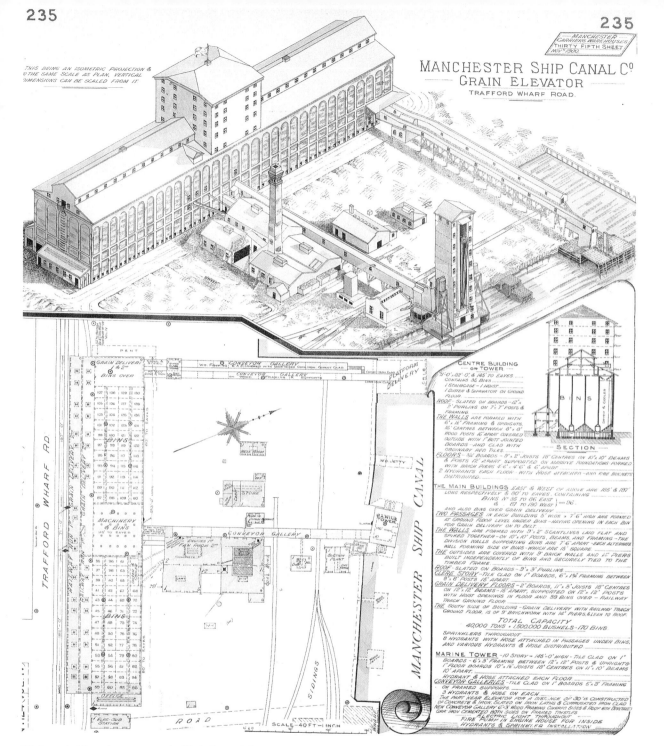

91. (*opposite*) In order to assess the likely fire risk for any particular structure it was essential to understand the internal hazard by detailing construction materials, layout, and usage. Goad's fire-insurance plans gave special consideration to warehousing districts, port facilities and factories, particularly those with higher fire risks–showing the layout in a ground plan and also presenting a three-dimensional representation of the structure which is often unique and largely disregarded. Information is given on the number of storeys, different door and window types, the location of skylights and so on. The Manchester Ship Canal Co. Grain Elevator, opened in 1898 and destroyed by enemy action in December 1940, is represented in ground plan, section and 'isometric projection'. Details are given of dimensions, construction materials and methods, fire precautions, and lighting. Since the 'Isometric Projection' is to the same scale as the plan, 'vertical dimensions can be scaled from it.'

'MANCHESTER CARRIERS WAREHOUSES THIRTY FIFTH SHEET NOV.R 1900.
MANCHESTER SHIP CANAL C.O TRAFFORD WHARF ROAD.'

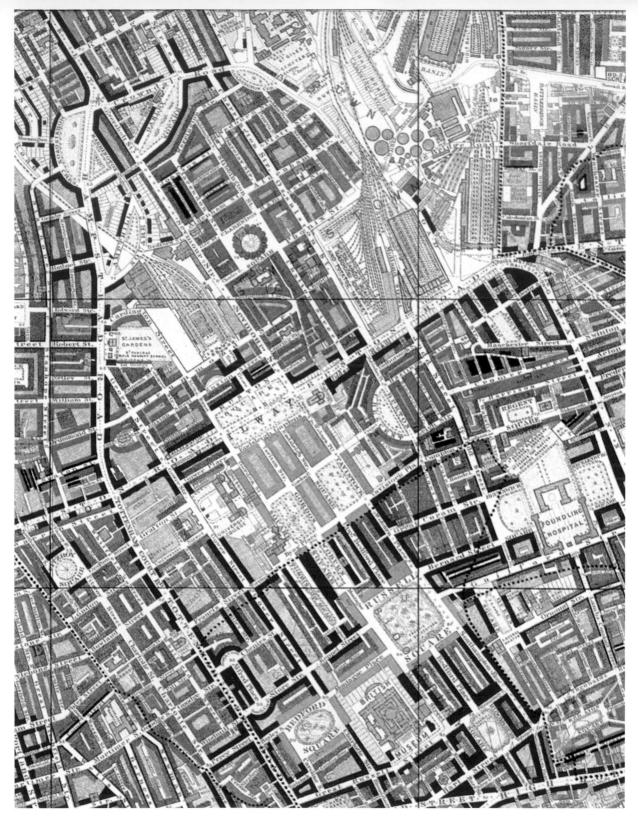

104. Charles Booth constructed a revealing picture of social differentiation using a seven-colour code of social class, ranging from yellow for streets of wealthy families with three or more servants to black for the lowest grade of occasional labourers, 'loafers' and semi-criminals.

'DESCRIPTIVE MAP OF LONDON POVERTY 1889.' (Detail)

Burdett, for example, prepared a useful survey (1769) for the projected Liverpool Canal but it was not sufficient to save the scheme.[2]

Detailed engineering plans clarify individual schemes and illustrate an engineer's work. Plans, for example, for the English and Bristol Channels' Ship Canal project (1824) are usually credited to Telford who signed the report, but, in fact, they illustrate the work of James Green, a local engineer who prepared them and who had previously proposed a canal over the same route.

Since deposited transport plans formed the basis of legislation and were subject to the scrutiny of opposers they must be regarded as relatively accurate cadastral records. However, particularly during railway 'mania' when schemes were promoted in great numbers, railway surveyors were heavily criticized and there was much suspicion that surveys had been constructed from any maps to hand, thus not truly presenting the contemporary landscape. Generally, though, deposited plans represent local topography reasonably accurately. However, both route and engineering features may well have been amended during the parliamentary approval process, and delineation may not represent the final form of a scheme.

Other maps frequently derived their transport information from deposited plans and prospectuses. The latter were particularly misleading sources since they were frequently sketchy and selective in topographical delineation. All too often compilers of county maps, in particular, took the prospectus at face value, depicting a scheme as shown when in practice it might well have been modified or, indeed, never built at all. Schemes never ever built sometimes enjoyed a happy cartographic existence for decades. Few map-makers were as conscientious as Bradshaw, who apparently had his transport maps checked against the original plans by the engineers themselves. In contrast, Hennet typically marked canals and railways not yet opened on an otherwise splendid map of Lancashire (1830). Transport schemes were particularly prone to anticipation, since the opening of a project in the near future would not then render a map obsolete. In assessing maps of transport and communications the original, skilled, accurate surveys must always be distinguished from plagiarized, edited versions derived by commercial map-makers.

Select Bibliography

BOND, M.F., 'Materials for transport history amongst the records of Parliament' (*Journ. Trans. Hist.*, 4; 1959–60)

JOHNSON, L.C., 'Historical records of the British Transport Commission' (*Journ. Trans. Hist.*, 1; 1953–54)

Road maps

Road delineation was one of the main reasons for constructing medieval maps. Itinerary maps show spatial relationships along a single line, concentrating on correct ordering of places and general direction, but paying scant attention to exact direction or distance. Thus, Paris's maps mark the pilgrim route to Dover as a straight line, identifying major stopping places, monasteries and monastic guest houses along the route. Other features are placed in relationship to the route rather than to each other, causing many deliberate distortions particularly in southern England. The 'Gough' map (*c*.1360) depicts a route system of some 2940 miles covering most of England, although several well-known roads are missing and important towns are not connected to the network at all. Almost 40 per cent of the routes shown coincide with the alignment of Roman roads. New road directions reflect changing and developing needs.[1] This apparently official map seems to have been amended for use in certain areas, showing, for example, networks of local roads in south-east Yorkshire and Lincolnshire. Although interpretation of the 'Gough' map is difficult, since neither its purpose nor maker are known, it clearly shows a national road system radiating from London, reflecting the increasing centralization of government. The most notable local medieval itinerary map, dating from the late fourteenth or early fifteenth century, shows little apart from the names of villages lying on routes through Sherwood Forest. Generally, however, roads were little mapped before the seventeenth century and only during the eighteenth were they more or less routinely shown. In Ireland, for example, before the mid eighteenth century, only a few map-makers, such as Bartlett, bothered to mark communication lines at all.

Maps of national or regional highway systems developed naturally from medieval itinerary maps. General maps of England and Wales by such as Carr (*c*.1668) Ogilby (1675), and Adams (*c*.1695) delineate the networks within which local action took place at particular dates. In Scotland roads were only generally shown in detail on maps from 1725 when military roads began to be constructed. Annual reports by commissioners appointed in 1803 to construct roads and bridges in the Highlands contain general maps of roads under construction or repair. Small single-sheet maps produced by such as Petty, Browne, Morden and Seller first delineated Ireland's roads in the seventeenth century and in the eighteenth the Board of Public Works produced crude sketch-maps. In general, maps of the road system tend to be sketchy until the spread of coaching, turnpiking and the postal system forced comprehensive and relatively accurate coverage.

In the late seventeenth century post roads spread, stagecoach services multiplied and a rash of coaching inns appeared. Until coaching declined from the mid-1830s, map-makers, such as Andrews (1800), catered specifically for coach travellers with general maps of coaching and postal routes, marking 'the distances from Town to Town according to the Mile Stones and other exact admensurations'. A combination of factors such as low traffic density and readily available water transport retarded road development in Ireland. In 1805 the Post Office proposed new mail-coach routes and commissioned plans and sections of supposedly rigorous accuracy. In the next 11 years Post Office engineers surveyed 2068 miles of Irish road, initially considering existing main routes but rejecting the steepest and most circuitous. However, some survey work was the subject of contemporary criticism; Larkin's surveys, for example, were said to have been made by 'young lads' without proper supervision. In the event, little actual construction resulted and few maps survive, perhaps because they did not meet the standards required by the 1805 Post Office Act.

Turnpike roads formed the backbone of the coaching and postal systems. From 1663 until about the 1840s turnpike trusts were authorized by Parliament to improve roads and recoup expenses by levying tolls on road users. A General Turnpike Act (1773) intensified trust development. From 1813 plans had to accompany proposals submitted to Parliament for new roads or deviations of over one hundred yards. Since few turnpikes bothered about improving road alignment, most proposals did not involve land acquisition and bare outline sketches were sufficient. However, in contrast, turnpike plans at large scales show land on each side of a proposed route in accurate detail. Separate plans of bridges, toll

houses, etc., may be inset at larger scales and the route may be portrayed in section with gradients. From the early 1860s to the early '90s widespread determination to remove the trusts and their annoying tolls led to steady dissolution, often accompanied by the mapping of the road to be disturnpiked.

Ireland adopted the trust system in 1729, and the power to alter roads was extensively used, particularly for straightening out crooked routes. From 1765 maps had to accompany applications to Parliament for new roads. However, there was less scope for turnpike development in Ireland because it was more economically backward than elsewhere and there were other bodies active in road improvement. During the eighteenth century many acts for local road construction emanated from the grand juries which considered proposals for any new public road; but only from 1818 did the Grand Jury Act lay down elaborate instructions about plans and sections accompanying road applications. However, it is unlikely that the Act's high standards were often achieved. Following the mail-coach road improvements of the early nineteenth century, Ireland entered an era of road construction by local landlords, financed by government loans and grants. During this period engineers of the calibre of Griffith, Nimmo and Bald, who had worked for the Bogs Commission and the grand juries, surveyed new roads for the Board of Works.

Although many trusts were notoriously inefficient, others kept well-ordered records which often include maps. Joseph Salway, for instance, mapped the road from Hyde Park Corner to Counter Bridge in 1811 for the Kensington Turnpike Trustees, showing it in plan and vertical section and indicating surface quality and drainage.[2] Other bodies promoted general road improvement. The South Wales Association for the Improvement of Roads, for instance, employed Cary to engrave the 'Road

---

51. A 'Comparative View' juxtaposes the mileages by different routes, noting savings in distance along proposed routes. 'Intended Improvements' are recorded and distances and toll bars are marked on all roads.

'Plan of the Several Turnpike Roads BETWEEN LEEDS & DONCASTER, by Way of Ferry Bridge, Wakefield, and PONTEFRACT; and also, from Aberford to Doncaster, by way of Ferry Bridge & by the Roman Bridge, through PONTEFRACT, Surveyed in Oct.ʳ 1822, by Chaˢ Fowler, LEEDS.'

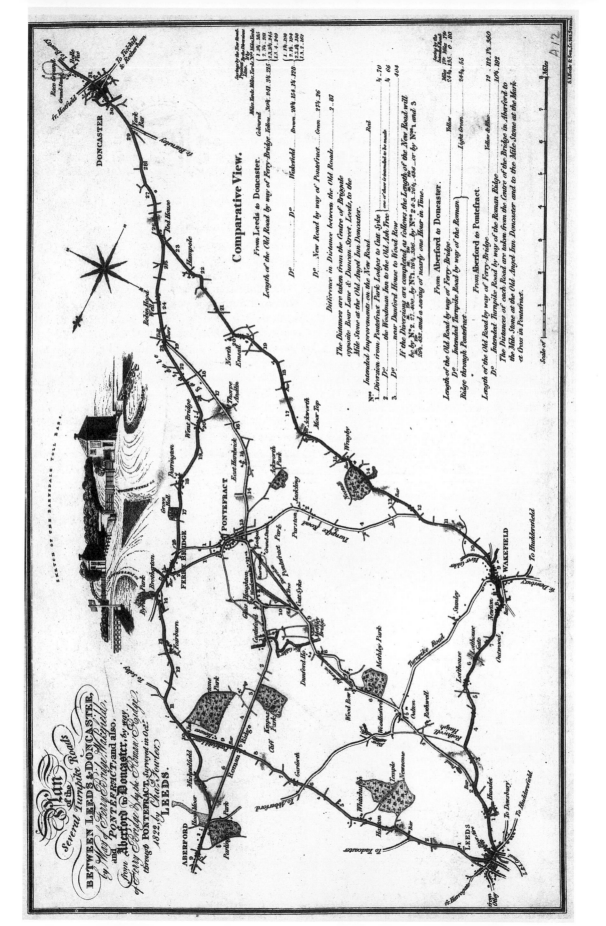

from the New Port of Milford, to the New Passage of the Severn, & Gloucester' (1792) to facilitate trust rationalization in readiness for the expected packet service between Milford and Waterford. The result is a detailed map of a two-mile wide strip, at 2 inches to the mile, along the main South Wales mail-coach route on 17 long, folding sheets which together form a plan nearly nine yards long.

General turnpike maps, such as Fowler's 'Turnpike Roads between Leeds and Doncaster' (1822), illustrate alternative routes with distances, comparing their economic advantages. With so many comprehensive large-scale plans available for reference, general maps should have been accurate. However, even Cary, the engraver of so many detailed plans, managed to show some Sussex turnpikes only as minor roads and others not at all on a turnpike map 'corrected in 1802'. He also

confused different roads and marked projected turnpikes that were never constructed.[3]

Other large-scale plans record local roads. Maps appeared with sale notices and deeds when former roads were to be sold, as at Warnford (1776); they clarified minor alterations such as the building of a level crossing; and they detailed the state of road repairs for urban sanitary authorities, as for the Southsea roads in 1877–80. Detailed engineering plans, with their vertical sections, continued to be produced in numbers when responsibility for roads was taken over by local authorities in the later nineteenth century. Quarter Session records frequently contain a prolific series of road and footpath diversions and stopping-up references with plans made when existing rights of way were diverted and highways, bridleways and footpaths closed. The commonest reason for diversion or closure was the making and expansion of parks, particularly during Georgian estate improvement, when a path or roadway close to the mansion became a nuisance and an invasion of privacy. The disappearance of houses and fields as parks were enlarged also made rights of way superfluous. Landlords suppressed the existence of unwelcome

---

52. 'PLAN SHEWING PROPOSED DIVERSION OF ROAD AT HURST IN THE PARISH OF BEXLEY IN THE COUNTY OF KENT verified before us two of Her Majesty's Justices of the Peace for the County of Kent on the Oath of Thomas Hennell Surveyor the 4.th day of March 1865.' (Detail)

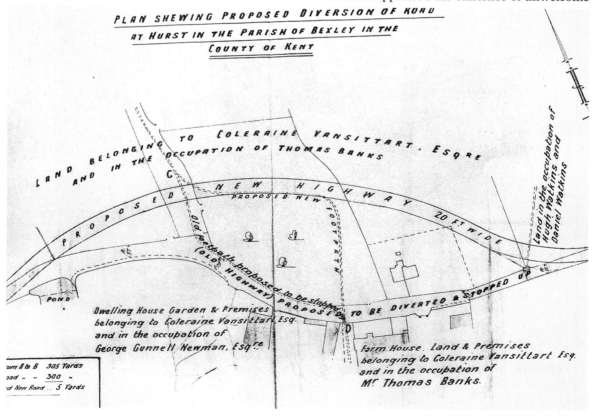

routes by eliminating them from their estate plans, hoping that this would allow denial of any right of way. In 1697 an Act established procedure for highway closure with provision for reference to Quarter Sessions and from 1773 diversion by order of two or more justices of the peace became legal. Justices could close or divert unnecessary roads and footpaths, provided that the new way was more convenient to the public and not subject to appeal, and that the order and accompanying map were confirmed and enrolled by the Quarter Sessions. Plans accompanying most diversion and closure cases may show routes to be diverted, proposed alternative new roads, field names, agricultural improvements, buildings, ownership, and aggrandizement by landlords in the small area covered. They improved considerably in quality, accuracy, and detail from about 1800.

Pilgrim guides evolved into books estimating distances along main roads, produced by Tudor topographers and chroniclers such as Holinshed, Leland, Smith, Stow and Norden. Distance books developed in turn into road-books containing written descriptions of routes, settlements and sights along the way. Essential details were presented in tables noting 'stages', facilities, distances, crossroads and connections with other main routes. Road-book text eventually became so elaborate and cumbersome that cartographic representation was recognized as being more convenient, especially when travelling. Both general road maps and strip maps of individual routes were added to written descriptions. As road travel increased, stimulated by expanding coaching and turnpiking, production of road-map books blossomed until inflated demand was punctured by railway development.

Road strip maps were introduced by Ogilby in his detailed topographical work *Britannia* (1675), which contains a hundred strip maps and over two hundred pages of text. It appeared in several editions until 1698. Ogilby covered 7519 miles of road on maps each delineating about 70 miles on six or seven strips, $2\frac{1}{4}$–$2\frac{1}{2}$ inches wide, reading from bottom left to top right. The major routes of England and Wales are carried outwards from their starting point on a continuous strip whose folds are engraved side by side. Longer routes appear on four or five sheets. In order to save space, maps represent each stretch of road as comparatively straight, but compass-roses placed at intervals indicate changes of direction.

In an age of cartographic plagiarism, *Britannia*

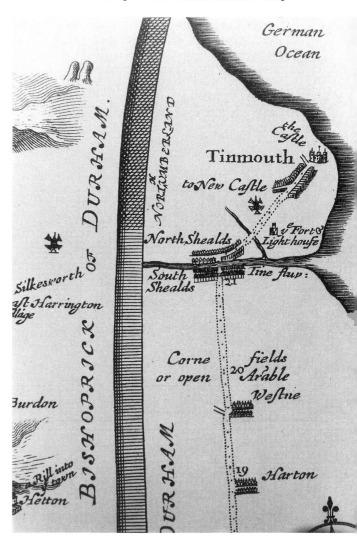

53. 'The Road from Whitby in Com. Ebor. to DURHAM By IOHN OGILBY Esq[r]. His Ma[ties] Cosmographer.' 1675. (Detail)

was unusual in being constructed from original field work using the measuring wheel or 'waywiser' to record distance and probably the magnetic compass, chain and quadrant to survey along roads by compass traverse. The use of the statute mile of 1760 yards, first made legal in 1593 but adopted only around London, did much to establish it throughout the country. Similarly, use of a scale of 1 inch to the mile helped popularize it for county cartography during the next two centuries. Ogilby's distinction between enclosed and open land was important since it allowed position to be fixed roughly when no other recognizable features were in sight. Ogilby's strip maps establish road location before turnpiking diversions and common-land enclosure. They indicate ascents and descents, and mark bridges (often detailing construction), fords, early tollgates, road conditions and wayside landmarks – such as gallows, beacons and maypoles. Figures indicate mileages and dots mark furlongs. 'Turnings out of the Road to adjacent Places . . . are generally inscrib'd, to such a Place . . . . sometimes the reputed Distance of the said Place . . . is likewise signify'd by Figures affixt'.

Ogilby's maps are particularly useful sources for features adjacent to roads. Land use is specified in notes such as 'Enter a more' and 'arrable'. The impact of agrarian change has been emphasized by comparing the relatively empty countryside of heaths and marsh bordering Ogilby's roads with the high level of contemporary commercial cultivation.[4] Roadside development is recorded by windmills and watermills, and in notes such as 'a Moore with a great many Colepitts' and 'Led furnace'. 'Capital Towns are describ'd Ichnographically, according to their Form and Extent' representing the street plan, often for the first time, and clearly showing the concentration of suburban building along the few roads leading from gaps in fortifications. 'Lesser Towns and Villages, with . . . Mansion Houses, Castles, Churches, Mills, Beacons, Woods, &c.' are represented 'Scenographically, or in Prospect'. Many of the large number of inns located and identified subsequently disappeared; the Porcupine Inn on the Rye Road, for example, was still marked in a road-book of 1785 but is now lost. However, Ogilby often positioned roads incorrectly; inserted imaginary curves and ignored existing bends; located villages on the wrong side of the road; and on occasion adapted routes in order to fit them on to particular sheets.

Although *Britannia* was immediately popular, running through several editions in 1675–76, it was a cumbersome, unwieldy, expensive folio volume, some 21 inches high, weighing about 4½ lbs. Whilst suited to the gentleman's library, it was not adapted to travelling. Nevertheless, it served its purpose, for although its circulation must have been limited no effort was made to replace it until some 40 years later when reduced versions began to appear for the pocket, only occasionally introducing minor revisions. Senex (1719), Gardner (1719), and Bowen (1720) published road-books, claiming to be up-to-date, 'very much corrected'

and 'improved', which in reality plagiarized Ogilby to a greater or lesser extent.[5] None of the detail was based on systematic field revision of Ogilby's work, although Senex perhaps copied less uncritically than others, and much was omitted to fit the smaller format. Ogilby was again copied in strip maps for the *Universal* and *Gentleman's* magazines in the 1760s and '70s,[6] and Kitchin plagiarized Senex.

Only from the late eighteenth century did coaching and turnpike development stimulate demand for new road-books by such as Bowles, Armstrong, Paterson, Mogg, Smith, and Laurie & Whittle. Cary was appointed to survey some 9000 miles of road for the General Post Office to prevent further disputes concerning distances. The first edition of his *Itinerary* (1798) was based on this 'Actual Admeasurement'. A further 1000 miles were measured for its second edition (1802).

From the late eighteenth century many road-books also presented road information on small-scale county or local maps. County maps in works by Gray and the like are essentially just route maps marking distances. Local maps in road-books such as Cary's survey of high roads around London contain greater detail. The affluent market able to afford wheeled travel was flattered by the detailed representation of country houses and estates, with owners named. However, there is little indication of road quality or the nature of adjoining countryside. Generally, milestones, tollgates, turnpikes and inns are marked. Notes on tolls and arrangements between trusts, particularly where they overlapped, explain how to achieve maximum distance from tickets. Road-books up-dated for re-issue, such as Cary's *Survey* which appeared in 1790, 1801 and 1810, provide a useful record of changes in property ownership.

Although road-books of England and Wales increasingly also covered southern Scotland, the slower pace of road improvement in Scotland and

---

54. Cary's small road maps show much non-road information including canals, parks, woods, commons, towns, villages, hamlets, and gentlemen's houses, with owners or occupiers named. Industrial sites such as paper mills, powder mills and iron works are located, as are such features as burial grounds. Estate layout is delineated and footpaths through woods and across marsh and heath are shown.

Cary's Actual Survey of the Country Fifteen Miles Round London. On a scale of one Inch to a Mile . . ., 1786. (Detail)

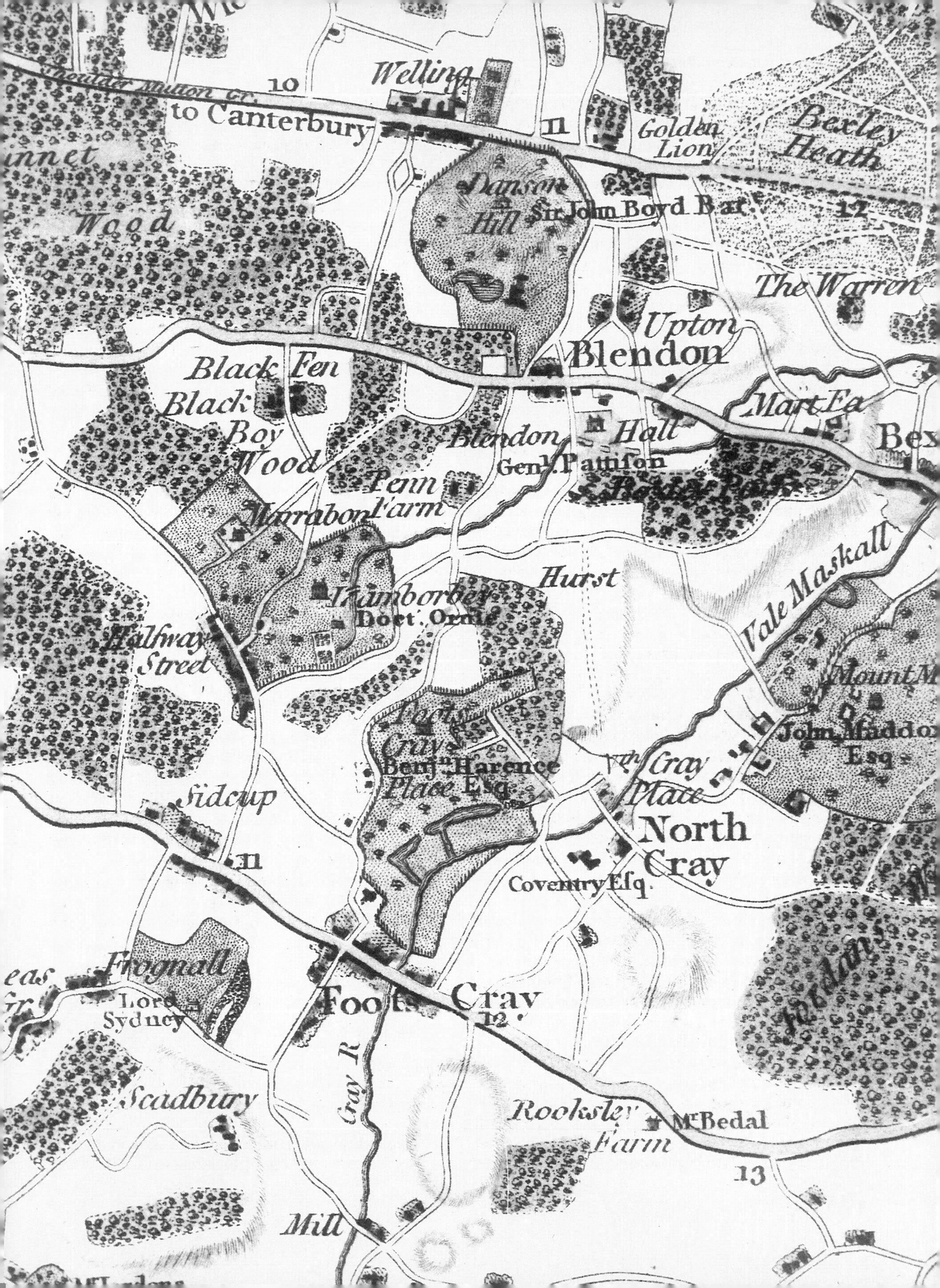

Welling

to Canterbury

10

11

Golden Lion

Bexley Heath

12

Danson Hill

Sir John Boyd Bar.

The Warren

Upton

BLENDON

Black Fen

Black Boy Wood

Blendon Hall

Gen.l Pattison

Mart Ea

Bex

Bexley Post

Penn Farm

Marrabone

Hurst

Vale Maskall

Halfway Street

Wimborden

Doct. Orme

Lady Guy's

Benj.n Harence Place Esq

Mount M

John Maldon Esq

Cray Place

Sidcup

North Cray

Coventry Esq.

Frognall

Lord Sydney

Foots Cray

12

Scadbury

Cray R.

Rooksley Farm

Mr Bedal

13

Mill

Ireland held back and reduced production opportunities for both road maps and road-books of those countries. In Scotland some maps were produced in 1725–35 for General Wade, who constructed 258 miles of road. Taylor & Skinner, who also mapped the 'Great Post Roads' between London, Bath and Bristol (1776), published strip maps of over 3000 miles of Scottish roads (1776) and some 8000 miles of Irish roads (1778).[7] Again these maps concentrate on information likely to appeal to potential buyers by emphasizing 'all . . . noblemen and gentlemen's seats with . . . . names of . . . . proprietors annexed'. Nevertheless, Taylor & Skinner's maps are the most accurate road representations for Scotland and Ireland of the period. A reduction of the Scottish survey was produced *c.*1805 by Thomas Brown in a smaller, handier format. In 1785 Taylor produced a beautiful and informative manuscript road-book containing 103 separate pages of maps mainly of southern Scotland, some showing more detail than those of the 1776 survey, but some less.[8] Some, particularly those of country around Edinburgh and Aberdeen, have pale red lines superimposed to delineate cultivated land. Most are faced with manuscript descriptions of places and people connected with the area.

Roads first appeared on printed county maps in the late sixteenth century, pioneered by Norden on Middlesex (1593) and Hertfordshire (1598) and Symonson on Kent (1596). William Smith's maps (1602–3) show many local routes serving market towns in addition to great highways. Scottish roads were first delineated on Pont's 'Lothian and Linlitquo' *c.*1610; but for Ireland no detailed county road maps appeared before the mid eighteenth century. Despite the increasing importance of roads many map-makers continued to exclude them from county maps. Saxton and Speed, for example, concentrated instead on river crossings, which held greater significance than routeways for both traveller and military. Similarly, in Ireland before 1650 only bridges, routes through wooded areas, and causeways appeared with any frequency. Despite the importance of bridges, they were carelessly recorded. Saxton omitted many important bridges. Smith's bridges often have no road connection, whilst roads cross streams where no bridges are shown, presumably at fords if bridges had not been carelessly overlooked. A particular difficulty in establishing bridging or fording points from early maps is that routes crossed rivers in different places at different times as, for example,

the London-Rye road did over the Darent. Similar difficulties occur in cartographic study of trackways – for they wandered over available public open space and frequently altered course to firmer ground in bad weather.

The Statute of Bridges (1531) placed responsibility for maintenance of public bridges and roads 300 feet either side on the county or corporate town in which they stood unless responsibility was assumed by others. Designs for new bridges and plans of repairs and improvements to bridges and approaches, along with other related maps, are found not only in the bridge records of statutory bodies but also in those of Quarter Sessions, parish, and landowners of crossing points.[9] From 1813 proposals for bridge construction seeking Parliamentary approval had to be accompanied by large-scale plans.

Maps of hundreds often delineate road patterns with some accuracy; Hasted's Codsheath Hundred (1778), for instance, portrays both a difficult section of the Rye Road and its replacement route at an easier gradient authorized in 1748. Dugdale's Warwickshire hundreds seem to reflect local knowledge, and Beighton's later replacements offer even greater detail. However, roads shown on hundred, county, and other general topographical maps have inevitably been selected, often ruthlessly so, usually without indication of the basis for selection. Lea, for example, re-issued Saxton's maps in 1693 with roads added for the first time. Whilst he largely copied Ogilby, he did not follow him exactly and his Warwickshire, for instance, excludes roads recorded by Smith (1603) and Dugdale (1656) still important at that later date. Lea also seems to have adopted his own road classification system based on traffic density, but gave no key to his signs. Roads are scarce on 'Down Survey' maps and liable to disappear suddenly. Bowen & Kitchin's county maps treat roads unsatisfactorily: although mainly copied from earlier sources such as Ogilby and Moll, many routes have been inexplicably omitted; places are isolated without any apparent connections; and winding routes generally have been straightened.

Roads shown on early county maps cannot be trusted. Comparison of two early Kent maps concluded that Symonson's roads are more accurate than those on the third issue of 'The Shyre of Kent'.[10] Although the latter map first appeared probably in the 1570s (the only known example of the first state is inserted in a copy of Lambarde's *Perambulation of Kent*, published in 1576), the version with roads was apparently issued only in the 1720s. However, the roads must have been engraved shortly after its original production, sometime during the 10 years preceding publication of Symonson's map. Symonson's roads have, in turn, been found incorrect when compared with large-scale and obviously accurate estate plans which, for example, deny the existence of his road crossing Chevening Park.[11] Early cartographic evidence at small scales rarely establishes the exact route of a particular road.

Major lines of communication are fairly satisfactorily documented in turnpike records, on other large-scale road-improvement plans, and in road-

books. However, there is little record of minor roads. Only on large-scale county maps is the rural network serving hamlet and farmhouse laid out. County maps at scales of 1 or 2 inches to the mile could not or did not, record every track and footpath, but they do provide the first detailed delineation of local road systems. Burdett, for example, showed many stretches of Cheshire road for the first time. His delineation of some 2700 miles of road represented an enormous advance over cruder, small-scale Cheshire maps showing only main routes. Most early large-scale county map-makers copied Ogilby's routes, adopting his signs for open and enclosed roads. However, Ogilby's data was much revised and up-dated; Beighton, for example, painstakingly corrected Ogilby's Warwickshire road network, adding a detailed delineation of the minor road pattern. Turnpikes and roadside inns, whose frequency indicates traffic density, particularly concerned large-scale map-makers; their distribution on Beighton's Warwickshire, for instance, confirms the growing importance of Birmingham and Coventry at that time. Greenwood paid particular attention to turnpikes since they were of significance to subscribers concerned with road improve-

---

55. Proposals for the construction of an electric tramway in the district of Erith were submitted to Parliament in the 1903 Session. The project involved not only the laying of tramlines but the building of a depot for 16 cars and a new road to take a double track tramway.

'ERITH TRAMWAYS & IMPROVEMENT. Plans & Sections. NOVEMBER, 1902. W. C. C. Hawtayne, M.I.E.E. C. E. Stewart, M.I.C.E. Engineers. London. WATERLOW & SONS LIMITED, LONDON WALL & 49, PARLIAMENT ST. LONDON. TRAMWAY NO. 3. Sheet NO. 5. PLAN & SECTION.' 1903. (Detail)

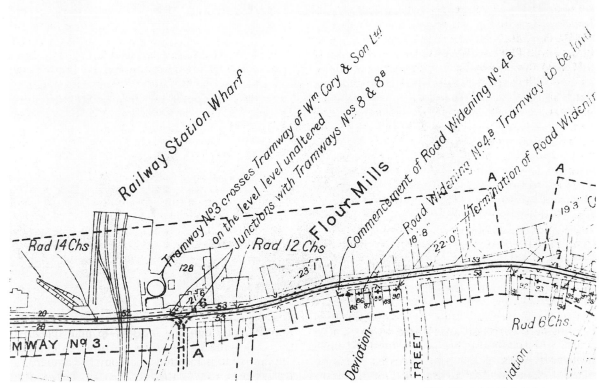

ment, stage-coach performance, and toll-gate income. Greenwood's turnpike information was revised for each new edition, emphasizing, for example, the increasing traffic density around Birmingham as it began to sprawl and develop suburbs. However, his minor roads were more often than not sketched in hurriedly without careful traversing. The intricate road pattern on Greenwood's maps is rarely delineated accurately and often it is difficult to identify which later routes are actually represented. Later, even the Ordnance Survey acknowledged that it was impossible to keep its road representation up-to-date.

Increasingly, detailed road delineation in road-books and large-scale county maps was transposed and plagiarized on to small-scale county maps. Roads became a feature of growing emphasis and, indeed, many county maps became little more than road maps. However, commercial pressures ensured that most small-scale county maps were carelessly prepared and their roads are untrustworthy. Predictably, Cary was probably the most accurate, particularly in his *New English Atlas* published in parts from 1801, but even his maps should not be regarded as reliable.

Suburban growth stimulated production of maps delineating cab, omnibus, and tramway services. For example, deposited plans of tramway proposals map in detail the immediate area showing tram lines and associated infrastructure; details of power supply; names of abutting streets and property; and industrial sites. Many have larger-scale insets of depots and junctions, and longitudinal sections. Maps of a whole network are often unreliable as town plans, but they do clarify routes, stops, and stands – and often they incorporate fare tables. Distance maps were produced in an effort to prevent overcharging by cab-drivers.[12] Transport developments also encouraged day trips and extended tours. Bacon, Philip and other opportunists grasped this chance to supply excursion maps concentrating on local facilities, particularly concerning cycling and places of interest. County maps overprinted with cycling information illuminate that recreation but should not be trusted either for accuracy or comprehensiveness; and general guide-book maps are of little value. However, some guides to specific roads, such as *The Dover Road Sketch Book* (1837), did model themselves on the road-book proper, with relatively detailed strip maps. Similar treatment of particular tours in guides published by Black and others provides an insight into Victorian road touring in scenic Britain.

122

Studies of roads and their use are frequently frustrated by the deficiencies of source material, particularly the maps. Roads for instance, are rarely represented on maps of Ireland before the mid eighteenth century, and few pre-1800 records from road-making bodies, such as grand juries and turnpike trusts, survive.[13] However, in contrast, where cartographic evidence does exist it facilitates reconstruction of routes. The Rye road, for example, has been recreated from the anonymous 'Shyre of Kent'; county maps by Symonson, Greenwood, and Andrews, Dury & Herbert; Ogilby's *Briannia*; Hasted's Codsheath Hundred; seventeenth-century estate maps; and editions of the Ordnance Survey.[14] Alternatively, road representation, particularly on larger-scale Ordnance sheets, can be used to locate particular road developments from their characteristic features, as can be done, for instance, for roads created or altered by enclosure.[15]

Select Bibliography

BOWEN, E., *Britannia Depicta, or Ogilby Improved*. Introduction by J.B. Harley. (1970)

BOX, E.G., 'Hampshire in early maps and road books' (*Hants. Field Club. Papers Proceedings*, 12; 1931)

BOX, E.G., 'Kent in early road-books of the seventeenth century' (*Archaeologia Cantiana*, 44; 1932)

DUCKHAM, B.F., 'Turnpike records' (*History*, 55; 1968)

FORDHAM, SIR H.G., *Notes on British and Irish Itineraries and Road Books* (1912; reprinted in *Studies in Carto-Bibliography*, 1914 & 1969)

FORDHAM, SIR H.G., *Studies in Carto-Bibliography British and French and in the Bibliography of Itineraries and Road-Books* (1914; reprinted 1969)

FORDHAM, SIR H.G., 'Roads and travel before railways in Hertfordshire and elsewhere' (*Trans. Herts. Nat. Hist. Soc.*; 1915)

FORDHAM, SIR H.G., 'Road-books and itineraries bibliographically considered. [With a catalogue of the road-books and itineraries of Great Britain and Ireland to the year 1850]' (*Library*, 13; 1916)

FORDHAM, SIR H.G., 'The roadbooks and itineraries of Ireland 1647–1850, a catalogue' (*Journ. Biblio. Soc. Ireland*, 2, 4; 1924)

FORDHAM, SIR H.G., *Road-Books and Itineraries of Great Britain 1570–1850* (1924)

FORDHAM, SIR H.G., 'Paterson's roads. Daniel Paterson, his maps and itineraries, 1738–1825' (*Library*, 4; 1925)

FORDHAM, SIR H.G., 'John Ogilby (1600–1676). His *Britannia* and the British itineraries of the eighteenth century.' (*Library*, 4; 1925)

FORDHAM, SIR H.G., *Roads on English and French Maps at the End of 17th Century* (1926)

FORDHAM, SIR H.G., 'The road books of Wales with a catalogue 1775–1850' (*Archaeologia Cambrensis*, 82; 1927)

FORDHAM, SIR H.G., 'The earliest tables of the highways of England and Wales, 1541–1561' (*Library*, 8; 1927)

NICHOLSON, T.R., *Wheels on the Road. Road Maps of Britain 1870–1940* (1983)

OGILBY, J., *Britannia. A Coloured Facsimile* (1939)

OGILBY, J., *Britannia, Volume the First: or, an Illustration of the Kingdom of England and Dominion of Wales – 1675.* Bibliographical note by J.B. Harley. (1970)

OGILBY, J., *Ogilby's Road Maps of England and Wales from Ogilby's Britannia, 1675.* Introduction by Roger Cleeve. (1971)

PARKER, J.A., 'The old tracks through the western Highlands. (As shown on Roy's map of Scotland)' (*Scot. Mountaineering Club Journ.*, 20; 1934)

POWELL, R.F.P., 'The printed road maps of Breconshire 1675–1870' (*Brycheiniog*, 18; 1978–9)

WERNER, E., 'Road-maps for Europe's early post routes 1630–1780' (*Map Collector*, 16; 1981)

WERNER, E., 'Maps and road books of Europe's mail coach era 1780–1850' (*Map Collector*, 16; 1981)

Waterway maps

Until railways became established, waterways offered the most efficient inland transport. River improvement extended the network from the sixteenth century, creating a system of navigable rivers later linked by canals. The Lea was one of the first English rivers to be mapped with its adjacent lands at a large scale.[1] Lord Burghley drew a rough sketch-plan (1560) at about 2 inches to the mile to help resolve conflicts over its improvement and the use of riverine lands; and a strip map (1594), attributed to Humphry Gyfforde, shows riverside land after the construction of the New Cut at about 9 inches to the mile detailing sluices, weirs, shipping, mills, fish traps, heronries, field boundaries with names, and suggesting some land use. Disputes also arose over use of water to drive mills because river flow had to be regulated and banks and weirs repaired. Plans were prepared to illustrate disputes between riverside landowners when a new mill robbed an old of its water supply; in 1514, for example, part of the Ouse was mapped for a case between the Abbot of Ramsey and the tenants of Godmanchester. In 1606 Saxton mapped Swinden Brook as evidence for the Duchy of Lancaster Court, and he surveyed maps, to accompany litigation, of Horbury (1598) and Luddenden (1599; 1601) both on the Calder. Disputes continued to use river maps in evidence. In 1774, for example, 'Part of the River Tweed disputed by Sir Francis Blake and James Couts, Esq.'

was drawn by Ainslie, showing ringnet fishing, fords, boat landings, and a dam dyke.

In 1662 the Thames was mapped from Westminster to the sea for the Navy Office.[2] Although only riverside communities with naval connections are shown in any detail, London is represented in full with the latest buildings and streets, making this the earliest map of Charles II's city and the only one accurately recording the position of one of the Civil War forts encircling the city.

River ports, such as Boroughbridge and Northallerton, were emphasized as early as *c.*1250 by Matthew Paris. Many once important medieval ports, such as Heacham and Snettisham, are recorded by maps dating from the sixteenth and seventeenth centuries. River ports on tidal waters frequently possess full cartographic records of improvement and development; numerous plans, for instance, document improvement and drainage of the Great Ouse around Kings Lynn, and Yarranton's unimplemented improvement scheme for the Dee Navigation is recorded on a rather crude map of the upper estuary (1674).

Parliamentary sanction was sought for river navigation schemes. However, plans were statutorily required to accompany applications for canal, navigation or river schemes only from 1794. Surveying and levelling were first mentioned only in the investment boom of the early 1720s when river improvements were an important class of proposed projects. Small-scale plans showing only the general line of a proposal display limited topographical information. In contrast, large-scale plans such as Adair's 20 inch to the mile map of the Clyde (1731), usually in the traditional strip format, offer great detail, including depths and velocity; riverside property ownership, noting frontage; fords, weirs, dams, sluices, reservoirs, bridges; notes on erosion; ferries, boatman's houses, lines of canalization, wharves, industrial sites; shipyards and basins; sandbanks and channels; navigation limits; and so on.

In the late eighteenth century the new civil engineers, such as Smeaton and Rennie, began to produce high quality plans, establishing new standards of accuracy and content not only for maps of ambitious schemes but also of limited improvements such as individual harbour installations, locks, sluices, and weirs. Sections, such as Telford's profile of the Lea, appeared both separately and on the plans. The map of the proposed Chelmer and Blackwater Navigation (1792–94), at 6.6 inches to the mile, surveyed under Rennie's direction, shows detail up to a mile on each side of the river and its new cuts. Lizars's plan (1824) of Baird's proposed improvements to the Leven records Dumbarton in sufficient detail to identify gasworks, limeworks, and other industrial sites. Larger-scale insets show greater detail; an enlarged plan of Dumfries, for example, on a map of the Nith (*c*.1805) locates the infirmary, toll houses, collector's and lock-keeper's houses, mills, and bridges.

Thematic river maps may be informative. Moxon, for instance, mapped the Thames (1684)

'as it was lately frozen over, describing the Booths, Foot-paths, and the various Representations upon it'. In the nineteenth century, rivers were increasingly used for leisure and maps were specifically designed for anglers, oarsmen, and so on, by Taunt and others, showing facilities along the river. Maps of steamship routes and facilities were prepared to accompany trips on rivers and lakes, among islands, and across seas.

Although the Exeter Canal had been constructed in the mid 1560s, canal construction only became widespread as agrarian and industrial revolutions gathered pace in the late eighteenth century. The urgent need for improved water transport was satisfied by linking the existing framework of navigable rivers with man-made canals. The building of the Duke of Bridgewater's canal to carry his coal to market in Manchester heralded the modern canal age. In order to raise money on mortgage for his canal, a map over a yard square was prepared in 1764 of the Duke's Manor of Worsley, distinguishing land use and identifying tenant holdings with acreages. A book of enlarged plans of the estate, naming fields and noting acreages, was prepared slightly later, probably for the same purpose.[3] Plans

56. When appointed engineer of the Forth and Clyde Canal in 1785, Robert Whitworth commissioned a survey by John Laurie which was engraved by John Ainslie. The depth soundings, marked in feet, show that part of the shallow channel of the Clyde was scarcely navigable. Efforts to deepen the river by confining it to a narrow faster-flowing channel which would deepen by enforced scouring are indicated by short parallel lines, representing walls built out from the banks. The double arrow-head sign locates locks on the canal.

'A PLAN OF THE GREAT CANAL From FORTH to CLYDE By ROB.^T WHITWORTH ENGIN.^R: AND MR JOHN LAURIE.' *c*.1790. (Detail)

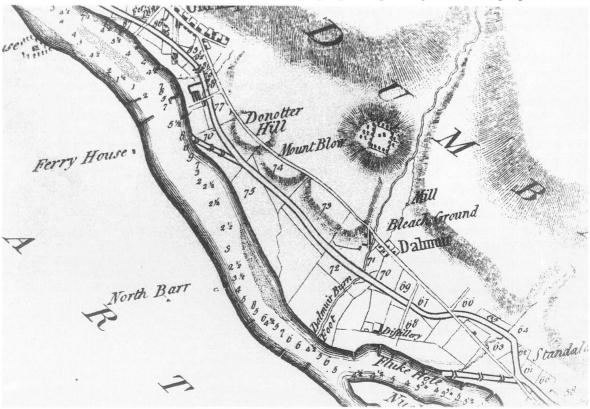

of estates involved in canal schemes are commonplace; Cary, for example, mapped land at Paddington in 1812 'proposed to be leased & exchanged, by the Bishop of London & his lessees and the Grand Junction Canal Company', showing lands involved and distinguishing enclosures.

When a canal company was formed a private act of Parliament was required permitting the project to go ahead. During the canal 'mania' (1791–94) Parliament passed some 81 canal and navigation bills. From 1794 applications entailing compulsory purchase had to be accompanied by an exact plan of land to be taken (but not a section of proposed works), a Book of Reference and a Consents' List. From 1795 plans had to be at a scale of at least $\frac{1}{2}$ inch and from 1814 at not less than 3 inches to the mile. Further plans had to be submitted if a route was to be altered even slightly or a branch added. Many canals were eventually purchased by railway companies, occasioning the preparation of further plans, and since a projected railway route often followed a canal's line, large-scale railway plans frequently also show canals in detail.

For promoters to choose the most suitable route, it was essential to make a feasibility survey and take levels, but this rarely recorded much topographical detail. Leading canal engineers either made preliminary surveys themselves or were called in to judge the technical viability of suggested routes surveyed by local engineers. These 'principal engineers' sometimes prepared the Parliamentary plans, but often they simply checked those supplied by the local man, as in the case of Telford and Green. They were also responsible for preparing the canal's detailed engineering working plans. Actual canal construction was supervised by a 'resident engineer' responsible for surveying deviations in the line, sites for wharves, and so on.

Large-scale canal plans show a strip of land at least a field wide on each side of the proposed route. Features marked include named fields; woods, land parcels, buildings, coal pits, industrial sites, roads, footpaths, lock-keeper's cottages, stables; 'Navigation' or 'Canal' inns at junctions with main roads; tunnels, reservoirs, locks, branches; and sometimes land use. Notes record mineral reserves which might be potential cargoes. Other information found on plans includes estimated costs, tidal levels, distance tables, and plans and drawings of tunnels and bridges. Some plans include sections of the proposed route; a Cary sketch-plan (1793), for example, portrays a 'Section shewing the amazing rise of the proposed Rochdale Canal from Manchester to Deanhead'. Larger-scale insets of towns or

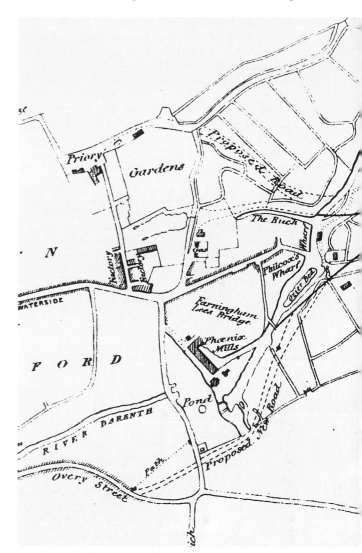

57. A canal linking Dartford to the Thames was proposed in order to give industrial areas access to the open river. The plan of the scheme locates not only details of the proposed canal and new roads but also such features as the workhouse and gasworks and names farms, bridges and wharfs.

'PLAN of a PROPOSED CANAL from the RIVER THAMES, to the TOWN OF DARTFORD, KENT; with a Branch to Crayford Creek: ALSO A FERRY from the entrance of the Canal to the opposite Shore at PURFLEET IN ESSEX. Surveyed and Drawn (under the direction of W. Tierney Clark Esqr Civil Engineer) by W. Hubbard, Dartford, 1835.' (Detail)

estates detailing wharves, basins, warehouses, industrial sites and boat-building yards, are particularly important for the canal ports which grew with unprecedented speed.

Many leading map-makers published plans derived from deposited canal plans to satisfy popular interest. Cary even published an atlas of canal plans, in parts 1795–1808, containing 16 plans at about $\frac{1}{2}$ inch to the mile, showing roads, rivers, streams, existing and proposed canal lines, towns, villages, parks, woods, and heaths. Canal maps prepared from deposited plans will be relatively accurate and may even be more informative than the original. Cary's plan of 'Proposed Deviations of the Somersetshire Coal Canal' (1793), for example, is almost a direct copy of the deposited plan, but seems to incorporate course changes made after deposition plus other additional information, probably culled from Day & Master's county map (1782). In contrast, plans derived from a project's prospectus are of questionable reliability, as are pamphlets and broadsheets published unofficially by supporters or opposers.

River and canal networks were frequently mapped as a whole or in regional units. General maps illustrated contemporary histories;[4] were included in atlases and topographies; and were published separately. General maps are usually highly inaccurate, frequently incorporating canals that were never constructed. More accurate are those by the canal engineers themselves; 'Navigable Canals now making in the Inland Parts of the Kingdom', for example, were mapped by Brindley (1769), being drawn and later revised by Whitworth. Bradshaw's plans are particularly reliable, notably the maps produced for the south and Midlands in 1830.[5] Most accurate are network maps prepared for official purposes such as that printed in 1852 for the Committee of Privy Council for Trade and those appearing in the monumental 12-volume Royal Commission report on *Canals and Inland Navigations of the United Kingdom*, 1906–11.

58. In August 1774 the *Gentleman's Magazine* published a plan of a canal proposed to by-pass portions of the River Aire difficult to navigate. A reference table details lands through which the canal would pass; this has been altered by hand, presumably to take account of later variations in route and the acquisition of land for the project. Landowners are named.

'PLAN of the proposed CANAL from the River Air at HADDLESEY to the River Ouse at SELBY by W. Jessop, Engineer.' 1774.

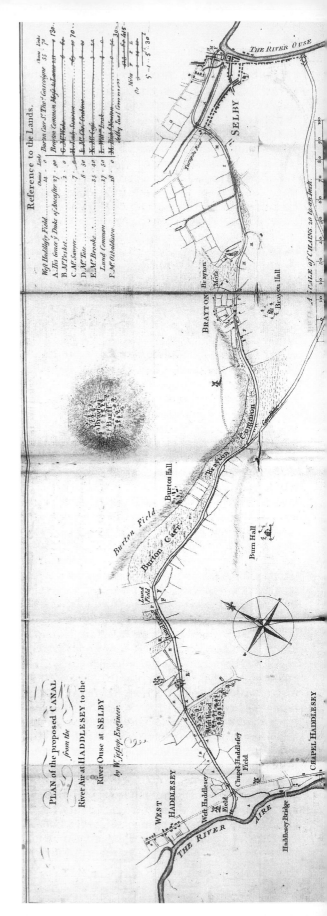

River and canal maps were issued in popular journals, histories and topographies such as Gooch's *General View* of agriculture in Cambridgeshire (1813) and Hutton's *History of Birmingham* (1809). Small-scale maps, particularly of canals, often appeared in the *Gentleman's Magazine* and other journals, plagiarizing earlier maps, particularly from prospectuses.

Waterways were a significant feature of county maps from the days of Saxton, who featured rivers prominently. However, only from the canal age did county map-makers represent them at all well and even then delineation remained unsatisfactory. Although some map-makers, such as Taylor and Budgen, indicated navigable rivers on large-scale county maps, usually by marking navigation limits, others such as Greenwood did not. The great canal age coincided with the great era of large-scale county cartography. Consequently canals were depicted boldly, and new signs were added to cartographic language, most notably the arrow-head sign for locks. Nevertheless, canal representation on large-scale county maps is disappointingly unreliable. Yates, for example, attempted to keep up-to-date by showing not only completed canals but also those proposed and under construction on his Warwickshire (1793); unfortunately the map's key makes no distinction, creating the impression of a denser network than actually existed. Since most small-scale county maps took their topographical detail from large-scale predecessors, they too are inevitably inaccurate. Even Cary, whose wide-ranging commissions for canal cartography should have given him detailed knowledge of the network, managed to portray canals incorrectly on his county maps, showing, for example, canals authorized but never built.

For some areas waterway plans may be the most detailed contemporary maps available; for instance, canal 'mania' in South Wales produced Dadford's Monmouth-Brecon Canal plan (1792) and Sheasby's Swansea Canal plan (1793), which are both vital topographical sources for the area. Canal plans are particularly important sources for industrial sites; for example, Rennie's survey of a proposed canal linking Newbury and Bath (1793) provides incidently a view of working coalpits in the Somerset coalfield. However, the difficulties of interpreting canal plans are well illustrated by conflicting studies of the Somersetshire Coal Canal.[6] Contemporary maps have never established whether the Radstock branch was ever opened and, if so, whether it was ever connected with the main line at Midford before the Radstock tramroad opened. Nor has the exact site of Weldon's famous canal lift been determined. Indeed, the best guide to its location seems to be Greenwood's large-scale Somerset (1822) which marks 'Cassion Locks' and 'Cassion House' and suggests the existence of two caissons rather than the one hitherto presumed built.

Select Bibliography

COBB, H.S., 'Parliamentary records relating to internal navigation' (*Archives*, 9; 1969)

HADFIELD, C., 'Sources for the history of British canals' (*Journ. Trans. Hist.*, 2; 1955–6)

Railway maps

Early railway development was closely connected with waterways, as the first railways (or tramroads, dramroads, or waggon ways) were built to transport minerals and stone to the quayside by horse-drawn truck. In the eighteenth century some canal companies obtained legislation allowing construction of tramroads and mineral lines, but since many lines were privately run by colliery owners on their own land, plans were not necessarily deposited with Parliament. However, plans were required from 1803. Since many tramroads were constructed as canal feeders, they were frequently delineated on canal plans rather than on separate tramroad plans. Large-scale tramroad plans can be very detailed; Grainger's plan, for example, for a horse-drawn railway 'from Monkland coalfield to the Forth and Clyde Canal' (1823), at 200 yards to the inch, documents land ownership, field boundaries, houses, farms, mills, limestone pits, limekilns, quarries, coal pits and engines. Tramways are sometimes marked on large-scale county maps and are occasionally shown on regional maps such as Gibson's map of the North-East coalfield (1788).

The modern railway dates from the opening of Stephenson's Stockton-Darlington line in 1825. The 6621 miles of line open by 1850 had required perhaps 85,000 acres of land, and the 13,000 miles constructed by 1870 perhaps 200,000 acres; all this and much more had to be mapped. Unlike other major transport developments, the modern railway was required to deposit large-scale plans with Parliament from its very beginning. Plans accompanied proposals to create companies; to construct and run lines; to deviate from the original

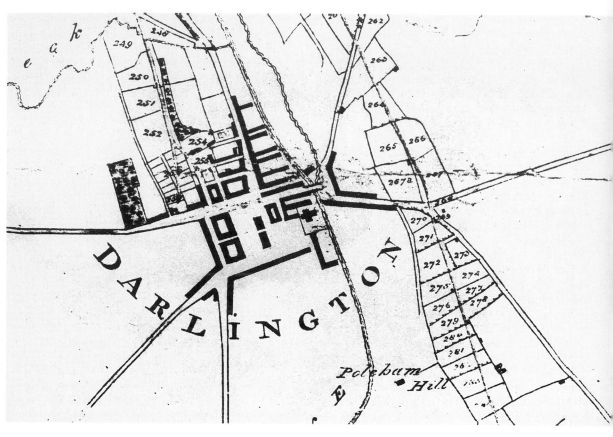

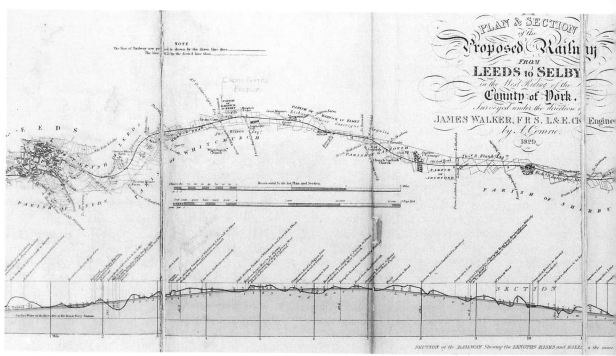

59. 'Plan AND Section of the intended RAILWAY OR TRAMROAD FROM STOCKTON BY DARLINGTON TO THE COLLIERIES NEAR WEST AUCKLAND IN THE COUNTY of DURHAM and of several BRANCHES therefrom and of the Variations and Alterations intended to be made therein respectively, and also of the ADDITIONAL BRANCH of Railway or Tramroad Proposed to be made 1822. Geo. Stephenson Engineer.' (Detail)

scheme; to add branch lines, extensions, and doublings; and for other minor works. From 1853 proposals were accompanied by plans submitted with 'demolition statements'.[1]

Although actual construction was fairly evenly spread in time, railway promotion was concentrated in two short periods of speculative fever in 1835–37 and 1844–47, creating a bunching in the demand for surveys. In 1844, for example, plans for 248 projects were lodged with the Board of Trade, and in the following year 815. Consequently, during railway 'mania' there was a frantic demand which the supply of competent surveyors could not meet, resulting in the employment of unskilled exponents with little training. Many of the resultant plans were virtually worthless, offering inaccuracies in both plan and levels to a scheme's opposers. Even surveys by conscientious and skilled surveyors, often attracted from the Tithe and Ordnance Surveys by high rates of pay,

were rushed because field work had to be sandwiched in the autumn between the end of harvest and the onset of winter. Every available short cut was taken to speed survey. Existing maps, particularly tithe maps, were incorporated into railway surveys despite uncertain reliability and uneven quality. Most commonly, proposed routes were superimposed on to Ordnance sheets whenever available, making only minor alterations to topographical detail from field observations. However, in the event, many schemes never advanced beyond the proposal stage. In fact, poor plan quality often contributed to the defeat and rejection of a scheme.

As 'mania' dissipated, so specialist engineers increasingly monopolized railway surveying, producing authoritative plans not only of the entire scheme but also of its engineering works. The Great Western Railway, for example, followed a policy of mapping its installations in urban areas at 40 feet to the inch, incidently recording much of the surrounding areas. In 1847 *Returns and Plans of Iron Bridges* were submitted to the Railway Department by most companies following the failure of an iron bridge over the Dee; drawings were annexed to some returns. Plans for the building, extension or alteration of stations and termini not only delineate them in minute detail but also record surrounding property due to be cleared. Special plans, some-

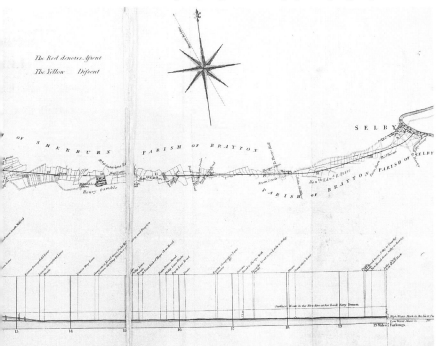

60. The plan accompanying the *Report to the Committee of the proposed railway from Leeds to Selby* (1829) shows fields, with owners named, and many other features of the land through which the line was to run from Marsh Lane, Leeds, to Selby.

'PLAN & SECTION of the Proposed Railway FROM LEEDS to SELBY in the West Riding of the County of York. Surveyed under the direction of JAMES WALKER, F.R.S.L. & E. Civil Engineer, by A. Comrie. 1829.'

129

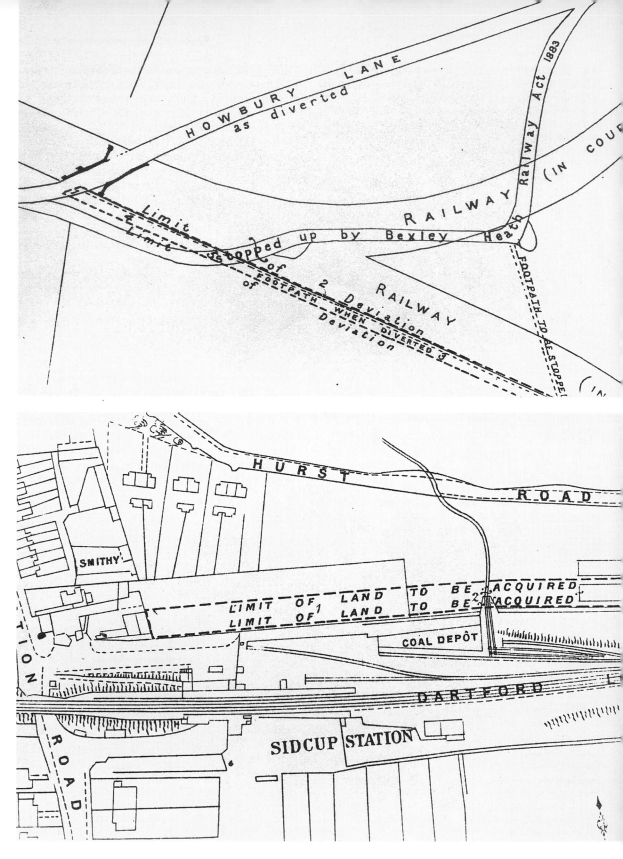

HOWBURY LANE
as diverted

Limit of 2 Deviation

Limit of Deviation

FOOTPATH WHEN DIVERTED 3

RAILWAY Railway Act 1883 (IN COUR

RAILWAY stopped up by Bexley Heath

RAILWAY

FOOTPATH TO BE STOPPE

HURST ROAD

SMITHY

LIMIT OF 1 LAND TO BE ACQUIRED

LIMIT OF 1 LAND TO BE ACQUIRED

COAL DEPÔT

DARTFORD L

SIDCUP STATION

ROAD

130

61. The construction of the Bexleyheath Railway, eventually opened in 1895, required the closing and diversion of roads and footpaths, including Howbury Lane, which had to be diverted when the Slade Green to Barnehurst section (sanctioned by Parliament in 1883) was constructed.

'BEXLEY HEATH RAILWAY. FOOTPATH DIVERSION. SESSION 1893.' (Detail)

---

times with sections of footpaths, bridges and subways, were drawn up to deal with footpath diversion either when crossed by a proposed line or when moved to serve a new station or to allow station expansion.

Large-scale plans, prepared for the railway companies by nationally known map-makers such as Wyld, show a mass of detail concerning the railway and the land it was to cross. Branch lines to collieries, mills and other works emphasize industrial location. Plans have frequently been annotated by engineers and have added details of local population and possible freight. Archaeological sites exposed during railway excavation sometimes appear on later plans. Special maps occasionally portray the scene of an accident.

Railway plans are the most numerous of transport plans because so many bodies were interested in railway development and had plans deposited with them. Railway works proposed to cross or encroach on harbours, estuaries, and tidal and navigable waters were examined by the Admiralty's Harbour Department until 1864, and after by the Board of Trade's Harbour Department. The impact of railway construction on the Ordnance Office's military land was mapped in 1840–56, as was the effect on fortifications and other Ordnance works, particularly in southern England – as at Dover in 1868. Plans accompanied sale of Crown lands to railway companies, and reports were prepared on the effects of proposed construction; for instance, in 1834 plans were produced showing the effect of the proposed London-Windsor Railway on Windsor Park and Castle. Similarly, plans assessed the potential impact of proposals on the

---

62. The opening of the Dartford Loop Line in 1866 stimulated development in a relatively poor agricultural area to the south-east of London. The creation of a New Town at Sidcup and its subsequent growth demanded an expansion of Sidcup station.

Proposal for the acquisition of land for an expansion of Sidcup Station, on the Dartford Loop Line, 1902. (Detail)

Duchy of Lancaster's lands. Proposals to run railways through forest land were sometimes recorded for the Forestry Commission; and plans were prepared when improvements initiated by the Commissioners of Works affected railway land, or vice versa. Maps and plans were also drawn for the Treasury, and, particularly, for the Board of Trade's Railway Department.

For the railway historian, the most reliable network maps are those produced on a semi-official basis by employees of the Railway Clearing House or later by the House itself. Macaulay's 'Station Map' of Great Britain (1851) appeared in at least 21 editions until 1893. It shows the relationship of every station, its ownership and the ownership of routes serving each station. Although Clearing House information was undoubtedly used in preparation, the map's accuracy is questionable; certainly on occasion Macaulay showed lines in use long before actual opening and reference to what was, or was not, open is risky. However, Macaulay and later publishers of his maps did try to keep them up-to-date. His 'Metropolitan Railway Map' (1859) is found in at least three variants of the first edition and four of the second, and throughout its 11 editions, appearing until 1875, stations and lines were added, deleted, or re-located. This map, showing railways around London, indicates ownership by colouring; displays junctions and distances; and distinguishes lines open from those merely sanctioned.

John Airey, another Clearing House employee, prepared what were essentially working maps for railwaymen. In 1867 he published a book of diagrams derived from the Clearing House's own hand-drawn coloured diagrams of inter-company junctions, which shows through-running facilities and the precise points of ownership change. Supplements to these *Railway Junction Diagrams*, with additional, and later revised, diagrams, were published annually and further editions of the book appeared with ever more diagrams. Since title-pages are often dated with the year of issue in books sold with up-dating supplements between editions, they give the false impression of being a new edition rather than a re-issue of mainly unrevised maps. New editions of the junction diagrams appeared in 1870, 1872, 1875, 1883, 1888 and 1894, but individual sheets were dated only from 1892 and only the new and revised sheets were dated for the 1894 edition. Airey probably issued a few copies of each new edition to railway companies for comment prior to publication. Copies exist which are clearly in a proof stage before correction. Airey's maps were 'compiled with great care from details supplied by the Railway Companies, all of which have been duly certified'. Junction diagrams were prepared in order to calculate rates; to arrange 'running' powers of one company on another's lines; and to settle disagreements.

---

63. Official inquiries investigated the functions and operations of the railways and many published reports contained maps both of particular lines and of the whole network. In 1906 a commission was set up to make recommendations on how the Irish rail network might be improved. Its report contained several maps, including one showing the system near the peak of its development with about 3500 miles of line, distinguishing standard and light railways and tracks shared by railway companies.

'VICEREGAL COMMISSION on IRISH RAILWAYS including LIGHT RAILWAYS 1906.' 'Prepared and Printed at the Ordnance Survey Office, Southampton, 1907.' (Detail)

Junction diagrams did not adequately cover areas, such as London and Manchester, congested with railways because even a simple routing required reference to several diagrams. From 1869 Airey produced larger 'railway diagrams' of such areas plus smaller-scale maps of regional networks eventually covering the whole British railway system, except for north and central Wales. Initially only railway information was shown but later details of canals, rivers, and nearby towns were added. Maps were dated only from January 1876, specifying the month for the first six months but thereafter only the year.

Despite Airey's high reputation, many of his maps are difficult to date and some were certainly prepared by careless and inexpert staff. Diagrams are found with the colour key incorrectly painted, thus interchanging companies, and with inaccurate colliery branches.[2] The Clearing House purchased Airey's stocks in 1895; henceforth, maps were issued as 'Official Railway Maps' in the name of H. Smart, the Clearing House secretary.

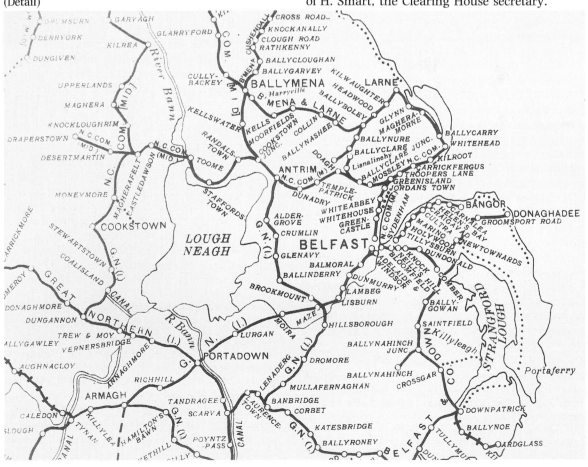

Sketchy general maps of a line appeared at the proposal stage to attract potential shareholders, being generally copied from existing small-scale maps. Additional information found on prospectus maps includes population and industries of towns served and comparative mileages by rival routes. Newspapers also frequently carried maps of new lines. Detailed working maps of a company's network differentiate the lines of different companies showing 'running' powers. Little detail other than specifically railway information is shown, although street outlines are sometimes delineated.

Small-scale reductions of working maps were produced by companies such as the District Railway to advertise their services and facilities, being distributed free to publishers for inclusion in guidebooks. Although railway information was kept roughly up-to-date, little attention was paid to topographical detail which was mostly copied from whatever Ordnance maps were to hand, often being dramatically out-of-date. Other reasonably accurate guide maps appeared in Bradshaw's various railway periodicals. Commercial publishers, such as Mogg and Wyld, also issued handbooks for railway travellers and guides to particular lines containing strip maps on which 'the Tourist has pointed out to him without any troublesome reference . . . objects of interest in his vicinity . . . rivers and canals he is crossing . . . remarkable places he is passing, and the distance he is travelling.' Many guide maps incorporate fare scales and distance tables. Illustrated railway guides, containing topographical maps, route guides, and plans of towns and environs at a small scale were produced of scenic areas served by railways.

Despite their reluctance to develop suburban services, demand forced railway companies to provide commuter facilities. Maps showing the close duplication of lines and stations by rival companies in towns were produced by such as Bacon for 'those who would understand the labyrinth of the Railway Systems'. Similar plans of railway provision in urban and suburban areas appeared when railways companies sought entry to a town, or accompanied proposals to combine all railways in one central amalgamated station.

General maps of regional and national networks appeared in great numbers. Most reliable are those prepared for official bodies and those published by Bradshaw, who corrected and enlarged his maps periodically. The Ordnance Survey published a railway map of Ireland on six sheets, at $\frac{1}{4}$ inch to the mile, for the 1836 commission considering railway provision. Although prepared from older surveys of varying accuracy, it proved perhaps the most successful single map of Ireland ever produced by the Ordnance. Probably the best regional railway maps prepared by other commercial map-makers are those in 'Cassell's Railway Atlas . . . of 20 Folio Maps (four being Double) of the principal English Railway Routes' (c.1863–).

Railways were considered a vital component of small-scale county maps and map-makers frequently revised nothing but railway information for a new edition. All too often railways were simply superimposed on topographical maps, sometimes of alarming antiquity, with the title changed to suggest the production of an up-to-date 'railway' map; Cruchley, for instance, altered many of Cary's county maps in this way. In such cases neither railway information nor topographical detail is dependable for the date of issue, although where a firm had a particular interest in railways, such as W.H. Smith & Son, information may be more accurate. Stations, when shown at all, are seldom named and usually inexactly located. Rapid railway development made it difficult for map-makers to keep maps up-to-date; J. & C. Walker issued their county maps with railways added by hand, and Fisher, Son & Co. suggested that purchasers of their county atlas should draw in railways as they were sanctioned by Parliament. In such cases, railway information is generally unreliable. Thus, railway evidence should only be cautiously used to date topographical detail. Since railways on county maps were frequently derived from prospectus or deposited plans, routes shown, even when accurately copied, were often incorrectly placed, taking no account of Parliamentary revisions. The safest source of railway information on general topographical maps is the Ordnance Survey, which took great pains to keep its railway representation up-to-date and accurate.

Select Bibliography

Railway Maps and the Railway Clearing House. The David Garnett Collection in Brunel University Library. A collection of articles mainly by David Garnett. (Brunel Univ; 1986)

FOWKES, E.H., 'Railway history and the local historian' (*E. Yorks. Local Hist. Soc.*; 1963)

SHIRLEY, R.W., 'Mapping Great Britain's industrial revolution: two classic maps of the 1830s' (*Int. Map Colls. Soc. Journ.*, 7, 1; 1987)

WARDLE, D.B., 'Sources for the history of railways at the Public Record Office' (*Journ. Trans. Hist.*, 2; 1955–56)

Communications maps

Communications maps occasionally illuminate local provision. However, only maps produced by or for official bodies are reliable and the 'postal' and 'railway and telegraph' maps plagiarized by opportunists such as Collins and Cruchley should be disregarded.

From 1807, regional and national maps were produced by postal officials for the General Post Office to show letter circulation over mail routes, distinguishing types and regularity of delivery. In the early nineteenth century limits of 'Free Delivery' areas were marked on town maps and during 1790–1836 rough sketches of local post routes accompanied reports on local arrangements.

Although mainly used as wall charts in postal offices or for internal reference, postal maps were occasionally published. They also sometimes accompanied reports on the Post Office, such as those by Wyld for the report of the Committee on Post Office Management (1837).

The telegraph network is best recorded on maps produced by telegraph companies, such as that of its network published by the Electric Telegraph Company in 1853, and by specialist maps such as the 'Diagram exhibiting the Radial System of Electric Telegraph Communication in England and Wales' and the 'Submarine and European and British Telegraph Companies lines and connections with Europe', both of *c.*1850.

14

Marine charts

Land detail on marine charts is generally reduced to a minimum and shown only as an aid to position fixing. Whenever possible marine surveyors simply plagiarized existing topographical maps, only bothering to locate landmarks with any accuracy. However, until Ordnance maps became generally available for coastal areas, hydrographic surveyors were often forced by lack of other sources to conduct their own land surveys, although their primary concern was never the accuracy of topographical detail. Hence, in some cases, marine charts may be the only source of data concerning coastal areas at a particular time. Since so much of the British Isles lies very close to the sea, marine charts can provide historical evidence for many places and areas, as well as giving a broad picture of coastal defence and sea-borne trade.

Written or printed sailing directions, often known as 'rutters', commonly issued with charts and in marine atlases, supplement chart evidence. Their descriptions may be unique, including, for instance, information on hinterland production, port commerce and coastal inns.

Defence requirements, in particular, stimulated chart production. Lord Burghley built up a significant collection of maps of southern coastal areas most threatened by the Spanish. Early charts of Irish waters were prepared by English ships watching for Spanish invasion and intercepting Scottish aid to Ulster. From the Tudor period, strategic considerations caused coasts around naval installations, fortifications, and possible invasion sites to be mapped more comprehensively than other areas.

Coastal charts concentrate on features for the navigator, such as landmarks, leading lines, anchorages, landing places, rocks, and soundings, which are shown on all charts with variable accuracy and completeness. Land representation evolved from the primitive coastal sketch drawn in perspective to the true plan; first showing features in bird's-eye view illustrating the general nature of the hinterland; secondly in detailed coastal profiles as seen from sea with silhouetted landmarks; and finally as a detailed topography stretching some distance inland from the coast.

The earliest depictions of British coasts appear on portolan or compass charts, showing, at a small scale, a highly conventionalized coastline with harbours and river mouths, and occasional other coastal features important to the navigator.[1] Although portolan charts represent the British Isles poorly and gross errors survived uncorrected for long periods, they have their uses. For instance, they provide better evidence of the site of the medieval port of Ravenser Odd than confused written sources. Ravenser existed from c.1235–c.1360 on a small sandbank close to the headland of Spurn, as a fishing and trading port that in its day rivalled Grimsby. It was washed away c.1360 and its location is now arguable. It was marked on portolan charts from 1339, although sometimes placed on the Wash instead of the Humber. Similarly, a portolan chart by Maggiola proves the existence of the Stony Binks shoal at the mouth of the Humber c.1508–10, showing its nature and extent.[2]

The first printed sea atlas with charts and sailing directions assembled systematically was produced by Waghenaer (1584–85), covering Western Europe.[3] Its highly inaccurate small-scale charts were the first to standardize hydrographical knowledge and include only observed facts essential for good pilotage. They show estuaries, harbour approaches, and other areas of difficult pilotage at scales larger than the remaining coastline, to emphasize depths, harbours, anchorages, rocks and dangerous shoals. Shores appear in elevation with landmarks, but surrounding sea and land are represented in plan. Place-names are limited to the coastline and inland there is virtually no topographical detail. Waghenaer's great work was published in English as the *Mariners' Mirrour* (1588) with charts copied from the Dutch, but with sea surfaces left blank to allow amendment.

Waghenaer's panoramic coastal profiles, as seen from a ship out at sea, precisely locate landmarks such as windmills, beacons, churches and even individual trees. Trinity House officially recognized the importance of landmarks and in 1566 an act prohibited the removal of prominent landmarks for passing sailors 'to save and kepe them and the Shippes in their Charge from sundry Daungers'. Although not new, being derived from earlier French and Portuguese hydrographic works, coastal elevations were new for British coasts. Coastal profiles were often adopted by marine charts and atlases after Waghenaer and became a standard feature of Admiralty charts; Seller's chart of the Thames (*c.*1671), for example, includes five crude profiles on the same page locating churches, windmills, and other buildings and landscape features, and the 'blue-back' chart of Spithead (1833) by Heather, revised by Norie, has two coastline views showing the 'Appearance of Hurst Beach' and the western tip of the Isle of Wight with detailed representations of the old and new lighthouses, the Needles light, the castle, a tavern and beacons. Profiles became an art form when special marine artists, often serving naval officers, produced beautiful watercolour sketches and views of coasts and harbours.

Waghenaer's charts were rapidly followed by those of other Dutch publishers, notably Blaeu, whose improved charts show more accurate, less pictorial, coastlines without exaggeration of important coastal features.[4] Blaeu included many more lights, beacons, and buoys, and defined approach courses and shoals more clearly, but he largely relegated the useful coastal profiles from chart to text. He issued more new editions with revisions than his predecessor.

Dutch marine atlases dominated the market well into the seventeenth century. Moxon's 'sea plats' (1657) failed to dent their monopoly. In the late 1660s Seller published an English marine atlas using old plates purchased from the Dutch and re-engraved in London. Some plates had been in use since the 1620s and were derived from even earlier material. Only the charts of the Thames, Humber and Tyne were drawn from original English sources. Despite its plagiarism and Seller's business failure, his *English Pilot* proved immensely popular, being republished until 1803.

From the reign of Henry VIII British coasts were charted in manuscript through the private initiative of resident pilots and masters, officers of Trinity House and the Customs Service, and other local men. The 'Thames School', trading from the late sixteenth to the early eighteenth century, produced portolan-style manuscript charts.[5] Generally, manuscript chart coverage in the seventeenth century was uncoordinated and unbalanced; no such charts of north-west England, for example, exist for this period. Privately-produced chartlets were sometimes published hoping for sufficient sales to cover costs, being often characterized by relatively abundant land detail, but a lack of truly hydrographic information as were many of the larger privately-published charts. They were, thus, of limited value for navigation. Until the Admiralty Hydrographic Office began charting British waters effectively in the mid nineteenth century, private publishers such as Heather, Norie, Laurie & Whittle and Steel attempted to chart British coasts but failed to produce any sort of comprehensive picture.

Dissatisfaction with Seller's accuracy in particular and the lack of original surveying in general led to Collins's appointment to survey Britain's coasts in 1681.[6] In just seven years Collins prepared 120 plans of harbours and coasts, but only 48 of these were engraved for publication (1693).[7] His atlas, containing a general chart, charts of the entire English and Welsh coast and eastern Scotland, a few Irish harbour plans, and two pages of coastal profiles, appeared largely unchanged in numerous editions (although five charts covering limited areas by local hydrographers were added) and was in use at sea for a hundred years. Despite showing estuaries and harbours at larger scales, Collins's maps are often highly inaccurate, being surveyed only with measuring chain, compass and leadline in an underfunded operation. He seems to have used local knowledge only once and his charts aroused much dissatisfaction and criticism; the Lizard, for example, is hardly recognizable, being very generalized and placed too far north.[8] However, despite their inaccuracies, Collins's charts are good historical sources, being based on fresh survey and relatively free from distortion. The chart of the Dee estuary, for instance, offers decisive evidence of the speed of silt accumulation in the upper estuary before 1684.[9] They show the contemporary location of shifting sands and the hazardous routes across them. The chart of the Exe estuary is the earliest to record soundings. More significantly, Collins's chart may well be the best land map available for some areas in an age of poor county mapping.

John Adair, who had charted the Firth of Forth (1688), surveyed the eastern Scottish coast just after Collins. Although more disorganized than Collins, he was more thorough, producing charts by elementary triangulation which prove highly accurate in comparisons of distance and bearing. Some of his work was engraved for a single atlas edition (1703), but most of the manuscript surveys were never engraved and many are lost.[10]

Extensive surveys were sometimes supported by port officials and merchant interests. An early chart of the Wash (1693), for example, was commissioned from Merit to show position and depths of the buoyed channel and alternative routes in case the existing approach should silt up. Similarly, Fearon & Eyes were commissioned, 'in consequence of the dangerous sands' of Liverpool harbour, to survey the coast from Anglesey to Furness – producing four outstanding charts (1738). Since shoals were constantly shifting, Eyes had to re-chart Liverpool Bay in 1764 to show changes. Even this new chart was soon out-of-date and manuscript additions are known showing lights recently erected to mark the changed passage. Emanuel Bowen, who engraved the four charts, used their data on his county maps, making his treatment of Lancashire coastal waters unusually informative for such a map. Murdo Downie was encouraged by the Newcastle Trinity House to prepare charts of the north-east coast and eastern Scotland which were highly thought of, the latter being published together in 1792. Charts were also sometimes commissioned by other official bodies, such as Nimmo's Irish fishery board charts (c.1820).

In an effort to bring order to the haphazard charting of home waters in the early eighteenth century, the Admiralty encouraged and sometimes commissioned private individuals to conduct hydrographic surveys. Lewis Morris, land surveyor and Holyhead customs officer, obtained Admiralty agreement to survey the Welsh coast from Llandudno to Milford Haven.[11] His first 11 manuscript charts were drawn on scales ranging from 1 inch to the mile for the general chart of Anglesey (1737) to 33 inches to the mile for the detailed plan of Holyhead harbour (1737). In 1748 Morris published a general chart of the Welsh coast and St George's Channel and a small volume of 25 plans of harbours and bays. Lewis's work was revised by his son William who published a large chart of St George's Channel (1800) and a revised edition of the atlas (1801) containing additional charts extending coverage to Liverpool and Cardiff. Morris's work was copied in 1766 in a map of the Welsh coast by Williamson, who added a large inset of Liverpool and Parkgate harbours.

The Admiralty extended its support of private chart making after 1750, particularly through its association with the elder Mackenzie. His surveys of the Orkneys and the west coast really began the systematic charting of the Scottish coasts. They established new levels of accuracy in hydrographic surveying, being based on rigid triangulation with a measured baseline and angles measured by a theodolite sighted on beacons erected on hilltops. In 1750, Mackenzie published eight fine charts, six of them at 1 inch to 1 mile, in his *Orcades* atlas– delineating that intricate coastline, with its dangerous rocks and shoals, accurately and for the first time.[12] His work is notable for the detail of its land representation; lead deposits, for example, being noted in parts of the Orkneys. The atlas was re-issued in 1767, 1776, and 1791.

After charting the Orkneys, Mackenzie surveyed the entire Scottish west coast and its outlying islands (an area previously neglected by hydrographic surveyors), Ireland, and the west coast of England and Wales, as far south as Pembrokeshire, publishing the completed charts in 1776. Although a great improvement on all earlier maps, these charts were apparently not prepared by detailed triangulation and inaccuracies are very noticeable. In 1781 and 1790, Huddart prepared new charts of the west Scottish coasts, but Mackenzie's charts were only partially corrected.

Mackenzie's nephew, Murdoch Mackenzie junior, surveyed the Thames estuary in 1777, followed by the coast between Plymouth and Bognor using the new survey technique of fixing by sextant angles and plotting by station pointer. As a preliminary to hydrographic work, he carried out detailed topographic surveys of the coastal region, using triangulation to fix the position of landmarks. Mackenzie's charts show more land detail than corresponding 1-inch Ordnance sheets published almost 30 years after. Some of his surveys were adopted later as the official Admiralty charts.

Although the Hydrographic Office was established in 1795, only 44 Admiralty charts of home waters had appeared by 1829, covering the area from the Wash through the Dover Strait to Land's End.[13] Francis Beaufort became head of the Hydro-

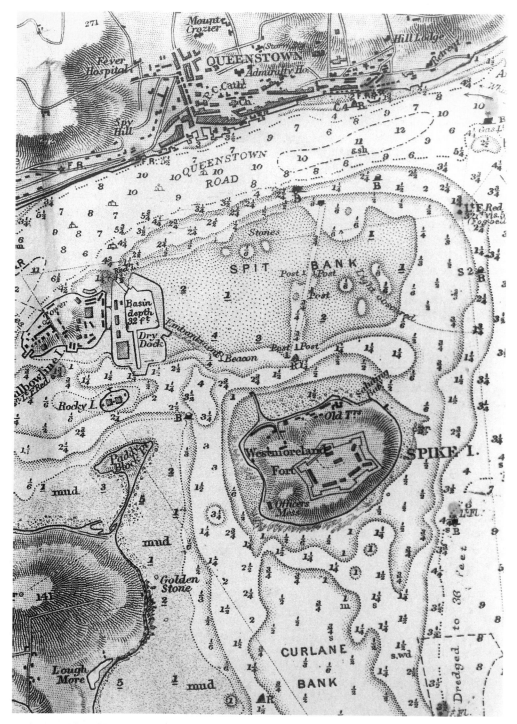

64. 'IRELAND—SOUTH COAST. CORK HARBOUR AND
APPROACHES SURVEYED BY STAFF COMMANDER
W.E. ARCHDEACON, R.N. 1888 . . . Coast line and
Topography from the Ordnance Survey.' 1891. (Detail)

graphic Office in May 1829, initiating his 'Grand Survey' which transformed the charting of British coasts.[14] During 26 years in office, Beaufort successfully re-charted practically all the coasts and inshore waters of the British Isles. The survey of Britain and eastern Ireland was completed in 1855, with 255 charts available, and by 1860 over 300 charts were listed. Subsequently the unfrequented coastline of western Ireland was surveyed by Bedford. Catalogues of *Charts, Plans . . . published by the Admiralty* provide full details of official charts available at particular dates. Many of these charts still form the basic survey data for modern charts, particularly of Ireland and Scotland.

Admiralty charts vary considerably in size and scale, with some general charts of open coasts at scales below 1 inch to the mile. Continuous chart revision recording the constantly changing seabed, particularly along the east coast and in estuaries, created a series of 'editions' and 'corrections' showing successive coastal changes and developments in some areas. In 1832 the *Nautical Magazine* was started specifically to give information for chart correction and in 1834 this function passed to the *Admiralty Notices to Mariners*. (Many other charts were corrected during use by manuscript annotations.) Admiralty chart imprints note publication date with later revisions dated in separate notes; however, unless the precise date of a particular change can be identified from Hydrographic Department records, revision dates should be considered only as approximate.[15] Topographical detail on Admiralty charts was selected carefully from land maps to show only features useful to seamen. However, some Admiralty surveyors went further; Thomas, for example, recorded archaeology and geology in his survey of the Shetlands (1810–36), and the survey of the Aberdeenshire coast (1834) produced detailed information to about three miles inland.[16]

Information useful to sailors was made a feature of large-scale maps of coastal counties such as Donn's Devon (1766) and Donald's Cumberland (1774). The Ordnance Survey also recorded some hydrographical data and sometimes marine improvements were superimposed on its sheets; the Irish Board of Works, for example, delineated new piers and harbours on lithographed extracts of the 6-inch maps (1852–3).

The main purpose of marine charts was to show hydrographical information such as hazards and navigational aids. Since the coastline frequently had to be portrayed in sufficient detail to allow identification by physiographic character, cliffs were often shown in elevation on early charts while the shore remained in plan. The lie and position of navigational aids was generally mapped. However, on early charts sailing marks like buoys and beacons are a notable omission; and what beacons are shown, usually by an upright stake supporting a fire bucket, were for defence rather than navigation. Much other topographical information also appears incidentally on marine charts. Conversely, many charts were prepared for non-navigational reasons, showing hydrographic information only incidentally to their main purpose. A chart of the Yorkshire coast and Humber estuary (*c*.1569), for example, was prepared to assess coastal defences. It pictures not only fortifications and harbour works but also churches and beacons; the towns of Grimsby and Hull are also shown and legends and notes document invasion fears and sea-wall breaches.[17] This chart is the earliest delineation of any part of Yorkshire on so large a scale. Similarly, Bruce's chart of Loch Sunart and the adjacent coast of Mull (1730) was really constructed to highlight mineral wealth and to stimulate road building.

Coastal change and its effects may be studied from marine chart, military plan, and topographical map. Norden's very large and complete survey of Sir Michael Stanhope's estates between Aldeburgh and Orford (1600–1) records the state of that much-altered coast at the time; and a chart of coastal defences (*c*.1533–4), probably by Lee, is the earliest cartographic evidence of the length of Orford Spit. Johnson's large-scale maps of sites in the same area (*c*.1800) present the situation about two hundred years later. Military maps also reveal the nature of coasts at particular dates. Fear of Spanish invasion *c*.1587, for example, brought forth a map showing 'all the places of descente alongste the sea coaste' of Sussex.[18] Fortification maps by such as Popinjay, Poulter, Adams and Norman convey much incidental physical information about the coast. Despite their imperfection and unreliability, early maps help recreate successive cycles of destruction and regrowth of Spurn Point during the period of greatest change, allowing the location of Ravenspurn, Ravenserspurn or Ravenspurgh where Henry IV and Edward IV landed respectively in 1399 and 1471, but which was washed away *c*.1608. Similarly, Pont's manuscript map (*c*.1590) of the Buchan district locates the Kirk of Forvie which was engulfed by encroaching sand, possibly as early as the fifteenth century, and generally early maps of the area record the position and extent of Rattray, which decayed after being cut off from the sea *c.*1720. Early coastal maps make an important contribution to overall evidence, and they can be adjusted to known points to control what they show, in order to compare them. The study of Spurn Point illustrates the value of sixteenth-century maps for a period when other evidence is meagre and also highlights the inadequacy of the English version of Waghenaer's chart compared to manuscript military charts. In contrast, studies of Orford Spit show that sixteenth-century cartographic evidence may be interpreted to demonstrate a relative coastal stability not supported by written evidence.[19] Colonel Hellard, the Director-General of the Ordnance Survey, concluded in evidence to the Royal Commission on Coast Erosion (1906) that 'old surveys or maps' were unreliable and, therefore, useless for the accurate comparison of the 'very small distances' necessary in determining coastal change and that non-Ordnance 'charts or maps' in the Survey Office 'would give . . . no evidence of any real value'.

Estuary charts can be particularly useful; an unsigned manuscript map of 'Waterford River' (*c.*1603), for example, is one of the best maps of the southern Irish coast. Controversies over new estuarine channels often generated a series of maps recording different proposals and developments; Mackay's plan (1732), prepared in opposition to the Dee navigation bill, shows much more detail in the upper estuary than Collins's chart (1689) from which it was derived. Medieval river ports situated in or at the mouth of estuaries (if they can be so described) were mapped, as at Blakeney (1586) and Wells-next-the-Sea (1668). Information on estuaries may be derived from many different types of maps. For instance, for the Exe estuary: an estate plan shows the extent of creeks in 1787; Collins's chart (1693) establishes tidal range; a plan of Topsham (1836) indicates the difficulty of harbour entry and the extent of waterfront development; and generally a variety of maps establish the existence of Woolcomb's Island and the shift in the main channel which led to Starcross's decline.[20]

Ports are recorded in detailed maps showing the development of harbour facilities and coastal fortifications; for example, at least 18 maps, specifically of the harbour, and 24 sets of plans, specifically of the dockyard (including copies and derived plans), produced before 1801, document Portsmouth and its immediate environs. Locally-drawn sixteenth-

century charts of harbours and their approaches or adjacent coasts are usually highly-coloured bird's-eye views, often giving a unique picture of the contemporary appearance of coastal settlements and the first delineation of roads. Many such charts were produced by government engineers, like Popinjay and Digges, whose primary concern was coastal defence and who mapped hydrographical information only incidentally. Digges's Dover (1581) shows not only the harbour and proposed development sites, but also the castle, town and fields inland. Thus, in mapping defences, engineers produced the earliest native attempts to map their own coasts.

Repeated French assaults during Henry VIII's reign stimulated the first concerted effort to map important harbours and initiated proposals for port improvement. Henry commissioned charts of harbours and estuaries from the Bristol Channel round to Newcastle. A chart drawn *c.*1536, for instance, depicts the coast and hinterland between Exmouth and the headland of Tor, showing the little harbour of what is now Torquay; a similar plan of Poole harbour, produced in the closing years of his reign, gives considerable prominence to defensive beacons. Fear of Spanish invasion during Elizabeth I's reign generated maps of Irish harbours, such as Jobson's plan of Waterford (1591) 'with the new fortification there' and Candell's map of Cork and Kinsale harbours (1587), which was perhaps copied from Jobson's similar map or vice versa.[21]

Proposals and estimates for harbour improvements were accompanied by detailed plans and, sometimes, by records of past works. Completed schemes were also mapped. A map (*c.*1548) illustrating attempts to re-open Sandwich's silted harbour was certainly consulted by Lord Burghley when considering further schemes in the 1570s. Sandwich's continued decline became increasingly serious, since it left no harbour of refuge close to the Goodwin Sands. Over a long period, plans were prepared showing proposals to improve an alternative refuge at Ramsgate by engineers from Brett & Desmaretz to Smeaton and Rennie. At least 17 contemporary plans or picture-maps record harbour improvement carried out or contemplated at Dover in the sixteenth century.[22] Harbour plans were produced not only by marine cartographers like Caundish and Borough, but also by land surveyors; a large-scale plan of Dover harbour, for example, by Symonson or possibly his father accompanied improvement proposals sent to the Council of State *c.*1583. It is often impossible to ascertain whether what is shown in such early harbour plans represents then existing works or projects which may or may not have been carried out, particularly as plans are often not dated or signed.

The seventeenth and eighteenth centuries witnessed increased production of harbour surveys by local pilots, by Trinity House, by military engineers, and by private surveyors such as Eyes, who mapped Liverpool docks for the Corporation (1742), and Burdett, who charted its harbour (1771). In some cases elaborate large-scale charts resulted. There was a general movement to improve small harbours, particularly along the south coast, where the continued silting combined with increasing draught to create a desperate need for improvements. Desmaretz, for example, one of the most prolific surveyor-engineers of the age, surveyed Shoreham (1753) making proposals for a new harbour entrance, and Watson planned an intended new harbour at Rye (1756). Generally, however, schemes rarely led to actual construction because costs far outweighed likely benefits.

Military engineers mapped strategically important harbours in manuscript. In 1698, Edmund Dummer, surveyor of the Navy at Portsmouth, organized the surveying of 18 harbours along the south coast in just two months, producing sketches, now in the Royal Geographical Society, which, although appearing superficial and rushed, are often the best contemporary harbour representations. Talbot Edwards, in command of the Portsmouth station from 1716, drew several plans, as did Lempriere; and Christian Lilly, responsible for the Plymouth Division, produced detailed surveys in 1714–17. Desmaretz's activities were particularly wide-ranging since he was not attached to a specific dockyard. He covered harbours and their defensive works all over southern England.[23] Generally, military harbour plans were produced at large scales; Desmaretz surveyed Harwich harbour and approaches (1732) at 15 inches to the mile, and the plan of Ramsgate harbour (1755), made with Admiral Sir Piercy Brett, is at the exceptionally large scale of 30 inches to the mile.

Unwieldy harbour charts at large scales were sometimes reduced for publication. Although many of Lewis Morris's plans remained in manuscript, those considered most useful appeared in a small volume (1748) of 25 plans of harbours and bays, on scales of a half to eight inches to the mile. William Morris re-issued the work (1801), with the plans re-engraved and an added plan of Amlwych harbour. Despite little alteration, the re-engraved plans do demonstrate the continuing unchecked silting of Welsh harbours.

The Lords Commissioners of the Admiralty, who had persuaded Morris to publish his surveys, also promoted the publication of other plans. Mackenzie junior produced large-scale surveys of harbours from Plymouth to Bognor. In 1793, Mackenzie's one-time assistant Spence reported on the suitability of harbours along the Galloway coast for naval and customs' patrol boats, producing detailed large-scale harbour surveys of Garleston Bay, Port Yarrock, Whithorn and Port Nessock. Eventually, the Admiralty began to publish its own harbour plans, at 10–20 inches to the mile and upwards, both separately and as insets on general charts.

From 1800 plans of docks and harbours accompanied proposals presented to Parliament and from 1813 these were to be at a minimum of 1 inch to the mile, as were plans of bridges, ferries, piers and quays. The Harbour of Belfast Improvements Bill (1831), for instance, was illustrated by a plan of the proposed wet dock and other improvements; and proposals for further development in 1898 were accompanied by an atlas of eight plans. Harbours and port facilities were mapped by the most eminent engineers of the day. Port Patrick, for example, was surveyed by Telford (1809) for possible use as a packet station for Northern Ireland; by Rennie (1815 and 1819) for a scheme to build piers to protect its exposed harbour; and again by Rennie (1846) for a proposal to build an outer harbour. Many large-scale plans have detailed insets or attachments showing engineering works proposed for the planned harbour construction.

Many types of map show port and dock development. The early growth of London's dockland, for example, is recorded in an inset of the Isle of Dogs and the India Docks added to Bowles & Carver's 'Two-Sheet Plan' of London (1805). The sweeping improvements in the dock system in the early nineteenth century are more effectively portrayed on sheets added to Horwood's London for its second edition (1807), extending it eastwards to the Lea to cover the East and West India Docks. Over the map's four editions the effects of dock development are dramatically demonstrated in the building of short terraced streets to house increasing numbers of dockers in the fields off the Commercial Road. Extension sheets covering developments were also added to their maps by such as Cary and Wallis. However, actual development is more reliably

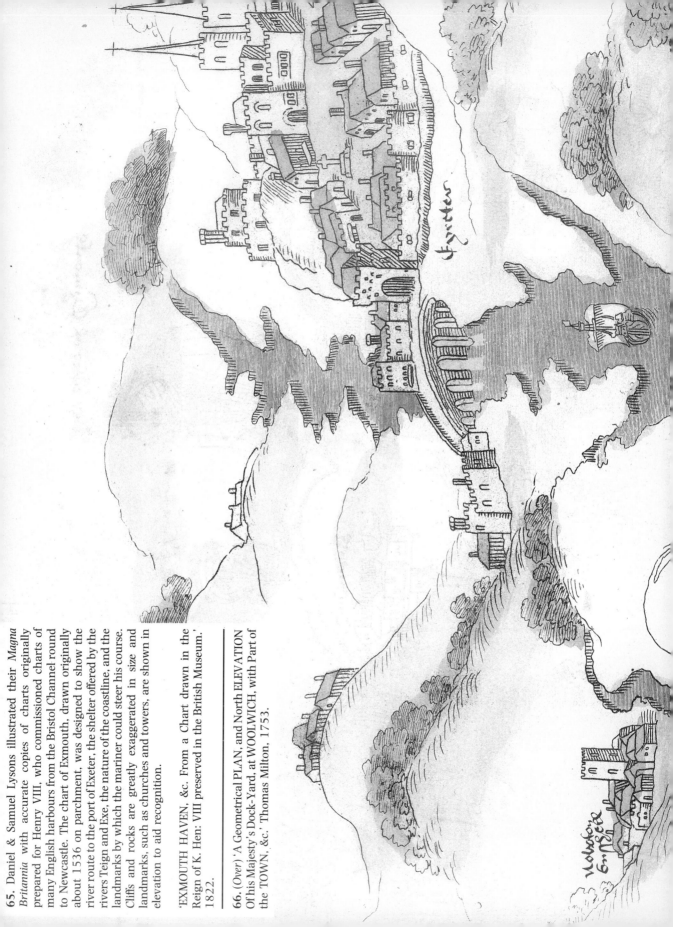

65. Daniel & Samuel Lysons illustrated their *Magna Britannia* with accurate copies of charts originally prepared for Henry VIII, who commissioned charts of many English harbours from the Bristol Channel round to Newcastle. The chart of Exmouth, drawn originally about 1536 on parchment, was designed to show the river route to the port of Exeter, the shelter offered by the rivers Teign and Exe, the nature of the coastline, and the landmarks by which the mariner could steer his course. Cliffs and rocks are greatly exaggerated in size and landmarks, such as churches and towers, are shown in elevation to aid recognition.

'EXMOUTH HAVEN, &c. From a Chart drawn in the Reign of K. Hen: VIII preserved in the British Museum.' 1822.

66. (*Over*) 'A Geometrical PLAN, and North ELEVATION Of his Majesty's Dock-Yard, at WOOLWICH, with Part of the TOWN, &c.' Thomas Milton, 1753.

EXMOUTH HAVEN, &c.

From a Chart drawn in the Reign of K. Hen: VIII.
preserved in the British Museum.

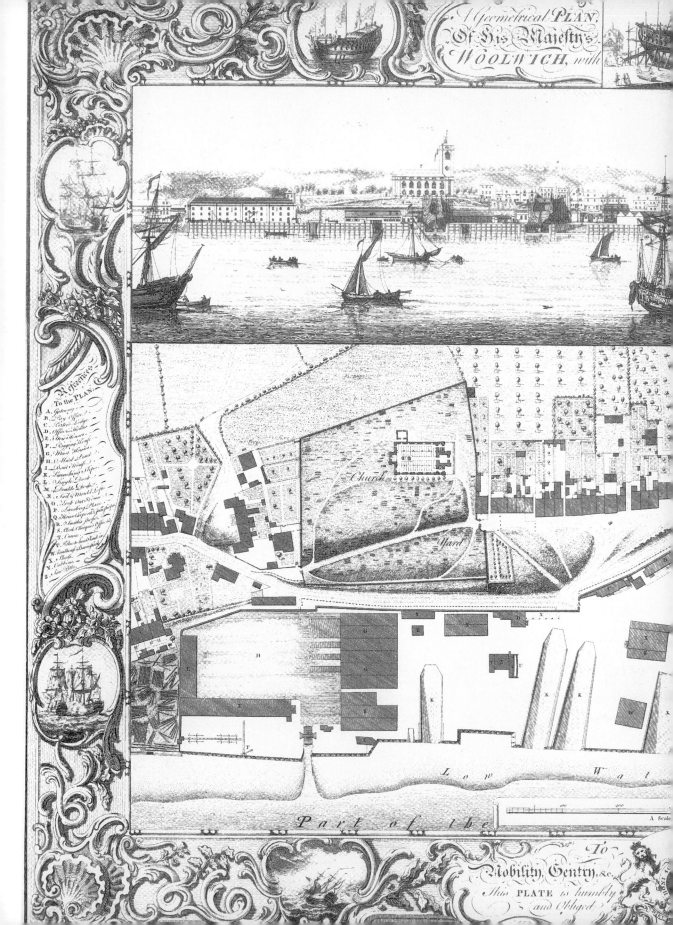

A Geometrical PLAN, Of His Majesty's WOOLWICH, with

References
To the PLAN.
A. Gateway
B. Pay Office
C. Porter's Lodge
D. Officers Houses
E. New Houses
F. Rigging House
G. Mast House
H. O. Mast Pond
I. Boat House
K. Launching Slips
L. Single Dock
M. Double Dock
N. Sail & Model Loft
O. Look Out House
P. Landing Place
Q. House Carpenters, pitch, & c.
R. Smiths Shops
S. Clerk Cheques Office & c.
T. Crane
U. Place to haul boats in
W. Smiths & Anvil
X. Docks
Y. Cabbins
Z. Saw Pits

Church

Yard

Low Wat

Part of the

A Scale

Nobility, Gentry, &c.
This PLATE is humbly
and Obliged

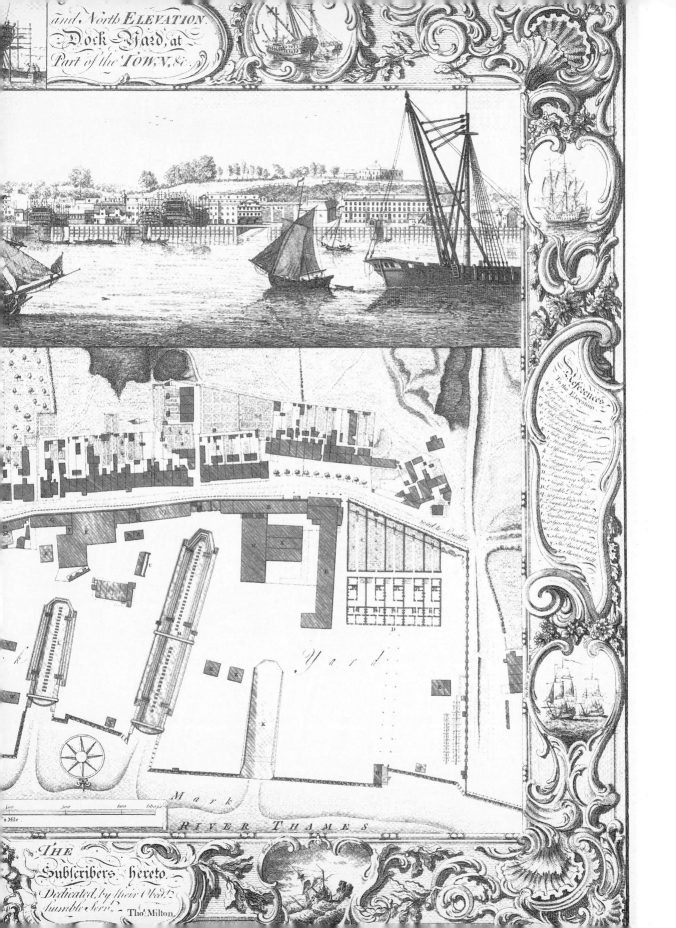

Yard

Mark

RIVER THAMES

THE
Subscribers hereto.
Dedicated by their Obed.t
humble Serv.t
Tho.s Milton.

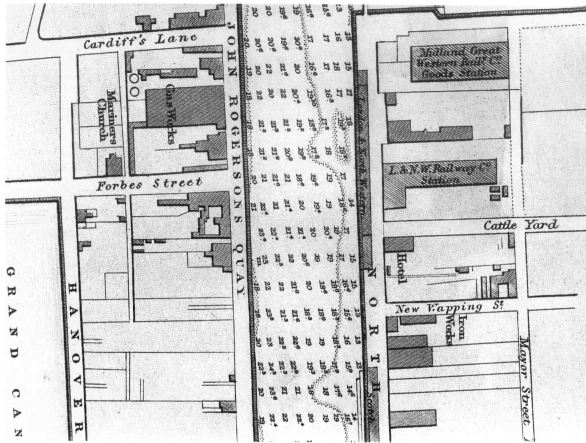

67. 'IRELAND. DUBLIN BAR AND THE RIVER LIFFEY
TO O'CONNELL BRIDGE Surveyed by CAPTAIN GEORGE
PIRIE R.N. May, June 1899.' Inset of Dublin Docks.
'London – Published at the Admiralty 15th June 1899.'
(Detail)

recorded in detailed plans of the docks themselves, both proposed and constructed. In 1796, for instance, a Parliamentary report on provision of adequate port facilities for London was illustrated by plans, five engraved by Cary, including 'Mr. S. Wyatt's plan of the proposed docks at the Isle of Dogs'. Similarly, of over 50 schemes put forward in 1765–1900 for the improvement of the Port of Bristol (vividly illustrating the caution, hesitancy, and delay caused by lack of purpose and capital), 25 were accompanied by plans delineating proposed development and sometimes also surrounding areas.[24] Successive maps showing harbour areas obviously document port development, as for Greenock for the period 1734–1947.[25]

Care must be taken when comparing charts of different dates. Comparison of charts of the Scilly Isles, for example, by Collins and Tovey & Ginver separated by some 80 years, shows that areas of sand and mud exposed at low water were more extensive and of different shape in 1779 than in 1693, suggesting a cycle of tidal and weather conditions favouring growth of sandbanks and mudflats in the interim. However, such a conclusion would have to be verified by other evidence, since the accuracy of the maps cannot be trusted. The study of Orford Spit underlines the benefits and difficulties of abstracting marine information from all types of maps and topographical information from marine charts. Sixteenth-century cartographic evidence was found contradictory and written records were more useful. Cartographic information before 1800 was limited by small scale, including the charts of Seller and Collins; by small area covered, as in Agas's work; and by its accuracy, as with Norden's estate plans. The derived nature of content negated the value of works such as Seller's charts, Hodskinson's large-scale county map (1783), and the first edition of the Ordnance Survey. Nineteenth-century marine surveys were found more accurate and gave a better understanding of the Spit's development. There were reservations about some nineteenth-century maps and charts including the large-scale county maps of Greenwood and Bryant. Generally, hydrographic charts were found a valuable source of data which, however, diminished with the decline of small harbours and increasing dependence on the Ordnance Survey for topographical detail.

Select Bibliography

BLEWITT, M., *Survey of the Seas: A Brief History of British Hydrography* (1957)

CLARKE, R.S.J., 'Early printed charts of Irish waters' (*Proceedings and Reports*, Belfast Nat. Hist. Phil. Soc., 2, 10; 1983)

DAVID, A.C.F., 'Alexander Dalrymple and the emergence of the Admiralty chart' in D. Howse (ed.): *Five Hundred Years of Nautical Science 1400–1900* (1981)

DAWSON, L.S., *Memoirs of Hydrography* (2 vols; 1883–85)

DAY, SIR A., *The Admiralty Hydrographic Service 1795–1919* (1967)

EDGELL, SIR J., *Sea Surveys: Britain's Contribution to Hydrography* (1965)

EDWARDS, H.S. (ed. R.V. Tooley), 'Alexander Dalrymple, F.R.S. (1737–1808), first Hydrographer to the Admiralty' (*Map Collector*, 4; 1978)

FLOOD, D.T., 'The earliest chart of Dublin Bay' (*Dublin Hist. Rec.* 29; 1975–76)

HOWSE, D., & SANDERSON, M., *The Sea Chart: An Historical Survey Based on the Collections in the National Maritime Museum* (1973)

ROBINSON, A.H.W., 'The charting of the Scottish coasts' (*Scot. Geog. Mag.*, 74; 1958)

ROBINSON, A.H.W., *Marine Cartography in Britain. A History of the Sea Chart to 1855* (1962)

SKELTON, R.A., 'King George III's maritime collection' (*Brit. Museum Quart.*, 18; 1953)

SKELTON, R.A., 'The hydrographic collections of the British Museum' (*Journ. Inst. Navig.*, 9; 1956)

15

Settlement plans

Settlement sites have often been short-lived and many have been deserted, being recorded only on maps and plans. Early plans of sites later deserted picture the medieval village. A plan of Boarstall (1444), one of the earliest surviving village plans, shows the church and moated site surrounded by houses with the village fields beyond. It is proved reasonably accurate by comparison with remaining earthworks, even to the extent of the surrounding ridge and furrow.[1] Similarly, a plan of Grafton Flyford (c.1700) displays features exactly corresponding to remaining earthwork patterns; a plan (1759) records Cranstoun which housed nearly two hundred people c.1781 but had apparently disappeared by 1812; a late-eighteenth-century map of Atcham shows part of the village, with prospects of various buildings, which was demolished when Attingham Park was extended; and a plan (1736) shows Middleton Stoney, which was gradually submerged by the park extensions of the Earls of Jersey until moved completely in 1825.

Deserted settlements are also recorded in the mapping of earthworks and remains, as on Ordnance sheets. A plan of East Layton (1608), for instance, portrays empty crofts – 'the scyte of the houses' – adjoining the village green; a plan (1586) shows 'The place where the towne of whate boroughe stoode'; and a plan of Fallowfield (1583) marks deserted plots.[2] The contraction of villages such as Coughton and Kinwarton is well recorded by estate plans. A plan of Dowles (1784), for example, shows only three cottages left standing near the church. Plans record settlement disappearance in calamitous circumstances; the Suffolk Fire Office, for instance, mapped fire damage at Needingworth (1847), and a plan records the destruction of Graffham House by fire (1813), incidentally showing the moats of two earlier houses. Norden marked 'decayde places', but these seem to refer to ruins of castles, abbeys and the like.

Depopulated places were apparently first recorded at a smaller scale by Dugdale's Warwickshire hundreds (1656).

Map comparison may reveal settlement disappearance. Small farms along the Ayr-Galston road shown by Ross (c.1760), Home (1773), Wilson (1813), and Thomson (1832) are absent from the Ordnance first edition (1858), indicating their suppression during enclosure. Ordnance sheets, in particular, indicate deserted settlements by showing isolated or ruined churches, large empty areas in a populated countryside, and footpath intersection for no apparent reason. However, disappearance from maps may have been caused simply by a change of name and quite possibly many settlements shown by early cartographers survived under new names. Even the most diligent mapmakers rarely recorded all settlements; consequently, omission does not denote disappearance. Comparison of the most important maps of the Buchan District, for example, shows that only 139 settlements appear on all despite the fact that Pont showed 425 as early as c.1590 on the map with the fewest settlements.[3] It is very unusual for all settlements to appear on all maps of an area and, therefore, continuity of cartographic existence should not be expected.

---

68. Many medieval villages failed to survive and remain today only as a complex of earthworks. The village of Wootton Underwood in Buckinghamshire was cleared by the Grenville family in order to create a landscaped park out of the medieval fields and all that remains is the church. However, it was mapped in 1649 using colour to distinguish common fields, enclosures, moor and wasteland, and naming landowners and tenants.

'A PLOT AND true Description of the Mannour of Wooton-Underwood in the County of Bucks For the Wo[r] Richard Grenville Esq[r] Admeasured An[o] 1649. Per me Georgium Sargeint Supervisorem.'

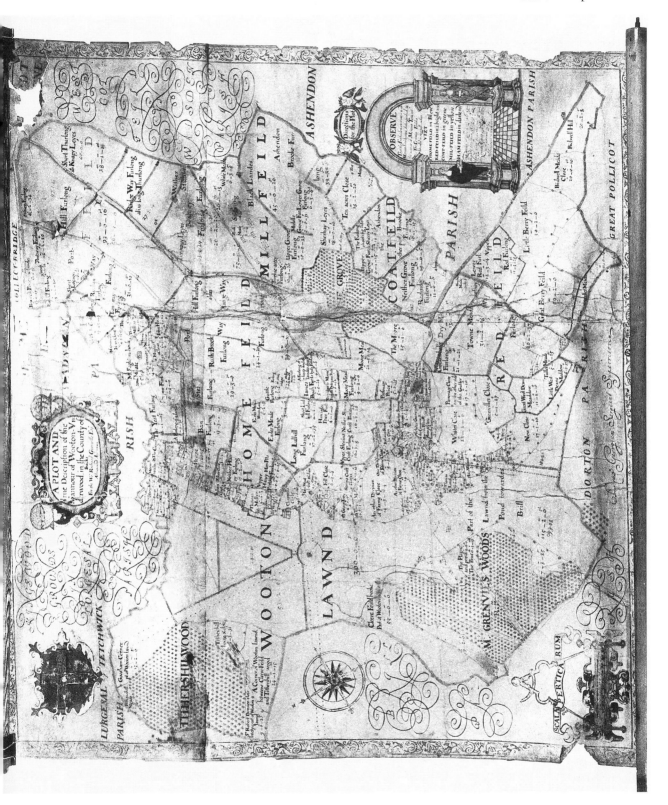

The trewe Platt of the newe' byldyng, upon true' pyllers it' ttonn, betwixt the Church Ttyles of kyngſbrydge . . . 1586

This is Sir' John Peters' Lande' called Norton.

This water is called the myle leate of kyngſbridge

Gorge french' lande

garden

the Church yeard of kyngelbridge

George french his land

Gardens

George french

the newe byldyng

The Wetter parte of the Towne of kyngelbridge

The Eaite ende of the Towne of kyngsbridge

the pellery

The Cheape houte of kyngſbridge

Garden

hindes houte and Garden

G.P.Harris del. March 1799, from the Original Plan 1586.

Longmate sc.

69. Popular, pseudo-scholarly journals such as the *Gentleman's Magazine* published not only maps of current developments such as turnpikes and canals but also reproductions of early plans, sent in by readers, many of which have since disappeared. Mr Urban contributed a 'bird's-eye view' of Kingsbridge, Devon, – 'So correctly does it seem to have been executed, that prior to the year 1796, when considerable alterations were made, it continued an almost faithful representation of the place.'

'. . . . Platt of the newe byldyng . . . . of kingsbridge.' 'G.P. Harris del, March 1799, from the Original Plan 1586.' (*Gentleman's Magazine*, May 1799)

In contrast to maps of extinct settlements or those destined to disappear, plans were prepared to propose new settlements, often indicating land use and existing buildings.

Settlements are incidentally portrayed on all kinds of maps; estate plans, military maps and marine charts provide some of their earliest representations. However, town plans are an independent cartographic genre. As early as 1455, a Gloucester rental showed occupants in double columns representing the sides of the street with tiny pictures of landmarks sketched in position in the lists. But this is not a map, for nothing is drawn in plan. Neither is the view of Bristol in Ricart's *Maire's Kalendar* (1479). The Tudor adoption of the bird's-eye view marked the beginnings of British town mapping proper, with towns shown in perspective as seen from an elevated viewpoint, within a surrounding countryside enlivened by figures and rural scenes.[4] Bird's-eye views are

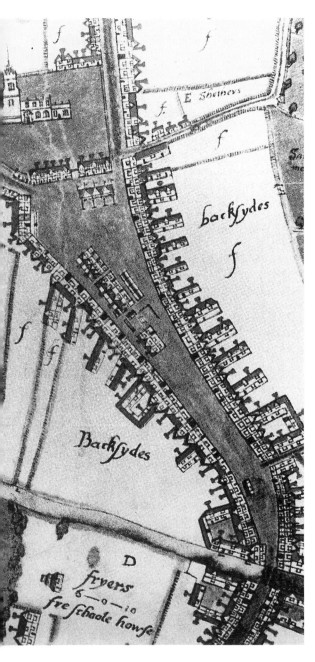

70. John Walker senior's map of the manor of Bishop's Hall, drawn for Sir Thomas Mildmay, shows 'the Towne in true proporcion', even distinguishing the fish and leather stalls. Colour differentiates types of landholding. Fields, woods and meadows were surveyed and drawn accurately so that '. . . by the Scalle you may presently measur the same'.

'A Trew Platt of the Mannor and towne of Chellmisforde. By John Walker, Architector.' 1591. (Detail)

closely allied to the panoramic view, traditionally used on medieval maps, which represents the town in elevation from a low viewpoint. This was also developed by such Tudor cartographers as Smith and it is sometimes difficult to distinguish between panorama and bird's-eye view. Together they may provide inter-related evidence about the town. Bird's-eye town representation became a recognized and well-developed form of topographical art, most effectively demonstrating the town's extent, character, and architecture. Pictorial representation in elevation on a ground plan provides vital information on fortifications, buildings (many since demolished), and other features, set within the main street pattern and surrounded by surburban development. Obviously, horizontal scale varies in accuracy; smaller streets are obscured by neighbouring houses; the relations between buildings and open spaces and between areas are false; and beyond the built-up area the angle of view gradually decreases and scale is progressively compressed. Despite their drawbacks and errors, bird's-eye views are important sources for town study; a view of St Andrews, for example, *c.*1580, carefully portrays property boundaries and building detail.[5] Although only a proportion of all existing buildings is shown in bird's-eye views, it is unlikely that this ratio varied much from place to place, allowing comparison of building density between areas.

Cunningham's Norwich (1558) is probably the earliest engraved view of a British town, although the incomplete 'copperplate' map of London may predate it. By the end of the sixteenth century several other important towns had been mapped. Some remained in manuscript, such as Smith's Bristol (1568) and Walker's Chelmsford (1591); but others were printed: Cambridge by Lyne (1574) and Hamond (1592); Oxford by Agas (1578–88)[6]; and Exeter by Hooker (1587).

Some plans are remarkably detailed; the so-called 'Agas' map of London (1588), for example, portrays, amongst other features, water supply, food markets, and forms of recreation and entertainment.[7] Hamond's Cambridge is extraordinarily accurate with valuable information on demolished buildings and house structure and arrangement, despite elementary mistakes in labelling and even drawing.[8]

Smith derived most of his manuscript collection (1588) of plans and profiles from earlier works, with only Bristol and perhaps Bath and Canterbury from original surveys. Norden intended to include plans in his *Speculum Britanniae*. His manuscript description of Northamptonshire (1591) contains large-scale plans of Higham Ferrers and Peterborough; and Middlesex (published in 1593) portrays Westminster and London.[9] The inset bird's-eye view of Chichester on his Sussex (1595) is the city's earliest known plan.

Not only the great cities and other places of particular importance were mapped. The earliest known plan of Leeds (*c*.1560) was produced to illustrate a dispute over the building of a corn mill.[10] Agas produced a magnificent plan of Toddington (1581) on 20 sheets, showing the small town within its open fields and pasture; he also mapped Dunwich (1587). Saxton surveyed Manchester (1590) and Dewsbury (1600), although the former plan is now lost, if, indeed, it was ever prepared. Plans of villages and small towns aid particularly the understanding of open-field settlement.[11]

Increased plan production in the late sixteenth century was perhaps stimulated by the success of Braun & Hogenberg's atlas, which eventually included finely engraved, detailed but derivative plans or views of 18 towns in the British Isles.[12] Chester (*c*.1595), for example, reveals the remarkable extent of ornamental gardens within the city walls; and London (1572), showing it in the 1550s, is one of the city's most important extant pre-Fire plans. However, no matter what their age, only minimal effort was made to update plans for later editions or when plagiarized. Similar miniature plans by Meisner appeared in *Politica-Politica*, *c*.1700.

Existing surveys were most systematically plagiarized by Speed for insets on his county and provincial maps, creating the most comprehensive Tudor collection of town plans and views.[13] Speed's own crude and cursory surveys are supposedly distinguished by his 'Scale of Paces', whilst derived plans have no scale. However, this is a doubtful indication of source because Newcastle has both scale and an attribution to Mathew. Although about three-quarters of the plans bear Speed's scale, he only claimed directly to have surveyed plans on Cardiganshire and Pembrokeshire.[14] Almost certainly Speed derived his Irish plans from existing but unidentified sources, although possibly he did visit Dublin and make personal observations.[15] Each county usually has two or three insets of its important towns; Reading was transferred to Buckinghamshire because of lack of room on Berkshire. A key usually lists streets, churches,

principal buildings, gates, mills and other important sites. Scales vary generally from about 5–10 inches to the mile, although there are both larger and smaller scales. Inevitably much detail is lacking. They are true ground plans but important features are represented in relief, giving the plans the informative character of perspective views and creating a vivid picture of contemporary life. Exaggerated street widths, however, produce a misleading impression of spaciousness.

Speed's plans are undoubtedly his most important contribution to British topography, providing the essential basis for Tudor town reconstruction, despite the errors in street-names common to most early plans.[16] They show, particularly, the extent of ribbon development along main roads beyond city walls, and suburbs around cities like York and Worcester. Building representation seems on occasion to differentiate the number of storeys and in Monmouth houses with gable-ends or side-walls to the street front are even distinguished. However, apart from obvious errors of distance and direction, other inaccuracies are apparent; Southampton, for instance, shows the castle, which was by then a ruin, and far too many houses in streets where the exact number is known at about the same date. Tudor town plans in general portray street layout; locate walls and gates, many of which had been totally or partially destroyed by the late seventeenth century; identify sites and appearance of demolished buildings; and show the extent of suburban development which could be measured accurately despite rapid survey.

Unfortunately, Speed's work provided a source which could readily be plagiarized for the next 150 years. His maps, with their insets, were issued until the 1770s. Plagiarized plans were added as insets to Saxton's maps by Web (1645) and Lea (*c*.1694). Similarly, his plans were copied by Hermannides (1661), Beer (1690), and van der Aa (1729). Speed's plans also appeared in later versions with only the most obvious new features added; New Radnor, for instance, was copied with additions by

---

71. The earliest known printed plan of Cambridge is a bird's-eye view of the town from the south. A description of the town is inset in the corner of the plan. Colleges and churches are drawn in detail to a larger scale than that of the town generally. Buildings are crammed together more closely than they were in reality and the outskirts of the town are contracted.

'CANTEBRIGIAE.' Richard Lyne, 1574.

CANTEBRIGIA

CANTEBRIGIA vrbs celeberrima a Granta fluuio vicino, Cantgra a primo non tam vrbis quam Academiæ conditore Cantabro, magni nominis Hispano, Cantebrigia, a Saxonibus Grauntecestre, et Grantebrige iam olim nuncupata est: Fluuius ho dic antiquum nomen retinens, flexuosis riparum anfractibus ab austro in aquilonem mari tenus longissimo tractu protenditur. Vrbs uero conditoris nomen et memoriam sempiternam reddens etiam Academiæ dignitatem multo quam olim fuit illustriorem conseruat. Muro fuisse cinctam historiæ referunt sed eum pictis Danicis et Saxonicis bellis (ut et veterem vrbis faciem) concidisse. Henricus tertius Angliæ Rex circa annũ Dñi. 1265. fossa et portis Cantebrigiam muniuit. Quo tempore ibm contra exhæredatorũ iniurias, et excursiones, q Eliensem Insulam occupabant se defendit. Muro etiam iam tun rursus cinxisset, nisi eo absente Londino Gilberto Clarensi duce occupato, nouæ calamitati pspicere fuisset coactus. Hui' fossæ ab eo tempore Regiæ nomen obtinuit vestigiũ quoddam in hac charta cernitur. Sed q ad vrbis ambitu et defensionẽ altissimis, fuit, et latissimis fossionibus primum apparatu expurgandis platearũ sęcib'. eluendisq in Gratã fluuiũ sordibᵈ non male nunc inseruit. Q si Cantebrigienses cõiunctis opib' efficerent vt q est ad vadũ Trumpingtomiæ amniculus fossam hanc allueret, non esset Cantebrigia vrbs vlla elegantior, tantiq facti memoria non tam posteris grata quam ipsis iucunda et fructuosa existeret.

St Clemens

The Kinges diche

Jesus Colledge

Barnwell ca

silia lane

Gray Friers

Walles lane

St Johns Colledge

Trinitie Coll. Chap. A

Civitas Colledge cwalle

lesiluer lane

St Michaell

Christ Coll.

Peyte

Trinitie Church

ſgate Barnewell

Shoema ker lane

Shereres lan

Market hill

Common Schols

Kinges Colledge

Petti curie

Market warde

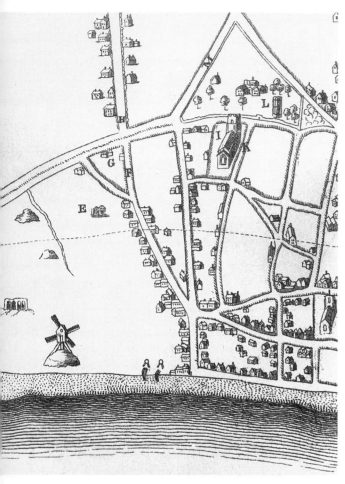

72. Dunwich was a city of size and importance until 1347, when coastal erosion began to attack it. A storm carried away 400 houses, shops and windmills. Further serious losses occurred periodically over the centuries; virtually nothing of Dunwich remains today. In 1753 Thomas Gardner published a copy of a plan of 1587 by the local land surveyor Ralph Agas. Gardner's plan was in turn copied in the late nineteenth century by the leading East Anglian map publishers Jarrold & Sons. Coastal profiles of the Dunwich area drawn in the 1680s by Capt. Greenvile Collins show a town still of considerable size a century later, but with some of the more prominent coastal features, such as the windmill to the south of the town, absent.

'A PLAN Exhibiting the Remains of the antient City of Dunwich, A.D. 1587. Also its' River, Part whereof is Southwold Haven, with Places of Note bordering thereon.' (*An Exact Fac-Simile OF* Gardner's Folding Plan *Of the Ancient CITY OF DUNWICH, 1587. With its Rivers, Churches, and Antiquities. PRICE ONE SHILLING. JARROLD & SONS, LONDON, NORWICH, YARMOUTH, & CROMER*). (Detail)

Le Keux (1855), his plan reappearing in 1859, and again in 1905 dated 1800!

Speed mapped only Limerick, Cork, Dublin and Galway outside England and Wales. Sixteenth-century town mapping in Scotland and Ireland tended to be a by-product of military concerns and action; the earliest Edinburgh plans, for example, relate to the battle of 1544 and the siege of 1573. Gordon's manuscript Fife (1642) includes small plans of Cupar and St Andrews; and he surveyed Edinburgh (1647) and St Andrews (1661), continuing representation partly in plan and partly in view and elevation. However, the next Scottish town plan did not appear until Edgar mapped Edinburgh (1742).

This dearth of original town survey was found generally in the early seventeenth century. Millerd's Bristol (1673) continued representation in plan and view, despite being the city's first measured plan. However, a new age was heralded by London's Great Fire (1666), which required rigorously surveyed plans to sort out confused property rights following the destruction. The first scientific survey of the pre-Fire city centre was made by Leake (1669), showing the layout of burnt-out streets with many names and ground plans of medieval churches and some major buildings in the burnt area. The most influential map was of the rebuilt city by Ogilby & Morgan on 21 sheets at 100 feet to the inch, completed in 1677, which provides a remarkable record of both post-Fire rebuilding and the destroyed pre-Fire medieval city.[17] Ogilby produced a true plan without portraying buildings in elevation, although Morgan reverted to traditional style in 1681–82.[18] The Great Fire was an unprecedented catalyst and many plans were produced in the ensuing years, notably by Hollar.[19]

Ogilby's *Britannia* was planned to include views and topographical descriptions of English cities. This scheme failed, but Ogilby did survey Ipswich in 1674. This remarkable map was eventually published in 1698 on nine sheets at 100 feet to the inch, showing: house plots, sometimes naming owners; church ground plans; land use beyond the town boundary; and industrial sites. Ogilby's practice of publishing explanatory booklets with his large-scale plans listing street- and place-names was followed by Rocque and others, providing an invaluable source of identification for many alleys and yards. Ogilby also surveyed Malden, but the draft has not survived and seems never to have been engraved.

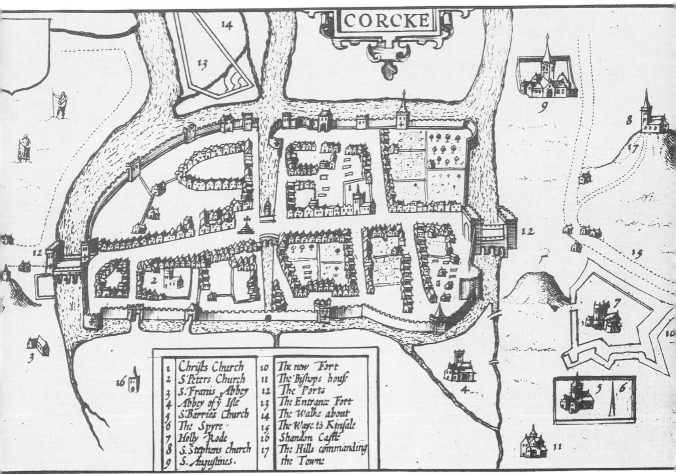

The new Fort, The Bishops house, The Ports, The Entrance Fort, The Walks about, The Waye to Kinsale, Shandon Castle, The Hills commanding the Towne, S. Augustines.

1	Chrifts Church	10	The new Fort
2	S. Peters Church	11	The Bishops house
3	S. Franis Abbey	12	The Ports
4	Abbey of y̆ Ifle	13	The Entrance Fort
5	S. Barries Church	14	The Walks about
6	The Spyre	15	The Waye to Kinfale
7	Holly Rode	16	Shandon Castle
8	S. Stephens church	17	The Hills commanding the Towne
9	S. Augustines		

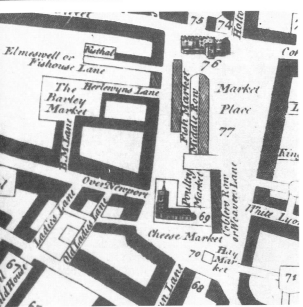

73. Plans of 'Lymericke' and 'Corcke' were incorporated as insets by John Speed on his map of the Province of Munster. No scale is given.

'CORCKE.' John Speed, 1611.

74. Norwich was one of the most comprehensively mapped English towns in the eighteenth century, with important plans published by Cleer (*c.*1696), Corbridge (1727), Blomefield (1746), and Hochstetter (1789), from which other plans were derived.

'A PLAN of the CITY of NORWICH.' Francis Blomefield, 1746. (Detail)

155

Mr Middletons
Rope Walk

CABLE STREET

Mr John Bury

Mr Williamson

Mr John Bury

JOHN STREET

BURY STREET

Mess. Bateman & Sherratts Iron Works

UNION STREET

DEAL STREET

BREAD STREET

Trinity
Chapel

CLOWES

Salford
Company

Rope Walk

Legendre
Starkie Esq.

COOKE STREET

Rope Walk

HARDMAN STREET

STREET

Salford
Compa

Mr Wilkinson

LOOM STREET

BROUGHTON STREET

STREET

BACK STREET

QUAY STREET

WOOD STREET

BROWN STREET

GARDEN STREET

Salford
Compa

SPAW STREET

JOHNSON STREET

MEADOW

Salford
Quay

GORE STREET

LIKE STREET

NEW BAYLEY STREET

BROWNS

BOLTON

BREWERY

FALKNER STREET

STREET

New Bayley Prison

New Bridge

NEW BRI

IRWELL STREET

WELL

BOOTH STREET

STANLEY STREET

STREET

Bath Inn

New Warehouse

WATER STREET

IRWELL

SOMERSET STR

WILLMOTT STR

WATER STREET

BACK STREET

DOL FIELD

IRWELL STR

Ogilby established new standards of accuracy and a new magnitude of scale which were increasingly adopted during the eighteenth century, despite continued portrayal in perspective view, particularly of picturesque places such as Bath and Shrewsbury. Large-scale, accurate plans of growing towns appeared with increasing frequency; but provincial towns with little manufacture were mapped only infrequently and poorly, and towns in relative decline not at all. Important centres like Norwich, portrayed by Cleer (1696) and others in the next century, were recorded at successive stages of development. New centres were mapped for the first time in plans surveyed during the crucial early years of expansion; Birmingham, for example, was delineated by Westley (1731), Bradford (1751) and Hanson (1778). Many notable plans appeared during the eighteenth century – Taylor's Hereford (1757), Hunter's Chester (1789), Hochstetter's Norwich (1789) and Green's Manchester & Salford (1794) are outstanding.

Predictably, London generated the century's supreme surveys. Rocque published three stunning plans: of the environs on 16 sheets at $5\frac{1}{2}$ inches to the mile (1746); on 24 sheets at 26 inches to the mile (1746); and on eight sheets at 13 inches to the mile (1755), based on the previous map but with additions.[20] Rocque also mapped Bristol (1742), Exeter (1744), and Shrewsbury (1746). Probably the greatest eighteenth-century plan is Horwood's London (1799), on 32 sheets at 26 inches to the mile.[21] Horwood intended to number every house but this proved impossible; nevertheless, every house is shown, with courts, alleys, and vacant spaces away from street frontage. The plan remained the finest delineation of the metropolitan

area until coverage by the 25-inch Ordnance Survey in the 1860s. Horwood also mapped Liverpool (1803) at the same scale.

Scottish town plan production, excepting Edinburgh, really dated only from the mid eighteenth century. McArthur, for example, mapped the whole of Glasgow for the first time at a large scale on four sheets (1778). Ainslie mapped Edinburgh (1804), covering the entire city with Leith and the suburbs for the first time, but this was almost entirely superseded by Kirkwood's plan (1817) at about 14 inches to the mile, which is the finest early-nineteenth-century plan of the city, recording even house numbers. In Ireland, Cork was mapped by Carty (1726) and Dublin by Brooking (1728). Rocque delineated Dublin (1756) on four sheets in such minute detail that he claimed landowners could colour their own properties.[22] Rocque not only published five separate maps of Dublin and vicinity, but also plans of Armagh and Newry (as insets on his county map of Armagh {1760}), Thurles (1755), Kilkenny (1758), and Cork (1759). Scalé published revised versions of some of Rocque's plans; his own notable map of Waterford (1764); and Allen's survey of Wexford (1764). Enniskillen (c.1750), Drogheda (1749), Galway (1818), Limerick (1769), Tralee (1756), and Londonderry (1747 and 1799) were mapped by the early nineteenth century; and Belfast, Dublin, Cork and Waterford had been covered several times by the mid 1830s.

Original eighteenth-century town surveys were frequently plagiarized for popular single-sheet versions, particularly by printsellers such as the Bowles family, Overton and Sayer. Thomas Bowles, in fact, published London maps varying in scale from a tiny waistcoat-pocket map (1725) to a huge folding map measuring $6\frac{1}{2}$ by 2 feet (1731), and was the first to show houses numbered in London streets (1738).

Until the 1840s plans were produced in the traditional way by private map-makers such as Shakeshaft, who mapped Preston (1809) at about 20 inches to the mile;[23] Netlam & Francis Giles who surveyed Leeds (1815); and Bennison who mapped Liverpool (1835). But all too often early-nineteenth-century demand was satisfied by re-issues of older maps, revised to various unsatisfactory degrees. New London maps, for instance, only started to appear in the 1820s and as late as c.1840 Wyld's plan was still produced by adapting some of Horwood's plates of 1799. However, increasingly map-makers could derive materials from official

---

75. Green's plan of Manchester and Salford on nine sheets at 1″:60 yards shows the ownership of the enclosed fields on the town's outskirts and the sites of industrial undertakings, distinguishing numerous dye works, a vitriol works, printing works, cotton works, an iron foundry, and so on. The great density of building in some areas is apparent, as is the spread of terraced back-to-back housing. The social landscape is represented by a dispensary, an infirmary, a lunatic asylum, workhouse, churches and chapels, etc.

'A PLAN OF Manchester AND SALFORD DRAWN from an ACTUAL SURVEY, BY William Green, Begun in the Year 1787 and Compleated in 1794.' (Detail)

surveys conducted by the Tithe or Ordnance Surveys. Similarly, local authorities increasingly commissioned their own official surveys, providing further reliable sources for plagiarization; the Lochmaben town council, for instance, mapped its burghal territories in 1786.[24] No matter how much the source was disguised by simplification of topographical detail and addition of marginal views and other sales gimmicks, the debt to official plans is readily apparent in a vast number of privately-published town plans. The best plans, often at very large scales, not only derived from but also influenced by official sources, became steadily more authoritative and comprehensive as the century progressed. Stanford, for example, produced 'the most perfect map of London . . . ever . . . issued' (1862) at 12 inches to the mile from the Ordnance's sheets prepared for the Commission of Sewers; and Weller compiled a map in the same period (1861–2) which shows even more information than Stanford's, including industrial sites and local authority buildings. Bartholomews derived its Edinburgh (1891) from the Ordnance's 5-feet plan. In Ireland the appearance of Ordnance plans was followed by derived publications such as O'Hagan's Londonderry (1847), Guy's Cork (1852), the Marlow brothers' Kilkenny (1861), and Ward's Belfast (1864).

The Irish Survey mapped towns from 1830 at 12, 20, and 24 inches to the mile and Belfast (1833) at 3 chains to the inch. Between 1833–42 plans of about a hundred Irish towns, all places with more than a hundred houses, were produced mainly at 5 feet to the mile by the Survey for the Valuation Office. Only the Ordnance's survey of Dublin (1840–47) was engraved and published. Since these plans were never intended for publication, they vary more in accuracy, style, and content than maps of any other Ordnance series, with accuracy ranging from 'very good' at Kilkenny (1841) to 'bad' at Wexford (1840). Although the valuation plans were intended to be 'skeleton' maps showing no more than the 6-inch survey, many surveyors fortunately included additional data, often in minute detail. Revision of the 24-inch Londonderry plan (1830) was authorised in 1847 and the re-survey of Belfast at 5 feet to the mile in 1854, but there was no comprehensive programme for town revision. The Towns Improvement Act (1854) empowered towns to provide themselves with large-scale maps and in 1855 the Ordnance agreed to supply 5-feet plans if the local authority met part or all of the cost depending on circumstances. In the event, only Lurgan and Portadown within areas where the 6-inch maps were being revised were surveyed, and they (respectively in 1856 and 1857) and Belfast (1858) were engraved and published.

Growing anxiety about sanitary conditions and public health led to the decision to survey towns in Great Britain at the 5-feet scale as they were covered by the 6-inch survey. The 5-feet scale was authorised for towns with over four thousand inhabitants north of the Hull-Preston line in 1840, starting with St Helens whose plan appeared in 1843–4. Rapidly there followed 5-feet plans for most towns in Lancashire and Yorkshire, the London area, and Southampton (c.1846). In Scotland after 1843 the 5-feet scale was adopted for towns with a population of over four thousand during the period of the 6-inch survey. Most 5-feet plans were published before 1855, although a few towns were surveyed on the same scale after the main series had been abandoned, including Kingston-upon-Thames (1865–66) and Windsor (1866–67). In all 59 plans were published at this scale in England and 15 in Scotland.

In practice the 5-feet scale proved too small to show necessary sanitary detail. Pressure from the newly-formed Board of Health and towns wishing to 'improve' against cholera persuaded the Ordnance Survey to prepare plans at 10 feet to the mile where local boards were willing to meet part of the cost. In England and Wales 30 towns were mapped at this scale in 1848–52, showing sanitary features in great detail. However, only 18 were published, the rest apparently remaining in manuscript with town authorities. Later, some surveys were either engraved and issued by the Ordnance as the towns' basic plans, or, elsewhere, new surveys were made and published at this scale.

Although the Ordnance Survey produced some plans, most were prepared either by a board's own surveyor or were contracted to private surveyors. All were required to conform to the Board of Health's instructions and standards. Around Liverpool, for example, Gotto mapped Garston (1855) and West Derby (1855), Mills & Fletcher mapped Wallasey (1855), Terbutt mapped St Michael's Hamlet in Toxteth Park (1856), and Orridge mapped Wavertree (1854). 'Two plans will be required. A general plan of the district under the jurisdiction of the Local Board, to a scale of two feet to the mile, and a detailed plan of the town portion of the district to a scale of 10 feet to the mile.' Scales were subject to negotiation under special circum-

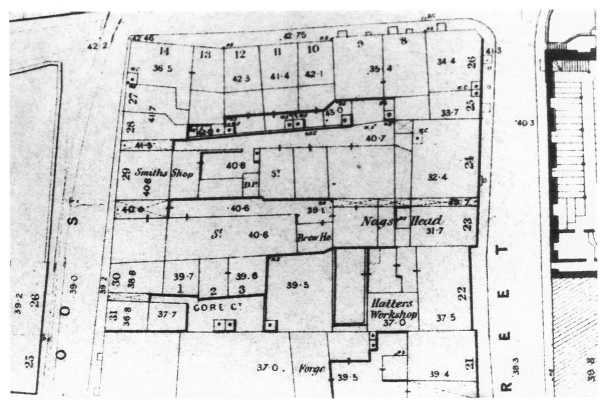

77. 'Swansea Local Board of health 1852. Survey of the Borough of Swansea. SCALE, 44 FEET TO AN INCH.' 'Surveyed & Drawn under the Superintendence of S. C. Gant, C.E. Surveyor to the Board.' Scale : 10':1m. (1:528). (Detail)

stances, as for Wallasey. Plans had to be drawn in accord with Board of Health specimens and were submitted to it for approval. 'The detailed plan must exhibit in it true position every permanent object . . . varieties of paving, of other surface material . . . distinguished by colour . . . numbers of all houses . . . all properties under one occupation . . . distinguished by . . . reference letter or sign, according to its class.' However, these instructions seem to have left considerable room for personal interpretation. At least some plans were sealed as 'first class' despite not conforming exactly to specification as, for example, Leamington which lacks house numbers (although possibly the streets were not numbered in 1852).[25] Some plans were eventually lithographed for general distribution. The need for large-scale plans was accepted by towns and cities not covered by the Public Health Act. Plans were commissioned such as the 10-feet survey conducted from 1850 to the Board of Health's specifications for the Birmingham Street

Commissioners. Cartographic action on public health not only records sanitary features in remarkable detail but portrays much else besides.

Local boards also prepared designs of drainage systems for Board of Health approval; sometimes simply superimposing the design on the recent tithe map. The Ordnance produced special diagrams showing sanitary districts. 'Superintending Inspectors' added maps to reports to the Board on local boards, as, for example, in the map of the pollution of the Wensum (1851).

Recognition of the inadequacy of the 5-feet scale led to the introduction of a scale of 10.56 feet to the

78. (*Over*) Warwick Corporation commissioned the Ordnance Survey to map the town at 10.56':1m., to facilitate the laying of sewers. The built-up area was covered on 17 coloured manuscript sheets, each measuring approximately 2' × 3'. The tiny numbers on each property indicate heights above sea level, so that sewers could be planned with a proper fall.

'WARWICK LOCAL BOARD OF HEALTH PLAN OF DISTRICT 1851. Surveyed in 1851 by the Ordnance Survey Department in accordance with the provisions of the Public Health Act.' Scale : 10.56':1m. (1:500). (Detail)

mile for all towns of over four thousand inhabitants in Great Britain in 1855. However, in practice unless towns paid most of the survey costs to obtain priority in the regional mapping timetable, they could find that survey at public expense might be scheduled far in the future and then only of a restricted area. Exeter, for example, was surveyed out of the regular sequence, with expenses met partly by the city.[26] By 1894 when the series was discontinued, 365 towns had been mapped at this scale in England, 32 in Wales, and 56 in Scotland, with Nottingham (*c*.1882), for example, covered by 352 sheets, Liverpool (1890–91) by 304, and Manchester & Salford (1891) by 262.

Irish towns of more than one thousand inhabitants were mapped at 10.56 feet to the mile from 1859, excepting those already published or in preparation at 5 feet. However, certain towns were revised (for example, Belfast 1871–73) or re-surveyed (Londonderry 1870–73) out-of-turn in recognition of special importance and rapid development. To cope with the extra burden, some of the

largest towns had to be plotted at the older scale of 5 feet instead of 10.56. In the event the population threshold qualifying towns for survey was raised to four thousand in 1872. Complaints that the 10.56-feet scale was too large led to the restoration of the 5-feet scale, firstly for the largest towns and for all from 1879. Large-scale town plans were discontinued in Ireland in 1893, except for those already in progress or under contemplation. In all, 42 towns were published at the 5-feet scale plus Greater Dublin (1847–89) which was covered by 10 separately titled sections; and 66 towns were published at 10.56 feet to the mile. At the Valuation Office's special request, the Ordnance again produced 5-feet town surveys which were eventually sold generally. However, these are merely photographic enlargements of 25-inch plans, containing no additonal detail. The Valuation Office also produced its own large-scale plans of certain small towns not separately mapped by the Ordnance; sometimes showing features not found on the Ordnance's 6-inch sheets.

79. 'Sheet XXXVIII.II.5 Chester (Caer-Lleon). Surveyed in 1874. Re-zincographed and printed in 1884.' Ordnance Survey. Scale : 10.56':1m. (1:500). (Detail)

80. Leeds. Sheet CCIII. Surveyed 1888–1890. Photo-zincographed and published at the Ordnance Survey Office, Southampton, 1890–1891. Scale: 10.56':1m. (1:500). (Detail)

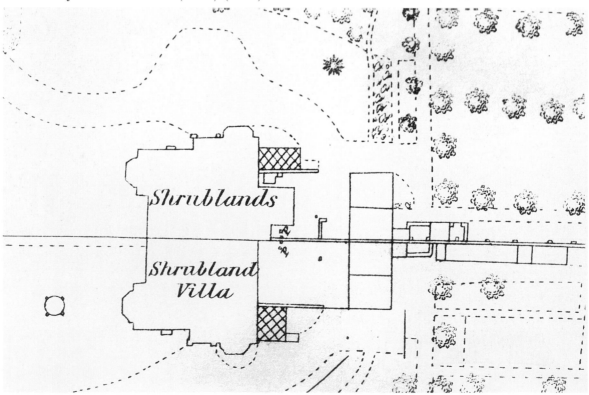

Generally, only a first edition of most plans appeared because no fresh surveys or revisions were carried out after 1893/4, although some plans certainly underwent a process of continuous, often un-noted, piecemeal revision. The Exeter plans, for instance, were reissued in 1883 with significant topographical changes. The Ordnance revised some existing plans at the town's expense in 1898–1908 at the 10.56 feet scale, such as those of Aberdeen (revised 1899–1900) and Dundee (revised 1900–1). Other towns conducted their own revisionary surveys. Sometimes revisions do not cover the whole area of the original plans. In Ireland a few towns had been revised by 1909 at the 5-feet scale; Greater Dublin, for instance, being revised again in 1907–9.

Ordnance town plans note date of survey, publication and revision on each sheet. Fairly complete details of published plans, with dates of survey and publication and the number of sheets, are given in the catalogues of Ordnance publications. Index maps were published, mainly at the 6-inch scale, to each town's sheets.

Some Ordnance plans represent the Survey's earliest large-scale coverage, predating the 25-inch plans and offering additional information such as building names and commercial/industrial use. The plans show an immense amount of detail, down to every lamp post and pillar box. The layout of the larger public buildings is shown particularly clearly, often giving detail of individual rooms; the 10-feet plans of Alnwick (*c*.1852 and 1866), for example, portray the workhouse, specifying functions of rooms and buildings.[27] However, content was simplified on later sheets in the cause of economy. Irish plans, for instance, omitted minor detail such as flower beds after 1872 and greatly restricted the delineation of interior walls in public buildings after 1881. Modern development makes Ordnance coverage appear uneven, with many seemingly unimportant towns mapped.[28]

Planning and construction of a new London sewer network required large-scale surveys showing levels. London was surveyed at its own expense by the Board of Ordnance, producing three sets of skeleton maps published by 1852 at scales of 6 and 12 inches and 5 feet to the mile. These maps are simply block plans showing only street outline and bench marks. An index was published at the 1-inch scale.[29] At the same time, the Metropolitan Commission of Sewers surveyed existing sewers, entering details on the engraved 5-feet skeleton sheets as they became available. The maps and their accompanying field notebooks illuminate the practical problems of the survey and the state of streets and sewers. The Commission surveyed some areas at 10 feet to the mile because the 5-feet scale could not detail house drainage adequately; 13 sheets cover the riverside upstream from the Houses of Parliament and 15 sheets the Kennington area. The skeleton plan offers a framework, trigonometrically correct and complete as far as street information was concerned, which could be used as a foundation for more accurate and detailed maps. Private map-makers surveyed and added topographical detail; notably Stanford, whose 'Library Map' (1862) to some extent filled the gap until detailed survey could be undertaken. The in-filling of the skeleton plans was surveyed in 1863–71, producing the largest and most detailed plan of any city ever made, published at the 5-feet scale by 1876 on 326 sheets. However, skeleton sheets remained on sale, some being updated to show topographical developments without changing the original imprints. Engraving of 25-inch sheets reduced from this survey was not completed until 1880. Because of the expense of the 5-feet survey, London was never mapped at any larger scale. The series was completely revised in 1891–95 and a new edition was published from 1893, with houses stippled rather than blank. The final sheet of the '1894–96 edition', or 'New Series', appeared in 1898. A further revision took place in 1906–9, extending coverage to substantial surrounding areas. In 1898–1905 the Land Registry also revised large sections of the 5-feet map for its own purposes and extended the survey into neighbouring built-up areas, showing only detail necessary for land registration and creating maps of lesser value than the fuller Ordnance edition.

Large-scale Ordnance plans are rivalled in historical value by fire-insurance plans. These were first produced by fire-insurance companies from the late eighteenth century to detail structures to be insured, adjacent structures, fire-fighting facilities, and distribution and concentration of policy holders. Manuscript plans were prepared for the company's exclusive use; the Sun Insurance Office, for example, produced 80 plans, now in the Guildhall Library, covering 35 different trades in 1794–1807 – presenting a perfect cross-section of London industry.[30] In 1857 James Loveday, 'Surveyor of Risks' at the Phoenix Fire Office, published plans of London's waterside at 30 feet to the inch, pinpointing likely fire locations and estimating size and severity;[31] and Freeman produced similar plans in the early 1860s. From 1885 Goad produced fire-insurance plans particularly related to warehousing and transport facilities, usually at 40 feet to the inch.[32] All sets of Goad's plans have a key plan at about 200 feet to the inch. In some cases, particularly in south-east England, a key sheet was produced but no full survey, as at Cambridge, Bury

St Edmunds, and Guildford, due to lack of interest from potential customers. These plans, together with Goad's selective plans of congested areas and those of individual buildings and sites, offer the most detailed land-use information for British urban centres in the late nineteenth and early twentieth century. Separate indexes list streets, buildings, and firms.

Companies could not base risk assessment and premium calculation on out-dated plans. Hence, fire-insurance plans were revised far more frequently than other town plans. Goad's plans were never sold, being leased to subscribers on a long-term basis; thus effectively limiting the distribution of and access to them. On completion of a new survey subscribers returned plans to Goad for revision. Minor revisions, such as new ownership of a few plots, were made by pasting paper overlays or 'correction slips' on to the plan; major revisions, however, might require preparation of a completely new sheet. Goad updated plans usually every five or six years, although larger, complex, and more important centres might be re-surveyed every year or two. Goad's plans provide unrivalled data for increasingly complex areas, particularly

---

81. Fire-insurance plans were designed to give the underwriter, at a glance, all the information needed to determine the degree of fire risk and a fair premium. In addition to the nature of the structure itself and its use, it was essential to place it in a spatial context in order to understand the risks of fire developing in neighbouring premises and spreading to the insured property, and the proximity of fire fighting provision. Goad's plans offer a mass of information by colour and sign on: land use; building construction; height; street widths; property numbers and lines; the location of fire hydrants, water pipelines and reservoirs; means of access to and egress from premises; occupancy, product line, and usage; and so on. Transport facilities and storage operations are recorded in great detail. Building materials are identified by hand-colouring, thus providing guidance to the flammability of the various structures.

Fire insurance plan of Crayford. 1908. (Detail)

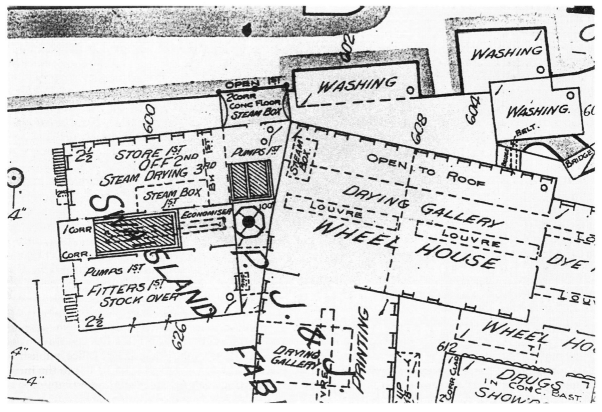

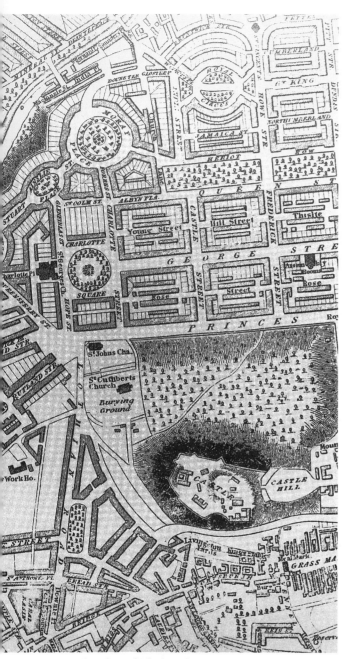

82. The plan of Edinburgh engraved by John Bartholomew senior for W. & D. Lizars's *Post Office Directory* of 1826 was reissued without alteration in the editions of 1827 and 1828. It was a landmark in Scottish town cartography and the first of many plans of the city to be produced by the Bartholomew firm.

'PLAN OF EDINBURGH DRAWN & ENGRAVED FOR THE GENERAL POST OFFICE DIRECTORY. on Steel by W. H. Lizars.' 1826. (Detail)

relating to architecture and planning. They facilitate, for example, study of the changing location and nature of retailing through the appearance, disappearance, and movement of shops and their changing size. Goad's plans are a vital but underused source for both economic and social history in general, and for the history of architecture and planning in particular.

Many town plans are found in histories, topographies, directories, guides and town atlases. They were frequently specially surveyed and often represent the most valuable portrayal at a particualr date; Perry's Liverpool, for example, produced for his *History of Leverpool* (1769), is one of the best delineations of the Georgian city. Hooker's Exeter (1587), Loggan's Oxford (1675) and Cambridge (1690), and Clarke's Penrith (1787) all illustrated histories or topographies. More ambitious works may contain several plans; Coxe's *Monmouthshire* (1801) includes six excellent plans by Morrice, and Hutchins's *Dorset* (1774) boasts seven splendid plans.

In the eighteenth century, street plans became a prominent feature of guide-books and local directories. Such plans are often useful sources for comparison with other, more obvious, surveys. Bentley's directory map of Dudley (1839), for instance, records building extension since Treasure's survey (1835); and Sketchley's Birmingham directories complement maps by Westley (1731) and Bradford (1751).[33] Conscientious publishers frequently revised directory maps: Gore's Liverpool directory, for example, often commissioned a new plan for its latest edition; and Bartholomew's 6-inch maps in Glasgow's *Official Post Office Directory* after 1865 were carefully revised annually from Ordnance and actual survey. Amongst the best directory plans are those published by Baines in his directories of Yorkshire (1822–23) and Lancashire (1824–25). However, all too often publishers, claiming accuracy and novelty, simply inserted poor earlier maps of dubious quality, without revision or acknowledgement: The growth of holiday and spa resorts led to street-plan production both for individual sale and insertion in guide-books. Other less obvious works may contain useful plans; the early-nineteenth-century growth of Cheltenham, for example, is graphically portrayed by a plan in Jameson's treatise on *Cheltenham Waters and Bilious Diseases* (1809).

Particularly in the nineteenth century, town plans were added to general atlases as Birmingham, Dublin, Edinburgh, Liverpool and London

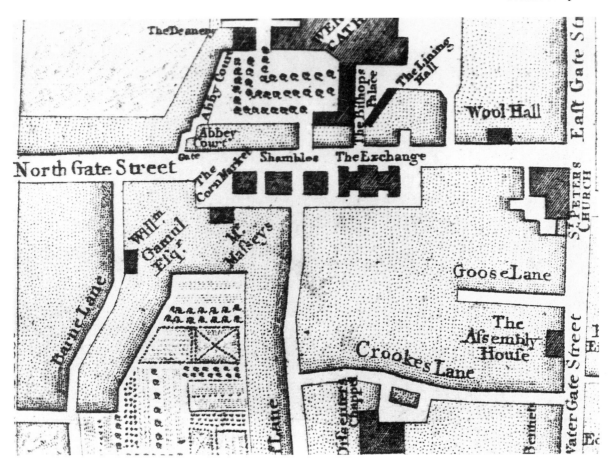

The Deanery

Abby Court

The Bishops Palace

The Lining Hall

Wool Hall

East Gate St

North Gate Street

Abber Court

Gate

The Corn Market

Shambles

The Exchange

St Peters Church

Willm Gamul Esqr.

Mr Masseys

Goose Lane

Barne Lane

The Assembly House

Crookes Lane

Lane

Disquiard Chappl

Bennet

Water Gate Street

83. Alexander de Lavaux, an experienced officer in the engineer branch of the Board of Ordnance, was sent to Chester to supervise improvements to the city's decayed fortifications in the face of the threat from Bonnie Prince Charlie's rebellion. Like many of his fellow engineers, De Lavaux used his training in military surveying to map the locality in which he was stationed. His map of Chester is the first to represent the main street plan with accuracy, although it fails to depict the small alleys and lanes running off the main streets or single houses and garden plots. Public buildings and larger houses, with owners named, are differentiated.

'PLAN of the City & Castle of Chester Survey'd and Drawn BY Alexander De Lavaux ENGINEER.' 1745. (Detail)

were by the Society for the Diffusion of Useful Knowledge (1833). Tallis added especially decorative plans with elaborately engraved borders and vignettes to his atlas *c.*1850;[34] Cole & Roper brought together 21 plans, previously issued in parts, in 1810, although most of it was secondary material;[35] Thomson included plans of several burghs in his Scottish atlas (1832); Moule pub-

84. Mazell's plan of Southampton was designed as a guide for visitors drawn to the spa and its various attractions, and as an advertisement for the proposed development of the Polygon. The intention of the promoters was to build an estate of houses for upper-middle-class owners in the shape of a polygon. Town maps of the period show the proposed final layout, but the scheme actually went no further than the first few houses. The plan's purpose as a visitors' guide dictated which streets should be shown and which buildings should be represented in the numbered key. It is difficult to distinguish the stippled built-up areas from areas of marsh and common fields, and the curious layout of small land parcels outside the east walls seems slightly improbable.

'A PLAN of SOUTHAMPTON and of the POLYGON.' 'P.Mazell Sculp!' 1771.

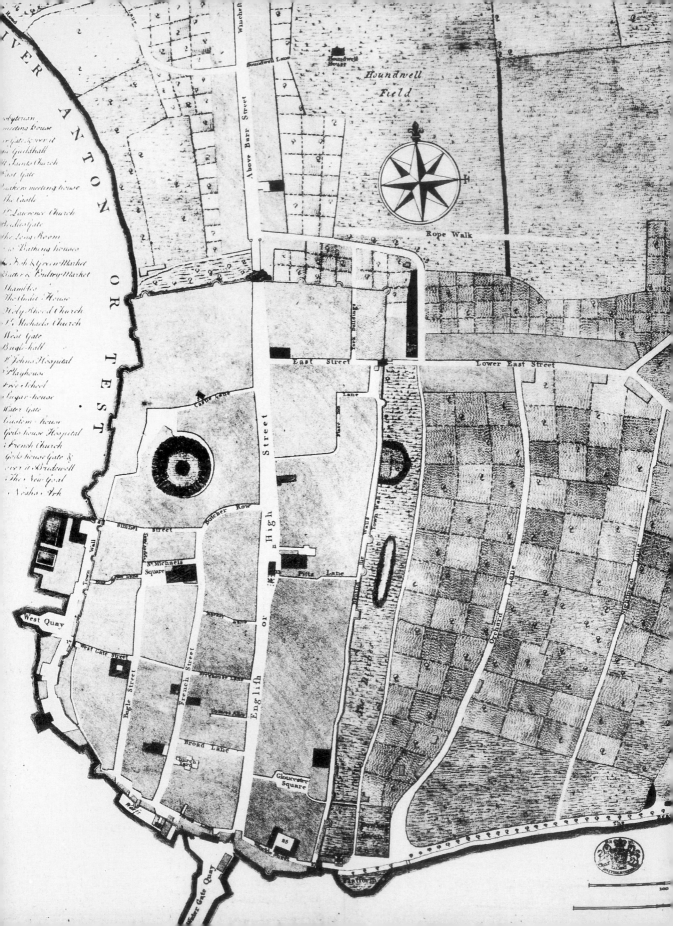

RIVER ANTON OR TEST

Houndwell Field

Houndwell House

Houndwell Lane

Rope Walk

Above Barr Street

Winchester Lane

Presbyterian
meeting House
Gate over it
Guildhall
St Saints Church
East Gate
Quakers meeting house
The Castle
St Laurence Church
Bridlesgate
The Long Room
The Bathing houses
The Fish & Green Market
Butter & Poultry Market
Shambles
The Audit House
Holy Rhood Church
St Michaels Church
West Gate
Bugle hall
St Johns Hospital
Playhouse
Free School
Sugar house
Water Gate
Custom house
Gods house Hospital
French Church
Gods house Gate &
over it Bridwell
The New Goal
Noahs Ark

East Street

Lower East Street

Lane

Castle Lane

Vork Buildings

Butcher Row

Town Walls

High Street

English or High Street

Ditch

Orchard Lane

Simnel Street

Street

St Michaels Square

French Street

Town Wall

Pitts Lane

West Quay

West Gate Street

Bugle Street

Broad Lane

Church Yard

Gloucester Square

Platform

Water Gate Quay

A

PLAN

of

SOUTHAMPTON

and of the

POLYGON.

RIVER ITCHIN

Foot way to Northam

Mary's Church

Chaple Mill

Itchin Ferry

Cross House

The Marsh

THE POLYGON

New Road

New Road

1. The Hotel.
2. Conduit Head.
3. Four Posts.
4. Road to Rumsey.
5. Road to Redbridge.
6. King John's Pond.

River Anton or Tut

PLAN

of the Intended

POLYGON

SCALES.
Yards.

500

longs or ¼ of a Mile.

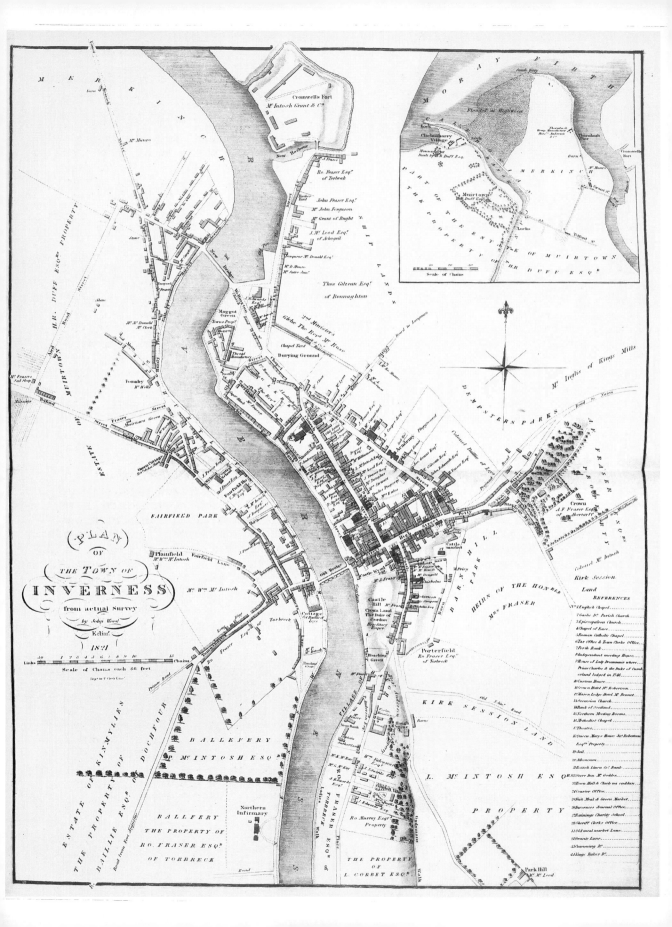

PLAN OF THE TOWN OF INVERNESS from actual Survey by John Wood Edin. 1821

85. John Wood published the finest collection of nineteenth-century town plans in his *Town Atlas* of Scotland. Whenever possible, Wood derived his plans from existing reliable surveys but for most, such as Inverness, he carried out his own new and accurate surveys. The atlas was first issued in 1828, containing plans of 48 towns but inexplicably omitting some which Wood had already surveyed and published individually.

'PLAN OF THE TOWN OF INVERNESS from actual Survey by John Wood Edin.ʳ 1821'.

lished a few plans in his county topographies (1830–36); plans were prepared in white line on a black ground for Pinnock's *Guide to Knowledge* (1833–36); and Dower produced plans for Partington's *British Cyclopaedia* (c.1833). As the century progressed the atlases and map series of Bacon, Bartholomew and the like incorporated ever more plans of towns and maps of environs at small scales, but these were generally unoriginal and little revised in successive issues.

Complete town atlases were also produced. The large-scale town plans of Rocque, Lavaux, and others were, for example, reduced to pocket size by Dury (1764). Dawson derived plans from Ordnance maps to accompany enquiries into municipal government in 1832 and 1837. Undoubtedly the finest town atlas was published of Scottish towns in 1828 by Wood who also produced important plans 1820–c.1847 of, at least, 58 towns in England and Wales, although these were never collected together and Grantham remained in manuscript.[36] The sectional atlas was introduced when the largest towns became too large to be accommodated on a normal sized folding map at anything but the smallest scales. Although most were pocket sized, some large-scale maps were divided in this way. The *Weekly Dispatch*'s London, for instance, was used by Bacon for a whole series of atlases from 1879.[37] No other atlases cover so large an area of Greater London, give so much topographical detail, or contain such full and extensive indexes; in fact, little of the information recorded on Bacon's largest-scaled London plans is to be found on other maps, even on the largest-scale Ordnance plans of the day.

General topographical maps identify settlements existing at particular times, showing their distribution, location, and layout. For individual districts they usually represent the best and most comprehensive sources on settlement patterns available. In particular, large-scale county maps often provide the first cartographic evidence of many lesser

rural settlements by locating and naming a vast number of country houses, farms and hamlets. Inevitably, settlements and buildings have been selected and many omitted. Signs rarely represent disposition of individual buildings; delineation is often generalized; and relative settlement size cannot be deduced with any certainty. From the 1740s towns began to be shown in plan, with white roads passing between blocks of buildings. Although obviously limited, this provides an idea of street layout. Yates's Staffordshire (1775), for instance, shows Dudley with extensive ribbon development along the Wolverhampton road. Urban layout on Greenwood's maps is precise and detailed; and Donn's Devon tries to portray many settlements authentically. Often the block plan is the earliest record of the shape and size of many towns and larger villages. Generally, settlements are easily identified on all topographical maps. Once established and named, the major ones tended to be shown on most large-scale maps. However, problems of identification do arise when spellings vary; where similar names appear in close proximity; and where settlements are un-named in a closely-populated landscape which does not allow certain identification from position alone; where a single name covers a number of settlements collectively, perhaps to save space; and where established settlements have been omitted, as could happen to a monumental extent on even the most reliable maps. Nevertheless, despite the problems, general topographical maps present essential evidence of the settlement pattern; for example, they appear to confirm the view that agricultural improvement in Scotland brought with it a transition in settlement from grouped ferm-touns to dispersed single farms.

Town plans also appear as insets on many large-scale county maps. Some are accurate, detailed, based on original survey, and of primary importance. The first recorded Glasgow plan, for instance, is found on Ross's Lanark (1773), and the first important Edinburgh plan after the start of building in the New Town is inset on the Armstrongs' map of the three Lothians (1773). Jefferys made new town surveys for his county maps; Yorkshire (1771–72), for instance, has six larger-scale inset plans. Other high quality insets include Davis's Oxford (1797) and Donn's Plymouth and Exeter (1766). However, other insets plagiarized from earlier surveys are out-of-date compared with the main map. Burdett's Chester inset (1777), for instance, was copied from

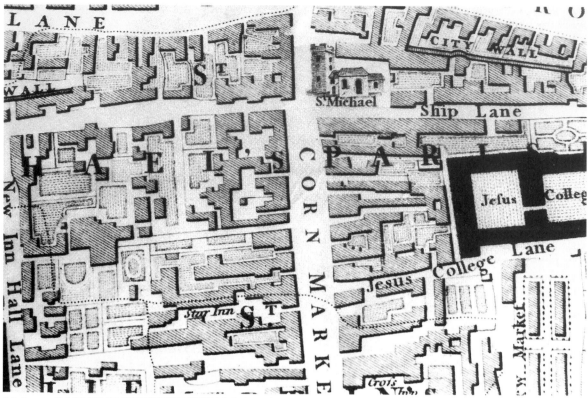

86. Inset of 'A PLAN OF THE UNIVERSITY AND CITY OF OXFORD' from 'A New MAP of THE COUNTY OF OXFORD.' Richard Davis, 1797. (Detail)

De Lavaux's plan (1745), following it by failing to record the old city's intricate pattern of alleys and incorporating only the most obvious revisions. Other unreliable insets appear in the *Large English Atlas*, on Strachey's Somerset (1736), and Prior's Leicestershire (1779). Some insets were revised for later editions of a map. Successive issues of the Armstrongs' Lothians of 1773, 1775, 1778, and 1787, for instance, demonstrate the rapid progress in the building of Edinburgh's New Town; and Faden substantially improved Burdett's Chester by adding street names and numerous topographical features for his re-issue of 1794 (no further changes were, however, made for the issue of 1818).

Town expansion could easily be added to existing plans for later editions by simply engraving new development in what was previously a generalized rural setting, or adding extra sheets to larger-scale maps. Nevertheless, the extra expense usually deterred updating and fringe development may appear on printed maps only many decades after it

actually occurred. The addition of 'improvements' within an already built-up area was more difficult and expensive since extensive re-engraving and revision was required. Consequently, only the most obvious, unavoidable, and interesting develop-

87. Unlike Davis's fine inset plan of Oxford, the inset plan of Leicester, on the otherwise excellent map of Leicestershire by John Prior, was a disappointingly inferior, little-revised adaptation of Thomas Roberts's plan published in 1744 but probably originally drawn in 1712. Although the Exchange (built in 1746), the Assembly Rooms (*c.*1750) and the Infirmary (1771) have been added to indicate contemporary development, other notable new buildings are missing and urban expansion has generally been ignored. Samuel Carte's plan of 1722 is almost identical in the built-up area shown, suggesting no urban development between 1712 and 1804! Inset plans on large-scale county maps were often at too small a scale to show buildings in any way other than as schematic representations of blocks of buildings and groups of houses; it was frequently impossible to position individual buildings precisely.

Town plan of Leicester from '. . . MAP of LEICESTERSHIRE from an actual Survey, Begun in the Year 1755, and finished in the Year 1777 . . .' John Prior, 2nd. edn., 1804. (Detail)

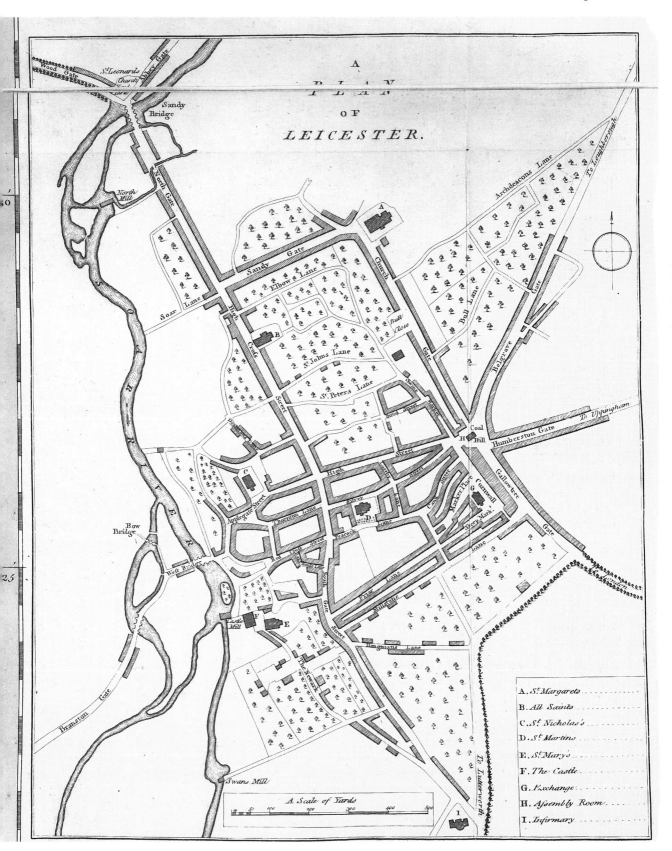

A
PLAN
OF
LEICESTER.

A Scale of Yards

A. St Margarets
B. All Saints
C. St Nicholas's
D. St Martins
E. St Mary's
F. The Castle
G. Exchange
H. Assembly Room
I. Infirmary

ments were generally added for later issues. In contrast, plans were sometimes updated regularly and comprehensively: the Bowles' family, for instance, minutely recorded Georgian town planning on their London plans; sequences of Edinburgh maps published by Knox, Brown, and Lothian in the 1820s show very clearly the speed of building in various city areas; and Millerd's Bristol was brought up to date for each of its four re-issues before 1730. Plans derived at least partly from earlier surveys and then revised in piecemeal fashion, usually as cheaply as possible, are composite sources embodying features of different origin from several dates. They do not accurately portray the town at a particular date.

Most town plans, such as most of those of London published 1800–24, are copies or re-issues of earlier maps. Periodically, an enterprising map-maker would prepare a new survey which would then become the common source for derived plans over the ensuing years. Thus, Hunter's Chester (1789) replaced De Lavaux's (1745) as the basis for the city's maps; and the outdated and unreliable London maps of the early 1850s only improved as Stanford emerged as the capital's leading cartographer. Major towns have maps and plans in plenty for the late-Georgian and Victorian years, but very many are small, unreliable, and carelessly and hastily made. Of the main classes of town cartographers, engineers stationed locally and local surveyors will, as a general rule, prove more reliable than others. Settlement maps and plans are obviously uneven in local availability, depending on numerous factors. Some towns are far more comprehensively covered than their neighbours. Many provincial towns have a series of plans dating from the sixteenth century, whilst others may have no cartographic record until the nineteenth. For well-mapped towns, plans provide crucial evidence of rapid and complex changes.

Select Bibliography

ASPINALL, P.J., 'The use of nineteenth-century fire insurance plans for the urban historian' (*Local Hist.*, 2; 1975)

BAGLEY, J.J., 'County maps and town plans' in *Historical Interpretation No. 2: Sources of English History 1540 to the Present Day* (1971)

BRAITHWAITE, L., *Exploring British Cities* (1986)

CAMBLIN, G., *The Town in Ulster* (1951)

CONZEN, M.R.G., 'The use of town plans in the study of urban history' in H.J. Dyos (ed.): *The Study of Urban History* (1968)

ELLIOT, J., *The City in Maps: Urban Mapping to 1900* (1987)

FORDHAM, A., *Town Plans of the British Isles* (Map Colls. Circle, 22; 1965)

LOBEL, M.D., 'The value of early maps as evidence for the topography of English towns' (*Imago Mundi*, 22; 1968)

Public Record Office of Northern Ireland, *Northern Ireland Townplans, 1828–1966. A Catalogue of Large-scale Townplans prepared by the Ordnance Survey and deposited in the Record Office* (2nd edn.; 1981)

RAVENHILL, W., 'Early town mapping' in 'British cartography in the Renaissance' in J.B. Harley & D. Woodward (eds) *The History of Cartography*, 3, *Cartography in the Age of Renaissance and Discovery* (Forthcoming)

WEST, J., *Town Records* (1983) [Contains a 'Gazetter of town maps and plans c.1600–1900' based mainly on the plans of England and Wales listed in the *British Museum Catalogue of Printed Maps, Charts and Plans* (1967)]

Town Bibliography

The parts of R.V. Tooley's series on 'Large scale English county maps and plans of cities not printed in atlases', which appeared in the *Map Collector* from 1978 with notes on many town plans, are listed by county in the 'County Bibliography'. See also the 'Notes' to this chapter for further references.

Aberdeen

ANDERSON, P.J., 'Ms. maps of Aberdeen' (*Scot. Notes Queries*, 2, 6; 1905)

BARNETT, M.J.F., 'Early map-makers and nineteenth-century surveyors of Aberdeen' (*Scot. Geog. Mag.*, 79; 1963)

FRASER, G.M., 'Aberdeen maps and views' (*Scot. Notes Queries*, 2, 7; 1905)

---

88. The Greenwoods' map of London at 7":1m. was the first to be published on a large scale for many years. However, it was never the most reliable of surveys, with many minor roads wrongly positioned and developments depicted that were never put into effect. The map, first published in 1827, enjoyed a long life, being last issued by Smith & Son in 1856. Although it was issued 10 times in all, significant revisions were made only for the issue of 1830. The most important metropolitan improvements were added to new editions but suburban development was lamentably neglected and, by 1856, what had always been a relatively unreliable survey was one of the most misleading maps available.

'MAP of LONDON From Actual Survey, COMPREHENDING THE Various Improvements to 1856.'

Ayr

FORSYTH, J.W., 'Maps and plans' in A.I. Dunlop (ed.): *The Royal Burgh of Ayr* (*Coll. Ayrshire Arch. Nat. Hist. Soc.*, 2, 2; 1950–52)

Bedford

CHAMBERS, B., *Printed Maps and Town Plans of Bedfordshire 1576–1900* (1983)

Belfast

EWART, L.M., 'Belfast maps, a record of plans of the town chronologically arranged, with a copy of a manuscript plan of Belfast dated 1680 in the British Museum' (*Ulster Journ. Arch.*, 1; 1894–5)

GETTY, E., 'The true position of the Ford of Belfast' (*Ulster Journ. Arch.*, 4; 1855)

Public Record Office of Northern Ireland, *How to Use the Record Office Series: Maps and Plans. No. 17, Belfast, 1570–1860* (*c.*1969)

Bristol

Bristol and Gloucestershire Archaeological Society, *A Gloucestershire and Bristol Atlas* (1961)

PRITCHARD, J.E., 'Old plans and views of Bristol' (*Trans. Bristol Gloucs. Arch. Soc.*, 48; 1928)

Cambridge

CLARK, J.W., & GRAY, A., *Old Plans of Cambridge 1574–1798* (2 pt.; 1921)

Carrickfergus

SWANTON, W.M., 'Maps of Carrickfergus, in the British Museum' (*Ulster Journ. Arch.*, 2; 1895–96)

Carlow

HORNER, A.A., 'Two eighteenth century maps of Carlow town' (*Proc. Roy. Irish Acad.*, 78, C; 1978)

Chichester

BUTLER, D.J., *The Town Plans of Chichester 1595–1898* (1972)

Cork

CARBERRY, E., 'The development of Cork city as shown by the maps of the city prior to the Ordnance Survey maps of 1841–42' (*Cork. Hist. Soc. Journ.*, 48; 1943)

MACCARTHY, C.J.F., 'Notes on maps and plans of Cork interest' (*Cork. Hist. Soc. Journ.*, 73; 1968)

Drogheda

THOMAS, A., 'Drogheda in 1574' (*Louth Arch. Soc. Journ.*, 18; 1975)

Dublin

CLARK, M., *The Book of Maps of the Dublin City Surveyors, 1695–1827; An Annotated List with Biographical Notes, and Introduction* (1983)

COSGRAVE, E.M., *A Catalogue of Engravings of Dublin* (1905)

COSGRAVE, E.M., 'On two maps dated 1751 and 1753, of the Essex Bridge District, Dublin' (*Journ. Roy. Soc. Antiquaries Ireland*, 48; 1918)

JOYCE, W. ST J., 'Old maps of Dublin and its district' in *The Neighbourhood of Dublin* (2nd edn., 1921; reprinted 1971)

MCCROSSAN, J.L., 'Notes on some Dublin city maps' (*Irish Booklover*, 26; 1938)

MALONE, J.B., 'Maps and the Liberties' in E. Gillespie (ed.): *The Liberties of Dublin* (1973)

Dundalk

O'SULLIVAN, H., 'Rothe's Castle, Dundalk and Hugh O'Neill, a sixteenth century map' (*Louth Arch. Soc. Journ.*, 15; 1963)

TEMPEST, H.G., 'A seventeenth century map of Dundalk' (*Louth Arch. Soc. Journ.*, 6; 1926)

TEMPEST, H.G., 'A seventeenth century map of Dundalk and Castletown' *Louth Arch. Soc. Journ.*, 14; 1957)

Dungarven

POWER, P., 'An old map of Dungarven, 1760' (*Waterford S.E. Ireland Arch. Soc. Journ.*, 14; 1911)

Edinburgh

COWAN, W., *The Maps of Edinburgh, 1544–1929* (2nd edn., revised with census of copies in Edinburgh libraries; 1932)

MEADE, M.K., 'Plans of the New Town of Edinburgh' (*Archit. Hist.*, 14; 1971)

Royal Scottish Geographical Society, *The Early Views and Maps of Edinburgh, 1544–1852* (1919)

SIMPSON, D.C., 'City plans and the New Town' (*Univ. Edin. Journ.*, 23; 1967–68)

Eniskillen

LOWRY CORRY, S.R., EARL OF BELMORE: 'Ancient maps of Eniskillen and its environs' (*Ulster Journ. Arch.*, 2; 1896)

Exeter

CONSTABLE, K.M., *The Early Printed Plans of Exeter, 1587–1724* (Reprinted from the *Trans. Devonshire Assoc.*; 1932)

Galway

TRENCH, W.F. (et al.), 'Notes on a seventeenth century pictorial map of Galway town' (*Galway Arch. Soc. Journ*, 4; 1905–6)

Glamorgan

MOORE, P., 'Glamorgan town plans: a survey of sources through three centuries 1600–1900' in S. Williams: *Glamorgan Historian*, 9 (1976)

Glasgow

BROWN, J.A., 'The cartography of Glasgow' (*Scot. Geog. Mag*, 37; 1921)

HILL, W.H., 'Maps and plans relating to Glasgow and its neighbourhood' in *Reference Catalogue of Books, Pamphlets and Plans, etc. relating to Glasgow in the Library at Barlenark* (1905)

KINNIBURGH, I.A.G., 'John Ainslie's map of Port Glasgow in 1806' (*Scot. Geog. Mag.*, 76; 1960)

Hawick

SINTON, J., 'Local maps' in *Bibliography of Works relating to, or published in, Hawick* (1908)

Inverness

ANDERSON, P.J., 'Maps and plans' in *A Concise Bibliography of the Printed and Ms. Material on the History, Topography and Institutions of the Burgh, Parish and Shire of Inverness* (1917)

Kilmallock

ANDREWS, J.H., 'An Elizabethan map of Kilmallock' (*N. Munster Antiq. Journ.*, 11; 1968)

Kingston-upon-Hull

SHEPPARD, T., *The Evolution of Kingston upon Hull as shown by its Plans* (1911)

Leeds

BONSER, K.G, & NICHOLS, H., *Printed Maps and Plans of Leeds, 1711–1900* (Thoresby Soc.; 1960)

Liverpool

BROWN, R.S., 'Maps and plans of Liverpool & district by the Eyes family of surveyors' (*Trans. Hist. Soc. Lancs. Cheshire*, 62; 1911)

London

The Guildhall Library, the London Topographical Society, and Harry Margary (Lympne Castle, Kent) publish facsimile early plans of London.

DARLINGTON, I,. & HOWGEGO, J., *The Printed Maps of London, c.1553–1850* (1964; reprinted 1978 wih revisions).

FISHER, J., Introduction to *A Collection of Early Maps of London 1553–1667* (1981)

GLANVILLE, P., *London in Maps* (1972)

HYDE, R., *Printed Maps of Victorian London, 1851–1900* (1975)

MARTIN, W., 'The early maps of London' (*Trans. Lond. Middx. Arch. Soc*, 3; 1917)

Londonderry

COLBY, T., *Ordnance Survey of the County of Londonderry: Memoir of City and N.W. Liberties* (1837)

Manchester

LEE, J., *Maps and Plans of Manchester and Salford 1650–1843* (1957)

Manchester Public Libraries, *Maps of Manchester, 1650–1848* (1969)

Newcastle West

O'CONNOR, P., 'An eighteenth century plan of Newcastle West, county Limerick' (in *Annual Observer* (Newcastle West Hist. Soc. Journ.), 2; 1981)

Norwich

CHUBB, T., & STEPHEN, G.H., *A Descriptive List of the Printed Maps of Norfolk, 1574–1916; Descriptive List of Norwich Plans and the Principal Early Views 1541–1914* (1928)

Oxford

SALTER, H., 'Oxford topography', (*Oxford Hist. Soc.* 39; 1899)

SALTER, H., *Survey of Oxford, 1772* (Oxford Hist. Soc.; 1912)

Paisley

MCCARTHY, M., 'Maps' in *A Social Geography of Paisley* (1969)

Perth

MCCLAREN, T., 'Early plans of Perth' (*Trans. Perthshire Soc. Nat. Science*, 10; 1938–42)

Portsmouth

HODSON, D., *Maps of Portsmouth before 1801* (Portsmouth Rec. Ser., 4; 1978)

Shrewsbury

Field Studies Council, *Old Maps of Shrewsbury* (n.d.)

Southampton

Southampton Corporation, *Southampton Maps from Elizabethan Times* (1964)

WELCH, E., 'The earliest maps of Southampton' (*Cart. Journ.*, 2; 1965)

Warwick

Warwickshire Museum, *Warwick Town Maps 1610–1851*. Reproductions of five original maps, with the names of the inhabitants of the principal streets transcribed from contemporary records. (Warwick County Museum; 1984)

Waterford

DOWNEY, E., *The Story of Waterford* (1914)

16
Specialized urban plans

From the late seventeenth century urban conditions were improved by bodies of commissioners who sought Parliamentary sanction to control such 'improvements' as paving, cleaning and lighting. From c.1760 many local acts were passed creating improvement commissions which 'improved' the urban environment until well into the nineteenth century. Commissions often prepared their own large-scale plans, if necessary for Parliamentary submission; such a map of Exeter (1840), for example, names landowners and shows land to be built on in detail. Large-scale 'improvement' surveys became common from the eighteenth century. From 1811, proposals for 'improvements' and street and paving schemes made to Parliament had to be accompanied by large-scale plans. Before the 1840s plans were generally drawn in manuscript to a variety of specifications. Reports to town authorities, containing ever more information on transport services, housing, sewerage, drainage and so on, were frequently illustrated by similar maps; for instance, a report to Norwich Corporation's Sewage and Irrigation Committee (1885) recorded sewers on an outline street plan. A later report (1893) mapped the new main drainage works.

The creation of water, electric-lighting and gas companies in the nineteenth century generated maps usually with information simply superimposed on to Ordnance sheets. Large-scale plans were statutorily required by Parliament to accompany proposals for gas, electricity and heating schemes. In London, for example, the Metropolitan Gas Act (1860) required each company to prepare a map showing mains, at a minimum of 6 inches to the mile, to be deposited with the local Clerk of the Peace and made available for public inspection; maps were to be updated and corrected annually to show new mains. Reports on public utilities were illustrated by maps such as that of

London's 'thoroughfares to be lighted by electricity' (1882–3).

From the eighteenth century, large-scale surveys relating to drainage, sewerage and water supply became particularly common. Applications to Parliament for approval of schemes for water supply and drainage had to be accompanied by large-scale plans. From the 1830s and '40s urban sanitary surveys tended to cover the entire urban area, rather than part of it, at larger scales than before. Various Leeds' plans, for example, show proposed lines of sewers, main drainage and water supply at a time of rapid change in the 1860s; and Smyth mapped Belfast's water pipes (1790), adding useful elevations of the poor house and the infirmary. Concern over pollution caused the mapping of the older streets of Norwich, showing drains and sewers flowing into the Wensum (1851). Richard Kelsey, surveyor to the City's Commissioner of Sewers, compiled the earliest printed London sewer map (1841), but it was far from satisfactory, failing to show levels and directions of fall and flow. Kelsey's replacement William Haywood prepared improved surveys (1854) and, henceforth, London's sewer system was delineated in detail, particularly on Ordnance large-scale base maps. Sanitation reports, both official and unofficial, may yield unexpected cartographic treasures: Thompsons' essay on the *Sanitary Condition of Stourbridge* (1848), for example, contains not only a sanitary town plan, but also an environs' map; designs for waterworks, reservoirs, sewerage schemes, water supply, a proposed public garden, model housing, and improved ventilation; and plans and elevations of baths and wash houses. As large-scale Ordnance sheets extended in coverage, so increasingly, sewer plans were superimposed on to them; Erith's main sewers, for instance, were added in manuscript to 6-inch sheets (1878) and its entire system was superimposed on to the 25-inch (1879). Water-supply plans may also record distant areas and supply routes; proposals to supply water to Birmingham *c*.1894, for example, included maps of Radnorshire showing watersheds and sites of proposed reservoirs and dams, and in 1790 Yates mapped the route of water pipes from Bootle to Liverpool.

Sanitary requirements and plumbing needs often necessitated the mapping of individual building or buildings groups. The earliest English representation of objects entirely in plan occurs on a large-scale plan dating from the early thirteenth century, showing the arrangement of springs, cisterns, and pipes at Wormley for supplying water to Waltham Abbey.[1] An even earlier pair of plans (*c*.1165) portray waterworks at Canterbury Cathedral on a ground plan of variable scale with bird's-eye views of buildings.[2] A mid-fifteenth-century plan shows conduits bringing water to the Charterhouse from springs two miles away; this 10-feet parchment roll includes a plan of the Charterhouse, showing individual cells and other rooms. Lyne's Cambridge records a scheme to bring running water to the King's Ditch to improve sanitation, and, indeed, may have been produced in connection with the scheme.

Individual buildings were mapped for other reasons. Ecclesiastical records contain not only maps of church lands but also plans of church properties. Glebe terriers from *c*.1600, and occasionally slightly earlier, contain descriptions of church houses and notes on income sources with occasional plans. For later centuries there are copious records concerning the building and re-building of parsonages. Exeter's diocesan records, for instance, contain a plan and survey report (1779) on the old vicarage at Kentisbury, together with a proposed plan of the new vicarage. In Scotland, the records of heritors, responsible for kirk and manse upkeep, contain plans of all sizes of ecclesiastical building.

Many different records include plans showing distribution and nature of buildings, with details of construction, alteration and repair. For example, plans, elevations and perspective drawings often accompanied estimates for great mansions, new farm houses, mills, stables, or even estate workers' cottages. Buildings plans were prepared in England from at least the late fourteenth century. A plan of *c*.1390 shows part of a court in Winchester College – but it is not a scale drawing. Similarly, plans of building plots in the Bridge House estates in the 1470s give full measurements and show plots

roughly the right shape but they are not to scale. Building plans drawn by architects or master masons before the mid sixteenth century are approximate outlines with written room dimensions. The scale drawing of non-military building plans seems to have been introduced by military engineers already skilled in the art. Plans of the royal manor house at Hull (*c*.1542/3) by Rogers, at about 16 feet to the inch, seem to be the earliest English non-military scale building plans. Plans steadily approximated ever more closely to a consistent scale and by the 1570s scale plans were being drawn by such as Browne for Hull's custom house and Symonds for works at the Cursitors Hall and at Havering Palace.

Landlords required plans of their properties. In particular, in the early seventeenth century, population pressure on dwelling space and high land prices in the larger towns created an urgent need for plans distinguishing tenement ownership in buildings. Space was at a premium and buildings often had upper floors which pushed into and over adjacent tenements; to avoid disputes it was essential to record room size and property ownership accurately. Landowners like the Clothworkers' Company and Christ's Hospital engaged surveyors, such as the Treswell family who surveyed numerous properties in and around London in 1585–1617,[3] to produce plans of both single structures and blocks of buildings, including not only houses but also taverns, inns, company halls, and other specialized buildings. Treswell's plans for the Clothworkers' Company, for example, drawn probably to accompanying leases of 1607–11, show its London property with accompanying text describing the upper storeys of each building wtih measurements.[4] Generally, tenants are named in the rooms they occupied. Most plans are ground plans showing doorways, stairs, chimneys, yards and gardens. When studied with accompanying text they provide information on room use; number of rooms in a tenancy; proportion heated; and so on.

It is particularly fortunate that institutional property in London was mapped in the early seventeenth century, for the Great Fire destroyed more than two-thirds of the medieval city.[5] Confusion over property lines following any extensive fire highlighted the inadequacies of traditional written surveys, persuading many more institutional landlords and large private owners to map their property. The practice of appending plans to leases, introduced by the City Lands Committee following

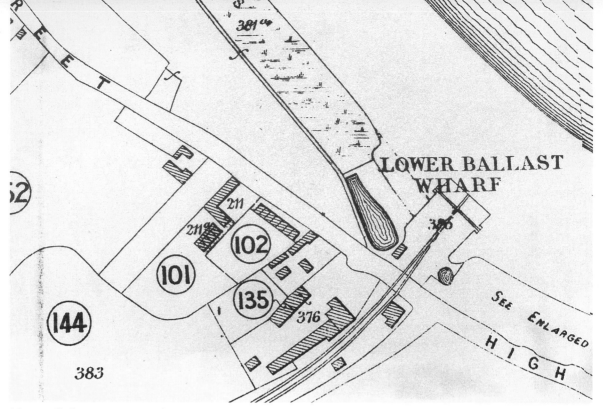

89. Pencilled annotations on the plan detail buyers and prices paid.

'Plan of the LENNEY PARK ESTATE ERITH, KENT. For Sale by DANIEL SMITH SON & OAKLEY. 1874.' (Detail)

---

the Great Fire, was increasingly adopted elsewhere. Ground plans were commonly prepared to accompany leases and conveyances. Many plans also illustrated sale catalogues, which themselves often contain valuable written information, both being sometimes annotated with details of buyers and prices paid. Landlords' property plans became common after 1700 and prolific after 1800. The best recorded properties are generally those of the municipal corporations, the Church, the Crown, and of other ancient institutions such as the City Guilds, Dulwich College, Christ's and St Bartholomew's Hospitals, and the Livery Companies, but a vast number of private landlords also mapped property in detail. The corporation estate in Drogheda, for example, was mapped by Newcomen & Cockayne as early as 1657; and Christ's

---

90. The Clothworkers' Hall, on the east side of Mincing Lane in London, was surveyed for the Clothworkers' Company by Ralph Treswell in 1612. The building shown was damaged in the Great Fire of 1666 and has since been twice rebuilt.

Untitled plan of the Clothworkers' Hall. 1612.

Hospital's Abbey Wood estate was surveyed by Stenning in 1900. In the nineteenth century many more building plans were prepared for fire-insurance purposes. New types of landowners emerged, such as the railway companies, which acquired and mapped large estates in many towns. Building Control Plans were submitted with planning applications to local authorities from the late nineteenth century.

Many towns have the history of their public buildings recorded in copious plans of town halls, hospitals, courts, markets, prisons, board schools, technical institutes, libraries, slaughterhouses, workhouses, and so on. The opening of Leeds town hall (1858) even generated a plan 'showing Her Majesty's route'. Similarly, other important buildings were frequently portrayed, providing a valuable record especially of those which fell into disrepair or were demolished. Urban 'improvement' often involved the construction of completely new streets or the creation of housing estates. Initially, land for 'improvement' had to be purchased by municipal authorities; plans were prepared to facilitate purchase showing ownership and tenancy, ranging from the very complex to the very simple where rural land outside the built-up area was purchased in one unit from a single owner. Reports and proposals to and by improvement commissioners and seeking Parliamentary sanction were illustrated by large-scale plans of

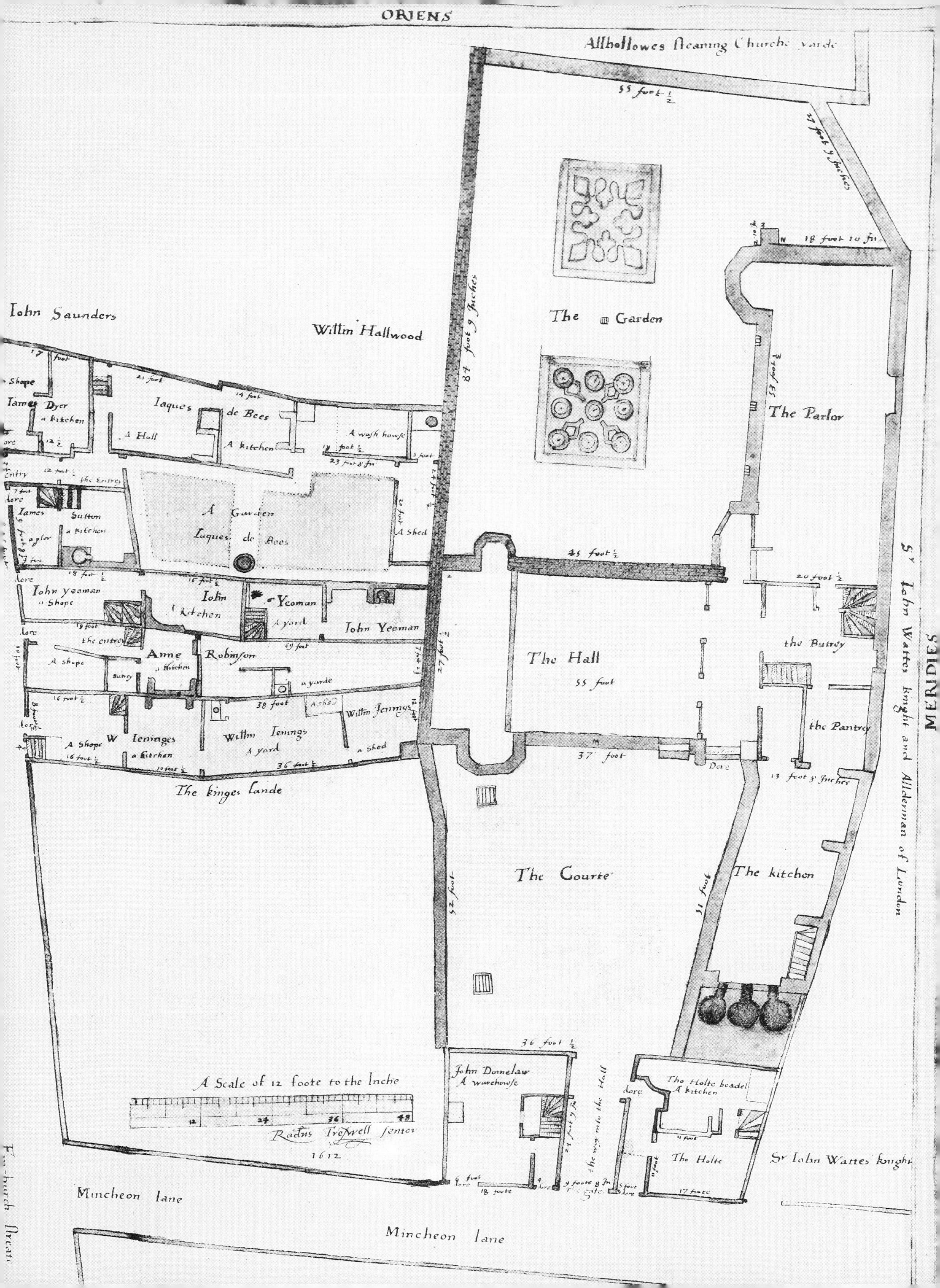

Allhallowes ſteaning Churche yarde

55 foot ½

57 foot 9 Inches

John Saunders

Willm Hallwood

The Garden

The Parlor

17 foot

Shope

21 foot

Iaques de Bees

14 foot

18 foot 10 Inches

James Dyer a kitchen

A Hall

A kitchen

A wash houſe

12 ½

23 foot 8 In

5 foot

84 foot 9 Inches

Entry

12 foot

the Entry

7 foot dore

A Garden

A shed

James Sutton a kitchen

Luques de Bees

a plor

18 foot ½

16 foot ½

dore

John yeoman a Shope

John Kitchen

Yeoman

45 foot ½

20 foot ½

19 foot

the entry

Iohn Yeoman

A yard

29 foot

the Butrey

Sʳ Iohn Wattes knight and Allderman of London

Anne Robinson a kitchen

The Hall

the Pantrey

A shope

butry

55 foot

16 foot ½

38 foot

a yarde

A: 5580

Willm Jenings

37 foot

Dore

13 foot 8 Inches

W Ienninges a kitchen

16 foot ½

10 foot ½

Willm Iennings A yard

A shed

36 foot

The kinges lande

52 foot

The Courte

51 foot

The kitchen

36 foot ½

A Scale of 12 foote to the Inche

12   24   36   48

Radus Treſwell ſenior

1612

John Donnelaw A warehouſe

the way into the Hall

24 foot 9 in

Tho Holte beadell A kitchen

dore

9 foot dore

18 foote

a foote 9 in the gate

5 foot dore

11 foot

Tho Holte

Sʳ Iohn Wattes knight

17 foot

Mincheon lane

Mincheon lane

Fenchurch ſtreate

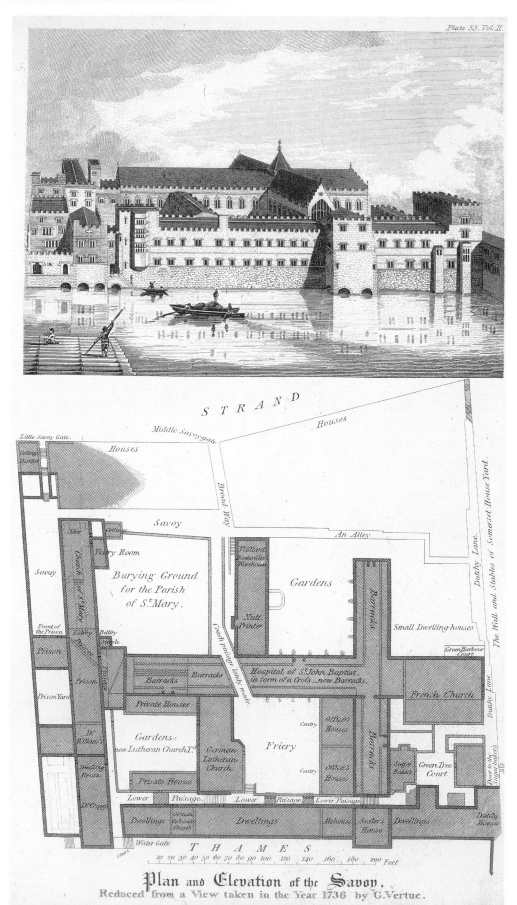

Plate 33. Vol. II.

S T R A N D

Little Savoy Gate.

Houses

Middle Savoy gate.

Houses

Cutting Distiller

Savoy

Broad Way

An Alley

Dudley Lane.

Bar

Cutting

Vestry Room

Hallard Bookseller Warehouse

Savoy

Church of St Mary

Burying Ground for the Parish of St Mary.

Gardens

The Wall and Stables of Somerset House Yard.

Front of the Prison

Lobby

Bellfry

Nall Printer

Small Dwelling-houses

Prison

Prison

Coach passage lately made.

Green Harbour Court

Prison Yard

Barracks

Barracks

Hospital of St John Baptist, in form of a Crofs... now Barracks.

French Church

Private Houses

Centry

Officers Houses

Barracks

Dudley Lane.

Dr Wilkins's

Gardens: now Lutheran Church Y.^d

German Lutheran Church.

Friery

Sugar Bakers

Green Tree Court

Dwelling House.

Private Houses

Centry

Officers Houses

Door to the Sugar Bakers

Dr Gray's

Lower Passage. Lower Passage. Lower Passage

Dwellings

German Calvinist Church

Dwellings

Alehouse

Sutler's House

Dwellings

Dutch House.

Water Gate

Stairs

T H A M E S

10 20 30 40 50 60 70 80 90 100 120 140 160 180 200 Feet

Plan and Elevation of the Savoy.

Reduced from a View taken in the Year 1736 by G. Vertue.

N.º 12. of R. ACKERMANN'S REPOSITORY of ARTS &c. Pub. Decr 1. 1816.

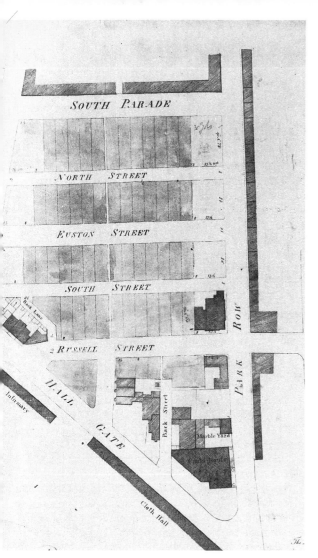

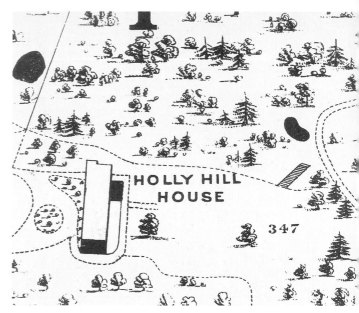

94. 'This Plan is an Enlargement of the Ordnance' at about 50":1m., showing that part of the estate that had already been sold off and locating new house building and a gravel pit.

'Plan of HOLLY HILL HOUSE, BELVEDERE. – KENT. 1889 R.W. SCOBELL. Surveyor, 25, Bucklersbury, E.C. PALMER, SUTTON & ROBINS, 34, CRUTCHED FRIARS, LONDON. E.C.' (Detail)

92. (*Opposite*) The Palace of the Savoy, named after Peter of Savoy to whom it was granted by Henry III, was by the early eighteenth century occupied by a variety of groups and individuals. The plan of the palace buildings in 1736 differentiates uses, and even names occupants. The buildings of the palace deteriorated markedly in the next half-century and what remained was demolished to form the approach to Waterloo Bridge.

'Plan and Elevation of the Savoy, Reduced from a View taken in the Year 1736 by G. Vertue. N.º 12. of R. ACKERMANN's REPOSITORY of ARTS &c. Pub. Dec.r 11 1816.'

93. (*above*) The Land here described is now to be sold by private Contract in building Lots for Houses, Warehouses &c.'

'A Plan of an Estate situate in Leeds in the COUNTY of YORK, belonging to Mess.rs Thompson & Makins as the same is divided into Building Lots for Sale Made in April 1819 by Jonat.n, Tayler, LEEDS.'

proposed street, housing, and other developments; the *First Report of the Commissioners for Improving the Metropolis* (1844), for instance, contains a plan of proposed changes on the Chelsea waterfront. Reductions of official plans of such popular schemes as London's Regent Street satisfied widespread interest.

One of the earliest residential estates was that developed at Hatton Garden in London. It was mapped on completion in 1694 by Abraham Arlidge, showing site numbers and frontage measurements and naming every tenant.[6] Housing schemes, both public and private, proliferated from the eighteenth century, begetting plans of land available for sale and proposed development. Large-scale plans show individual lots, house plots set out for development, and those already built on, sometimes naming the first purchasers. Such plans record suburban growth street by street and estate by estate.

Landowners of scattered properties required plans showing property dispersion; foundations such as Christ's Hospital held widespread estates which required accurate boundary delineation. As early as *c.*1550 St Paul's parish, Canterbury, was mapped for the Church of England. Such property plans offer much useful information; plans of urban glebe lands belonging to Shalford parsonage (1617), for example, include a plan of Guildford. An appreciation of town development requires an understanding of land-ownership structure. Unfortunately, there are few maps showing landlords' boundaries; the picture must usually be constructed from estate plans, sale catalogues, deeds and other documents. For London: Stanford's 'Library Map' (1891) was coloured to show the boundaries of 17 major estates; Lloyd marked estates on the 25-inch Ordnance plans c.1892; and some 35,000 estates over 114 square miles were delineated on the 25-inch Ordnance sheets to create the 'Ground Plan of London,' completed in

1910.[7] Where landownership plans exist, comparison with other maps may reveal relationships between ownership and development; the interrelationship between ownership and other urban factors; and the nature of estate management, development and redevelopment.

Map-makers frequently anticipated the adoption of proposals and marked them as fact on general urban maps, usually failing to remove them subsequently if the scheme was shelved. Some, however, were conscious of the dangers; advertisements for Lancefield's Edinburgh (1851), for example, claimed that 'all improvements in progress are shown, whilst care has been taken to exclude all those intended improvements which may never be erected, and which, in former plans, give such a false impression of extent to the city.' Maps showing suggested and sanctioned 'improvements' were prepared by superimposing information on to existing town plans, as Wyld, Stanford and Smith did many times for London and W. & A.K. Johnston did for Edinburgh, creating often simplified versions of even larger-scale plans. Wyld, for instance, overprinted his large London map (c.1848–9) with sewer levels and also adapted it to show the 'Gas Companies' Districts and Stations' (c.1870). Such maps were often produced specifically to meet official demand, sometimes on an annual basis as were Stanford's of London. General 'improvement' maps, particularly those prepared for official purposes, provide a wealth of useful information in a very clear form. Collectively they can portray urban expansion and development with great accuracy, identifying crucial influences and changes.

95. 'NOTE. This plan is provided merely to assist intending Purchasers in identifying the property for sale and the Vendor does not guarantee its accuracy.' Manuscript notes record buyers and prices paid.

'Plan of part of WESTHEATH HOUSE ESTATE ABBEYWOOD, KENT. For Sale by Auction by THURGOOD & MARTIN at The Wheatley Hotel, Erith ON 25TH APRIL 1907. ROBT J. COOK & HAMMOND. LITH. 2 & 3, TOTHILL ST WESTMINSTER.' (Detail)

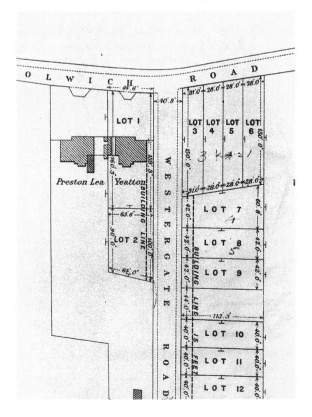

96. Many proposals for urban development were accompanied by detailed plans such as Cooke's plan for the 'erection of an Amphitheatrical Area . . . and upwards of sixty Houses fit for the occupation of opulent Citizens . . .'. The proposal was never carried through. All too often, such plans were copied and proposals could appear as fact on the plans of plagiarizing map-makers, confused and harassed by the scale of urban change but making some attempt to delineate the alterations.

'IMPROVEMENTS PROPOSED BY THE HON. CORPORATION OF LONDON BETWEEN THE ROYAL EXCHANGE AND FINSBURY SQUARE. Engraved by John Cooke, Engraver to the Hon. Board of Admiralty Jany 1802.'

IMPROVEMENTS PROPOSED
BY THE HON. CORPORATION OF LONDON BETWEEN THE ROYAL EXCHANGE AND FINSBURY SQUARE.

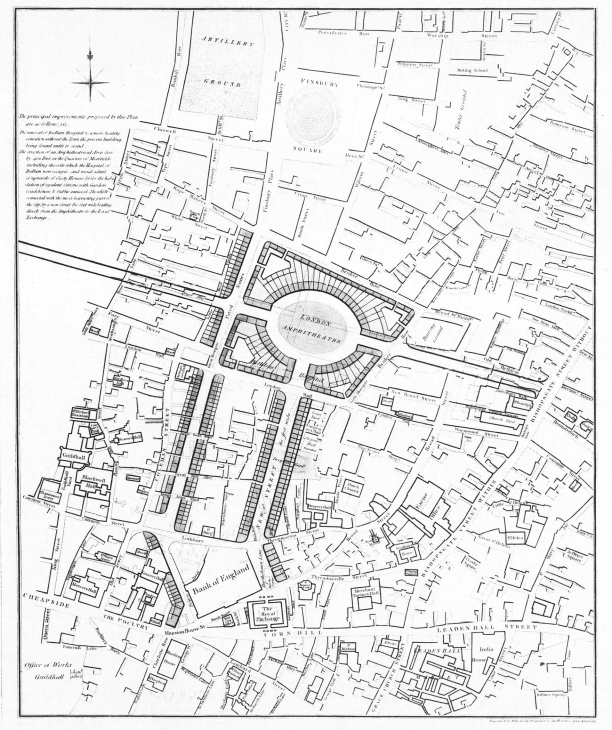

17
Other parish plans

Parishes were mapped as individual units in tithe, estate, and other types of maps. They were also sometimes delineated separately for administrative purposes or to illustrate a parish history. A late-fifteenth-century manuscript, illustrated with a map of the area around Barholm, may well be the earliest English parish history. Particularly, from c.1870–1914 many parish histories were published, often containing maps; some being as large as earlier county histories but others being no more than enlarged church guides.

Petty's 'Down Survey' produced detailed manu-

97. In the eighteenth century Daniel O'Brien produced this copy of Farrand's parish map of 'Doonabrooke & Tannee' prepared in the 'Down Survey'. Detailed parish maps, showing basically only the name, acreage and boundaries of each forfeited townland, were produced to accompany descriptive 'terriers' which listed former proprietors.

'the parrish^s Of Doonabrooke & Tannee in the $\frac{1}{2}$ Barony of Rathdowne by Wm Farrand.' 1655–57. (Detail)

98. The second and last undated revision of Peter Potter's detailed plan, at 26":1m., of St Marylebone was issued c.1832. This first plan of St Marylebone as a separate parish, first published in 1821, shows it shortly before the development of St John's Wood. The map was largely modelled on Horwood's map of London (1792–99) but Potter's house numbering is more complete and accurate, and licensed public houses are marked. In both its revisions, numbers were not generally given to additional houses and, therefore, in most cases where a street is not numbered, it was added on one of the later revisions.

'Plan OF the Parish of SAINT MARY LE BONE, IN the County of MIDDLESEX. Constructed pursuant to an Order of the Vestry, 1st July 1820. . . . . BY PETER POTTER.' c.1832. (Detail)

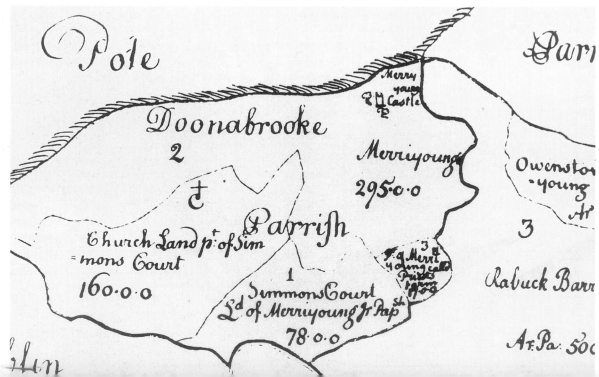

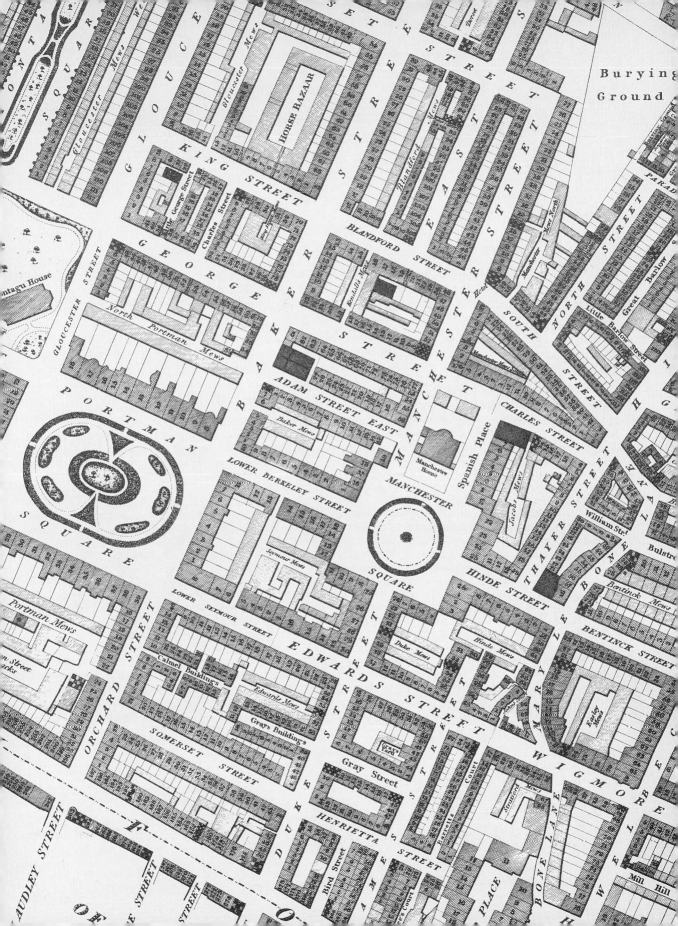

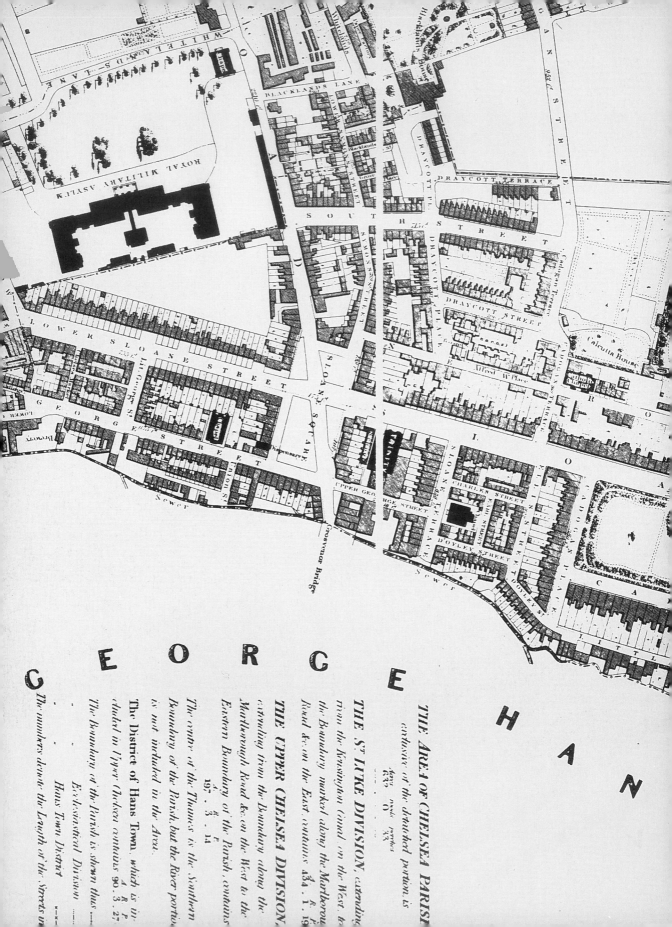

WHITELANDS-LANE

ROYAL MILITARY ASYLUM

BLACKLANDS LANE

Blacklands Lane

DRAYCOTT PL

SLOAN STREET

Blackland

DRAYCOTT TERRACE

DRAYCOTT PLACE

Cadogan Terrace

DRAYCOTT STREET

SOUTH

MOSSOP STREET

STREET

Calcutta House

Alfred Place

Parish Church

LOWER SLOANE STREET

SLOANE SQUARE

LIt George St

GEORGE STREET

Dispensary

LOWER

CHURCH

GEORGE

Brewery

TRINITY

SLOANE TERRACE

CHARLES STREET

CADOGAN

SLOANE TERRACE

C A

UPPER GEORGE STREET

GEORGE STREET

DOYLEY STREET

Sewer

Grosvenor Bridge

Sewer

LITTL

GEORGE HAN

G E O R G E H A N

THE AREA OF CHELSEA PARISH
exclusive of the detached portion, is

acres roods perches
632   0   33

THE St LUKE DIVISION, extending
from the Kensington Canal on the West, to
the Boundary marked along the Marlborough
Road &c. on the East, contains 434 . 1 . 19

THE UPPER CHELSEA DIVISION,
extending from the Boundary along the
Marlborough Road &c. on the West, to the
Eastern Boundary of the Parish, contains
    197 . 3 . 14
                    A.   R.   P.
The centre of the Thames is the Southern
Boundary of the Parish, but the River portion
is not included in the Area.

The District of Hans Town, which is in-
cluded in Upper Chelsea contains 90 . 3 . 27
                                      A.   R.   P.
The Boundary of the Parish is shown thus ———
        .   .   Ecclesiastical Division ———
        .   .   Hans Town District ———
The numbers denote the Length of the Streets in

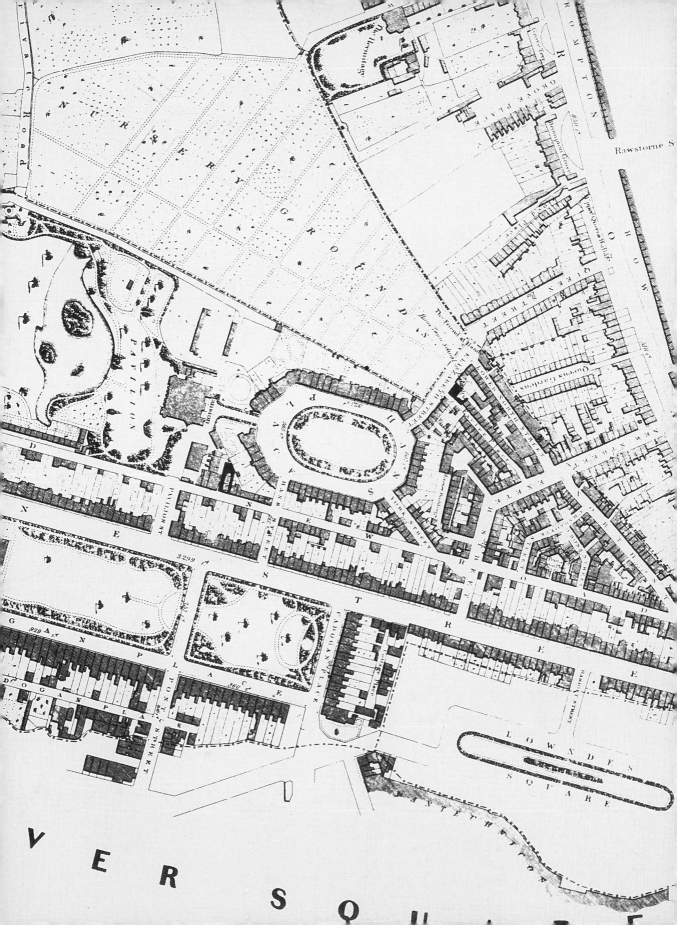

99. (*previous pages*) Sheet 1 of 2 : '. . . . MAP OF CHELSEA, FROM A NEW AND ACTUAL SURVEY, Shewing the Ecclesiastical Divisions of S.^T LUKE AND UPPER CHELSEA, and the DISTRICT OF HANSTOWN and containing that portion of the Parishes of KENSINGTON AND S.^T MARGARET'S WESTMINSTER, lying between the BOUNDARY OF CHELSEA AND THE FULHAM ROAD . . . . LONDON, PUBLISHED BY F.P. THOMPSON, SURVEYOR &c 10 BURY STREET NEAR THE NEW CHURCH CHELSEA. JULY 4.th 1836.' (Detail)

script parish maps at scales usually of 3.2–6.4 inches to the mile, containing information concerning landownership and land quality and accompanied by books of reference. The Surveyor-General's authenticated copies of these parish maps, amongst other items, were destroyed during the Irish Civil War (1922). Fortunately, in some cases copies have survived elsewhere, made for or by bodies such as the Quit-Rent Office, the Ordnance Survey, and possibly the Irish Record Commission, and by local government officials and private individuals.[1] However, as with the parish history, detailed administrative parish maps only came to be produced in quantity during the nineteenth century as the growing complexity of urban areas gave greater importance to the smaller parish unit. For example, in Ireland, from 1867, plans of new parishes were required to be lodged in the council office in Dublin Castle.

Parish vestries frequently needed accurate, large-scale plans in order to administer parish property; control the parish purse; assess and levy rates; supervise constables, overseers, and waywardens; light and pave streets; and so on. Parish plans were commissioned by the vestry or were produced privately by subscription, often accompanied by books of reference. Thus, Horner was commissioned to map Clerkenwell, producing a giant map (1808) at one chain to an inch, covering not only the parish but also property owned by it in other areas in insets. His survey distinguishes each building with its street number

and differentiates parish property, building types, and private estates. Potter's plan of St Marylebone (1820) includes an extensive area not covered by Horwood's London, showing every individual house, licensed premises, outhouses, mews and manufactures. Marylebone was again mapped splendidly by Davies in 1834.

The Parochial Assessments Act (1836) enabled the Poor Law Commissioners to 'order a Survey, with or without a Map or Plan, on such a scale as they may think fit, to be made and taken of the Messuages, Lands and other Heraditaments liable to Poor Rates.' As a result, some four thousand out of 15,000 parishes in England and Wales had been surveyed and revalued by 1843. The standards, style and scale (usually 3 chains to the inch) of Parochial Assessment surveys owe much to Dawson's recommendations for tithe surveys. However, in the event less than half were sealed as 'first class'. At best, as in the surveys of Hardwick and Tress, the Assessment map provides a minutely detailed ground plan of every building in the parish. Generally, surviving Parochial Assessment maps represent the most dependable local maps of the period.

In the nineteenth century most parishes held at least some simple parish plan in church records for administrative purposes. Most parish surveys commissioned by the vestry remained as single-copy working documents in manuscript, but on occasion they were published. Dent's survey of Islington (1805–6), for example, was reduced and published by Starling (1831) 'including all the recent and projected improvements'. The vestry of St Michael le Querne even had their parish plan (1853) lithographed, presenting it framed and glazed to every parishioner.

Select Bibliography

HYDE, R., 'The *Act to regulate parochial assessments* 1836 and its contribution to the mapping of London' (*Guildhall Studs. Lond. Hist.*, 11; 1976)

18
London and other ward plans

The City of London is divided into wards, each of which elects an alderman for life and a varying number of common councilmen for one year. Strype's version (1720) of Stow's London survey (1598) introduced clear and accurate ward plans and henceforth London's wards were mapped periodically.[1] These plans were carefully updated for the edition of 1754–5. In 1756 Maitland issued the second edition of his London survey with ward plans engraved by Cole, but these were mainly copied from Strype's plans. Cole cribbed the illustrations of City churches from *Perspective Views of all the Ancient Churches* (1736) by West & Toms, and made many mistakes, such as misnaming churches and assigning the wrong aldermen to wards. These plans are found without alteration in the 1760 issue of Maitland's survey, in two versions of it by John Entick of 1772 and 1775, and in *English Architecture or the Publick Buildings of London and Westminster* (c.1760). The *London Magazine* published a series of plans from 1766, probably mostly by Thomas Bowen, but these were to a greater or lesser extent copied from Cole's plans. Most were issued updated in 1773 in Noorthouck's *New History of London*. The last set of ward plans published as a series illustrated Thornton's *New and Universal History . . . of London* (1784) and Skinner's *New and Complete History . . . of London* (c.1795), but these were mainly copied from Noorthouck and are of no value as historical evidence. Maps of individual wards appeared throughout the nineteenth century, the most useful numbering houses. Outstanding is the plan of Farringdon Ward Within (1851) by Tress & Chambers.

A great wealth of topographical detail appears on manuscript ward plans prepared for the City of London by Meredith & Angell at 10 feet to the mile.[2] These Secondaries' ward plans of 1853–8 are more detailed than the Ordnance outline map of 1848 and earlier than the detailed Ordnance maps of 1875–8, preceding most Victorian street improvement and showing many of the still unchanged seventeenth-century boundaries.

Although no town had its wards mapped as comprehensively in series of plans as London, many individual wards were mapped, particularly in the nineteenth century, providing more detailed records sometimes than large-scale town and parish plans. The most widespread portrayal of wards resulted from the Municipal Corporations Act (1835) which led to investigation of municipal boundaries in 1837; the report was illustrated by maps precisely locating ward boundaries but disappointing in topographical content, being generally taken from the Ordnance Survey but with 'a great portion of the original surveys purposely omitted'. Ward plans are most useful for their clear depiction of street layout and the naming of streets. However, most ward plans were derived from earlier maps, being rarely based on original, up-to-date survey, and, certainly in the case of London, the majority offer little accurate historical evidence.

---

100. In addition to the large vignettes of the churches of St Stephen and St Michael, Cole's ward plan is decorated with tiny vignettes on the plan face of the Skinner's Hall, the Salter's Hall, the Waterman's Hall, Merchant Taylors School, and other churches and unnamed buildings. Despite Cole's claims that his plans were derived from 'a new survey', the plan was mainly copied from Strype and the vignettes from West & Toms.

'WALBROOK WARD AND DOWGATE WARD with their Divisions into PARISHES according to a NEW SURVEY.' Benjamin Cole, 1755.

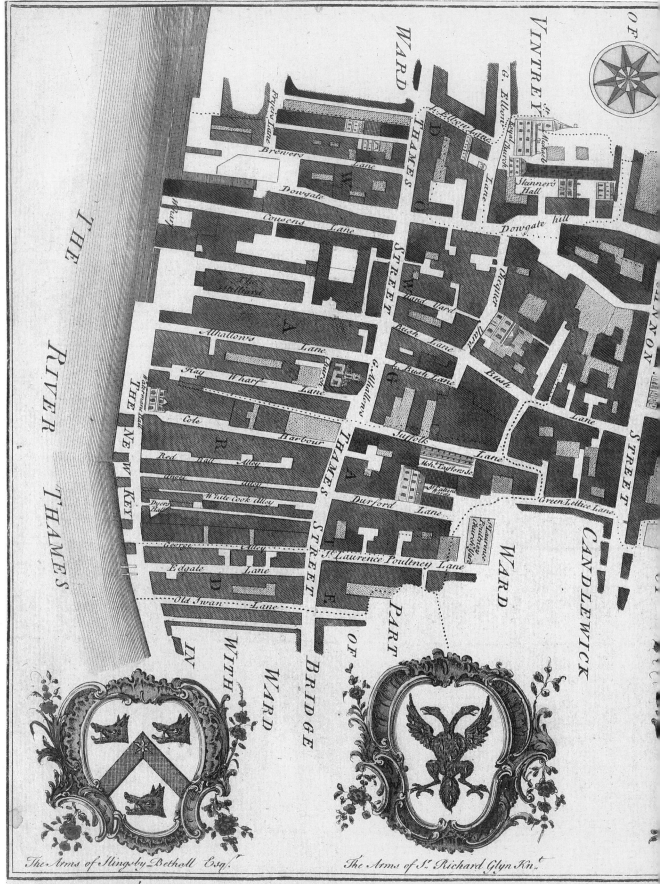

OF

VINTREY

St. Michael
Royal Church

G. Elliott little

J. Elliott little

WARD

Skinner's
Hall

Dowgate hill

Pryers Lane

Brewers

Lane

Dowgate

THAMES

STREET

Cousens Lane

Wharf

Walbrook Ward

Bush Lane

la Bush Lane

Bush Lane

CANNON

Dowgate

Walbrook Ward

THE

RIVER

THAMES

Allhallow's

Lane

Hay Wharf

Church
Lane

G. Allhallows
Lane

STREET

Suffolk

Lane

Green Lettice Lane

Mch. Taylors Sc.

St. Laurence
Church yd.

CANDLEWICK

Cole

Harbour

Red Lion Alley

Water man Hall

The New Key

Dyers Hall

White Cook Alley

George Alley

Edgate Lane

Old Swan Lane

Durford Lane

St. Laurence
Poultney
Church Yard

THAMES

STREET

Jo. Laurence Poultney Lane

WARD

PART

OF

BRIDGE

WARD

WITH

IN

This Plate is most humbly Inscrib'd to Slingsby Bethell Esqr. Lord Mayor of

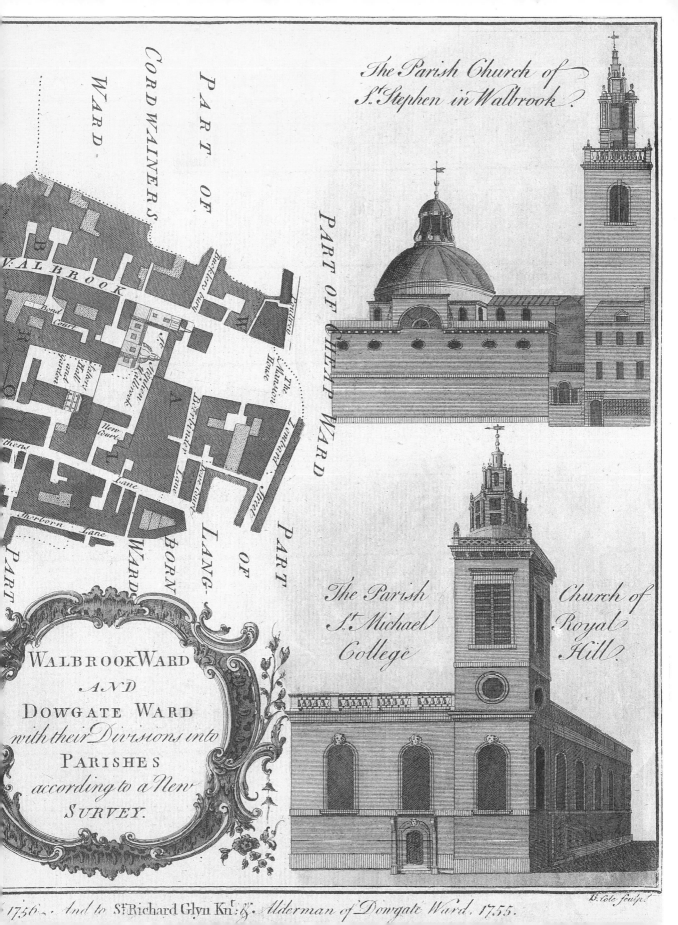

The Parish Church of
St. Stephen in Walbrook.

PART OF CHEAP WARD

PART OF CORDWAINERS WARD.

WARD.

WALBROOK

Bond Court

Salters Hall and garden

St Stephan Walbrook

New Court

Bucklers bury

Lombard Street

The Mansion House

Bearbinder Lane

PART OF LANG-BORN WARD

PART OF

St Swithens

Sherborn Lane

PART

The Parish   Church of
St. Michael   Royal
College   Hill.

WALBROOK WARD
AND
DOWGATE WARD
with their Divisions into
PARISHES
according to a New
SURVEY.

1756. And to Sr. Richard Glyn Knt. & Alderman of Dowgate Ward. 1755.

B. Cole sculpt.

19

Industrial maps

Industrial sites were portrayed at large scales. Darby's famous Coalbrookdale iron works, for instance, was mapped (1753), delineating forges, furnaces, blacksmiths' shops, moulding and charcoal houses, and a stamper mill. In 1817 Innes recorded industrial installations along the Dee; and in 1853 Craig drew a very detailed plan of the Carse Bridge distillery. Industrial sites were also delineated in detail in sale plans.

Maps were designed specifically to show widespread industrial features, and industrial information was recorded in topographical maps generally. Estate maps often show manufacturing sites scattered over an industrial but still rural countryside, failing only to represent 'cottage' production. They illuminate a micro-pattern of early industrial activity which does not emerge even on large-scale county maps. A map of Loughor Parish (1729), for example, reveals not only existing coal pits with their coal roads but also old workings, and ruined roads and engines no longer used.

Large-scale county map-makers portrayed a detailed industrial landscape, revealing for a wider area the essentially rural nature of industry. Tuke, for example, emphasized the low degree of urbanization in the Yorkshire woollen-producing area (1787). The cartographer's perceptions and interests determined the extent of industrial portrayal and no map-maker achieved comprehensive coverage. Burdett's treatment of Cheshire's industrial countryside, for instance, is of mixed quality, with some industries well covered but others, such as silk production, partly or fully ignored. Similarly, Greenwood's industrial representation is patchy and sporadic, showing, for example, no evidence of systematic survey in Worcestershire. Other map-makers were less reliable; Hennet, for instance, made no serious attempt to map Lancashire's industry despite on occasion being more accurate than Greenwood; and Bowen & Kitchin showed

few industrial features in the *Large English Atlas*. Even when industrial features are shown it is rarely clear exactly what the conventional signs mean, as in the case of the depiction of mills on Thomson's Scottish county maps.

Inevitably, county cartographers selected features from the increasingly complex industrial picture. Inevitably, therefore, their records disagree. Windmills were frequently carefully recorded because of their importance in many triangulations. Generally, both wind and water mills received greater attention than most other industry, with use often stated; Rocque, for example, specified use for about half Surrey's watermills (*c*.1768). However, even for well-recorded features, all county maps are incomplete and comparison shows that each indicates sites not found on others. Maps of Cheshire, for instance, by Burdett (1777), Greenwood (1819), Swire & Hutchings (1830), and Bryant (1831) show between them 353 watermill sites, but only 66 appear on all four. Even accounting for industrialization, the intermittent nature of much mill work, inevitable changes of function, and site abandonment, clearly no Cheshire cartographer prepared anything like a full record.

---

101. Apart from roads, the sale plan of Marshall's Mills's estate shows only the 12 lots for sale at 5':1m. A reference table gives the area of each lot, but a manuscript addition notes that 'As these figures are compiled from old surveys accuracy of the same cannot be guaranteed.' The mill, engine house, offices, weaving shed, and stables are located, as are St John's Church, schools, Bethel Chapel, and the Mechanics Institute. Back-to-back housing is clearly defined in Brunswick Street and Back Derwent Street.

'PLAN OF MILLS, COTTAGES, BUILDING-LAND &c. AT HOLBECK, LEEDS THE PROPERTY OF MESS[RS] MARSHALL. FOR SALE.' 'J.W. CLARKE GISBRO.' 1893

PLAN OF
MILLS, COTTAGES, BUILDING-LAND &c. AT HOLBECK, LEEDS THE PROPERTY OF MESS.RS MARSHALL.

FOR SALE.

RIVER AIRE

CANAL

LOT 12
2467 Sq Yds

LOT 11
16.923 Sq Yds

SOLD

WATER LANE

LOT 10
1200 Sq Yds

LOT 9
4635 Sq Yds

LOT 7
10.555 Sq Yds

LOT 8

LOT 6

UNION PLACE

OFFICE

BOILERS

LOT 5
1790 Sq Yds

STABLES

ENGINE HOUSE

LOT 3
17.688 Sq Yds

MILL

LOT 4
9275 Sq Yds

LOT 2

WEAVING SHED

LOT 1
4334 Sq Yds

REFERENCE

LOT		Sq. Yds.
1		4334
2		753
3		17688
4		9275
5		1790
6		854
7		10555
8		287
9		4635
10		1200
11		16923
12		2467
Total Sq. Yds.		70.791

As these figures are
compiled from old sur-
accuracy of the sa
cannot be guarante

BRUNSWICK ST
BACK DERWENT ST
MARSHALL STREET

L & N W Ry
MIDLAND Ry

SWEET STREET WEST

St. JOHN's CHURCH

SCHOOLS   MECHANICS INSTITUTE   BETHEL CHAPEL

Scale 5 Ft. to 1 Mile 1856

J W CLARKE GISBRO

Industry is more adequately delineated on large-scale town plans. It was physically impossible for county cartographers to cram the wide variety of industry into their crowded townscapes, but on large-scale town plans individual factory and workshop use could be specified and even occupiers named. Such a relatively crude plan as 'Agas's' London can show tenter grounds for cloth drying and stretching. Similarly, London's 'copperplate' map (*c*.1553–59) depicts post-mills on rubbish tips in Finsbury Fields; a sack-hoist indicating their use for grinding corn, not for pumping water from surrounding marsh as sometimes assumed. The third important early London plan, by Braun & Hogenberg (1572), locates 'Ye Goounefowuders' a gun foundry also depicted by 'Agas' as a small cannon.

Industrial data is also given in production figures tabulated around such maps as Corbridge's Norwich (1727), and in notes on resources, such as those on timber and stone on a map of Belfast Lough (*c*.1570).[1] Industrial information on any type of map is probably never truly comprehensive, but, nevertheless, map evidence may be the sole record of an industrial activity; may provide the only means of tracing the changing function of power sites; and may, at least, establish the general industrial pattern.

20
Themes and thematic maps

Thematic maps concentrate on one or more themes, locating them on a topographical base using special signs or methods of statistical generalization to depict phenomena. Such physical, economic, political and social mapping developed from the seventeenth century, becoming particularly common in the nineteenth when printed colour was used to good effect. Good base maps, such as Ordnance sheets, were used to locate many themes. Stanford's map of the Metropolitan Board of Works' area (c.1865), for example, was exploited to illustrate election results, boundaries of gas company districts, administrative boundaries, and other topics; being so employed at least 47 times in all. Although thematic information is usually available to the historian elsewhere, thematic maps summarise it at a glance, presenting areal distributions in an easily comprehensible form.

As well as recording rock strata and land formation, geological and associated maps may provide landscape information for a particular date perhaps not found elsewhere. Packe's chart of 'East-Kent' (1743), for example, adds to its portrayal of valley systems: 'churches; city of Canterbury; towns, villages, streets, castles, camps, ruins . . . houses of noblemen and gentlemen with many others of lesser note . . . Downs, Parks, Groves, Tolls and Rows of Trees.'[1]

For mining districts, mineralogical maps may be the only means of tracing old mines and deposits exhausted or no longer exploited. Tudor mining development gave rise to disputes over boundaries of commons under which mineral rights were sought. Maps, such as those of the manors of Cowpen (1598) and Benwell (1637), were prepared to illustrate such disagreements. Maps continued to document disputes between mine-owners in later centuries, when plans were also produced recording underground workings in detail. Similar plans show quarries, describing the rock and

delineating the strata in section. Mineral deposits and mining activities sometimes also appear on estate plans.

Distribution of mineral resources and mining activity was mapped with increasing frequency as its economic importance grew. Lead and copper mine location was plotted on a simple outline map of south-west England and south Wales c.1570, possibly by Lord Burghley himself. Gibson added collieries and waggonways, with depths and lengths respectively, to topographical detail copied from Armstrong to create a map (1788) of collieries on the Tyne and Wear, presenting a different picture of pit distribution from Armstrong by omitting many pits marked on the earlier map, perhaps knowing them to be closed or incorrect, and by including two important mining areas missed. Gibson named the collieries 'by the Coals as they are Certified and sold at London Market'. Later, a 'Series of Plans of the Great Northern Coalfield' was produced by Bell 1843–61, and Archer mapped production of 'Coals for Gas Making Purposes' (c.1890) in Durham.

Before the Ordnance Survey, mining and quarrying were most comprehensively recorded by large-scale county map-makers, although even they provided only sporadic evidence of activity. Small, scattered, transient pits were easily overlooked, particularly in upland areas. The extent of mining mapping and reliability of delineation depended on the interests and priorities of individual cartographers, most of whom did not attempt to offer comprehensive coverage. Even when they marked pits, were they recording individual pits or shafts; or collieries comprising several shafts; or merely indicating active coalfield areas? The latter seems generally the case, making it impossible to estimate numbers of active collieries from large-scale county maps; Burdett's nine mines for Cheshire in the 1770s and Yates's some 150 for

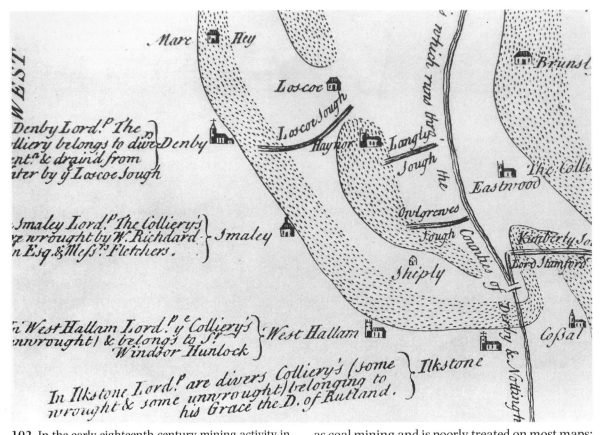

On the map, the following place-names and annotations appear:

Mare Hey

Loscoe

Loscoe Sough

WEST

Denby Lord.P The
lliery belongs to divers Denby
nt.s & drain'd from
ter by y Loscoe Sough

Haynor

Langly
Sough

Brunsl

The Colli

Eastwood

Smaley Lord.P The Colliery's
e wrought by W. Richdard
n Esq & Mess.rs Fletchers. } Smaley

Owlgreaves
Sough

Counties of Derby & Nottingh

Kimberty So
Lord Stamford

Shiply

West Hallam Lord.P y.e Colliery's
unwrought) & belongs to S.r
Windsor Hunlock } West Hallam

Cossal

In Ilkstone Lord.P are divers Colliery's (some
wrought & some unwrought) belonging to
his Grace the D. of Rutland. } Ilkstone

102. In the early eighteenth century mining activity in the Midlands was intensifying rapidly to meet growing demand, increasing the number of legal disputes between colliery owners. Drainage of seams caused the flooding of adjoining pits and Parliament was petitioned to prevent 'the wilful and malicious Destruction of COLLIERIES and COAL-WORKS.' The drainers were accused of intending 'to enhance the Price of Coals, and procure to themselves a Monopoly'. A counter-petition, accompanied by this plan, presented the case for the accused.

'A PLAN of several Veins of Coal within y.e Counties of Derby & Nottingham, also of several Soughs made by the late John Fletcher Esq.r his Son.s & Partner.s to unwater several Parts of the said Veins of Coal; as Survey'd in Jan.ry 1739. by Philip Hutchinson.' 1739. (Detail)

Lancashire in 1774 are underrepresentations of the true scale of activity. Greenwood's maps at least name some coal workings. Even the 6-inch Ordnance sheets fail to distinguish between individual shafts and collieries. The Survey generally never attempted to differentiate coal workings by their often distinctive names. Other mining and quarrying activity was rarely recorded in as much detail

as coal mining and is poorly treated on most maps; Burdett's Cheshire, for example, shows only three sites for salt production at a time when it was easily the most important industry in the county's central area.

Soil maps are relevant to the history of agricultural land use and road surfacing. Some of the county agricultural reports sponsored by the newly-formed Board of Agriculture from 1793 contain maps which use colours to indicate soil texture and fertility.[2] These crude maps, at 4–6 miles to the inch, were designed to show regional contrasts of soil and land use, but they also illuminate mineral location, use of regional names, and much else. The best provide broad land-use information: Davis's Wiltshire (1794), for instance, boldly defines water-meadows, arable, pasture, woods, and parks; and Middleton's Middlesex (1798) suggests the location and extent of market gardening around London using colours to differentiate arable, pasture and nursery grounds. However, despite updating for later issues, no great reliance should be placed on them. Middleton, for instance, failed to show market gardens and orchards between Brentford and Twickenham.

The principal advantage of land-use portrayal on maps is that the location of the data is normally precisely defined. Many maps record land use either directly or indirectly but, unfortunately, few maps concentrate solely on its depiction. At best, it was usually only possible to map broad usage categories rather than individual crops, tree species, and so on. The most detailed land-use map of an extensive area is Milne's 2-inch map of the London area (1800), which covers some 260 square miles and distinguishes 17 different land-use types by colours and key letters for each land parcel to show the state of cultivation.[3] Milne's

---

103. Rocque's Surrey distinguishes 'woods, parks, wildernesses, heaths or commons, marshes, grass, and ploughland' at the large scale of 2″: 1m.

'A TOPOGRAPHICAL MAP OF THE COUNTY OF SURREY, In which is Expressed all the ROADS, LANES, CHURCHES, NOBLEMEN and GENTLEMEN's SEATS, &c. &c. the Principal Observations, By the Late JOHN ROCQUE, Topographer to His MAJESTY, Compleated and Engrav'd by Peter Andrews.' *c.*1768. (Detail)

map adds substantially to knowledge of the land-use pattern in a major farming region just before it was engulfed by urban expansion, showing not only substantial areas of inner London still devoted to farming but also surrounding lands producing hay for the city's horses and market gardens and orchards located on the fertile Thames' banks.[4]

Land use, of course, appears incidentally on many regional maps. Cartographers of Elizabethan Ireland, for instance, delineated woods and bogs because of their importance as rebel hiding-places and obstacles to troop movements. Woodland and timber resources were often mapped carefully due to their significance for shipbuilding and iron smelting. Land use is, obviously, indicated in detail on many estate plans and tithe maps; Blagrave's 'Forest and Manor of Feckenham' (1591), for instance, portrays woodland, meadow, pasture, and 'corn ground' of varying qualities. Annotations on estate maps frequently detail current land use. In the late eighteenth century estate surveyors such as Rocque and Scalé developed representation of land use by conventional signs, undoubtedly

influencing particularly Irish map-makers such as Neville, who adopted their techniques.

Rocque's elevation from estate surveyor and *dessinateur de jardins* to county map-maker provided the opportunity to pioneer land-use representation on large-scale maps, using contemporary continental techniques. No longer would only woodland, parks and commons be marked on most maps. Rocque depicted land use on his large-scale maps by appropriate signs and shading in greater detail than ever before, offering a reliable, but not highly accurate, record. Middlesex (1754), for example, has been judged 'an excellent representation of the surface utilization'.[5]

Although later map-makers, such as Davis and Andrews, Dury & Herbert, followed Rocque's pioneering work, land-use treatment on large-scale county maps is patchy. Yates's Lancashire, for example, shows only boundaries between woodland and open country, and the fringes of moss and moorland appear to be imprecise; however, in fairness, Yates was the first to record the extent of mossland and cultivation limits in Lancashire even generally, providing a base for comparisons of the shrinking mossland and fluctuating moorland edge with later maps. Some map-makers, however, ignored land use; Burdett, for instance, did not show Cheshire's field boundaries and agricultural land use and represented woodland unsatisfactorily. Thus, he failed to portray the essentially agrarian character of a well-wooded county. In contrast, though, he did record many small areas of waste, common, green and heath destined to be lost in poorly- or un-documented enclosure. Forrest was precise in delineating Lanarkshire's moss and woodland. His map (1816) illuminates the extent of enclosure, yet gives little or no information on the distribution of arable and pasture. Greenwood mapped the general distribution of heath, common, and woodland adequately (although not naming individual woods), but failed to differentiate arable and pasture, or even to show cultivated land. Consequently, for example, he lost two of Worcestershire's most distinctive and important landscape features by not showing the extent of orchards and gardens surrounding rural dwelling on his large-scale county map (1822). Such detail as the naming of individual woods, which provides a clue to the type and use of woodland, was mapped and became generally available only with the coming of the Ordnance Survey.

Sample checks of large-scale county maps suggest that their broad land-use patterns are substantially correct. They pinpoint the main areas of change. In offering a broad picture of usage, they illuminate land-use distribution for cultivation, pasture, woods, parks and commons, and the extent of enclosure and the survival of open fields. Greenwood's Worcestershire, for instance, offers a fairly accurate representation of the distribution and boundaries of woodlands, heaths, commons and parks – difficult to reconstruct from other documents from a time of woodland clearance and waste reclamation. From the most comprehensive large-scale county maps it is possible to calculate areas devoted to various types of use. Large-scale county maps are often the only land-use information source in the absence of other cartographical, statistical or documentary evidence, although they must always be treated with caution when drawing purely local conclusions.

The manuscript drawings made for the first edition Ordnance 1-inch maps offer land-use evidence of variable quality. Those surveyed at 6 inches to the mile show land use in colour and, with the exception of arable and grassland, by conventional signs. Drawings at 3 inches to the mile are in more varied style, usually differentiating arable land and grassland by colour or shading. Most drawings are at the 2-inch scale and there is great variation between them in land use shown. Some record little more than the printed 1-inch maps. Although the 1-inch maps offer more land-use information than other contemporary map series, they are difficult to interpret for any large area, because of the time taken to survey them. On the manuscript drawings for the Irish 6-inch maps, land use is shown by conventional signs for gardens, woodland, bog and mountain.

In 1855–1918 the Ordnance Survey conducted what was essentially a national land-use survey as an integral part of its cadastral mapping. Although emphasis was placed on non-cultivated land, arable and permanent pasture were consistently recorded and no less than 26 either single or combined land-use types were specified for identification in the field. The Ordnance aimed to show as much vegetation as a scale would allow. Pre-1881 6-inch maps show considerable land-use detail, including market gardens and orchards, but fail to divide cultivated land into arable and grassland. Later maps, reduced photographically from the 25-inch series, are less informative, since it was necessary to simplify the larger-scale plans to allow legible reduction. Generally, however, large-scale

Ordnance maps offer much useful land-use information, particularly for areas surveyed to high standards at critical periods of change.

Nineteenth-century waste reclamation gave particular significance to the boundary line between cultivated and non-cultivated land, making it a primary concern which the Ordnance Survey systematically surveyed and carefully recorded. Ordnance maps have been used to identify areas of former tillage now covered by rough pasture in Scotland and areas reclaimed from the waste in Ireland.[7]

Despite the quality of the Ordnance's land-use treatment, there are problems of interpretation. It is not always clear what is shown and how it was selected. Specification for inclusion probably changed as the Survey's expenditure was increasingly questioned, demanding reduced vegetation detail. There was a tendency for woodland in particular, and other types of vegetation and land use to a lesser extent, to be simplified. The second and third editions of the 25-inch sheets show much less detail than the first. Further problems stem from the unification of different uses under one sign, when they had previously been treated separately. In 1897, for example, rough pasture, rough heathy pasture and bog were subsumed in a single sign for rough pasture. Similarly, replacement of hand-drawn and hand-engraved signs by standardized stamped signs lost minor variation and individual character. Changes in punch design also suggest vegetation changes which never occurred. Generally, as for the 1-inch maps, large-scale Ordnance maps were prepared over too long a period and lacking supporting documentation for effective comparison.

In addition to the land use shown on the 25-inch maps, from 1855 a series of pamphlets recorded the types of land use identified during cadastral mapping and revision.[8] These separate Parish Area Books (called Books of Reference after 1872) were published for each parish, identifying parcel numbers on the 25-inch plans, giving their acreages, and noting the state of cultivation. From sometime in 1880 land descriptions were omitted, although parcel areas were still listed. The Books were entirely discontinued in 1888 before national coverage at the 25-inch scale had been completed. However, by *c.*1880 land-use data for several thousand parishes had appeared, covering about a quarter of England and Wales, mainly in southeast England and parts of lowland Scotland. In Ireland only the parishes in County Dublin were covered by Books of Reference. Thus, for many parishes land-use distribution at a key stage in agricultural development can be reconstructed using the reference numbers and notes in the Books.[9]

Comparison of land-use data from the Books and maps is problematical because the information covers a lengthy period during which the maps were surveyed slowly by the Ordnance. It is not clear what the land-use terms used exactly mean; after 1872 when the 25-inch sheets were filled to the sheet edges the Books ceased to collate precisely with the new plan format; it was difficult to revise Books in line with map revisions; and the quality of the information is unknown. In most cases the Ordnance's material should be reliable but, certainly, in one instance at least data from adjacent parishes does not match up in the Books because the same types of land use were assigned to different categories by different examiners.[10]

Accurate field and farm portrayal is a crucial factor in the interpretation of local land use. In general, only pre-enclosure field boundaries on estate maps and on enclosure maps showing existing enclosures can be considered at all reliable, and even then not always. An elaborate picture-map of the manor of Sherborne (1569–74), for example, shows a detailed landscape but its field boundaries are imaginary.[11] In contrast, Rocque and Scalé not only depicted boundaries accurately but even named fields and distinguished types of fencing on the best of their Irish estate plans. Even large-scale cartographers of high repute created imaginary field landscapes to fill in areas between roads. Rocque's Surrey (*c.*1768) and Armagh (1760) field boundaries are 'diagrammatic';[12] Andrews & Dury's Hertfordshire (1766) boundaries show a much simpler pattern than do the 6-inch Ordnance sheets (1872–84), although fields would probably have become larger rather than smaller in the interim; and Davis's Oxfordshire (1797) is no more reliable.[13] Of the few large-scale maps which depict field boundaries, only Yeakell & Gardner's Sussex (1778–83) was prepared from a survey of every enclosure. A few regional maps portray field boundaries, such as Richardson, King & Driver's 4 inch-to-the-mile map of the New Forest (1789) which was reduced from their magnificent 8-inch manuscript survey (1787) made for the Commissioners for Woods and Forests and now preserved in the Public Record Office. Field shapes on Milne's London land-use map correspond closely with those shown on the Ordnance's original 2-

inch drawings. However, it seems likely that boundaries on most of the 2-inch drawings are either incomplete or diagrammatic. Drawings at 3 and 6 inches are more accurate.[14] Comparison of the manuscript drawings with farm surveys and other maps for Wales shows that the field boundaries were interpolated and that no reliance can be placed on them. Field boundaries were not at first marked on the fair drawings for the Irish 6-inch maps, but they were shown after 1835 and for the southern half of the country the field pattern on the plans seems complete. Tithe surveys, of course, show field boundaries for areas covered for the period 1836–c.1850. Notwithstanding such provision for limited areas, in general fields were only mapped accurately and comprehensively for the whole country by the Ordnance's 6-inch sheets. Even then, interpretation of farm boundaries can still be ambiguous on tithe and large-scale Ordnance maps, for there is usually nothing to indicate their nature; the problem is sometimes reduced by the presence of tree signs along the boundary on the 6-inch sheets and on some tithe maps. Since Ordnance sheets are more accurate than virtually all predecessors, field shapes, sizes, and positions rarely correspond with those shown on earlier maps. Fields are usually named on estate plans and most comprehensively on tithe maps, but seldom on enclosure plans. In addition to their obvious uses, field names aid the identification of archaeological sites and earthworks.[15]

The country house and park was one of the most important elements of the rural landscape. It was given special emphasis by map-makers from the sixteenth century onwards, initially being indicated by the traditional but outdated sign of an area surrounded by a paling fence. Many parks subsequently disappeared as they were divided between freeholders or consolidated into single farms and the map may represent the only evidence of existence; Flitteris Park on the borders of Rutland and Leicestershire, for example, appears on Saxton's county map but has long since been disparked. In Ireland demesnes and private parks were more fully mapped than any other kind of rural land use, and deerpark walls appear on maps such as those of the 'Down Survey' and early county maps which show no ordinary fences. From the early eighteenth century cartographers regularly named landowners on their maps. As the century progressed, more and more attention was paid to the country house and estate. Rocque's special interest in parks and gardens caused him to

delineate them in great detail on his county maps, often to the extent of incorporating simplified versions of his elaborate plans of formal gardens. Other map-makers, such as Greenwood, Bryant, Cary, Bowles and Dury, had more mercenary motives for detailed delineation, using it to secure patronage and a ready market. In contrast, others paid scant attention to parks; Burdett, for example, indicated only approximate extent. Since map-makers were anxious not to offend important potential customers, it is safe to assume that country seats were generally comprehensively and correctly mapped and that none were given prominence at the expense of others.

Different interpretations of land use by surveyors bedevils analysis of usage from a series of maps of one area or any comparison of regions through maps of the same period. In any case, large-scale county maps were rarely surveyed at even roughly the same time. Surveyors regarded the importance of land-use representation differently. Since it was often incidental to a map's main purpose, they frequently portrayed it in highly conventionalized form with little care for exact delineation. Changes revealed by comparison may be nothing more than differing interpretations. These are particularly common where uses slid imperceptibly into each other and it was difficult to locate the division, or where use was commonly classified in different categories in different areas.

Similarly, varying accuracy of land-use location can suggest changes over time which never occurred. This is particularly troublesome when comparing earlier maps with the more accurate Ordnance sheets. Thus, it is difficult to establish whether specific changes actually occurred, let alone when. Further complications arise from the habit of incorporating material from earlier surveys into maps.

However, despite the difficulties and dangers, cartographic data is commonly used to reconstruct past land use. The chief contemporary sources for land-utilization study in Lanarkshire in the late eighteenth century, for example, have been identified as the large-scale maps of Ross (1773) and Forrest (1816) and the soil map accompanying Naismith's report to the Board of Agriculture.[16]

As statistics emerged as a separate technique and body of thought in the early nineteenth century, so statistical maps were developed. Maps were devised to represent population density, traffic flow, freight density, education, housing standards, livestock values, crime and so on, by new and highly successful graphical presentation techniques such as flow lines, aquatint shading, and graduated circles.[17] From the 1850s economic maps were prepared to illustrate the production and movement of goods and to pinpoint industrial location. Petermann's map of 1851 is considered to be the first map exclusively concerned with marking industrial concentrations by point symbols, thus presenting a useful summary of industrial development.

Boundaries have always been an important concern of map-makers; as early as 1531–33, for instance, south-west Fylde was mapped as evidence in a boundary dispute.[18] However, in preparing estate maps as evidence in boundary disagreements, the surveyor was likely to favour his client's side of the argument. More reliable are boundary maps prepared for official purposes, particularly from the nineteenth century, when boundaries were increasingly superimposed on to accurate base maps. Maps defining proposals for new constituencies and of finalized boundaries accompanied Parliamentary reform in the early 1830s, produced under Dawson's supervision based on the Ordnance Survey, generally at scales of 1–6 inches to the mile. Unofficial versions were published by Samuel Lewis (1840), showing not only the old and new boundaries but also areas of dense housing, bridges, workhouses, churches, rectories and so on. Further enquiry into municipal boundaries in 1837 produced maps delineating ward boundaries. Irish Parliamentary and municipal boroughs were mapped respectively in 1832 and 1837, under Larcom's supervision, to meet requests for clarification of the new arrangements from other government departments. Further maps of altered Parliamentary boundaries accompanied reports of the Boundary Commissions of 1867, 1885 and 1888; boundaries and other information such as polling places being superimposed on to Ordnance maps.[19] Many local authorities commissioned their own boundary reports. A report investigating Belfast's 'municipal affairs' (1859), for instance, contains maps and plans including one showing 'the municipal boundary of the borough before its extension of 1853; after its extension; the boundary of the lighted and watched districts and the boundary of water commissioners jurisdiction'. As local government grew, more complex administrative maps were produced by overprinting reliable base maps; Stanford's London and Johnston's Edinburgh maps, for example, were overprinted to show many

different boundaries. The Ordnance Survey sometimes produced special printings of its sheets showing changes in local government boundaries.

Generally, boundaries were delineated in a fairly cavalier fashion on all maps except estate, plantation, and enclosure plans before the appearance of large-scale county maps, and, as a rule, they should not be trusted. Gascoyne (1700) and Martyn (1748) showed parish boundaries rather crudely on their maps of Cornwall, and their example was followed by Rocque and others, but only Greenwood mapped them for most of the country in his county maps. Greenwood also portrayed many other boundaries, including those of detached areas, some of which were not delineated again until the Ordnance's 6-inch survey. However, despite Greenwood's impressive achievement, which must have been based on a ground survey and assiduous collection of local information, many errors are immediately apparent, and his maps cannot be considered reliable for parish or other boundaries. Others were even less reliable; Bryant, for example, over-generalized many boundaries and omitted most detached areas. On many later nineteenth-century maps parish boundaries are rarely distinguished from those of townships and smaller parish sub-divisions. In Ireland parishes were delineated by the 'Down Survey' and subsequently on many county maps of the eighteenth and nineteenth centuries. Irish boundaries tended to be recorded carefully and some surveyors were brave enough not to resort to conjecture in cases of doubt. Elsewhere, parish boundaries were first marked on tithe maps. A special printing of current revisions of the 'Old Series' Ordnance sheets known as the 'Index to the Tithe Survey' (*c*.1851) delineates and names parishes covered by tithe surveys by superimposing them on the Survey's topographical detail. Apart from the tithe plans themselves, these index maps are often the first reliable printed depiction of parish boundaries and are particularly useful for showing detached areas. For Ireland, the county index maps to the 6-inch sheets are the earliest medium-scale record of the names and boundaries of civil parishes. Large-scale town plans can show a profusion of boundaries. Some publishers even produced sets of administrative maps such as 'Philips' "Citizen" Series of MUNICIPAL MAPS . . . OF LONDON Showing the Divisions of the various Governing Bodies'.

Ordnance Survey maps offer the most reliable administrative representation. However, boundaries recorded varied according to current policy. The Irish Survey, for example, decided to show demesnes by distinctive shading in 1834 after three counties had already been published. Subsequently, demesnes were generally defined on the owner's authority. They are most clearly represented on the county indexes to the 6-inch sheets. Similarly, the Irish Survey decided to add municipal boundaries to its 6-inch maps in 1868 and to remove initial letters showing the exact position of townland boundaries from its 25-inch sheets in 1899. Specifications of boundaries to be shown on Ordnance sheets were altered at various dates. For England and Wales, for example, ecclesiastical parishes, hundreds and wapentakes were discontinued in 1879 and were replaced by civil parishes; and in 1887 urban district boundaries were added, as were those of poor law unions in 1888 and rural districts in 1899.

The Ordnance also produced maps concentrating especially on boundary delineation. The outline index map showing the sheet numbers of the 6-inch series of Great Britain formed the basis for subsequent 'Administrative Diagrams' at $\frac{1}{4}$–$\frac{1}{2}$ inch to the mile, showing various boundaries. In the late 1880s county diagrams began to appear at the quarter-inch scale; in 1885 new parliamentary divisions were illustrated; in 1888 civil parish boundaries and the limits of sanitary districts; and new series appeared throughout as boundary revision occurred showing such administrative units as petty sessional divisions. By 1900 a series of county administrative diagrams at the $\frac{1}{2}$-inch scale were also being produced showing such units as poor law unions, rural and urban districts, sanitary districts, boroughs and civil parishes.

Amongst the earliest Irish Survey maps were manuscript boundary sketches prepared in 1826–41, not only by Ordnance surveyors but also by a separate boundary department. These latter sketches depict county, barony, parish and townland boundaries, with an indication of the boundary's physical character, often set within its local topography showing streams, roads, buildings, prehistoric earthworks, and even minor landmarks such as stones, trees and fence intersections. Occupiers' names are recorded for many houses and some large residences are shown in perspective rather than in plan. Proposed alterations to these boundaries from 1854 were marked in colour on a set of 6-inch maps by the Valuation Office. The index diagrams for the Irish 25-inch sheets, which show the boundaries of townlands,

baronies, rural and urban districts, and county boroughs are the clearest portrayal of the ancient land divisions of Ireland, bringing out their many variations in size, form and nomenclature. The Irish Survey mapped poor law unions in 1881, and rural and urban districts in 1899.

Religious boundaries were frequently specially mapped. For instance, maps accompanied Orders-in-Council for the creation and alteration of ecclesiastical parish boundaries. James Backhouse mapped boundaries of meetings of the Society of Friends, their meeting days and places, and routes and distances between meetings in northern England (1773). The distribution of religions was also recorded. The religious state of England, for example, was mapped by Hume (1860) and the biased *Royal Standard* cartographically exposed London's 'Romish establishments' and 'public institutions' infiltrated by 'Romish priests' (1871). The Puritan Norden was equally biased in his promotion of chapels-of-ease and suppression of 'bishop's sees' on all but one of his county maps. In contrast, Arkell published an objective survey of the extent of Jewish settlement in east London, showing the proportions of Jews and Gentiles (1899).[20]

Social commentators sought to establish links between social conditions and religion, as, indeed, they did with other themes such as drink and disease. The 1841 Irish Census pioneered social mapping with maps recording classes of housing and literacy by differential shading, and in a plan of Dublin coloured to differentiate classes of residential and shopping districts. Chadwick's report on sanitary conditions (1842) was illustrated by maps of Bethnal Green and Leeds, showing classes of housing and distribution of disease incidence. In 1858 Hume recorded Liverpool's levels of poverty, crime and immorality in relation to the location of churches, chapels, and schools. In 1889 Booth published the first volume of what was to be the finest nineteenth-century social survey, eventually portraying London poverty in minute detail. His poverty map of East London in Volume 1 is a direct descendant of the Dublin sanitary map, classifying streets by colours according to class. Volume 2 contains an appendix of maps showing seven coloured classes of poverty overprinted on to Stanford's 'Library Map'. In subsequent issues maps were updated, corrected, and extended to cover a much larger area. Consecutive revisions record the changing fortunes of individual streets as demolition, rebuilding, and expansion changed population character and distribution. Despite their limitations, particularly in representing streets with a mixture of poverty and wellbeing, Booth's maps unemotionally reveal the abject state of a large part of Victorian London's population. They indicate the influence of London's ground plan on poverty distribution, showing how cul-de-sacs tended to be occupied by the 'semi-criminal' classes and how poverty was trapped by physical barriers such as railways, canals, new buildings and new streets which cut off districts from the mainstream of urban life.[21]

Drink was thought to be one of the principal causes of poverty. Public-house distribution was mapped in an effort to link poverty and alcohol. Although generally location is simply represented by a dot distribution, some maps, such as those of Norwich (1875) and Kings Lynn (1892), distinguish breweries, fully-licensed premises, beer houses, spirit dealers, and so on, and some even name individual public houses.[22] However, 'drink' maps prepared by temperance propagandists may not be very reliable. It is perhaps wiser to rely on later maps from non-partisan sources such as Booth who mapped 'Houses Licensed for the Sale of Intoxicating Drinks' (1900) and the Local Government and Taxation Committee of the London County Council, which prepared a 6-inch plan showing licensed premises (1903). Since most of the few drink maps were created by overprinting suitable base maps, they rarely throw any other new light on town topography.

The spread of educational provision in some towns is well recorded on maps prepared for local school boards showing school sites and proposed sites; deficiencies in school places; distribution of different types of schools; and so on. Detailed plans record proposals for school buildings and extensions to existing buildings, illuminating the environment of nineteenth-century education; Habershon & Pite's plan of alterations to 'Middle Class Schools for the Erith School Board' (1874), for example, shows even the 'Masters Desk', the 'Porch for Hats &c', coal bunkers, and individual water closets.

It was increasingly recognized that one of the main causes of poverty was disease. Cholera epidemics were mapped both nationally and locally with data superimposed usually on a suitable base map, establishing a tradition of medical mapping which was well entrenched by the mid nineteenth century.[23] Medical maps accompanied official reports and surveys, accounts of outbreaks, and

tracts on the nature and cause of disease. The best of these can be surprisingly informative. Baker's report to the Leeds' Board of Health on the 1832 cholera epidemic was illustrated by a map, now lost, which distinguished between streets 'sewered and paved' by the town, townships, and private individuals. Locations of individual cholera deaths were mapped for Hull (1853) by Cooper and for London (1855) by Snow, presenting a picture of outbreak incidence; Shapter's Exeter (1849) records not only distribution of cholera deaths but also places where clothes were destroyed, cholera burying grounds, 'druggists', and soup kitchens; and for Oxford Acland distinguished between cases of cholera and choleraic diarrhoea (1856). Many other diseases such as smallpox, influenza, typhoid, scarlet fever and diptheria came to be mapped on a regular basis in the annual reports of medical officers of health. Where a series of such medical maps covers a number of years, it is sometimes a useful cartographic guide to piecemeal urban growth.

Thematic mapping also records leisure interests and pursuits. Archaeology, in particular, was a widespread interest amongst the classically-educated gentry. It enjoyed its greatest popularity after 1840, when many archaeological societies were established. General topographical maps from the days of Norden, Pont and Speed fed this interest of potential customers by marking at least a selection of antiquities. Maps showing site distribution were sometimes produced, often to accompany works on local archaeology. Roman camps and roads around Llandrindod Common were mapped, for instance, by Piece (1811). Many large-scale county maps distinguish a variety of antiquities, but the most comprehensive record of archaeological site location is offered by the Ordnance Survey, which became increasingly aware of the importance of field antiquities and added them in ever greater numbers to its maps, developing the use of writing style to record an impressive proportion of historic and prehistoric monuments.[24] Ordnance plans contain the most comprehensive survey of castle earthworks ever undertaken in Britain. Sometimes Ordnance surveyors even recorded earthworks and deserted village sites without realizing their significance. However, much of the Survey's early work is very variable since it depended on the interests, diligence, and aptitudes of individual surveyors. Even the Ordnance could not hope to record all sites, particularly at smaller scales where selection was inevitable; a study, for

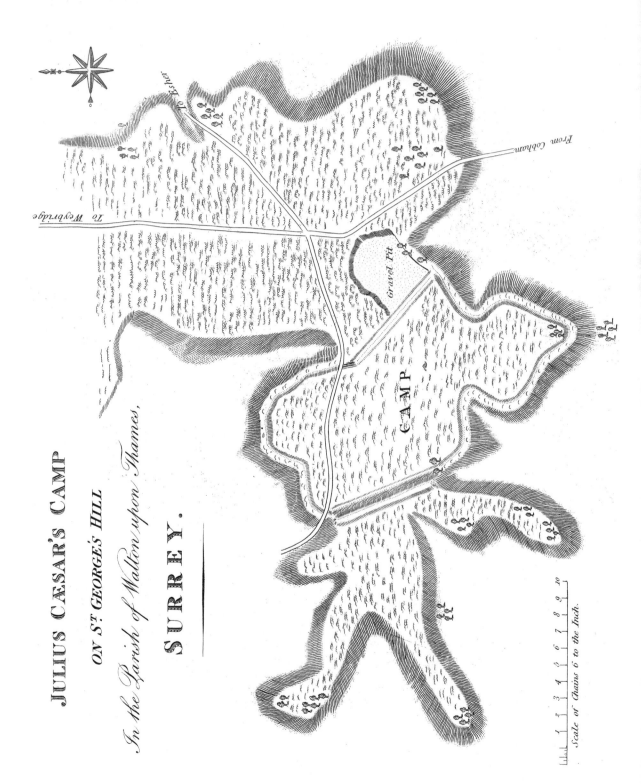

JULIUS CÆSAR'S CAMP

ON ST GEORGE'S HILL

In the Parish of Walton-upon-Thames,

SURREY.

Scale of Chains 6 to the Inch.

To Esher

From Cobham

To Weybridge

Gravel Pit

CAMP

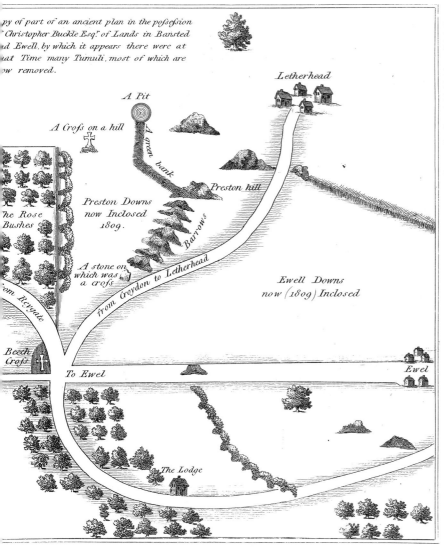

py of part of an ancient plan in the poſseſsion
Christopher Buckle Esq.ʳ of Lands in Banſted
d Ewell, by which it appears there were at
at Time many Tumuli, most of which are
ow removed.

A Pit

A Croſs on a hill

A green bank

Letherhead

Preston hill

Preston Downs
now Incloſed
1809.

he Roſe
Bushes

Barrows

A stone on
which was
a croſs

From Croydon to Letherhead

Ewell Downs
now (1809) Incloſed

om Reygate

Beech
Croſs

To Ewel

Ewel

The Lodge

105. 'JULIUS CAESAR'S CAMP
ON Sᵀ GEORGE'S HILL In the
Parish of Walton upon
Thames, SURREY.' 'Copy of
part of an ancient plan in the
possession of Christopher
Buckle Esqʳ of Lands in
Bansted and Ewell, by which it
appears there were at that
Time many Tumuli, most of
which are now removed.'
'Published by White & Cᵒ Fleet
Street, Janʸ 1. 1810.'

example, of moated settlements around the
Blackwater estuary identifies with certainty a total
of 39 sites from various maps including estate,
enclosure, tithe and large-scale county maps, but
of these only 21 appear as *Moats* on the Ordnance's
maps.[25]

Site features and settlement form are of greater
interest to the historian, particularly as many sites
have now disappeared. Such detail is well recorded
on the 6- and 25-inch Ordnance sheets and on a
few large-scale county maps like Warburton's
Yorkshire (1720) and Andrews & Dury's Wiltshire
(1773). However, the best record resulted from the
many large-scale surveys of individual sites; Strachey, for example, made a traverse survey of the

Fosse Way and drew plans of Iron Age hill forts.[26]
The greatest stimulus came from the work of
William Roy, who mapped sites from *c*.1752. Roy's
Military Antiquities of the Romans in North Britain
(1793) contains maps and plans illustrating his
field discoveries, either prepared from accurate
measurement or 'sketches' 'done by common
pacing only'.[27] Many of these plans provide the
only evidence of the original condition of many
Roman military works in Scotland and offer a
remarkably detailed picture. The fashion of mapping archaeological sites developed strongly in the
nineteenth century, with plans appearing in
numerous county histories, topographies and
other works; Colt Hoare's *Ancient History of Wilt-*

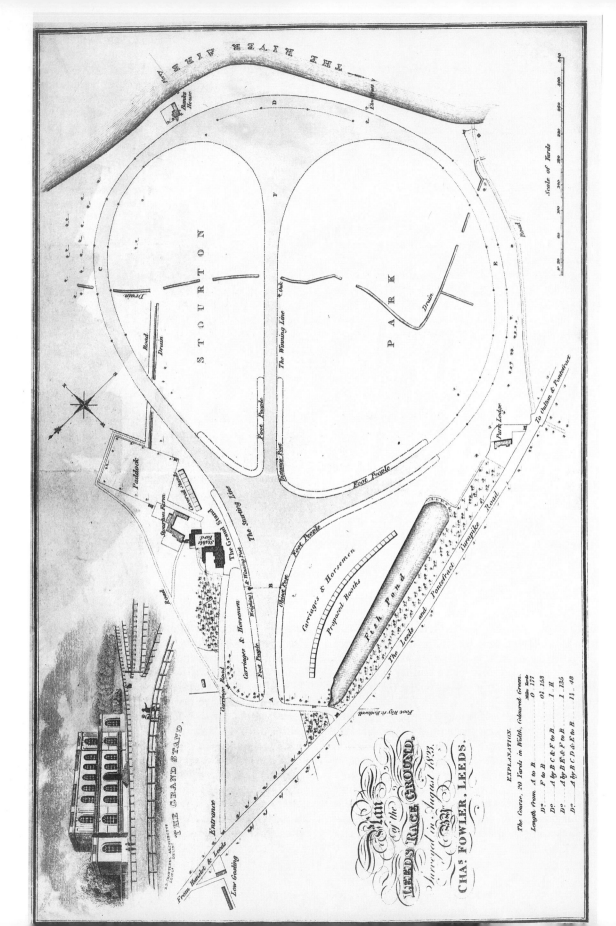

THE RIVER AIRE

Banks House

STOURTON PARK

Scale of Yards

Drain

Road

Drain

The Winning Line

Oak

Drain

Foot People

Distance Post

Foot People

Foot People

Road

Paddock

Queens Farm

Stourton Farm

Stable Yard

The Grand Stand

The Starting Line

Weighing & Winning Post

Object Post

Carriages & Horsemen

Foot People

Carriages & Horsemen

Proposed Booths

Fish Pond

Park Lodge

To Oulton & Pontefract

The Leeds and Pontefract Turnpike Road

Foot Way to Rothwell

Carriage Road

THE GRAND STAND

Entrance

From Hunslet & Leeds

Low Grating

R.D. CHANTRELL ARCHITECT, LEEDS.

EXPLANATION.

The Course, 20 Yards in Width, Coloured Green.

		Miles Yards
Length from A to B		0 . 177
D.o F to B		0 . 168
D.o A by B C & F to B		1 . 11
D.o A by B E & F to B		1 . 135
D.o A by B C D & E to B		11 . 48

Plan of the LEEDS RACE GROUND.
Surveyed in August 1823.
CHAS. FOWLER, LEEDS.

106. An Explanation gives measurements for parts of the course.

'Plan of the LEEDS RACE GROUND. Surveyed in August 1823. By CHAS FOWLER, LEEDS.' 1823.

---

shire (1812–21), for instance, is illustrated by a series of general distribution maps, a detailed map of Stonehenge, transect maps of antiquities along Roman roads, and detailed plans and views of individual sites. Even the Ordnance showed interest in publishing plans of individual sites, although it was less than usually successful in this respect; in 1865, for example, it published a separate plan of the megalithic cairns at Lough Crew and in the 1830s in Ireland a large number of megaliths, hill forts, raths, churches, and castles were surveyed or sketched.

Thematic maps of less intellectual pursuits include maps of grouse moors, locating shooting lodges, and golf courses, naming holes and bunkers and locating the clubhouse and 'club-maker's house'. Sporting venues were mapped particularly frequently; Fowler's plan of 'Leeds Race Ground' (1823), for instance, illustrates the grandstand and locates and names buildings, stands, paddock, drains, and ferry.

Select Bibliography

BASSETT, D.A., *A Source-Book of Geological, Geomorphological and Soil Maps for Wales and the Welsh Borders (1800–1966)* (1967)

Mines Department of the Board of Trade, *Catalogues of Plans of Abandoned Mines* (5 vols. Supplements; H.M.S.O.; 1928–39)

University of Reading, *The History and Development of Geological Cartography. Catalogue of the Exhibition of Geological Maps in the University Library* (1967)

Notes

Preface

1 See, for example: SKIPP, V., *Medieval Yardley* (1970); and: WHITEHEAD, J., *The Growth of Stoke Newington; a model for other local studies* (1983)

2 Appendix to G. Bradshaw's 'Map of the Canals and Navigable Rivers of the Midland Counties of England' 1829.

Introduction

1 See, for example:
CLOSE, SIR C., 'The old English mile' (*Geog. Journ.*, 76; 1930)
SMITH, E.H., 'Lancashire long measure' (*Trans. Hist. Soc. Lancs. Cheshire*, 110; 1959)
WILLAN, T.S., & CROSSLEY, E.W. (eds), 'Three seventeenth century Yorkshire surveys' (*Yorks. Arch. Soc. Rec. Ser.*, 114; 1941)

2 See, for example: BIL, A., 'What is where: an introductory perspective of the content of Adair's map of Strathearn' (*Orb*, 6, 3; 1977)

3 See, for example: CRUMP, W.B., 'The genesis of Warburton's "Map of Yorkshire", 1720' (*Thoresby Soc. Misc.*, 28; 1928)

4 STONE, J.C., 'The preparation of the Blaeu maps of Scotland – a further assessment' (*Scot. Geog. Mag.*, 86; 1970). For examples of the way in which errors were perpetuated by such plagiarization, see: BURDEN, E., 'Stedes – the Berkshire village that never was' (*Map Collector*, 40; 1987), and: JONES, I.E., '"Unnear" – a Radnorshire example of plagiarism on eighteenth and nineteenth century maps' (*Trans. Rad Soc.*, 46; 1976)

5 See, for example: J. CLUTTON in E. RYDE, 'The Ordnance Survey of the United Kingdom' (*Trans. Inst. Surveyors*, 15, 1882–3) for criticism of the accuracy of contemporary colouring of Ordnance plans.

6 GREEN, J., *The Construction of Maps and Globes* (1717). See: CRONE, G.R., 'John Green, a neglected eighteenth-century geographer and cartographer' (*Imago Mundi*, 6; 1949)

7 GOUGH, R., *British Topography* (2 vols.; 1780)

Chapter 1: Sources

1 Sheffield Library, *A Guide to the Fairbank Collection of Maps, Plans and Surveyors' Books and Correspondence in the Reference Library* (1936). See: HALL, T.W., *The Fairbanks of Sheffield*, 1688–1848 (1932)

2 WALLIS, H., 'A banquet of maps' (*Map Collector*, 28; 1984)

3 BARBER, P., 'The manuscript legacy' (*Map Collector*, 28; 1984)

4 Public Record Office, Leaflet 49, *Maps in the Public Record Office* (n.d.)

5 ADAMS, I.H., 'The Scottish Record Office plan collection' (*Cart. Journ.*, 4; 1967)
SINCLAIR, C.J., 'Register House plans' (*Cart. Journ.*, 14; 1977)

6 CLARK, P., 'A useful collection of maps and charts' (*Map Collector*, 35; 1986)
See also:
CRONE, G.R., & DAY, E.E.T., 'The Map Room of the Royal Geographical Society' (*Geog. Journ.*, 121; 1955)
CRONE, G.R., 'Early books and charts in the Royal Geographical Society's collection' (*Journ. Inst. Navig.*, 6; 1953)
KELLY, C., 'The RGS archives: a handlist' (*Geog. Journ.*, 141, 1975; 142, 1976; 143, 1977)

7 Ministry of Defence, *Guide to Publications and Information Services of the Hydrographic Department* (*Nautical Pub.*, 95; 1985)

8 ANDERSON, J.P., *The Book of British Topography* (1881) also includes references to maps.

9 ADAMS, I.H., 'Large-scale manuscript plans in Scotland' (*Journ. Soc. Archivists*, 3; 1967)

10 By Ralph Hyde

11 The map was prepared in June 1850 by Messrs Banister, Preston & Alexander, costing £213 3s. It was tested by the Ordnance Survey. A reference in the minutes of the Croydon Local Board of Health led to its discovery by Brian Lancaster.

Chapter 2: Decoration

1 MEGAW, B.R.S., 'Farming and fishing scenes on a Caithness plan, 1772' (*Scot. Studs.*, 6; 1962)

2 ADAM, R.J. (ed.), *John Home's survey of Assynt* (Scot. Hist. Soc.; 1960)

3 MARKS, S.P., *The Map of Mid Sixteenth Century London* (*Lond. Topo. Soc.*, 100; 1964)

4 Ó DANACHAIR, C., 'Representations of houses on some Irish maps of *c.*1600' in G. Jenkins: *Studies in Folklife: Essays in Honour of Iorweth C. Peate* (1969). For comments on the representation of houses in an English road-book of 1802, see: SMITH, D., & WEBB, D., 'James Baker's picturesque plans of England and Wales' (*Map Collector*, 41; 1987)

Chapter 4: Estate plans

1 KERRIDGE, E., 'The manorial survey as an historical document' (*Amateur Historian*, 7; 1966)
See also
TAYLOR, E.G.R., 'The surveyor' (*Econ. Hist. Rev.*, 17; 1947)

2 PRICE, D.J., 'Medieval land surveying and topographical maps' (*Geog. Journ.*, 121; 1955)

3 HARVEY, P.D.A., *The History of Topographical Maps* (1980)

4 YATES, E.M., 'Map of Over Haddon and Meadowplace, near Bakewell, Derbyshire, *c.*1528' (*Agric. Hist. Rev.*, 12; 1964)

5 HARVEY, P.D.A., 'Estate surveyors and the spread of the scale-map in England, 1550–80' in J. Chartres (ed.): *Landscape and Townscape: Essays in Honour of M. W. Beresford* (Forthcoming)

6 DARBY, H.C., 'The agrarian contribution to surveying in England' (*Geog. Journ.*, 82; 1933)
See for example, the description of maps accompanying the *Buckhurst Terrier 1597–1598* (*Sussex Rec. Soc.*, 39; 1933)

7 I.H. ADAMS argues that the term 'estate plan' should be limited to plans made as inventories of an estate or for its management or improvement, and that 'farm plan' should be the term used for a single farm.

8 YATES, E.M., 'Map of Ashbourne, Derbyshire' (*Geog. Journ.*, 126; 1960)

9 For a discussion of maps prepared for Corpus Christi College, Oxford, by Nelson and Langdon, see: WOOLGAR, C.M., 'Some draft estate maps of the early seventeenth century' (*Cart. Journ.*, 22; 1985)
See also the village maps derived by R.A. Butlin from Norton's maps in 'Northumberland field systems' (*Agric. Hist. Rev.*, 12; 1964)

10 A group of Norden's manuscript surveys is reproduced in *Orford Ness, a Selection of Maps mainly by John Norden* (1966)

11 LAWRENCE, H., 'John Norden and his colleagues: surveyors of Crown lands' (*Cart. Journ.*, 22; 1985). See also: POLLARD, A.W., 'The unity of John Norden: surveyor and religious writer' (*Library*, 7; 1926)

12 See: SERGEANT, W.J., 'A further discovery of manuscript maps by Christopher Saxton' (*Geog. Journ.*, 132; 1966)
LAWRENCE, H., 'New Saxton discoveries' (*Map Collector*, 17; 1981)

LAWRENCE, H., & HOYLE, R., 'New maps and surveys by Christopher Saxton' (*Yorks. Arch. Journ.*, 53; 1981)

13 EVANS, I.M., & LAWRENCE, H., *Christopher Saxton: Elizabethan Map-Maker* (1979)

14 EDWARDS, A.C., & NEWTON, K.C., *The Walkers of Hanningfield: Surveyors and Mapmakers Extraordinary* (1984)
See also:
NEWTON, K.C., 'The Walkers of Essex' (*Bull. Soc. Univ. Cartographers*, 4; 1969–70)

15 See, for example: DUFFY, P.J., 'Farney in 1634: an examination of Thomas Raven's survey of the Essex estate' (*Clogher Rec.*, 10, 5; 1983)
GILLESPIE, R., 'Thomas Raven and the mapping of the Claneboy estates' (*Bangor Hist. Soc. Journ.*, 1; 1981)

16 ANDREWS, J.H., 'The French school of Dublin land surveyors' (*Irish Geog.*, 5; 1967)

17 HORNER, A.A., 'Cartouches and vignettes on the Kildare estate maps of John Rocque' (*Irish Georg. Soc. Quart. Bull.*, 14; 1971)

18 See, for example: MURPHY, P.J., 'Survey of Fontstown, co. Kildare, by Bernard Scale, 1764' (*Kildare Arch. Soc. Journ.*, 14; 1969)

19 MARTIN, J., 'Estate stewards and their work in Glamorgan, 1660–1760: a regional study of estate management' (*Morgannwg*, 23; 1979)

20 ADAMS, I.H., 'The land surveyor and his influence on the Scottish rural landscape' (*Scot. Geog. Mag.*, 84; 1968)

21 ADAMS, I.H. (ed.), *Papers on Peter May, Land Surveyor, 1749–1793* (*Scot. Hist. Ser.*, 15; 1979)

22 HYDE, R., 'Thomas Horner: pictural land surveyor' (*Imago Mundi*, 29; 1977)

23 ADAMS, I.H., 'Economic process and the Scottish land surveyor' (*Imago Mundi*, 27; 1975)

24 DUGGAN, G.C., 'An old Irish estate map' (*Geog. Mag.*, 27; 1954–55)

25 EDWARDS, R., 'Some notes on the 1785–1786 survey of the Manor of Kennington by Joseph Hodskinson and John Middleton' (*Lond. Topo. Rec.*, 25; 1985)

26 ROBERTS, B.K., 'An early Tudor sketch map: its context and implications' (*History Studies*, 1; 1968)

27 STEERS, J.A., 'Orford Ness; a study in coastal physiography' (*Proc. Geol. Assoc.*, 37; 1926)

28 EVANS, J.H., 'The Upchurch Marshes in the time of the first Elizabeth' (*Archaeologia Cantiana*, 76; 1961)
See also:
EVANS, J.H., 'The Rochester Bridge lands in Grain' (*Archaeologia Cantiana*, 68; 1954)

29 See, for example: GULLEY, J.L.M., 'The great rebuilding in the Weald' (*Gwerrin*, 3; 1961)

30 See, for example: EMMISON, F.G., *Some Types of Common-Field Parish* (Nat. Counc. Soc. Serv.; 1964)

31 GEDDES, A., 'The changing landscape of the Lothians, 1600–1800, as revealed by old estate plans' (*Scot. Geog. Mag.*, 54; 1938)

32 THIRD, B.M.W., 'Changing landscape and social structure in Scottish lowlands as revealed by eighteenth century estate plans' (*Scot. Geog. Mag.*, 71; 1955)

33 THOMAS, C., 'Estate surveys as sources in historical geography' (*Nat. Lib. Wales Journ.*, 14; 1966)

34 LEBON, J.H.G., 'The face of the countryside in central Ayrshire during the eighteenth and nineteenth centuries' (*Scot. Geog. Mag.*, 62; 1946)

35 RUSTON, A.G., & WHITNEY, D., *Hooton Pagnell. The Agricultural Evolution of a Yorkshire Village* (1934)

36 BATHO, G.R., 'Two newly discovered maps by Christopher Saxton' (*Geog. Journ.*, 125; 1959)

37 BAKER, A.R.H., 'Some early Kentish estate maps and a note on their portrayal of field boundaries' (*Archaeologia Cantiana*, 77; 1962)
See also:
BAKER, A.R.H., 'Local history in early estate maps' (*Amateur Historian*, 5; 1961–2)

38 See, for example: MCCARTHUR, M.M. (ed.), *Survey of Lochtayside 1769* (Scot. Hist. Soc., 1936)

39 THOMAS, D., *Agriculture in Wales during the Napoleonic Wars. A Study in the Geographical Interpretation of Historical Sources* (1963)

40 BAPTIST, SISTER M., 'Eighteenth-century maps and estate plans of Bromley, Beckenham and Penge' (*Archaeologia Cantiana*, 81; 1967)

41 MOISLEY, H.A., 'North Uist in 1799' (*Scot. Geog. Mag.*, 77; 1961)

42 FAIRHURST, H., 'The surveys for the Sutherland clearances 1813–1820 (*Scot. Studs.*, 8; 1964)

43 BAKER, A.R.H., 'Field patterns in seventeenth-century Kent' (*Geography*, 50; 1965)

44 See, for example: PRINCE, H.C., 'The changing landscape of Panshanger' (*Trans. E. Herts. Archit. Soc.*, 16; 1959)

Chapter 5: Enclosure plans

1 COX, J.C., 'Plans of the Peak Forest' in J.C. Cox (ed.), *Memorials of Old Derbyshire* (1907)

2 DODD, A.H., *The Industrial Revolution in North Wales* (1933; 2nd edn., 1951)

3 BOWEN, I., *The Great Enclosures of Common Lands in Wales* (1914)

4 HARRIS, A., *The Rural Landscape of the East Riding of Yorkshire 1700–1850* (1961)

5 SMAILES, A.E., *North England* (1960)

6 THOMAS, J.G., 'The distribution of the commons in part of Arwystli at the time of enclosure' (*Montgomeryshire Collections*, 54; 1955)

7 HARVEY, J.C., 'Early plans as a source for the study of field systems with special reference to the West Riding of Yorkshire' in *Early Maps as Historical Evidence* (Papers given at the Conference on the History of Cartography held at the Royal Geographical Soc.; 1967)

8 CHAMBERS, J.D., *A Century of Nottingham History* (1952)

9 WHYTE, I.D., *Agriculture and Society in Seventeenth-Century Scotland* (1979)

10 GONNER, E.C.K., *Common Land and Inclosure* (1912; 2nd edn., 1966)

Chapter 6: Tithe maps

1 KAIN, R.J.P., 'R.K. Dawson's proposal in 1836 for a cadastral survey of England and Wales' (*Cart. Journ.*, 12; 1975)

2 A reference index and cartographic analysis of the tithe maps and apportionments is currently being researched at the University of Exeter. It will ultimately furnish historians with a research tool to aid the use of tithe maps as sources of historical evidence.

3 WILLATTS, E.C., 'Changes in land utilization in the south-west of the London Basin, 1840–1932' (*Geog. Journ.*, 82; 1933)

4 CARPENTER, A.M., 'The value of the tithe surveys to the study of land ownership and occupancy in the mid-nineteenth century, with special reference to south Hertfordshire' (*Herts. Past Present*, 7; 1967)

5 See, for example: BUCHANAN, K.M., Part 68: 'Worcestershire' (1944)

Chapter 7: Regional maps

1 PARSONS, E.J.S., *The Map of Great Britain circa A.D. 1360 Known as the Gough Map . . .* (1958)

2 ELLISON, REV. C.C., 'Remembering Dr. Beaufort' (*Irish Georg. Soc. Quart. Bull.*, 18; 1975)

Chapter 8: Drainage maps

1 OWEN, A.E.B., 'Records of commissioners of sewers' (*History*, 52; 1967)

2 DARLINGTON, I., 'The London Commissioners of Sewers and their records' (*Journ. Soc. Archivists*, 2; 1962)
See also:
RIDGE, A.D., 'The records of the London Commissioners of Sewers' (*Journ. Soc. Archivists*, 1; 1957)

3 PERRY, J., *An Account of the Stopping of Dagenham Breach* (1721)

4 HAWKSHAW, J., 'Account of the cofferdam, the syphons, and other works constructed in consequence of the failure of the St. Germain's sluice of the Middle Level Drainage' (*Min. Proc. Inst. Civil Engineers*, 22; 1863)

5 COCK, F.W., 'The oldest map of Romney Marsh' (*Archaeologia Cantiana*, 30; 1911–12)

6 FORDHAM, SIR H.G., 'Descriptive list of the maps of the Great Level of the Fens, 1604–1900', in *Studies in Carto-Bibliography* (1914; 1969)
See also:
LYNAM, E.W., 'Early maps of the Fen district' (*Geog. Journ.*, 84; 1934)

7 LYNAM, E., 'Maps of the Fenland' in *Victoria History of the Counties of England: Huntingdonshire* (3; 1936)

Chapter 9: County maps

1 LYNAM, E.W., Introduction to *An Atlas of England and Wales. The Maps of Christopher Saxton engraved 1574–1579* (1934; introduction revised 1939). See also: SKELTON, R.A., *Saxton's Survey of England and Wales: with a Facsimile of Saxton's Wall-map of 1583* (1974).

2 HARLEY, J.B., 'Christopher Saxton and the first atlas of England and Wales, 1579–1979' (*Map Collector*, 8, 1979)

3 MANLEY, G., 'Saxton's survey of northern England' (*Geog. Journ.*, 83; 1932)

4 GARDINER, R.A., 'Philip Symonson's "New Description of Kent", 1596' (*Geog. Journ.*, 135; 1969)
See also:
HANNEN, H., 'An account of a map of Kent dated 1596' (*Archaeologia Cantiana*, 30; 1911–12)

5 STONE, J.C., 'Reverend map-maker' (*Geog. Mag.*, 45; 1973)

6 MEGAW, B.R.S., 'The date of Pont's survey and its background' (*Scot. Studs.*, 13; 1969)
See also:
CASH, C.G., 'The first topographical survey of Scotland' (*Scot. Geog. Mag.*, 17; 1901)

7 LEBON, J.H.G., 'Old maps and rural change in Ayrshire' (*Scot. Geog. Mag.*, 68; 1952)

8 STONE, J.C., 'Manuscript maps of north-east Scotland by Timothy Pont' (*Northern Scotland*, 1; 1972–73)
See also:
STONE, J.C., 'An evaluation of the Nidisdaile manuscript map of Timothy Pont' (*Scot. Geog. Mag.*, 84; 1968)
STONE, J.C., *A Locational Guide to the Pont, Gordon and Blaeu Maps of Scotland* (*O'Dell Memorial Monograph* No.3; 1971)
STONE, J.C., 'The settlements of Nithsdale in the sixteenth century by Timothy Pont: a complete or partial record?' (*Trans. Dumfriesshire Galloway Nat. Hist. Antiq. Soc.*, 50; 1973)
STONE, J.C., 'Problems in reading sixteenth century manuscript maps of Scotland' (*Proc. 13th Annual Summer School. Soc. Univ. Cartographers*; 1977)

9 ARLOTT, J. (ed.), *John Speed's England: A Coloured Facsimile of the Maps and Text from the Theatre of the Empire of Great Britain . . . 1611* (1953)

10 See, for example: WHITAKER, H., 'The later editions of Saxton's maps' (*Imago Mundi*, 3; 1939)

11 SHIRLEY, E.P., *The History of the County of Monaghan* (1879)

12 LARCOM, T.A. (ed.), *The History of the Survey of Ireland, commonly called the Down Survey . . . A.D. 1655–6* (1851)
See also:
STRAUSS, E., *Sir William Petty: Portrait of a Genius* (1954)

13 ANDREWS, J.H., Introduction to *Hiberniae Delineatio* (1970)

14 DOMHNAILL, S.Ó., 'The maps of the Down survey' (*Irish Historical Studs.*, 3; 1943)

15 ANDREWS, J.H., Introduction to *Noble and Keenan's Map of Kildare, 1752* (Irish Georg. Soc.; 1981)

16 RAVENHILL, W.L.D., 'Joel Gascoyne, a pioneer of large-scale county mapping' (*Imago Mundi*, 26; 1972)

17 COOPER, K., 'John Rocque's map of Surrey, 1768 – a disregarded historical reference' (*Bull. Soc. Univ. Cartographers*, 6; 1971)
See also:
HOOPER, W., 'Rocque's map of Surrey' (*Surrey Arch. Coll.*, 40; 1932)
LAXTON, P., Introduction to *A Topographical Map of the County of Berks, by John Rocque . . . 1761* (1973)
PHILIPS, H., 'John Rocque's career' (*Lond. Topo. Rec.*, 20; 1952)
VARLEY, J., 'John Rocque. Engraver, surveyor, cartographer and map-seller' (*Imago Mundi*, 5; 1948)

18 HARLEY, J.B., & HARVEY, J.C., Introduction to *A Survey of the County of Yorkshire by Thomas Jefferys, 1775* (1974)

19 HARLEY, J.B., 'The bankruptcy of Thomas Jefferys' (*Imago Mundi*, 20; 1966)

20 HARLEY, J.B., 'The Society of Arts and the surveys of the English counties 1759–1809' (*Journ. Roy. Soc. Arts*, 112; 1963–64)

21 HARLEY, J.B., 'The re-mapping of England, 1750–1800' (*Imago Mundi*, 19; 1965)

22 RAVENHILL, W.L.D., Introduction to *A Map of the County of Devon, 1765* (*Devon Cornwall Rec. Soc.*, 9; 1965)

23 HARLEY, J.B., FOWKES, D.V., & HARVEY, J.C., Introduction to *Burdett's Map of Derbyshire 1791* (Derbyshire Arch. Soc.; 1975)

24 WELDING, J.D., (ed.) *Leicestershire in 1777*. 'An edition of John Prior's map of Leicestershire with an introduction and commentary by members of the Leicestershire Industrial History Society' (Leics. Libs. Inf. Serv.; 1984)

25 DYMOND, D.P., Introduction to *The County of Suffolk Surveyed by Joseph Hodskinson . . . 1783* (*Suffolk Rec. Soc.*, 15; 1972)

26 PHILLIPS, A.D.M, Introduction to *William Yates's Map of Staffordshire 1775* (Staffs. Rec. Soc.; 1984)

27 WOOD, SIR H.T., 'The Royal Society of Arts. VI. The premiums (1754–1851)' (*Journ. Roy. Soc. Arts*, 60; 1911–12)

28 HARLEY, J.B., 'William Yates and Peter Burdett: their role in the mapping of Lancashire and Cheshire during the late eighteenth century' (*Trans. Hist. Soc. Lancs. Cheshire*, 115; 1964)

29 EMMISON, F.G.: Introduction to *A Reproduction of A Map of the County of Essex 1777 by John Chapman and Peter André* (*Essex Rec. Off. Pub*, 11; 1950)
See also:
GREEN, J.J., 'Chapman and André's map of Essex, 1777' (*Essex Rev.*, 19; 1910)

30 HARLEY, J.B., & LAXTON, P., Introduction to *A Survey of the County Palatine of Chester P.P. Burdett. 1777* (Hist. Soc. Lancs. Cheshire; 1974)

31 SKELTON, R.A., Introduction to *Two Hundred and Fifty Years of Map-Making in the County of Sussex* (1970)

32 INGLIS, H.R.G., 'John Adair – an early mapmaker and his work' (*Scot. Geog. Mag.*, 34; 1918)
See also:
LAING, D. (ed.): 'Collections of papers relating to the geographical description, maps and charts of John Adair F.R.S., Geographer to the Kingdom of Scotland 1686–1723' (*Bannatyne Club Miscellany*, 11; 1836)
MOORE, J.N., ' "A Mapp of the Parioch of Tranent": new aspects of the cartography of John Adair' (*Imago Mundi*, 39; 1987)

33 STRAWTHORN, J., 'An introduction to Armstrongs' map' in *Ayrshire at the Time of Burns* (Colls. Ayrshire Arch. Nat. Hist. Soc., 2, 5; 1959)

34 STORRIE, M.C., 'William Bald, F.R.S.E., c.1789–1857; cartographer and civil engineer surveyor' (*Trans. Inst. Brit. Geogr.*, 47; 1969)

35 ANDREWS, J.H., 'Ireland in maps: a bibliographical postscript' (*Irish Geog.*, 4; 1962)

36 ANDREWS, J.H., *Alexander Taylor and his Map of County Kildare* (Roy. Irish Acad.; 1983)

37 HARLEY, J.B., 'English county map-making in the early years of the Ordnance Survey: the map of Surrey by Joseph Lindley and William Crosley' (*Geog. Journ.*, 132; 1966)

38 LAXTON, P., 'John Rocque's survey of Berkshire, 1761' (*Journ. Durham Univ. Geog. Soc.*, 8; 1965–66)

39 HARLEY, J.B., & HODSON, D., Introduction to *The Royal English Atlas* (1971)

40 For Essex, see: EMMISON, F.G., & SKELTON, R.A., 'The description of Essex by John Norden, 1594' (*Geog. Journ.*, 123; 1957); and Hampshire, see: BOX, E.G.: 'Norden's map of Hampshire, 1595' (*Proc. Hants Field Club Arch. Soc.*, 13; 1935)
For a 'Summary of Norden's known work on English county maps' see: KINGSLEY, D., *Printed Maps of Sussex 1575–1900* (1982). Appendix IX.

41 PARRY, M.L., 'County maps as historical sources. A sequence of surveys in south-east Scotland' (*Scot. Studs.*, 19; 1975)

42 JONES, A.K., *The Maps of Yorkshire Printed in the Period 1577 to 1877 as Sources of Topographical Information* (Unpublished thesis; see *Int. Map. Colls. Soc. Journ.*, 6; 1986)

Chapter 10: Maps of county divisions

1 RAVENHILL, W.L.D., 'John Norden's maps of Cornwall: a problem in the historical cartography of south-west England' (*Cart. Journ.*, 7; 1970)
RAVENHILL, W.L.D., 'The missing maps from John Norden's survey of Cornwall' in K.J. Gregory & W.L.D. Ravenhill (eds): *Exeter Essays in Geography* (1971)

RAVENHILL, W.L.D., Introduction to *John Norden's Manuscript Maps of Cornwall and its Nine Hundreds* (1972)

2 BOYLE, J., *In Quest of Hasted* (1984)

3 ANDREWS, J.H., 'The maps of the escheated counties of Ulster, 1609–10' (*Proc. Roy. Irish Acad.*, 74, C, 4; 1974)

4 PETTY-FITZMAURICE, H.W.E., EARL OF KERRY, 'The Lansdowne maps of the Down Survey' (*Proc. Roy. Irish. Acad.*, 35, C, 12; 1920)

Chapter 11: Military maps

1 HARVEY, P.D.A., 'The Portsmouth map of 1545 and the introduction of scale-maps into England' in J. Webb, N. Yates, & S. Peacock (eds.): *Hampshire Studies presented to Dorothy Dymond* (1981)

2 HARLEY, J.B., 'The map collection of William Cecil, first Baron Burghley 1520–90' (*Map Collector*, 3; 1978)

3 ELLIS, H., 'Copy of a manuscript tract addressed to Lord Burghley, illustrative of the Border topography of Scotland, A.D.1590; with a platt or map of the Borders taken in the same year, both preserved in one of the Royal Mss. in the British Museum' (*Archaeologia*, 22; 1829)

4 O'NEILL, B.H.ST.J., 'Stefan von Haschenperg, an engineer to King Henry VIII, and his work' (*Archaeologia*, 91; 1945)

5 SHELBY, L.R., *John Rogers – Tudor Military Engineer* (1967)

6 SKELTON, R.A., 'The military surveyor's contribution to British cartography in the sixteenth century' (*Imago Mundi*, 24; 1970)
See also:
MERRIMAN, M., 'Italian military engineers in Britain in the 1540s' in S. Tyacke (ed.): *English Map-Making 1500–1650* (1983)

7 For background information, see:
MARSHALL, D.W., 'Military maps of the eighteenth-century and the Tower of London Drawing Room' (*Imago Mundi*, 32; 1980)
PORTER, W., *History of the Corps of Royal Engineers* (3 vols.; 1889). The development of the Corps of Royal Engineers to 1800 is outlined in D. Hodson: *Maps of Portsmouth Before 1801* (Portsmouth Rec. Ser., 4; 1978)

8 DE BOER, G., 'The two earliest maps of Hull' (*Post-Medieval Arch.*, 7; 1973)

9 PARNELL, G., 'Five seventeenth-century plans of the Tower of London' (*Lond. Topo. Rec.*, 25; 1985)
See also:
MAGUIRE, J.B., 'Seventeenth century plans of Dublin Castle' (*Journ. Roy. Soc. Antiquaries Ireland*, 104; 1974)

10 ANDREWS, J.H., 'The Irish surveys of Robert Lythe' (*Imago Mundi*, 19; 1965)
See also:
ANDREWS, J.H., 'An Elizabethan surveyor and his cartographic progeny' (*Imago Mundi*, 36; 1972)

11 MERRIMAN, M., 'The platte of Castlemilk, 1547' (*Trans. Dumfriesshire Galloway Nat. Hist. Antiq. Soc.*, 44, 1967)

12 HAYES-MCCOY, G.A., *Ulster and Other Irish Maps* (1964) See also:
HAYES-MCCOY, G.A., 'Contemporary maps as an aid to Irish history' (*Imago Mundi*, 19; 1965)

13 GAIRDNER, J., 'On a contemporary drawing of the burning of Brighton in the time of Henry VIII' (*Roy. Hist. Soc. Trans.*, 3, 1; 1907)
Reproduced in E.W. Gilbert, 'The growth of Brighton' (*Geog. Journ.*, 114; 1949)

14 LYNAM, E., 'English maps and map-makers of the sixteenth century' (*Geog. Journ.*, 116; 1959)

15 BROSNAN, C., 'When Irish towns were fortified' (*Ireland of the Welcomes*, 12; 1964)
See also:
O'SULLIVAN, M.D., 'The fortification of Galway town in the sixteenth and early seventeenth centuries' (*Galway Arch. Soc. Journ.*, 16; 1934)

16 BLAKE, M.J., 'A map of part of the County of Mayo in 1584; with notes thereon, and an account of its author, and his descendants' (*Galways Arch. Soc. Journ.*, 5; 1907–8)

17 See, for example:
MACCARTHY, C.J.F., 'Vallancey's plan for the defence of Spike Island' (*Cork Hist. Soc. Journ.*, 75; 1975)

18 ANDREWS, J.H., 'Charles Vallancey and the map of Ireland (*Geog. Journ.*, 132; 1966)
ANDREWS, J.H., 'Charles Vallancey's map of Ireland; a new reference' (*Geog. Journ.*, 146; 1980)

19 SKELTON, R.A., 'The military survey of Scotland 1747–55' (*Scot. Geog. Mag.*, 83; 1967). See also:
WHITTINGTON, G., 'The Roy map: the protracted and fair copies' (Scot. Geog. Mag., 102; 1986).
WHITTINGTON, G., & GIBSON, A.J.S., *The Military Survey of Scotland 1747–1755: a critique* (Hist. Geog. Res. Group; Inst. Brit. Geographers; 1986)

20 O'DELL, A.C., 'A view of Scotland in the middle of the eighteenth century' (*Scot. Geog. Mag.*, 69; 1953)
The map has also been used by R.A. Gailey to aid the analysis of 'Settlement and population in Kintyre 1750–1800' (*Scot. Geog. Mag.*, 76; 1960)

21 COULL, J.R., 'The district of Buchan as shown on the Roy map' (*Scot. Geog. Mag.*, 2; 1980)

22 O'DONOGHUE, Y., *William Roy (1726–1790): Pioneer of the Ordnance Survey* (1977)

23 WARNER, G.F., & GILSON, J.P., *Catalogue of Western Manuscripts in the Old Royal and King's Collections* (1921) lists annotations made by Burghley and others to this atlas.

24 FORDHAM, SIR H.G., 'A note on the "Quarter-master's Map" 1644' (*Geog. Journ.*, 70; 1927)

Chapter 12: Ordnance Survey maps

1 SEEBOHM, F., *The English Village Community* (1883)
2 THIRSK, J., Review of *The Victoria History of the County of Middlesex* (Vol. 3; 1962). (*Econ. Hist. Rev.*, 15; 1963)

3 WINTERBOTHAM, H.ST.J.L., *The National Plans* (Ord. Surv. Prof. Papers, 16; 1934)

4 ANDREWS, J.H., Appendix F: 'A note on the dating of Irish Ordnance Survey maps' in *A Paper Landscape* (1975)
CLARKE, R.V., 'The use of watermarks in dating Old Series One-Inch Ordnance Survey maps' (*Cart. Journ.*, 6; 1969)
MUMFORD, I., 'Engraved Ordnance Survey one-inch maps – the problem of dating' (*Cart. Journ.*, 5; 1968)
MUMFORD, I., & CLARK, P.A., 'Engraved Ordnance Survey one-inch maps – the methodology of dating' (*Cart. Journ.*, 5; 1968)

5 YATES, E.M., 'History in a map' (*Geog. Journ.*, 126; 1960)

Chapter 13: Transport and communications maps

1 MITCHELL, J.B., 'Early maps of Great Britain. The Matthew Paris maps' (*Geog. Journ.*, 81; 1933)
Reproduced in *Four Maps of Great Britain by Matthew Paris* (Brit. Museum; 1928)

2 HARRIS, J.R., 'Liverpool canal controversies 1769–1772' (*Journ. Trans. Hist.*, 2; 1955–56)

Road Maps

1 STENTON, F.M., 'The road system of medieval England' (*Econ. Hist. Rev.*, 7; 1936)

2 PRIDEAUX, W.F., 'Notes on Salway's plan' (*Lond. Topo. Rec.*, 3; 1906, & 5; 1908)

3 JOHNSTON, G.D., 'Roads from Arundel to the North' (*Sussex Notes Queries*, 17; 1968)

4 MACAULAY, T.B., *History of England* (1848)

5 Carto-bibliographical details of these and other road-books published before 1845 are found in D. Smith: *Antique Maps of the British Isles* (1982). For those published between 1837 and 1900, see the same author's *Victorian Maps of the British Isles* (1985)

6 TAYLOR, R.S., 'Road maps in 18th century magazines' (*Int. Map Colls. Soc. Journ.*, 6; 1986)

7 TAYLOR, G., & SKINNER, A., *Maps of the Roads of Ireland. 2nd. ed., 1783.* Introduction by J.H. Andrews. (1969)

8 FAIRCLOUGH, R.H., ' "Sketches of the Roads in Scotland, 1785"; the manuscript roadbook of George Taylor' (*Imago Mundi*, 27; 1975)
See also:
ADAMS, I.H., 'George Taylor, a surveyor o' pairts' (*Imago Mundi*, 27; 1975)

9 See, for example: SCROGGS, E.S., 'The records of Rochester Bridge . . .' (*Archives*, 2; 1954)

10 BOX, E.G., 'Lambarde's "Carde of this Shrye", third issue with roads added' (*Archaeologia Cantiana*, 39; 1926)

11 KNOCKER, H.W., 'Sevenoaks: the manor, church, and market' (*Archaeologia Cantiana*, 38; 1925)

12 HYDE, R., 'Maps that made cabmen honest' (*Map Collector*, 9; 1979)

13 ANDREWS, J.H., 'Road planning in Ireland before the railway age' (*Irish Geog.*, 5; 1964)

14 BOX, E.G., 'Notes on some west Kent roads in early maps and road books' (*Archaelogia Cantiana*, 43; 1931)

15 HOSKINS, W.G., *The Making of the English Landscape* (1955)

Waterway Maps

1 BULL, G.B.G., 'Elizabethan maps of the Lower Lea Valley' (*Geog. Journ.*, 124; 1958)

2 HOLMES, M., 'A seventeenth-century map of London and the Thames' (*Lond. Topo. Rec.*, 20; 1952)

3 WICKHAM, H., *Worsley in the Eighteenth Century* (1984)

4 See, for example: PHILLIP, J., *A General History of Inland Navigation, Foreign, and Domestic* (1792)

PRIESTLEY, J., *Historical Account of the Navigable Rivers, and Railways throughout Great Britain* (1831)

5 DE SALIS, H.R. (comp.), *Bradshaw's Canals and Navigable Rivers of England and Wales* (1904; reprinted 1928 & 1969)

6 TORRENS, H.S., 'Early maps of the Somersetshire Coal Canal' (*Cart. Journ.*, 11; 1974)

EYLES, J.M., 'A further study of the early maps of the Somersetshire Coal Canal' (*Cart. Journ.*, 12; 1975)

TORRENS, H.S., 'Further comments on the maps of the Somersetshire Coal Canal' (*Cart. Journ.*, 12; 1975)

Railway Maps

1 An example of such a plan is illustrated by H.J. Dyos in 'Some social costs of railway building in London' (*Journ. Trans. Hist.*, 3; 1957–58)

See also:

DYOS, H.J., 'Railways and housing in Victorian London' (*Journ. Trans. Hist.*, 2; 1955–56)

2 GARNETT, D., 'The railway maps of Zachary Macaulay and John Airey' (*Railway Canal Hist. Soc. Journ.*; 1959–71)

GARNETT, D., 'John Airey's undated maps' (*Railway Canal Hist. Soc. Journ.*, 17; 1971)

GARNETT, D., 'Macaulay's *Metropolitan Railway Map*' (*Railway Canal Hist. Soc. Journ.*, 21; 1975)

GARNETT, D., 'Airey's railway map of the East of England' (*Railway Canal Hist. Soc. Journ.*, 21; 1975)

GARNETT, D., 'Metropolitan District Railway maps: a tentative checklist' (*Railway Canal Hist. Soc. Journ.*, 23; 1977)

GARNETT, D., 'John Airey's undated early railway maps,' (*Map Collector*, 26; 1984)

Chapter 14: Marine charts

1 ANDREWS, M.C., 'The British Isles in the nautical charts of the XIVth and XVth centuries' (*Geog. Journ.*, 68; 1926)

2 DE BOER, G., 'Early maps as historical evidence for coastal change. The historical variations of Spurn Point: the evidence of early maps; (*Geog. Journ.*, 135; 1969)

3 GERNEZ, D., 'The works of Lucas Janszoon Waghenaer' (*Mariners' Mirrour*, 23; 1937)

KOEMAN, C., 'Lucas Janszoon Waghenaer': sixteenth century marine cartographer' (*Geog. Journ.*, 131; 1965)

KOEMAN, C., 'The history of Lucas Janszoon Waghenaer and his Spieghel der Zeevaerdt' (1964). [Introduction to facs. edn.]

SKELTON, R.A., Bibliographical note to the *Spieghel der Zeevaerdt* (1964)

4 SKELTON, R.A., Introduction to Blaeu's *The Light of Navigation (1612)* (1964)

5 SMITH, T.R., 'Manuscript and printed sea charts in seventeenth century London: the case of the Thames School', in N.J.W. Thrower (ed.): *The Compleat Plattmaker* (1978)

6 NAISH, G.P.B., 'Hydrographic surveys by officers of the Navy under the later Stuarts' (*Journ. Inst. Navig.*, 9; 1956)

7 VERNER, C., *Captain Collins' Coasting Pilot* (*Map Colls. Circle*, 58; 1969)

See also:

ELKINS, R., 'Charting a course for sober men' (*Map Collector*, 1; 1977)

8 RAVENHILL, W.L.D., 'Mapping the Lizard' (*Map Collector*, 13; 1980)

9 HARLEY, J.B., 'Ogilby and Collins: Cheshire by road & sea' (*Cheshire Round*, 1, 7; 1967)

10 MOORE, J.N., 'Scotland's first sea atlas' (*Map Collector*, 30; 1985)

See also

ROBINSON, A.H.W., 'Two unrecorded manuscript charts by John Adair' (*Scot. Geog. Mag.*, 75; 1959)

11 ROBINSON, A.H.W., 'Lewis Morris – an early Welsh hydrographer' (*Journ. Inst. Navig.*, 11; 1958)

See also:

ROBINSON, A.H.W., 'Lewis Morris, chartmaker extraordinary' (*Map Collector*, 8; 1979)

ROBINSON, A.H.W., Introduction to *Harbours, Bars, Bays and Roads in St George's Channel (1748)* (1987)

WALTERS, G., 'The Morrises and the map of Anglesey' (*Welsh History Rev.*, 5; 1970)

12 ROBINSON, A., 'Murdoch MacKenzie and his Orcades sea atlas' (*Map Collector*, 16; 1981)

13 RITCHIE, G.S., *The Admiralty Chart – British Naval Hydrography in the Nineteenth Century* (1967)

See also

CAMPBELL, T., 'Episodes from the early history of British Admiralty charting' (*Map Collector*, 25; 1983)

14 COLLINS, K. ST B., 'Admiral Sir Francis Beaufort' (*Journ. Inst. Navig.*, 11; 1958)

15 CAMPBELL, T., & DAVID, A., 'Bibliographical notes on nineteenth century British Admiralty charts' (*Map Collector*, 26; 1984)

16 RITCHIE, G.S., 'Early charts of the Buchan coast' (*Trans. Buchan Field Club*, 18, 2; 1972)

17 DE BOER, G., & SKELTON, R.A., 'The earliest English chart with soundings' (*Imago Mundi*, 23; 1969)

18 LOWER, M.A. (ed.), *A Survey of the Coast of Sussex, made in 1587* (1870)

19 CARR, A.P., 'Early maps as historical evidence for coastal change: the growth of Orford Spit: cartographic and historical evidence from the 16th century' (*Geog. Journ.*, 135; 1969)

20 CLARK, E.A.G., *The Ports of the Exe Estuary 1660–1860* (1960; republished 1968)

21 O'NEILL, B.H.ST.J., 'Notes on the fortifications of Kinsale harbour' (*Cork Hist. Soc. Journ.*, 2, 45; 1940)

22 MACDONALD, A., 'Plans of Dover harbour in the sixteenth century' (*Archaeologia Cantiana*, 49; 1937)

23 See: Appendix H: 'The manuscript harbour plans and charts of the military engineer' in A.W.H. Robinson: *Marine Cartography in Britain* (1962)

24 WILLIAMS, A.F., 'Bristol port plans and improvement schemes of the 18th century' (*Trans. Bristol Gloucs. Arch. Soc.*, 81; 1962)

25 KINNIBURGH, I.A.G., 'Greenock. Growth and change in the harbours of the town' (*Scot. Geog. Mag.*, 76; 1960)

Chapter 15: Settlement plans

1 Reproduced in: SALTER, H.E., & COOKE, A.H. (eds), 'Boarstall Cartulary' (*Oxford Hist. Soc.*, 88; 1930)

2 BERESFORD, M.W., 'Fallowfield, Northumberland: an early cartographic representation of a deserted village' (*Medieval Arch.*, 10; 1966)

3 COULL, J.R., *The Evolution of Settlement in the Buchan District of Aberdeenshire since the Late Sixteenth Century: The Evidence from Cartographic Sources and from the 1696 Poll Tax Assessment* (O'Dell Memorial Monograph No. 17; 1984)

4 RAVENHILL, W.L.D., 'Bird's-eye view and bird's-flight view' (*Map Collector*, 35; 1986)

5 BROOKS, N.P., & WHITTINGTON, G., 'Planning and growth in the medieval Scottish burgh: the example of St. Andrews' (*Trans. Inst. Brit. Geogr.*, 2; 1977)
See also:
SMART, R.N., 'The sixteenth century bird's-eye view plan of St. Andrews' (*St Andrews Preservation Trust Annual Report and Year Book*; 1975)

6 AGAS, HOLLAR, & LOGGAN, 'Old plans of Oxford' (*Oxford Hist. Soc.*, 38; 1898)

7 FISHER, J., Introduction to *The A-Z of Elizabethan London* (1979)

8 CLARK, J.W., 'John Hamond's plan of Cambridge, 1592' (*Proc. Camb. Antiq. Soc.*, 7; 1888)

9 WHEATLEY, H.B., 'Notes on Norden and his map of London' (*Lond. Topo. Rec.*, 2; 1903)

10 WILSON, E., 'A Leeds law suit in the 16th century' (*Pubs. Thoresby Soc. Miscellanea*; 1897–99)

11 BERESFORD, M.W., 'Maps and the medieval landscape' (*Antiquity*, 24; 1950)

12 SKELTON, R.A., Introduction to *Civitates Orbis Terrarum 1572–1618* (1965)
See also:
KEUNING, J., 'The "Civitates" of Braun and Hogenberg' (*Imago Mundi*, 7; 1963)

13 SKELTON, R.A., 'Tudor town plans in John Speed's *Theatre*' (*Arch. Journ.*, 106; 1952)

14 LAWRENCE, H., 'Permission to survey' (*Map Collector*, 19; 1982)

15 MACGIOLA PHADRAIG, B., 'Speed's plan of Dublin, 1603' (*Dublin Hist. Rec.*, 10; 1948–9)
See also:
ANDREWS, J.H., 'The oldest map of Dublin' (Proc. Roy. Irish Acad., 83, C; 1983)
BONAR LAW, A., *John Speed maps of Dublin* (Privately published; 1979)

16 See, for example: THORPE, H., 'The City of Lichfield: a study of its growth and function' (*Staffs. Hist. Coll.*; 1950–1)

17 HYDE, R., Introduction to *A Large and Accurate Map of the City of London – John Ogilby and William Morgan: 1676* (1976)

18 HYDE, R, Introduction to *London &c. actually surveyed – including A prospect of London and Westminster – Taken at several Stations to the Southward thereof – William Morgan: 1681/2* (1977)

19 LETHABY, W.R., & JENKYNS, R., 'Hollar's map' (*Lond. Topo. Rec.*, 2; 1903)

20 HYDE, R., Introduction to *The A-Z of Georgian London* (1982)
See also:
DAVIES, A., *The Map of London from 1746 to the Present Day* (1987)
HOWGEGO, J., Introduction to *An Exact Survey of the City's of London Westminster ye Borough of Southwark and the Country near 10 miles around London – John Rocque: 1746*
HOWGEGO, J., Introduction to *A Plan of the Cities of London and Westminster and Borough of Southwark – John Rocque: 1746*
London Topographical Society: *Index to Rocque's Plan of the Cities of London and Westminster and the Borough of Southwark, 1747* (1968)
WHEATLEY, H.B., 'Rocque's plan of London' (*Lond. Topo. Rec.*, 9; 1914)

21 LAXTON, P., Introduction to *The A-Z of Regency London* (1985)

22 ANDREWS, J.H., *Two Maps of Eighteenth Century Dublin and its Surroundings, by John Rocque. Introduction to facsimile reproductions of An Exact Survey of the City and Suburbs of Dublin, 1756, and An Actual Survey of the County of Dublin, 1760* (1977)
See also:
ANDREWS, J.H., 'Putting Georgian Dublin on the map' (*Ireland of the Welcomes*, 27; 1978)
BOWEN, B.P., 'John Rocque's maps of Dublin, 1756–c.1776' (*Dublin Hist. Rec.*, 9; 1947–48)

O'KELLY, F., 'John Rocque on Dublin and Dubliners, 1756' (*Dublin Hist. Rec.*, 1; 1938–9)

23 TOLLITT, S.S., 'William Shakeshaft, land agent' (*Lancs. Rec. Office Rep.*; 1964)

24 WILSON, J.B., 'James Tait's map of Lochmaben, 1786' (*Trans. Dumfriesshire Galloway Nat. Hist. Soc.*, 52; 1976–77)

25 HARLEY, J.B., 'The Ordnance Survey 1: 528 Board of Health plans in Warwickshire 1848–1854' in T.R. Slater & P.J. Jarvis (eds.): *Field and Forest: An Historical Geography of Warwickshire and Worcestershire* (1981)

26 HARLEY, J.B., & MANTERFIELD, J.B., 'The Ordnance Survey 1: 500 plans of Exeter, 1874–1877' (*Devon Cornwall Notes Queries*, 34; 1978)

27 CONZEN, M.R.G., *Alnwick, Northumberland: A Study in Town Plan Analysis* (1960) shows how large-scale maps and plans can be used in a detailed study of town growth.

28 The towns covered by the Ordnance Survey are shown in: ANDREWS, J.H., *History in the Ordnance Maps* (1974) [Ireland], and: HARLEY, J.B., *The Historian's Guide to Ordnance Survey Maps* (1964) [England, Wales, Scotland]

29 DARLINGTON, I., 'Edwin Chadwick and the first large-scale Ordnance Survey of London' (*Trans. Middx. Arch. Soc.*, 22; 1969)

30 HYDE, R.N., 'Notes on a collection of London insurance surveys 1794–1807' (*Journ. Soc. Archivists*, 4; 1970–73)
See also:
HYDE, R.N., 'More early insurance surveys come to light' (*Journ. Soc. Archivists*, 4; 1970–73)

31 LOVEDAY, J., *Loveday's London Waterside Surveys* (1857)

32 ROWLEY, G., *British Fire Insurance Plans* (1984)
See also
GOAD, C.E., 'Insurance plans – a historical sketch' (*Rep. Insurance Inst. Dublin, Session 1895–96*; 1896)
HAYWARD, R.J., 'Chas. E. Goad and fire insurance cartography' (*Assoc. Canadian Map Libraries. Proc. 8th Annual Conference*; 1974)
ROWLEY, G., 'An introduction to British fire insurance plans' (*Map Collector*, 29; 1984)
ROWLEY, G., 'British fire insurance plans: cartography at work' (*Bull. Soc. Univ. Cartographers*, 18; 1984)

33 For details of Sketchley's Birmingham directories, see: WALKER, B., 'Birmingham directories' (*Birm. Arch. Soc. Trans.*, 58; 1937)

34 See, for example:
MELLOR, R.E.H., 'A note on the plan of Aberdeen by John Tallis circa 1852' (*Aberdeen Univ. Rev.*, 48; 1979)

35 COLE, G., & ROPER, J., *Plans of English Towns . . . 1810* (Facs. edn.; 1970)

36 Anon: 'Wood's town atlas' (*Brit. Museum Quart.*, 27; 1963)

37 HYDE, R.N., Introduction to *The A to Z of Victorian London* (1987)

Chapter 16: Specialized urban plans

1 HARVEY, P.D.A., 'A 13th-century plan from Waltham Abbey, Essex' (*Imago Mundi*, 22; 1968)

2 WILLIS, R., 'The architectural history of the conventual buildings of the monastery of Christ Church, Canterbury' (*Archaeologia Cantiana*, 7; 1868)

3 SCHOFIELD, J., (ed.), *The London Surveys of Ralph Treswell* (*Lond. Topo. Soc. Pub.*, 135; 1987). See also: SCHOFIELD, J., 'Ralph Treswell's surveys of London houses, c.1612' in S. Tyacke (ed.): *English Map-Making 1500–1650* (1983)

4 GODFREY, W.H., 'The Clothworkers' Company: book of plans of the Company's property made in 1612' (*Lond. Topo. Rec.*, 18; 1942)

5 WHITTERIDGE, G., 'The Fire of London and St. Bartholomew's Hospital' (*Lond. Topo. Rec.*, 20; 1952)

6 HUNTING, P., 'The survey of Hatton Garden in 1694 by Abraham Arlidge' (*Lond. Topo. Rec.*, 25; 1985)

7 HYDE, R., 'Mapping London's landlords' (*Guildhall Studs. Lond. Hist.*, 1; 1973)

Chapter 17: Other parish plans

1 See, for example: MCNEILL, C., 'Copies of Down Survey maps in private keeping', and Simington, R.C., 'Origin of copies of Down Survey maps; (*Analecta Hibernica*, 8; 1938)

Chapter 18: London and other ward plans

1 HYDE, R., *Ward Maps of the City of London* (*Map Colls. Circle*, 38; 1967)

2 HYDE, R., 'A survey of the City of London re-discovered' (*Journ. Soc. Archivists*, 4; 1970)

Chapter 19: Industrial maps

1 ANDREWS, J.H., 'Christopher Saxton and Belfast Lough' (*Irish Geog.*, 5; 1965)

Chapter 20: Themes and thematic maps

1 CAMPBELL, E.M.T., 'An English philisophico-chorographical chart' (*Imago Mundi*, 6; 1949)

2 EAST, W.G., 'Land utilization in England at the end of the eighteenth century' (*Geog. Journ.*, 89; 1937)

3 HARVEY, J.H., 'The nurseries on Milne's land-use map' (*Trans. Lond. Middx. Arch. Soc.*, 24; 1973)

4 BULL, G.B.G., 'Thomas Milne's land utilisation map of the London area in 1800' (*Geog. Journ.*, 122; 1956)

5 WILLATTS, E.C., 'Middlesex and the London region' (1937). Part 79 of *The Land of Britain*.

6 HARLEY, J.B., *Christopher Greenwood County Map-Maker, and his Worcestershire Map of 1822* (1962)

7 See, for example:
PARRY, M.L., 'The mapping of abandoned farmland in upland Britain; an exploratory survey in south-east Scotland' (*Geog. Journ.*, 142; 1976)

PARRY, M.L., 'The abandonment of upland settlement in southern Scotland' (*Scot. Geog. Mag.*, 92; 1976)

8 HARLEY, J.B., *The Ordnance Survey and Land-Use Mapping* (*Hist. Geog. Res. Ser.*, 2; 1979)

9 See, for example:

HENDERSON, H.C.K., 'Our changing agriculture: the distribution of arable land in the Adur Basin, Sussex, from 1780 to 1931' (*Journ. Min. Agric. Fish.*, 43; 1936)

Other maps constructed from land usage recorded in the Area Books appear in the county memoirs of the Land Utilization Survey: *The Land of Britain*, parts: 63: Derbyshire (1941), 81: Surrey (1941), 83–4: Sussex (1942)

10 COPPOCK, J.T., 'The origin and development of agricultural statistics' in J.T. Coppock & R.H. Best (eds.): *The Changing Use of Land in Britain* (1962)

11 HARVEY, P.D.A., 'An Elizabethan map of manors in North Dorset' (*Brit. Museum Quart.*, 29; 1964–5)

12 STAMP, L.D., *The Land of Britain*. Part 81: Surrey (1941)

13 For a systematic study of land use and enclosure shown on Davis's Oxfordshire, see: LAMBERT, A.M., 'The agriculture of Oxfordshire at the end of the eighteenth century' (*Agric. Hist.*, 29; 1955)

14 COPPOCK, J.T., 'Changes in farm and field boundaries in the nineteenth century' (*Amateur Historian*, 3; 1958)

15 FIELD, J., *Field Names* (1972)

See also:

KERR, B., 'Dorset field names and the agricultural revolution' (*Dorset Nat. Hist. Arch. Soc.*, 82; 1961)

16 EAST, W.G., 'Land utilization in Lanarkshire at the end of the eighteenth century' (*Scot. Geog. Mag.*, 53; 1937)

17 For discussion of the various cartographic applications of statistical data, see:

ROBINSON, A.H., 'The 1837 maps of Henry Drury Harness' (*Geog. Journ.*, 121; 1955)

ROBINSON, A.H., *Early Thematic Mapping in the History of Cartography* (1982)

SMITH, D., 'The social maps of Henry Mayhew' (*Map Collector*, 30; 1985)

18 YATES, E.M., 'Blackpool, A.D. 1533' (*Cart. Journ.*, 127; 1961)

19 For bibliographical details of maps produced for the Boundary Commissions, see:

1832: SMITH, D., *Antique Maps of the British Isles* (1982)

1837; 1867; 1885; 1888: SMITH, D., *Victorian Maps of the British Isles* (1985)

20 The map illustrates C. Russell & H.S. Lewis, *The Jew in London* (1901)

21 REEDER, D.A., Introduction to *Charles Booth's Descriptive Map of London Poverty 1889* (*Lond. Topo. Soc. Pub.*, 130; 1985)

22 HYDE, R., 'Cartographers versus the demon drink' (*Map Collector*, 3; 1978)

For an analysis of public house location using maps, see: HARRISON, B. 'Pubs' in H.J. Dyos & M. Wolff (eds): *The Victorian City* (1973)

23 GILBERT, E.W., 'Pioneer maps of health and disease in England' (*Geog. Journ.*, 124; 1958)

24 HAVERFIELD, F.J, 'The Ordnance maps from the point of view of the antiquities shown on them' (*Geog. Journ.*, 27; 1906)

See also:

PHILLIPS, C.W., 'The Ordnance Survey and archaeology, 1791–1960' (*Geog. Journ.*, 127; 1961)

25 EMERY, F.V., 'Moated settlements in England', in A.R.H. Baker, J.D. Hamshere, & J. Langton (eds.): *Geographical Interpretations of Historical Sources. Readings in Historical Geography* (1970)

26 HARLEY, J.B., 'John Strachey of Somerset: an antiquarian cartographer of the early-eighteenth century' (*Cart. Journ.*, 3; 1966)

27 MACDONALD, G., 'General William Roy and his "Military Antiquities of the Romans in North Britain" ' (*Archaeologia*, 68; 1917)

Select bibliography

The Mapping of Scotland (IVth International Conference on the History of Cartography; 1971)

ANDREWS, J.H., *Irish Maps (Irish Heritage Series*, 18; 1978)

ANDREWS, J.H., 'Local maps and the Irish archivist' (*Bull. Irish. Soc. Archives*, 8; 1978)

ANDREWS, J.H., 'Maps and the Irish local historian' in *Group for the Study of Irish Historic Settlement. Bulletin 6* (1979)

ANDREWS, J.H, *Plantation Acres. An Historical Study of the Irish Land Surveyor* (1985)

BOOTH, J., *Antique Maps of Wales* (1977)

BOOTH, J., *Looking at Old Maps* (1979)

DOUCH, R., 'Geography and the local historian' (*Amateur Historian*, 3; 1958)

FORDHAM, SIR H.G, *John Cary Engraver, Map, Chart and Print-Seller and Globe Maker 1754 to 1835* (1925)

HARRISON, B., 'Reconstituting the medieval landscape', in A. Rogers (ed.): *Group Projects in Local History* (1972)

HISTORICUS, 'Topography and maps' (*Amateur Historian*, 3; 1956–8)

LAMBERT, A.M., 'Early maps and local studies' (*Geography*, 41; 1956)

MACFARLANE, A., HARRISON, S., & JARDINE, D., *Reconstructing Historical Communities* (1977)

SKELTON, R.A., 'Maps and the local historian' (*Middx. Local Hist. Counc. Bull.*, 11; 1961)

SMITH, D., *Antique Maps of the British Isles* (1982)

SMITH, D., *Victorian Maps of the British Isles* (1985)

TOOLEY, R.V., 'Large scale English county maps and plans of cities not printed in atlases', which appeared in the *Map Collector* in parts from 1978 and is listed by county in the 'County Bibliography', notes all types of non-county large-scale maps and plans as 'district maps' for most of the counties covered.

TYACKE, S., & HUDDY, J., *Christopher Saxton and Tudor Map-Making* (Brit. Library Ser., 2; 1980)

County bibliography

See also the *Notes* to *County Maps* for further references.

ENGLAND

Bedfordshire

CHAMBERS, B., *Printed Maps and Town Plans of Bedfordshire 1576–1900* (*Beds. Hist. Rec. Soc.*, 62; 1983)

HOPKINSON, M.F., *Old County Maps of Bedfordshire* (Luton Museum Art Gallery; 1976)

TOOLEY, R.V., 'Large scale English county maps and plans of cities not printed in atlases. Part I. Bedfordshire' (*Map Collector*, 5; 1978)

Berkshire

TOOLEY, R.V., 'Large scale English county maps and plans of cities not printed in atlases. Part 2. Berkshire' (*Map Collector*, 6; 1979)

Buckinghamshire

PRICE, U., 'The maps of Buckinghamshire 1574–1800' (*Recs. Bucks.*, 15; 1947–51)

TOOLEY, R.V., 'Large scale English county maps and plans of cities not printed in atlases. Part 3. Buckinghamshire' (*Map Collector*, 14; 1981)

WYATT, G. (eds. C. BIRCH & J. NUTTALL), *Maps of Bucks* (1978)

Cambridgeshire

FORDHAM, SIR H.G., *Cambridgeshire Maps: A Descriptive Catalogue of the Maps of the County and of the Great Level of the Fens 1579–1900* (1908)

TOOLEY, R.V., 'Large scale English county maps and plans of cities not printed in atlases. Part 4. Cambridgeshire' (*Map Collector*, 15; 1981)

Cheshire

HARLEY, J.B., 'From Saxton to Speed' (*Cheshire Round*, 1; 1966)

HARLEY, J.B., 'Maps of early Georgian Cheshire' (*Cheshire Round*, 1; 1967)

HARLEY, J.B., 'Cheshire maps 1787–1831' (*Cheshire Round*, 1; 1968)

HARRISON, W., 'Early maps of Cheshire' (*Trans. Lancs. Cheshire Antiq. Soc.*, 26; 1908)

MOORE, C., *Old Maps of Cheshire* (Published by the author; 1981)

TOOLEY, R.V., 'Large scale English county maps and plans of cities not printed in atlases. Part 5. Cheshire' (*Map Collector*, 17; 1981)

WHITAKER, H., *A Descriptive List of the Printed Maps of Cheshire, 1577–1900* (*Chetham Soc.*, 106; 1942)

Cornwall

QUIXLEY, R.C.E., *Antique Maps of Cornwall and the Isles of Scilly* (Published by the author; 1966)

TOOLEY, R.V., 'Large scale English county maps and plans of cities not printed in atlases. Part 6. Cornwall' (*Map Collector*, 21; 1982)

Cumberland

CURWEN, J.F., 'The chorography, or a descriptive catalogue of the printed maps of Cumberland and Westmorland' (*Trans. Cumb. Westm. Antiq. Arch. Soc.*, 18; 1918)

TOOLEY, R.V., 'Large scale English county maps and plans of cities not printed in atlases. Part 7. Cumberland' (*Map Collector*, 24; 1983)

Derbyshire

TOOLEY, R.V., 'Large scale English county maps and plans of cities not printed in atlases. Part 8. Derbyshire' (*Map Collector*, 27; 1984)

Devon

TOOLEY, R.V., 'Large scale English county maps and plans of cities not printed in atlases. Part 9. Devonshire' (*Map Collector*, 30; 1985)

Dorset

HOADE, W., 'Antique Dorset maps' (*Dorset. The County Mag.*, 77; 1979)

SUMNER, H., 'Old maps of Hampshire, Dorset and Wilts' (*Proc. Bournemouth Nat. Hist. Soc.*, 11; 1918–19)

TOOLEY, R.V., 'Large scale English county maps and plans of cities not printed in atlases. Part 10. Dorset' (*Map Collector*, 32; 1985)

Durham

MANLEY, G., 'The earliest extant map of the county of Durham' (*Trans. Arch. Antiq. Soc. Durham Northum.*, 82; 1936)

TOOLEY, R.V., 'Large scale English county maps and plans of cities not printed in atlases. Part 11. Durham' (*Map Collector*, 34; 1986)

TURNER, R.M., *Maps of Durham 1576–1872 in the University Library, Durham* (1954)

Essex

EMMISON, F.G., *County Maps of Essex 1576–1852. A Handlist* (1955)

Essex County Council: *The Art of the Map-Maker in Essex 1566–1860* (1947)

HUCK, T.W., 'Some early Essex maps and their makers' (*Essex Rev.*, 18; 1909)

TOOLEY, R.V., 'Large scale English county maps and plans of cities not printed in atlases. Part 12. Essex' (*Map Collector*, 36; 1986)

Gloucestershire

AUSTIN, R., 'Additions to, and notes on the "Descriptive Catalogue of Printed Maps of Gloucestershire 1577–1911" by T. Chubb' (*Trans. Bristol. Gloucs. Arch. Soc.*; 1917)

CHUBB, T., *A Descriptive Catalogue of the Printed Maps of Gloucestershire, 1577–1911* (*Trans. Bristol. Gloucs. Arch. Soc.*, 35; 1913)

TOOLEY, R.V., 'Large scale English county maps and plans of cities not printed in atlases. Part 13. Gloucestershire' (*Map Collector*, 38; 1987)

Hampshire

BOX, E.G., 'Hampshire in early maps and road books' (*Hants. Field Club. Papers Proceedings*, 12; 1931)

LAXTON, P., Introduction to *Two Hundred and Fifty Years of Map-Making in the County of Hampshire* (1976)

SUMNER, H., op. cit. (Dorset)

Hertfordshire

HODSON, D., *The Printed Maps of Hertfordshire, 1577–1900* (1974)

Kent

HEAWOOD, E., 'The earliest known maps of Kent' (*Geog. Journ.*, 92; 1938)

LIVETT, G.M., 'Early Kent maps (sixteenth century)' (*Archaeologia Cantiana*, 49; 1937)

LIVETT, G.M., 'Supplementary notes on early Kent maps' (*Archaeologia Cantiana*, 1; 1938)

WRIGHT, C., *Kent through the Years* (1975)

Lancashire

BAGLEY, J.J., & HODGKISS, A.G., *Lancashire: A History of the County Palatine in Early Maps* (1985)

HARRISON, W., 'Early maps of Lancashire and their makers' (*Trans. Lancs. Cheshire Antiq. Soc.*, 25; 1907)

WHITAKER, H., *A Descriptive List of the Printed Maps of Lancashire, 1577–1900* (*Chetham Soc.*, 101; 1938)

Leicestershire

GIMSON, B.L., & RUSSELL, P., *Leicestershire Maps: A Brief Survey* (1947)

Lincolnshire

GOSHAWK, E., 'Old Lincolnshire maps' (*Lincs. Historian*, 3; 1948)

Monmouthshire

MICHAEL, D.O.M., *The Mapping of Monmouth-Shire* (1985)

Norfolk

CHUBB, T., & STEPHEN, G.H., *A Descriptive List of the Printed Maps of Norfolk, 1574–1916: Descriptive List of Norwich Plans, 1541–1914* (1928)

Northamptonshire

WHITAKER, H., *A Descriptive List of the Printed Maps of Northamptonshire 1576–1900* (*Northants. Rec. Soc. Pub.*, 14; 1948)

Northumberland

WHITAKER, H., *A Descriptive List of the Maps of Northumberland, 1576–1900* (Newcastle-upon-Tyne Soc. Antiqs.; 1949)

Nottinghamshire

WADSWORTH, F.A., 'Nottinghamshire maps of the 16th, 17th and 18th centuries: their makers and engravers' (*Trans. Thoroton Soc.*, 34; 1930)

Shropshire

COWLING, G.C., *A Descriptive List of the Printed Maps of Shropshire A.D. 1577–1900* (1959)

Somerset

CHUBB, T., *A Descriptive List of the Printed Maps of Somersetshire 1575–1914* (Somerset Arch. Nat. Hist. Soc.; 1914)

HARLEY, J.B., & DUNNING, R.W., Introduction to *Somerset Maps. Day & Masters 1782. Greenwood 1982* (*Som. Rec. Soc.*, 76; 1981)

Staffordshire

BURNE, S.A.H., 'Early Staffordshire maps' (*Trans. N. Staffs. Field Club*, 54; 1920); with addenda in vol. 60 (1926)

KING, G.L., *The Printed Maps of Staffordshire 1577–1850* (1982)

Suffolk

Royal Institution of Chartered Surveyors, *Seven Centuries of Surveying in Suffolk* (1954)

SANFORD, W.G., *The Suffolk Scene in Books and Maps* (1951)

Surrey

RAVENHILL, W., Introduction to *Two Hundred and Fifty Years of Map Making in the County of Surrey: 1575–1825* (1974)

Royal Institution of Chartered Surveyors: *The Story of Surrey in Maps* (1956)

SHARP, H.A., *An Historical Catalogue of Surrey Maps* (1929)

Sussex

GERARD, E., 'Notes on some early printed maps of Sussex and their makers' (*Library*, 3; 1915)

GERARD, E., 'Early Sussex maps' (*Sussex County Mag.*, 1928)

KINGSLEY, D., *Printed Maps of Sussex 1575–1900* (1982)

SANFORD, W.G., *The Sussex Scene in Books and Maps* (1951)

Warwickshire

HARVEY, P.D.A., & THORPE, H., *The Printed Maps of Warwickshire, 1576–1900* (1959)

Westmorland

CURWEN, J.F., op. cit. (Cumberland)

Wiltshire

CHUBB, T., 'A descriptive catalogue of the printed maps of Wiltshire from 1576 to the publication of the 25 in. Ordnance Survey, 1855 (*Wilts. Arch. Nat. Hist. Mag.*, 37, 16; 1911)

SUMNER, H., op. cit. (Dorset)

Yorkshire

RAISTRICK, A., *Yorkshire Maps and Map-Makers* (1969)

RAWNSLEY, J.E., *Antique Maps of Yorkshire and Their Makers* (Published by the author; 1970; special edn., 1971)

WHITAKER, H., *A Descriptive List of the Printed Maps of Yorkshire and its Ridings, 1577–1900* (*Yorks. Arch. Soc. Rec. Ser.*, 86; 1933)

WALES

Brecon

LEWIS, M.G., 'The printed maps of Breconshire 1578–1900 in the National Library of Wales' (*Brycheiniog*, 16; 1972)

Cardigan

LEWIS, M.G., 'The printed maps of Cardiganshire 1578–1900, in the National Library of Wales' (*Journ. Card. Antiq. Soc.*, 2, 4; 1955)

Merioneth

LEWIS, M.G., 'The printed maps of Merioneth 1578–1900, in the National Library of Wales' (*Journ. Mer. Hist. Rec. Soc.*, 1, 3; 1951)

Radnor

JONES, I.E., 'The mapping of Radnorshire before the Ordnance Survey' (*Trans. Rad. Soc.*, 47; 1977)

LEWIS, M.G., *The Printed Maps of Radnorshire 1578–1900* (1977)

SCOTLAND

Aberdeen, Banffshire & Kincardineshire

JOHNSTONE, J.F.K., 'Maps' in *A Concise Bibliography of the History, Topography, and Institutions of the Shires of Aberdeen, Banff, and Kincardine* (Aberdeen Univ. Studs., 66; 1914)

WATT, W., 'List of maps of Aberdeen and Banff', in *A History of Aberdeen and Banff* (County Histories of Scotland; 1900)

Caithness

MOWATT, J., 'Old Caithness maps and mapmakers' (*John o' Groats Journ.*; 1938)

MOWAT, J., 'Maps, charts, plans, etc', in *A New Bibliography of the County of Caithness with Notes* (1940)

Dumfries & Galloway

MAXWELL, H.E., 'Principal maps of Dumfrieshire and Galloway' in *A History of Dumfries and Galloway* (County Histories of Scotland; 1896)

MOORE, J.N. 'Additions to *The early printed maps of Dumfriesshire and Galloway*' (*Trans. Dumfriesshire Galloway Nat. Hist. Soc.*, 58, 1983)

STONE, J.C., 'The early printed maps of Dumfriesshire and Galloway' (*Trans, Dumfriesshire Galloway Nat. Hist. Soc.*, 44; 1967)

Fife & Kinross

MACKAY, A.J.G., 'List of maps of Fife and Kinross' in *A History of Fife and Kinross* (County Histories of Scotland; 1896)

Inverness

ANDERSON, P.J., 'Maps and plans' in *A Concise Bibliography of the Printed and Ms. Material on the History, Topography & Institutions of the Burgh, Parish and Shire of Inverness* (Aberdeen Univ. Studs., 73; 1917)

Moray & Nairn

RAMPINI, C., 'List of maps of Moray and Nairn' in *A History of Moray and Nairn* (County Histories of Scotland, 1897)

Peebles, Roxburgh, & Selkirk

DOUGLAS, G., 'List of Maps of Roxburgh, Selkirk and Peebles' in *A History of the Border Counties (Roxburgh, Selkirk, Peebles)* (County Histories of Scotland; 1899)

West Lothian

West Lothian County History Society: *Hand-List of Maps of the County of West Lothian* (c.1966)

IRELAND

Antrim

MORTON, D., 'Some early maps of Co. Antrim' (*Bull. Ulster Place-Name Soc.*, 2; 1954)

Cork

MACCARTHY, C.J.F., 'Notes on maps and plans of Cork interest' (*Cork Hist. Soc. Journ.*, 73; 1968)

Index

Figures in **bold** (**25**) *refer to illustrations.*

Aa, Pierre van der 152
Abbey Wood 180, **95**
Abbey Wood estate 180
Aberdeen 95, 98, 120, 164
Aberdeen University Library 27
Aberdeen, William 33
Aberdeenshire 87, 139
Aberford 51
accuracy of maps: *see:* maps: accuracy
Ackermann, Rudolph **92**
Acland, Dr Henry Wentworth 205
Adair, John 54, 77, 83, 123, 137
Adams, John 113
Adams, John **20**
Adams, Robert 139
Addington Hills Water Works 28
Adlingfleet **34**
administrative maps: *see:* maps: administrative
Admiralty 136, 137ff, 146, **96**
Admiralty Notices to Mariners 139
advertisements 20, 133, 167, 184
Agas, Ralph 33, 36, 146, 151, 152, 154
'Agas' map of London; *see:* London: 'Agas' map
Aghrim, Battle of 94
Agrarian Revolution 46, 124
Ainslie, John 32, **16**, 44, 77, 83, 85, 123, 124, 157
Aire, River **4**, **58**
Airey, John 131f
Albin, John 68
Aldeburgh 95, 139
Alderney 68
All Souls' College, Oxford 27, 39
Allen, Joseph 157
Allen, William 85, 87
Alnwick 164
Ames, Israel 36
Amlwych harbour 141
Amyce, Israel 36
Ancient History of Wiltshire 207f
Anderston 30
André, Peter 84
Andrews, John **36**, 68, 114
Andrews, John; & Dury, Andrew 82, 207
Andrews, John; Dury, Andrew; & Herbert, William 73, 82, 88, **36**, 122, 200, 201
Andrews, Peter **103**
Angell, Samuel; & Meredith, Michael 191
Anglesey 43, 68, 84, 137
Angus 28, 85
Angus District Museums 28
Annandale 91
Annexed estates 43f

antiquities 100, 101, 102, 103, 105, **72**, 197, 204, 205ff
Antiquities of Warwickshire 80, 88, **42**
Antrim 63, 85, 103, 109, 111
apprentices 17, 41
Aram, John 48
Aran Islands 111
Arbroath Museum 28
archaeological maps: *see:* maps: archaeological
archaeological sites 101, 131, 197, 202, 205ff
archaeological societies 27, 28, 205
archaeology 107, 139, 205ff
Archdeacon, Commander W.E. **64**
Archer, John 46
Archer, Mark 197
architectural views **5**, 32ff, 164, 191, **100**
archives 25ff, 91
archways 35, 112
Area Book 54, 105
Arkell, George 204
Arlidge, Abraham 183
Armagh (City of) 95, **47**, 157
Armagh (County of) 73, 83, 88, 103, 109, 111, 157, 201
Armstrong, Andrew 73, 77, 82, 83, 84, 197
Armstrong, Andrew; & Armstrong, Mostyn John 82, 83, 171f
Armstrong, Mostyn John 82, 83, 95, 118
Arrowsmith, Aaron 68, 71
Artillery Ground (Garden) **46**
Arundel Castle 27
Arwystli 54
Ashbourne 36
Ashford 59
Ashstead 57
Assembly Rooms, Leicester **87**
Association of County Archivists 28
Assynt 33
Atcham 148
Athlone 95
Atkinson, Robert **25**
Attingham Park 148
Austen, Sir Robert **17**
authorship of maps: *see:* maps: authorship of
Ayr-Galston Road 148
Ayrshire **16**, 44, 46, 83, 111
Azerley 59, **28**

Back Derwent Street **101**
Backhouse, James 204
Bacon, George Washington 33, 122, 133, 167, 171
Badeslade, Thomas 71
Bainbridge, Thomas **22**
Baines, Edward **32**, 166

Baird, Hugh 124
Baker, Richard Grey 71
Baker, Dr Robert 205
Baker, T. 68, 86
Ballater 44
Bald, William 68, 77, 87, 114
Banagher 88
Banff 87
Bangor **13**
Bangor Borough Council **13**
Bangor, University College 27
Banister, Preston & Alexander 211
Bank House **4**
Bankside 33
Bansted **105**
Bantry Bay 91
Barholm 186
Barnehurst **61**
Barnsdale Toll Bar 32
barony maps: *see:* maps: barony
barrack plans: *see:* maps: barrack
Barretts Green **20**
Barrow Library 25
Bartholomew, John **82**
Bartholomew, John, & Co. 15, 158, 166, 167
Bartlett (or Barthelet), Richard 33, 92, 95, **47**, 98, 113
Barton 52
Bath 120, 127, 151, 157
Bath, Neville 77, 85
battle plans: *see:* maps: battle
Baugh, Robert 73, 77, 84
Bayly, John 80
Beaufort, Daniel Augustus 65
Beaufort, Admiral Sir Francis 137f
Beaurain, Jean, Le Chevalier de 68
Beckenham 48
Bedford, Capt. George Augustus 139
Bedfordshire 63, 73, **35**, 82, 86
Bedfordshire Record Office 41, 56
Beer, Johann Christoph 152
Beighton, Henry 73, 80, 82, 88, **42**, 120, 121
Belfast 26, 28, 95, 106, 157, 158, 162, 178, 203
Belfast Central Library 28
Belfast, Harbour . . . . Improvements Bill 141
Belfast Lough 196
Belfast Riots 95
Belfast Riot Commissioners, Report of 95
Belfast Volunteer Review Ground 95
Bell, John Thomas 197
Bellasis, Sir William 39
Belvedere **94**
Benbecula 68
Bennison, William 157
Bentley, Joseph 166
Benwell, Manor of 197

Berkshire 79, 82, 86, 152
Berwick 91, 92, 97
Berwickshire 83, 85, 87, 111
Bethel Chapel **101**
Bethnal Green 204
Bexley **15**, **17**, **26**, **52**
Bexley Local History Library 25
Bexleyheath Railway **61**
bibliographies 28
Bibliographical Account of the Principal Works relating to English Topography 28
Bibliothèque Nationale 88
bird's-eye views 33, 92, **42**, 94, **47**, 100, 135, 140, **69**, 150ff, **71**, 179
Birmingham 121, 122, 127, 157, 166, 179
Birmingham Canal 26
Birmingham Reference Library 26
Birmingham Street Commissioners 159
Bishop's Hall, Manor of **70**
Black, Adam & Charles 122
Blackadder, John 85
Blackwater estuary 206
Blaeu, Joan 21, 72
Blaeu, Willem 136
Blagrave, John 26, 36, 199
Blake, Sir Francis 123
Blakeney 140
Blomefield, Francis **74**
Board of Agriculture 198, 202
Board of Agriculture and Fisheries **29**
Board of Health 158f
Board of Health plans: *see*: maps: Board of Health
boards of health 26, 158f
Board of Ordnance 66, 91, 92, 98f, 131, 164, 167
Board of Public Works 114
Board of Trade 129
Board of Works, Irish 139
Boarstall 148
Boazio, Baptista 94
Bodleian Library **1**, 27
Bodley, Sir Josiah 17, 88
Bognor Regis 137, 141
Bogs' Commission 71, 114
Bonnie Prince Charlie 91, 167
Books of Reference 17, 35, 46, 105, 106, 112, 125, 190, 201
Booth, Charles **104**, 204f
Bootle 179
border: *see*: maps: border
Borough, William 140
Boroughbridge 123
Botley, Thomas 82
Boughill 51
boundaries 36, 40, 46, 50ff, 88, **41**, 97, 102, 103, 104, 105, 191, 203f
  administrative 77, 105, 110, 197, 203
  barony 72, 103, 204
  borough 203, 204
  civil parish 203, 204
  common 52, 197
  commonty 51
  county 76, 103, 110, 111, 203, 204
  county borough 204
  demesne 204
  detached area 203
  ecclesiastical parish **99**, 204
  enclosure 52, 54
  hundred 72, **36**, 204

farm 46, 59, 63, 100, 201
field **14**, 46, 53, 54, 59, 63, 67, 77, 98, 102, 105, 123, 127, **70**, **83**, 200, 201f
gas company district 197
lathe **36**
land use 200f
municipal 103, 191, 203, 204
open field 52
parish 58, 59, 63, 90, 103, 110, 191, 203, 204
parliamentary 203, 204
petty session 204
poor law union 204
property 43, 56, 59, 63, 97, 103, 151, 154, 165, 179ff, 190
religious 95, 204
rural district 204
sanitary district 159, 204
tenement 40, 103
tithe 59
town 154, 203
townland 41, 43, 63, 102, 103, 106, **97**, 204
urban district 204
vegetation 200f
wapentake 204
ward 191, 203
Boundary Commissions 203
boundary disputes 36, **12**, 38, 46, **41**, 197, 203
boundary plans: *see*: maps: boundary
boundary surveys 40, 43, 203
Bowen, Emanuel 118, 137
Bowen, Emanuel; & Kitchin, Thomas 79, 120, 194
Bowen, Thomas 191
Bowles, Carington 95, 118
Bowles family 157, 173, 202
Bowles, Thomas 157
Bowles & Carver 141
Bowra, John **17**
Boycot, William 38
Bradford, Samuel 157, 166
Bradley, J., & Son **28**
Bradshaw, George 113, 126, 133
Braemar Castle 94
Brampton Place 25
Brasier, William 38
Brassington, Charles 51
Brayley, Edward 37
Braun, George; & Hogenberg, Franz 33, 152, 196
Breaks [The] **4**
Brechin Museum 28
Breconshire 86
Brentford 198
Breton, Mr **2**
Brett, Admiral Sir Piercy 140, 141
Bridge House estates 179
bridges 28f, 35, 69, 105, 112, 113, 114, 118, 120, 123, 124, 125, 129, 131, 141, 203
bridge plans: *see*: maps: bridge
Bridgewater, Duke of 124
bridleways 54, 116
Brighton 94
Brindley, James 126
Bristol 32, 120, 146, 150, 151, 154, 157, 173
Bristol Channel 140, 143
Britannia 117f, 122, 154
British Cyclopaedia of Arts and Sciences 171

British Isles, maps of: *see*: maps: British Isles
British Library 25, 26, 98, 102
British Museum 143
British Railways Board 25
Bromley 48
Brompton **26**
Brooking, Charles 157
Brown, Thomas 120, 173
Browne, Christopher 114
Browne, John 98
Browne, William 179
Bruce, Alexander 139
Brunel University 27
Brunswick Street **101**
Bryant, Andrew 77, 79, 80, 86, 147, 194, 202, 203
Buchan 72, 139, 148
Buckinghamshire 79, 82, 86, **68**, 152
Buckinghamshire Archaeological Society 27
Buckle, Christopher **105**
Bucklersbury **94**
Budgen, Richard 73, 82, 127
Building Control plans 180
building plans: *see*: maps: building
building representation 33, 34, 41f, 46, 59, 61, **37**, 77, **41**, 91, 94, **47**, 98, 100, 101ff, **20**, 112, 117, 123, 125, 127, 136, **81**, 148ff, **83**, **86**, **87**, **91**, 178ff, **92**, **94**, **95**, 190, **100**, 204, 205, **106**, 209
building societies 27
Bullock, Henry **97**
Bull's Cross Farm **2**
Burdett, Peter Perez **3**, 25, 73, 77, 82, 84, 113, 121, 141, 171f, 194, 197, 198, 200, 202
Burghley, Lord 71, 91, 94, 95, 100, 123, 135, 140, 197
'Burghley-Saxton' atlas 100
Burley **18**
Burnett, Gregory; & Scott, William 87
Burrow Island **43**
Burton, Giles 46
Bury St Edmunds 165
Bury Street **99**
Bushey Park 18
Bute Collection of plans 48
Butler, Philip & Richard 85

cab services 122
cadastral maps: *see*: maps: cadastral
cadastral records 113
Caenarvonshire 84
Caesar, Julius; camp of **105**
Cahill, Daniel 77, 85
Calder, River 123
Calvert, Sir Harry 95
Cambridge 151, **71**, 165, 166, 179
Cambridgeshire 62, **33**, 71, 79, 86, 127
Cambridgeshire Record Office 26
Cambridge University 37, **71**
Cambridge University Library 27
camp maps: *see*: maps: camp
Campbell, I.C. 86
Campbell, Serg W. **76**
canal(s) 59, 102, 103, 105, 112, 113, 118, 123ff, 132, 133, 150, 205
  bills 35, 112, 123ff
  'mania' 125, 127
  plans: *see*: maps: canal
Canals and Inland Navigations of the United Kingdom 126

Candell, Francis 140
Canterbury 151, 183, 197
Canterbury Cathedral 25, 179
Canterbury Cathedral Archives 25
Canterbury Record Office 25
Carbery, Barony of **14**
Cardiff 137
Cardigan, Earl of **18**
Cardiganshire 48, 73, 84, 152
'card' revision 103, 111
Carew, Sir George 27, 92, 95
Carlisle 91, 92, 97
Carlow 85, 87, 109, 111
Carr, Richard 113
Carrickfergus 92
'Carrigfoile' castle **44**
Carse Bridge Distillery 194
Carte, Samuel 172
carto-bibliographies 28
cartometric testing 18
cartouche 17, 31f, 34
Carty, John 157
Carver, & Bowles 141
Cary, John 68, 73, 80, 84, 114, 116,
    118, **54**, 125, 126, 127, 133,
    141, 146, 202
*Cary's Actual Survey of the Country
    Fifteen Miles Round London* 118,
    54
Cary's New English Atlas 80, 122
Cary's New Itinerary 118
Cassell & Co. 133
Castlehill 33
Castlemilk 92
castle representation 40, 88, 90, 91ff,
    118, 123, 136, 140, 148, 152,
    197, 205, 209
catalogues 20
    Admiralty 139
    exhibition 28
    library, museum & archive 28
    map-sellers' 28
    Ordnance Survey 106, 164
    sale 26, 180, **93**, **94**, **95**, 184, 194
Catholicism 100, 204
*Catalogue of Maps and other Publications
    of the Ordnance Survey* 107
Caundish, Richard 140
Cavan 88, 109, 111
Cawdor, Lord **45**
Cecil, William; Lord Burghley: *see*:
    Burghley, Lord
Census of Ireland 204
'certificate' maps: *see*: maps: 'certificate'
Certificate of Capital Value 61
Certificate of Redemption of Tithe Rent-
    charge 62
Chadwick, Edwin 204
chainlines 17
Chambers, Francis; & Tress, Richard
    191
Chancery Lane **27**
Channel Islands 68, 92
Chapman, James 68
Chapman, John **2**, 77, 84
Chapman, John; & André, Peter 84
Charles I 95
Charles II 123
Charles Edward, Prince 91, 167
Charterhouse 179
*Charts, Plans . . . published by the
    Admiralty* 139
Chase, William 82
Chauncey, Sir Henry 80

Chelmer and Blackwater Navigation
    123
Chelmsford **70**, 151
Chelsea 183, **99**
Cheltenham 166
Cheltenham Waters and Bilious Diseases
    166
Cheney, Lord 100
Chertsey Abbey 36, **9**
Cheshire **3**, 77, 79, 84, 86, 110, 121,
    194, 197, 198, 200
Chester 152, 157, **79**, **83**, 171f, 175
Chester castle 92, **84**
Chesterfield Public Library 25
Chevalier de Beaurain, Jean: *see*:
    Beaurain, Jean, Le Chevalier de
Chevening Park 121
Chichester 152
cholera 158, 205
Christchurch tithe apportionment 61
Christie, E.F. **2**
Christ's Hospital 179, 180, 183
*Chronicles of England, Scotland, and
    Ireland* 94
Church 37, 62, 180
    Commissioners 25
    of England 57, 183
    of Ireland 27, 63
    property 25, 37, 57, 179
    records: *see*: ecclesiastical records
    representation 7, 40, 59, 71, 88, **36**,
        41, 90, 102, 103, 106, 118, 136,
        139, **65**, 148, 152, **71**, **72**, 154,
        75, 179, 191, **100**, 197, **103**,
        203, 204, 209
    Temporalities Commission 45
City Guilds 37, 180
City Lands Committee 179
Civil War: *see*: war: Civil
Clackmannanshire 85, 87
clan maps: see: maps: clan
Clandeboye **13**
Clandeboye, Lord 40
Clare 85, 88, 109, 111
Clark, W. Tierney **57**
Clarke, J.W. **101**
Clarke, James ('Land Surveyor' of
    Newport, Isle of Wight) 68
Clarke, James ('Land Surveyor' of
    Penrith, Cumberland) 166
Cleer, Thomas 155, 157
Clerke, Thomas 36
Clerkenwell 44, 190
clerks of the peace 51, 112, 178
Cliffe at Hoo 36
Clinker Collection 27
Cloncurry, Baron **21**
Clothworkers' Company 179, 180
Clothworkers' Hall **90**
Clutterbuck, Robert 80
Clyde, River 123, **56**
coaching maps: *see*: maps: coaching
Coalbrookdale 28, 194
coalfields
    Monkland 127
    Northumberland & Durham 127, 197
    Somerset 127
coastal profiles 135f, 154
Cockayne, Thomas; & Newcomen,
    Robert 180
Codsheath Hundred 120, 122
Coffey, James 87
Coke family 37
Cole, Benjamin 191, **100**

Cole, Charles Nalson 71
Cole, G.; & Roper, J. 167
Collins, Capt. Greenvile 136f, 140, 146,
    154
Collins, Henry George 134
colour 17, 21, 35, 42, 46, 48, 53, 59,
    88, 94, 95, 97, 102, 103, 108,
    109, 110, **43**, 131, 132, 148,
    149, 157, 158, 159, 165, 184,
    197, 198, 199, 200, 204, 211
Colt Hoare, Sir Richard 207
Coltman, Nathanial 80
Commercial Road 141
Commissioners for Improving the
    Metropolis 183
Commissioners for Woods and Forests
    201
Commissioners of Sewers 26, 69f, 158
Commissioners of Works 131
Committee of Privy Council for Trade
    126
Committee on Post Office Management
    134
commonty plans: *see*: maps: commonty
Commonwealth **1**, 36
communications' maps: *see*: maps:
    communications
compass charts: *see*: maps: compass
compass indicator 17, 117
Comrie, Alexander **60**
Connaught 40, 72, 98
Consents' Lists 35, 125
contemporary views of maps: *see*: maps:
    contemporary views of
conventional signs 17, 19, 20, 21, 41f,
    46, 58, **31**, 73, 77, 102, 120,
    121, 127, 159, 165, 171, 194,
    196, 197, 199, 200, 201, 202,
    203
Cook, Robert J.; & Hammond **95**
Cooke, John **96**
Cooper, H. 205
'copperplate' map: *see*: London:
    'copperplate' map
copying of maps: *see*: maps: copying
    see also: plagarism
copyright libraries 28
copyright notices 17
Corbridge, James 155, 196
Cork (City of) 154, **73**, 157, 158
Cork (County of) **14**, 72, 85, 98, 111
Cork Harbour **64**, 140
Cornwall 36, 38, 63, 73, 82, 86, 88,
    108, 203
Corporation of London: *see*: London:
    Corporation of
Corshill **16**
Cossins, John **5**
Couchman, Thomas 54
Coughton 148
Couling, William 48
Council of State 140
Counter Bridge 114
country houses: *see*: mansions
county divisions, maps of: *see*: maps:
    county divisions
county maps: *see*: maps: county
Court(s) 51
    of Chancery 50
    of Exchequer 39, 50
    of Session 26, 51
Coutts, James 123
Coventry 121
Cowcaddens 30

Cowpen, Manor of 197
Cowshott, Manor of **19**
Cox, Thomas **33**
Coxe, William 80, 166
Craig, J.M. 194
Cranstoun 148
Crawford, William 85
Crayford **81**
Crayford Creek **57**
Creighton, R. **6**
Crew, Lough 209
Crier Cut Ale House **4**
Crier's Cut **4**
Crimscote 63
criticisms of maps: *see*: maps: criticism
    of
Cromer **72**
Cromwell, Oliver 72f, 92, 100
Crosley, William 79, 84
Crown 36, 38, 43, 50, 51, 92, 131,
    180
Crown Surveyors 37
Croydon
    Board of Health plan 28, 211
    Enclosure **22**
    Tithe commutation **27**
Cruchley, George Frederick 66, 133,
    134
Crutched Friars **94**
Cubitt, Thomas 68
Culloden 98
Cumberland 82, 86, 110
Cumberland, Duke of 98
Cunningham, William 151
Cupar 154
Currabee estate **14**
Cursitors' Hall 179
Customs Service 136
cycling maps: *see*: maps: cycling

Dade, William **25**
Dadford, Thomas 127
Dagenham Breach 71
Darby, Abraham 194
Darbyshire, G.; & Sons **26**
Darent, River 120
Darlington 129
Dartford **57**
Dartford Loop Line Railway **62**
Dashwood, Francis **15**
dating of maps 17, 21, 102ff, 108,
    110, 132, 133, 139, 141, 164
Davies, Benjamin Rees 190
Davis, Richard 73, 84, 171, **86**, 172,
    200, 201
Davis, Thomas 198
Dawson, Robert Kearsley 57f, **32**, 171,
    190, 203
Day, William; & Masters, Charles
    Harcourt 73, **38**, 84, 126
Deanhead 125
decoration 17, 31ff, **5**, **6**, **7**, **8**, 41ff, 79,
    80, 167
dedications 17, 31, 34
deeds, maps in: *see*: maps: [in] deeds
Dee Navigation 123
Dee River 129, 136, 140, 194
Defence, Ministry of 27
demolition statements 35, 129
Denbigh 48, 82, 84, 110
Dent, Richard 190
Denver Sluices 71
depopulated sites 42, 106, 148, **68**,
    205

deposited plans: *see*: maps:
    parliamentary deposited
Derbyshire 82, 86, **102**
Derry: *see*: Londonderry
deserted villages: *see*: depopulated sites
Desmaretz, John **43**, 140, 141
Devon 56, 63, 73, **37**, 82, 86, **48**, 100,
    108, 139, **69**, 171
Devon, Earl of 41
Devonshire, Duke of 42
Dewsbury 152
Dickinson, John 80, 82
Dickinson, Joseph 18
Digges, Thomas 92, 140
diocesan records 61, 179
directories 67, 68, 166
directory maps: *see*: maps: directory
Directory of U.K. Map Collections 28
disease maps: *see*: maps: medical
disputes: *see*: litigation
distortion: *see*: maps: distortion
District Railway 133
dock plans: *see*: maps: harbour
Dogs, Isle of 141, 146
Doonabrooke Parish **97**
Donald, Thomas 82, 139
Donald, Thomas; & Milne, Thomas 84
Doncaster **51**, 116
Donegal 85, 95, 109, 111
Donn, Benjamin 73, **37**, 77, 82, **48**,
    100, 139, 171
Dorset 73, 82, 86
Douglas Navigation 26
Dover 91, 92, **20**, 113, 131, 140
Dover Road Sketch Book 122
Dover, Straits of 137
Dower, John 171
Dowgate Ward **100**
Dowlais Ironworks 26
Dowles 148
Down, County 40, 73, 77, 83, 85, 103,
    109, 111
Downie, Murdo 137
'Down' Survey 33, 40, 63, 72, 88, 90,
    106, 120, **97**, 186, 202, 203
drainage 26, 35, 65, 69f, 97, 114,
    123, 159, 164, 178f, 197, 209
drainage boards 26
drainage commissioners 26
drainage maps: *see*: maps: drainage
dramroads: *see*: tramroads
drawing of maps: *see*: maps: drawing
Dreenagh, Parish of **14**
drink maps: *see*: maps: drink
Drinkwater, John 68
Driver, Abraham & William 54, 201
Drogheda 157, 180
Dromeslawer, Robert 95
Dromiskin 51
Drury, Sir William **94**
Dublin 27, 44, 66, 73, 87, 95, 103,
    106, 146, 152, 154, 157, 158,
    162, 164, 166, 204
Dublin, Archbishop of 27
Dublin Castle 190
Dublin County 51, 63, 73, 77, 83,
    109, 111, 201
Duchy of Cornwall 37
Duchy of Cornwall, Surveyorship of 38
Duchy of Lancaster 36, 37, 38, 131
Duchy of Lancaster Court 36, 50, 123
Dudley 166, 171
Dugdale, Sir William 33, 71, 80, 88,
    42, 120, 148

Dulwich College 180
Dumbarton 124
Dumfries 124
Dumfriesshire 85
Dummer, Edward 141
Dunbartonshire 85, 111
Duncan, William 77, 87
Dundas, General 98
Dundee 164
Dunraven Collection of plans 48
Dunwich 152, **72**
Durham 27, 82, 86, 108, 110, **53**, **59**,
    197
Dury, Andrew 73, 82, 88, **36**, 122,
    171, 200, 201, 202, 207
Dutch War: *see*: war: Dutch
'Duvals' **20**

earthworks 73, 101, 106 148, 202,
    204, 205ff
East Anglia 34, 53, 154
East Greenwich 18
East Horndon 38
East India Docks 141
East Keswick **23**
East Layton 148
East Lothian 83, 85, 87
Eastoft **34**
East Riding **25**, 63, 79, 80, 86
ecclesiastical records 25, 27, 179,
    190
economic maps: *see*: maps: economic
Edgar, William 77, 83, 85, 154
Edgeworth, William 85, 87
Edgeworth, William; & Griffith, Richard
    87
Edinburgh 67, 94, 120, 154, 157, 158,
    88, 171ff, 184, 203
Edinburgh Castle 94
Edinburghshire 111
education maps: *see*: maps: education
Edward IV 139
Edwards, Talbot 141
Eglinton Estate 32, 44
electricity supply 35, 178
Electric Telegraph Company 134
Elford 36
Elizabeth I 40, 72, 92, 140, 199
Ellis, Thomas Joseph 79, 86
Elphinstone, John 77
Ely 71
Ely, Isle of **33**, 71
enclosure 36, **12**, 41ff, 46f, 50ff, 57,
    62, 63, **38**, 77, 97, 98, 105, 117f,
    121, 122, 125, 148, **75**, 200, 201
acts 50f
    General Enclosure Acts 50f
    awards 17, 27, 50ff
    commissioners 50ff
    plans: *see*: maps: enclosure
Enfield, William 68
Enfield Chase **1**
engineering plans: *see*: maps:
    engineering
*English Architecture or the Publick
    Buildings of London and Westminster*
    191
English and Bristol Channels' Ship
    Canal 113
English Channel 91
English Pilot 136
engraving 20, 21, 34, 101, 110, 111,
    136, 137, 141, 151, 157, 158,
    164, 171, 172, 201

Enniskillen 157
Enniskillen Castle 95
Entick, John 191
environs' maps: *see*: maps: environs
Erith **15**, **29**, **55**, 178, **89**, **95**
Erith School Board 205
Erne, River 95
Essex 36, 38, 56, 69, 72, 82, 84, 86,
    108, 110, **57**
Essex – Pembrokeshire line 108
estate(s) 36ff, 62, 65, 76, 126, 184,
    190
    agents 26, 27
    annexed 43f
    church 37, 180
    corporation 180
    Crown 36ff, 51, 180
    forfeited 38ff, 43f
    housing 180, **94**
    plans: *see*: maps: estate
    railway 180
    survey: *see*: survey: estate
    Trinity College 27
estuary charts: *see*: maps: estuary
Europe 92, 134, 135
evaluation of maps: *see*: maps:
    evaluation of
Evans, John 73, 84
Ewell **105**
Exchange, Leicester **87**
excursion maps: *see*: maps: excursion
Exe, River 136, 140, **65**
Exeter 68, **37**, 77, 99, 143, 151, 157,
    162, 164, 166, 171, 178, 179,
    205
Exeter Canal 124
exhibitions 28
Exmouth 140, **65**
Extraordinary Tithe Redemption Act 61
Eyes, John 137, 141
Eyre, Edward John 25
Eyre, Thomas; & Jefferys, Thomas 84

facsimiles 16, 17, 18, 25, **41**, 90, 106,
    150
Faden, William 108, 172
Fairbank, William 50
Fairbank Collection 25f, 27
Falkirk, Battle of 95
Falmouth Haven 92
Fallowfield 148
Famine, in Ireland 45, 51
Fannin, Peter 68
farm plans: *see*: maps: farm
Farrand, William **97**
Farringdon Ward Within 191
Fearon, Samuel; & Eyes, John 137
Feckenham, Manor of 199
Fellows' Library, Winchester College 27
Fens 36, 69f
Fens, maps of: *see*: maps: Fens
Fenton's Coal Staith **4**
Fermanagh 88, 109, 111
ferries 35, 68, 112, 123, **57**, 141, 209
Ferry Bridge 51
field(s) 36ff, **18**, 48, 50, **23**, 52, 53, 59,
    61, 62f, 69, 79, 88, 105, 106, **20**,
    112, 116f, 124, 125, **60**, 140,
    148, **70**, 152, **75**, 201
    boundaries: *see*: boundaries: field
    – name books 45, 101
    notes 20, **15**, 45, 51, 164
    sketches 20, **15**, 45, 164
    systems 46f, 202

Fife 83, 87, 111
Fife, Earl of 44
Figg, William 38
finance of map production 32, 77,
    136
Fineshead Priory 36
Finsbury Fields 33, 196
Finsbury Square **96**
fire insurance plans: *see*: maps: fire
    insurance
Fire of London: *see*: London: Great Fire
First World War 110, 111
Fisher, Son & Co. 133
Fishguard Bay **45**, 95
fishing 34, 137
Five Meadows **2**
Fleet Street **105**
Fletcher, John **102**
Fletcher; & Mills 158
Flint 48, 82, 84, 110
Flitteris Park 202
Fockerby **34**
Folkestone 34
Foot, 29th Regiment of 95
footpaths 53f, 59, 102, 112, 116, **54**,
    121, 124, 125, 131, 148
Foquett, William 68
Ford, Edward **1**, **2**
Forestry Commission 131
Forfar Museum 28
forfeited estates: *see*: estates: forfeited
Forrest, William 77, 85, 200, 202
Fort Augustus 94
Fort George 94
Forth and Clyde Canal **56**, 127
Forth, Firth of 137
Forth Valley 71
fortification plans: *see*: maps:
    fortification
Fort James **43**
Fort William 94
Forty Hall Estate **2**
Forvie, Kirk of 139
Fosse Way 207
Foster, George 82
Fowler, Charles 32, **51**, 116, **106**, 209
Fowler, William 87
'Fowlers' **20**
frame of map: *see*: maps: border
France 94, 95, 98, 136
freehold land societies 27
Freeman, C. 164
'French' school 41f
French Wars: *see*: war(s): Napoleonic
Fryer, John 86
Fulham Road **99**
Furness 137
Fylde 203

Galloway 141
Galston 148
Galway (City of) 154, 157
Galway (County of) 85, 88, 111
Gant, S.C. **77**
Garden, William 77, 85
gardens 59, 68, 102, 105, 106, 152,
    167, 178, 179, 200, 202
gardens, plans of: *see*: maps: garden
Gardner, Thomas 118, **72**
Gardner, William 41, 68, 73, 77, 84,
    99, 201
Gardner, William; & Cubitt, Thomas 68
Garleston Bay 141
Garnett Collection 27

Garristown 51
Garston 158
gas supply 35, 178, 184, 197
Gascoyne, Joel 73, 82, 203
General and Commercial Directory of Leeds
    32
General Turnpike Act 114
General View of the Agriculture of the
    County of Cambridge 127
Gentleman's Magazine 21, 91, 118, **58**,
    127, **69**
geology 139, 197
geological maps: *see*: maps: geological
Geological Survey 27
George III 50
Gibson, John 127, 197
Giles, Netlam & Francis 157
Gill, Valentine 77, 85
Ginver, N. 146
Glamorgan 48, 73, 84, 86, 110
Glamorgan County Record Office 26
Glasgow 30, 66, 157, 166, 171
glebe land 37, 53f
glebe terriers 37, 63
Gloucester 116, 150
Gloucestershire 50, 84, 86, 110
Glover, Moses 88
Goad, Charles E. 25, **81**, **91**, 164ff
Goddard, John; & Chase, William 82
Goddard, John; & Goodman, R. 82
Godfray, Hugh 68
Godmanchester 123
Gogerddan Collection of plans 48
Goldheaters Manor **2**
Gooch, Rev. W. 127
Goodman, R. 82
Goodwick Sands **45**
Goodwin, M.P. 68
Goodwin Sands 140
Goodwood Estates 41
Gordon, Duke of 44
Gordon, James 154
Gordon Riots 95
Gordon, William 73, 82
Gore, John 166
Gore, Johnson 166
Gosport **43**
Gotto, Edward 158
'Gough' map 65, 113
Gough, Richard 21, 73
Graffham House 148
Grafton Flyford 148
Grainger, Thomas 127
Grand Junction Canal Co. 125
grand juries 71, 73, 77, 114, 122
Grand Jury Act 114
Grant, James; of Grant 44
Grantham 171
Grassom, John 85
Gray, Andrew 68
Gray, George Carrington 118
Gream, Thomas 84
Great Britain 65, 77, 101, 110, 112
Greater London Record Office and
    Historic Library 26
Great Fire of London: *see*: London: Fire
    of
Great Level of the Fens 69, 71
Great Western Railway 129
Green, James 113, 125
Green, John 21
Green, William 157, **75**
Greenock 146
Greenwich 27

Greenwood, Christopher 32f, 73, 77, 79, 80, 84, 86, 87, 121, 122, 127, 147, 171, 194, 198, 200, 202, 203
Greenwood, Christopher & John **6**, **39**, 84, 86, 122, 147, 171, **88**
Grenville, Family 148
Grenville, Richard **68**
Griffith, Richard 114
Grimsby 135, 139
ground plans 32, 100, **91**, 151, 152, 179, 180, 190, 205
Guernsey 68, 99
guide books 65, 122, 133, 166
Guide to Knowledge 171
Guildford 165, 184
Guildhall Library 28, 164
Gunton, Nicholas **1**
Guy, 158
Gyfforde, Humphry 123

Habershon & Pite 205
Haddington 111
Haddlesey **58**
Haldenby **34**
Halsey **19**
Hammersmith 61
Hammond; & Cook, Robert J. **95**
Hamond, John 151
Hampshire 82, 84, 86, 99, 110
Hampton Court 41
Hanson, Thomas 157
Hanstown **99**
Harbour Department of the Admiralty 131
Harbour Department of the Board of Trade 131
harbour plans: *see*: maps: harbour
Hardwick, Philip 190
Harewood Common **23**
Harewood, Lord **23**
Harewood, Parish of **23**
Harpsden 26
Harris, G.P. **69**
Hartlepool 95
Harwich 141
Haschenperg, Stefan von 91
Hasted, Edward 88, 120, 122
Hatfield 57
Hatton Garden 183
Havering Palace 179
Hawkhurst **20**
Hawtayne, W.C.C. **55**
Hayward, William 71
Haywood, John 68
Haywood, William 178
Heacham 123
heating schemes 178, 179
Heather, William 136
hedges 52, 54, 59, 67, 105
'Hedingley', Manor of **18**
Hellard, Col. R.C. 140
Helmesden 39
Hennell, Thomas **52**
Hennet, George 86, 113, 194
Henry III 183
Henry IV 139
Henry VIII 91, 92, 136, 140, 143
heraldry 17, 31f, 69
Herbert, William 73, 82, 88, **36**, 122, 200, 201
Hereford 157
Herefordshire 77, 79, 82, 84, 86
Herm 68

Hermannides, Rutger 152
Hereford, Earl of 94, 95
Hertfordshire 38, 72, 79, 80, 82, 86, 110, 120, 201
Hexham, John 71
Hiberniae Delineatio 72
Higham Ferrers 152
highway bills 35
Historical Antiquities of Hertfordshire 80
Historical Inquiries concerning Forests and Forest Laws 65
Historical Tour in Monmouthshire 80, 166
histories 68, 80, 88, 91, 126, 127, 166, 186, 207
History and Antiquities of Holderness **25**
History and Antiquities of the County of Dorset (1774) 80, 166
History and Antiquities of the County of Dorset (1796–1815) 80
History and Antiquities of the County of Essex 88
History and Antiquities of the County of Hertford 80
History and Description of the City of Exeter and its Environs 68
History and Topographical Survey of the County of Kent 88
History of Birmingham 127
History of Enfield **1**
History of Hertfordshire 80
History of Leverpool 166
Hobson, William Colling 86
Hochstetter, Anthony 155, 157
Hodges & Smith 44
Hodgson, Thomas 86
Hodskinson, Joseph 73, 79, 84
Hogenberg, Frans; & Braun George 33, 152, 196
Holbeck **101**
Holdenby 36
Holderness **25**
Holinshed, Raphael 94, 117
Holland 72, 135, 136
Hollar, Wenceslaus 95, 100, 154
Holly Hill House **94**
Holyhead 137
Hombrestone, William 36
Home, John 33, 148
Hondius, Henricus 71
Honourable Artillery Company **46**
Hooker, John 151, 166
Hooton Pagnell 46
Horbury 123
Horner, Thomas 44, 190
Horsey Hill Fort 92
Horwood, Richard 141, 157, 186, 190
hotel representation 102, 106
Hounslow Heath 95
House of Commons 35, 164
House of Lords 35, 112, 164
House of Lords' Record Office 27
house representation 31, 41, **14**, **21**, 66, 71, 73, **37**, 91, 94, **47**, 98, 100, 102ff, 118, **54**, 120, 123, 125, 127, 148, 151, 157, **84**, **86**, **87**, 178, 179, 190, **101**, 197, **103**, 202, 204
Houses of Parliament 164
Hovenden, Warden 39
Howbury Lane **61**
Hubbard, William **57**
Huddart, Capt. James 137
Huggate 53

Hull 33, 91, 92, 139, 179, 205
Hull-Preston line 101, 103, 108, 158
Humber, River 92, 135, 136, 139
Hume, Rev. Abraham 204
hundred maps: *see*: maps: hundred
Hunslet **4**
Hunter, James 157, 175
Huntingdon County Record Office 92
Huntingdonshire 63, **33**, 82, 86
hunting grounds **1**
Hurst **52**
Hurst Beach 136
Hutchings, W.F. 79, 86, 194
Hutchins, John 80, 166
Hutchinson, Philip **102**
Hutton, William 127
Hyde Park Corner 114
Hydrographic Department, Taunton 27, 139
Hydrographic Office 136, 137f
hydrographic survey: *see*: survey: hydrographic

identifications of maps: *see*: maps: identification of
'IM' 100
imprints 17, 103, 107, 111, 139, 164
improvement 21, 26, 32, 41ff, 51, 117, 121, 123, 124, 131, 139, 140f, 146, 158, 171, 172, **88**, 180f, 184, 190, 191
  bills 35, 178
  commissions 26, 178, 180f
  plans: *see*: maps: improvement
Inclesmore 54
Incorporated Society for Promoting Protestant Schools in Ireland 27
Incumbered Estates Court 45
India Docks 141
industrial plans: *see*: maps: industrial
industrial representation 59, 66, **32**, 71, 73, **37**, 77, 79, 104, 105, 112, **54**, 122, 123, 124, 125, **57**, 126, 127, 131, 133, **91**, 154, **75**, 158, 164, 190, 194f, **101**, 198, 203f
Industrial Revolution 63, 124
infield–outfield system 43
Infirmary, Leicester **87**
Inland Revenue Land Valuation Department 106
Innes, John 194
inns: *see*: public house representation
instruments of survey: *see*: survey: instruments
insurance companies 164f
intentions of cartographer 19, 113, 194, 197, 202
Inverness 43, 98, **85**
Ipswich 154
Ireland 27, 33, 38ff, 44ff, 51, 63, 65, 71, 72f, 77, 79, 88, 91, 92ff, 101ff, 113, 114, 120, 122, 132, 133, 135, 136, 137f, 140, 141, 152, 154, 157, 158, 162, 164, 166, 186f, 199, 200, 201, 202, 203, 204, 209
Ireland: escheated counties of 106
Ireland from Maps 16
Irish Board of Works 139
Irish Civil War: *see*: war: Irish Civil
Irish Land Commission 45
Irish Record Commission 190
Irish Survey 103, 158, 190, 204

iron industry 73, 77, 106, 118, **75**, 194, 199
island maps: *see*: maps: island
Islay 68
Isle of Dogs 141, 146
Isle of Ely **34**, 71
Isle of Man 68, 108, 110
Isle of Mull 139
Isle of Wight 65, 68, 99, 102, 136
Isleworth Hundred 87
Islington 190
Italy 91
itinerary maps: *see*: maps: itinerary
Ivye, Paul 92, 95

Jacobite rebellion 43, 92, 94, 95, 98
Jalland, Richard 52
James I 36, 38, 40
James II 92
Jameson, Thomas 166
Jarrold & Sons **72**
Jefferys, Thomas 71, 73, **35**, **37**, 79, 80, 82, 84, 171
Jenkins, Alexander 68
Jenner, Thomas 100
Jersey 65, 68, 99
Jersey, Earls of 148
Jessop, William **58**
Jethou 68
Jobson, Francis 38, 72, 98, 140
Johnson, Isaac 139
Johnson, John 33
Johnson, Rowland 92, 97
Johnston, William & Alexander Keith 184, 203
Justices of the Peace **52**, 117

Keenan, James; & Noble, John 73, 83
Kelsey, Richard 178
Kennedy, Dr 83
Kennington 46, 164
Kensington 41, **99**
Kensington Turnpike Trustees 114
Kent 7, 38, **15**, **17**, 48, 56, **26**, **29**, 63, 72, 82, 84, 86, 92, 98, 99, **36**, **49**, **50**, 106, 108, **52**, 120, **57**, **89**, **94**, **95**, 197
Kentisbury 179
Kerry **42**, 111
Kildare 73, 77, 83, 85, 109, 111
Kildare, Curragh of 95
Kildare, Lord 42
Kilkenny 157, 158
Killarney 65
Kilwinning, Barony of **16**
Kincardineshire 77, 85, 87
King, William 54, 201
Kingsbridge **69**
King's County 73, 88
King's Ditch 179
King's Lynn 123, 205
Kingston-upon-Thames 44, 158
Kinross 83, 87, 111
Kinsale 94, 140
Kinwarton 148
Kirby, John 82
Kirkcudbrightshire 85, 111
Kirklees Hall 28
Kirkstall **18**
Kirkwood, Robert 157
Kitchin, Thomas 118, 120, 194
Knight, Charles 66
Knightlow Hundred **42**
Knight of the Valley 98

Knox, George 77, 85
Knox, James 85, 173

Lairde (or Laud) 43
Lake District 65
Laleham **9**
Laleham, Manor of 38
Lamaby House 25
Lambarde, William 92, 120
Lambert, James **20**
Lambeth Palace **6**
Lammermuir Hills 80
Lanarkshire 77, 83, 85, 111, 171, 200, 202
Lancashire 84, 86, 110, 113, 137, 158, 166, 194, 197, 200
Lancefield, Alfred 184
Landed Estates Court 45
Land Judges' Court 45
landmarks 17, 36, 117f, 135ff, 150
Land Registry 164
Land Registry Series 106
Land's End 137
land use maps: *see*: maps: land use
land use representation 39, 41ff, 53, 54, 56, 59, 61, 63, 65, **31**, 66f, 77, 79, 80, 88, 98, 101ff, 112, 118, 120, 123, 124, 125, **68**, 150, **70**, 152, 154, **81** 165, 198, 199ff, **103**
Land Utilization Survey of Britain 63
Langdon, Thomas 36
Larcom, Thomas 203
Large English Atlas 79, 172, 194
large-scale county maps: *see*: maps: large-scale county
Larkin, William 77, 85, 114
Laoighis 111
Laud (or Lairde) 43
Laurie, John 67, 77, 83, **56**
Laurie, Robert; & Whittle, James 91, **45**, 118, 136
Laurie, Robert Holmes 68
Laveaux, Alexander De 92, **83**, 172, 175
Laxton 59
Lea, Philip 120, 152
Lea, River 123, 141
Leake, John 154
Leamington 159
leases 179f
leases, maps in: *see*: maps: [in] leases
Leaven **25**
Le Chevalier de Beaurain: Beaurain, Jean, Le Chevalier de
Lee, Richard 91, 92, 139
Leeds **5**, 32, 45, 61, **32**, **51**, 116, 129, 152, 157, **80**, 178, **93**, **101**, 204
  Board of Health 205
  Central Library 26
  Race Ground **106**, 209
  town hall 180
Le Feuvre, C. 68
legal authority of maps: *see*: maps: legal authority of
legal disputes: *see*: litigation
Leicester **87**, 54, 172, **87**
Leicestershire 63, 84, 86, 172, 202
Leicestershire County Record Office 51
Leinster 98
Leinster, Duke of 42
Leith 157
Leitrim 85, 109, 111
leisure maps: *see*: maps: leisure
Le Keux, J.H. 152

Leland, John 117
Lempriere, C. 141
Lempriere, Clement 68
Lempriere, Thomas 68
Lendrick, T. 85
Lenney Park Estate **89**
Le Rouge, George Louis 68
lettering 17, 205
Leven, River 124
Lewis, Island of 68, 111
Lewis, Samuel 203
Lewis, Percival 65
libraries 25ff
Liddesdale 91, 95
Liffey, River **67**
Lilly, Christian 141
Limerick 72, 87, 98, 154, 155, 157
Lincoln Archives Office 26
Lincolnshire 53, **33**, 84, 86, 102, 113
Lincolnshire Fens **34**, 71
Lindley, Joseph; & Crosley, William 79, 84
Linenhall Library 26, 28
Linlithgowshire 111, 120
lithography 21, 44, 45, 61, 91, 139, 159, 190
litigation 18, 36, 38, 39, 44, 50, 118, 123, 152, 179, 197, 198, 203
Liverpool 68, 137, 141, 157, 158, 162, 166, 179, 204
  Canal 112
  Corporation 26, 141
  Corporation City Engineer's Dept., Private Streetworks Section 26
  and Manchester Railway 35
Livery Companies 27, 180
Lizard 136
Lizars, William Home **82**
Lizars, W. & D. **82**, 124
Llanaber 54
Llanbedr 54
Llanblethian 61
Llanddwywe 54
Llandrindod Common 205
Llandudno 137
Llanenddwyn 54
Llaniden Parish 48
Lloyd, John 184
local government 26, 158, 171, 180, 190
local history libraries 25
Local Maps of Derbyshire to 1770 28
Lochmaben 158
Loggan, David 95, 166
London **6**, 57, 66, 110, 113, 117, 118, 120, **62**, 131, 132, 136, 146, 164, 166, 178, 179, 183, 184, **96**, 197, 198, 205
  'Agas' map of 151, 196
  Bishop of 125
  City Lands Committee 179
  City of 40, 178, 191
  Commissioners for Improving the Metropolis 183
  Commissioners of Sewers 69, 158, 164, 178
  'copperplate' map of 33, 151, 196
  Corporation of **96**
  County Council, Local Government and Taxation Committee of 205
  docks 141
  environs of **31**, 67, 68, 95, 106, 157, 158, 184, 199, 201
  Fire of 152, 154, 179, 180

maps of 33, 34, 63, **31**, 66, 69, 79,
  95, 97, 118, 123, 141, 152, 157,
  158, 171, 173, 175, **88**, 178,
  186, 190, 199, 201, 203, 204f
Metropolitan Board of Works 197
Ordnance Survey of 66, 157, 164,
  184, 191
parish plans of 28, **98**, **99**
poverty map of **104**, 204f
–Rye Road 118, 120, 122
School Board 66
Wall **55**
ward plans of 191
and Windsor Railway 131
Londonderry (City of) 157, 158, 162
Londonderry (County of) 85, 103, 109,
  111
Londoners 40
London Magazine 191
longevity of maps: *see*: maps: longevity
  of
Longford 85, 88, 109, 111
Long Lane Farm **17**
Lothian, John 173
Lothians 77, 83, 98, 120, 171f
Loughor Parish 194
Louth 73, 77, 83, 85, 109, 111
Loveday, James 164
Luckombe, Philip 67
Luddenden 123
Lurgan 158
Luton 33
Lyne, Richard 151, **71** 179
Lyons, Manor of **21**
Lyons, Daniel & Samuel 143
Lythe, Robert 65, 92, 98

Macaulay, Rev. Kenneth 68
Macaulay, Zachary 131
MacDougall, P.L. 68
Mackay, John 140
Mackenzie, Murdock 137
Mackenzie, Murdock Junior 137, 141
Madden, Edward 46
Maggiola, Visconti 135
*Magna Britannia: being a concise
  topographical account of the several
  counties of Great Britain* 143
*Magna Britannia et Hibernia, Antiqua et
  Nova* **33**
Maire of Bristowe is Kalendar 150
Maitland, William 191
Makins & Thompson **93**
Malden 154
Man, Isle of 68, 108, 110
Manchester 124, 125, 132, 152, 157,
  75, 162
  Carriers Warehouses **91**
  Public Library 26
  Ship Canal Co. **91**
Manning, Richard 41
Manningham 38
Manorial & Tithe Documents Register
  28
manorial courts 50
manouvre maps: *see*: maps: manouvre
mansions 31ff, **10**, **20**, **21**, 66, **36**, **37**,
  79, 88, **41**, 116, 118, **54**, 120,
  171, 179, 197, **103**, 202
manuscript maps: *see*: maps:
  manuscript
maps
  accuracy 15, 17ff, 41ff, 51, 57ff, 63,
  73, 77, 79, 80, 98, 101ff, 113,

114, 116, 117, 118, 120, 121,
  122, 123, 126, 127, 129, 131,
  132, 133, 135, 136, 137, 139,
  143, 146f, 148, 151, 154, 158,
  164, 166, 167, 171, 172f, 179,
  184, 186, 191, 194, 200, 201f,
  203, 207, 211
administrative 67, 186f, 191
'Agas': *see*: London: 'Agas' map
archaeological 205f, **105**
authorship 17, 19, 102, 113
barony 17, 88f, 106
barrack 94, 95
battle **45**, 94f
'blue-back' 136
Board of Health 15, 26, 28, 158ff,
  76, **77**, **78**
border 17, 32, 111, 167
boundary 191, 203f
bridge 114
British Isles 28, 65, 135
building 179
cadastral 18, 57ff, 105, 106, 113,
  200
camp 95
canal **56**, **57**, **58**, 124ff
'certificate' 63
clan 95
coaching 114
commonty 51
'communications' 97, 134
compass 135
contemporary views of 21, 73, 77,
  137
'copperplate': *see*: London:
  'copperplate' map
copying 17, **1**, **2**, 21, 41, 44, 45,
  58f, 61, **29**, 72, 79, **41**, 80, 113,
  117, 118, 122, 126, 127, 133,
  135, 136, 137, 140, 143, 146,
  152f, **72**, 171, 175, 184, **97**, 191,
  203
county 15, 26, **3**, **6**, **7**, 54, 66, 72ff,
  35, **36**, **37**, **38**, **39**, **40**, 111, 113,
  117, 118, 120, 122, 127, 133,
  137, 152, 202
county divisions 88f, **41**, **42**
criticism of 21, 73, 77, 106, 113,
  114, 136, 158
cycling 122
dating: *see*: dating of maps
decoration: *see*: decoration
design 18, 41, 53, 59, 61, 72, 101,
  106, 158, 190, 200
[in] deeds 26, 116
diocesan 27
directory 32, 166
disease: *see*: maps: medical
distortion 17f, 110, 113, 136
dock: *see*: maps: harbour
drainage 34, 35, 69ff, **33**, **34**
drawing 17, 20, 21, 36, 58, 100,
  101f, 131, 151, 201
drink 205
economic 197, 203
education 202, 205
election 197
enclosure 15, 17, 18, 26, 28, 50ff,
  22, **23**, **24**, **25**, 106, 117, 125,
  75, 201, 202, 203, 206
engineering 35, 113, 116, 125, 129,
  141
environs 66ff, **30**, **31**, **32**, 88, 95,
  133, 171, 178

estate 15, 17, 25, 26, 27, 28, 32,
  36ff, **9**, **10**, **11**, **12**, **13**, **14**, **15**,
  16, **17**, **18**, **19**, **20**, **21**, 50f, 56,
  59, 63, 67, 79, 104, 106, 116,
  118, **54**, 121, 122, 124f, 140,
  146, 148, 150, 180, **90**, **93**, **94**,
  95, 184, 186, 194, **101**, 197,
  199, 201, 202, 203, 206
estuary 123, 135, 136, 137, 139,
  140
evaluation of 20, 21, 80, 102, 200,
  203
excursion 122, 133, **84**
farm 27, 36, 43, **17**, 46, 63, 102,
  202
Fens **33**, 71
fire insurance 25, 164ff, **81**, **91**, 180
fortification 27, 33, **43**, **44**, 91ff, **47**,
  139, 140
frame: *see*: maps: border
garden **10**, 41, 46, **20**, 178
geological 27, 197
glebe 63, 179, 184
Great Britain 112, 131, 204
harbour 35, 92, 94, 98, **48**, 123,
  135, 136, 137, **64**, **65**, **66**, **67**,
  139ff
hundred 33, 88, **41**, 120, 148
identification of 17
improvement 26, 35, 41ff, 178ff
industrial 26, 194f, **101**
index 164, 165, 203, 204
island 65f, 68
itinerary 113
land registration 106, 164
land use 63, 199ff
large-scale county 15, 66, 73ff, **35**,
  36, **37**, **38**, **39**, **40**, 72ff, 88, **48**,
  100, 102, 121, 122, 127, 139,
  146f, 157, 171, **86**, **87**, 194, 197,
  200, 202, 203, 205, 207
[in] leases **46**, 179f
legal authority of 18
leisure 124, 205, **105**, **106**
London: *see*: London: maps of
longevity of 20, 72, 120, 133, 136,
  152, 157, 175, **88**
manouvre 95
manuscript 18, 21, 27, 28, 35, 38,
  41, 44, 46, 56, 61, 71, 72, 73,
  77, 80, 88, 91ff, 101f, 103, 112,
  120, 126, 131, 133, 136, 137,
  139, 140f, 143, 151f, 154, 158,
  159, 164, 171, 178, 180, 184,
  186f, 191, 194, 199, 200f, 204
[in] margins 26
marine 15, 17, 27, 34, 92, 135ff,
  64, **65**, **66**, **67**, 150
medical 205
military 15, 27, 91ff, **43**, **44**, **45**, **46**,
  47, **48**, 139, 140f, 150, 152, 199
mineralogical 197f
mining 15, 25, 26, 27, **37**, 197f,
  102
[in] minutes of evidence 35
multi-sheet 21
national 15, 65, 112, 113, 126,
  133, 134
[in] newspapers 133
official 26, 28, 35, 91ff, 113, 126,
  63, 133, 134, 137, 140, 158,
  178, 184, 203, 205
open-field 36, **11**, 41, 46, 63, 105,
  152, 200

Ordnance Survey: *see*: Ordnance Survey maps
orientation 17
parish 26, 28, 46, 53, 56, 62, 63, 102, 104f, 106, 110, 111, 186f, 191, 194
park 41, 202
parliamentary deposited 15, 27, 35, 104, 112, 120, 121, 122, **52**, **55**, 125, 126, 127, **59**, **60**, **61**, 133, 140, 141f, 178, 180f
[in] petitions 35
physical 197
physical characteristics 17
picture 92ff, 140, 201
plantation 40f, 72f, 203
political 197
portolan 135f
postal 27, 114, 134
poverty 204f
pre-enclosure 46, 53, 112
projection 17, 110, 111, **91**
property **2**, 25, 27, 36ff, 56, 112, 122, 129, 179ff
[in] prospectuses 113, 126, 127, 133
provincial 98, 152
public utility 26, 28, 35, 178
purpose 18, 19, 21, 59, 113, 194, 197, 202
quarry **37**, 197f
railway 15, 25, 26, 27, 35, 112, 127ff, **59**, **60**, **61**, **62**, **63**
reduction 17, 21, 54, **25**, **34**, 79, 80, 101ff, 108, 110, 111, 118, 120, 133, 183, 190, 200
regional 65ff, 71, 113, 126, 127, 132, 133, 134, 199
Register House: *see*: Register House plans
reliability 18, 20f, 35, 41f, 46, 50, 53, 56, 58, 68, 72, 73, 77, 79, 80, 88, 98, 104, 113, 117, 120, 122, 126, 127, 129, 131, 132, 133, 134, 139, 140, 141f 146f, 152, 157, 171, 173, 175, 191, 194, 197, 198, 200, 201, 202, 203, 205
religion 27, 95, 179, 204
revision 17, 21, 44, 66, 68, 72, 79, **41**, 98, 101ff, 108, 109, 110, 111, 122, 129, 131, 133, 136, 137, 139, 141, 157, 158, 162, 164, 165, 166, 171ff, 175, 178, 186, 198, 201, 204
riot 95
river 35, 92, 123f
road 35, 54, 113ff, **51**, **52**, **53**, **54**, **55**, **56**, **57**
rundale 51
runrig 43f, **16**, 46, 48, 51
[in] sale catalogues and notices 26, 116, 180, **93**, **94**, **95**, 194, **101**
sanitary 35, 158ff, **76**, **77**, **78**, 178f, 184, 204, 205
scale 17f, 21, 31, 35, 36, 37, 43, 52ff, 57, 58f, 63, 66, 72ff, 88, 91f, 95, 98ff, 101ff, 112, 114, 122ff, 129, 132f, 135ff, 151ff, 178, 179, 190, 191, 198f, 203, 204, 205
'skeleton' 158, 164, 191
settlement 95, 148ff, **68**, **69**, **70**, **71**, **72**, **73**, **74**, **75**, **76**, **77**, **78**, **79**, **80**, **81**, **82**, **83**, **84**, **85**, **86**, **87**, **88**

Sheriff Court: *see*: Sheriff Court plans
social **104**, 197, 204f
soil 198, 202
sources: *see*: sources, acknowledgment of
see: sources, from which maps constructed
see: sources, where maps found
specialised urban 178ff, **89**, **90**, **91**, **92**, **93**, **94**, **95**, **96**
sport 209, **106**
statistical 202f
strip 112, 116ff, 123, 125, 133
symbolism: *see*: symbolism in maps
telegraph 134
tenement 38
terminology: *see*: terminology in maps
thematic 15, 34, 35, 195ff, **102**, **103**, **104**, **105**, **106**
'thumb-nail' **17**, 100
tithe 17, 18, 26, 28, 51, 57ff, **26**, **27**, **28**, **29**, 104, 106, 129, 159, 186, 199, 202, 203, 206
title 31, 133
town 15, 27, 32, 33, 34, **5**, **8**, 66, 67, 72, **37**, 77, 95, **47**, 118, 122, 123, 124, 125, 133, 134, 139, 140, **66**, 150ff, **70**, **71**, **72**, **73**, **74**, **75**, **76**, **77**, **78**, **79**, **80**, **81**, **82**, **83**, **84**, **85**, **86**, **87**, **88**, 178, 184, 191, 196, 203, 205
townland 46
tramroad 35, 127, **59**, 194
tramway 35, 55, 122
transport 35, 112ff, **51**, **52**, **53**, **54**, **55**, **56**, **57**, **58**, **59**, **60**, **61**, **62**, **63**
turnpike 26, 32, 35, 114f, **51**
ward 191
waterway **4**, 35, 92, 123ff, **56**, **57**, **58**
margins, maps in: *see*: maps: [in] margins
marine charts: *see*: maps: marine
Mariners' Mirrour 135
Marlow, James & brother 158
Marsh Lane, Leeds 129
Marshall, Messrs 101
Marshall's Mills' Estate **101**
Martin & Thurgood **95**
Martin, F.O. **26**
Martin, Martin 68
Martyn, Thomas 73, 82, 203
Masters, Charles Harcourt 73, **38**, 84, 126
Mathew, William 152
May, Peter 44
Mayo 77, 87, 88, 111
Mazell, P. **84**
McArthur, James 45
McArthur, John 157
McCrea Family 73, 77
McCrea, William 77, 85
McDougal, Stephen 68
Meath 73, 85, 109, 111
Mechanics Institute **101**
medical maps: *see*: maps: medical
Meisner, Daniel 152
memoirs 20, 101
Mercator, Gerard 65
Mercer, Charles 51
Merchant Taylors School **100**
Meredith, Michael; & Angell, Samuel 191

Merioneth 46, 84
Merit, C. 136
Methwold Warren 33
Metropolitan Board of Works 197
Metropolitan Commission of Sewers: *see*: London: Commissioners of Sewers
Metropolitan Gas Act 178
Middle Level Drain 71
Middlesex **31**, 72, 80, 82, 84, 106, 110, 120, 152, **98**, 198, 200
Middleton, John 198
Middleton Stoney 148
Midford 127
Midlands 53, 63, 102, 126, **102**
Midlothian 43, 77, 83, 85, 87
Mildmay, Sir Thomas **70**
Milford Haven 98, 116, 137
Military Antiquities of the Romans in North Britain 207
military engineers 39f, 91ff
military maps: *see*: maps: military
'Military Survey' of Scotland 79, 98
Millerd, James 32, 154, 173
mills 20, **4**, **9**, 59, **32**, 69, 71, **37**, 77, **41**, 102, 105, 118, **54** 123, 124, 127, 131, 136, 152, **72**, 179, 194, **101**, 196
Mills & Fletcher 158
Milne, Thomas 44, 46, 84, 199, 201
Milton, Thomas **66**
Mincing Lane **90**
mineral lines 127, 194, 197
mineralogical maps: *see*: maps: mineralogical
mineral representation **32**, **42**, 105, 118, 125, 127, 137, 139, 197f, **102**
Mines Record Office 27
mining plans: *see*: maps: mining
mining representation 59, **32**, **73**, **37**, 77, 105, 106, 118, 124, 125, 127, 131, 132, 194, 197f, **102**
Minshull, Samuel 48
Minster Manor 36
minutes of evidence, maps in: *see*: maps: [in] minutes of evidence
Mitchell, T. 87
Mogeely Estate 38
Mogg, Edward 118, 133
Moll, Hermann 120
Monaghan 72, 85, 109, 111
monasteries 36, 37, 113
dissolution of 36
Monkland 127
Monmouth 152
Monmouth-Brecon Canal 127
Monmouthshire 48, 80, 84, 86, 110
Montgomeryshire 84
Montrose Museum 28
Mooney, John 73
Moore, Sir Jonas **33**, 71
Moorfields 33
Moot Hall, Leeds **5**
Morant, Rev. Philip 88
Morden, Robert 114
Morgan, William **8**, 154
Morison, S.N. 87
Morrice, Thomas 166
Morris, Lewis 27, 43, 137, 141
Morris, William 68, 137, 141
Moule, Thomas 33, 167
Mountjoy, Lord; Lord Deputy of Ireland [later Earl of Devonshire] 92, 97

Moxon, Joseph 124, 136
Mudge, William 84, 108
Mull, Isle of 139
multi-sheet maps: *see*: maps: multi-sheet
Municipal Corporations 180
   Act 191
Munster 27, 38, 40, 92, 94, 98, 155
   plantation 40
Murton 39
museums 25ff

Naismith, John 202
Napoleon 91, 95, 99
Napoleonic Wars: *see*: war: Napoleonic
National Army Museum 27
National Coal Board 25, 27
National Library of Ireland 26
National Library of Scotland 26, 28,
   72
National Library of Wales 26, 43, 48,
   61
national maps: *see*: maps: national
National Maritime Museum 27
Nautical Magazine 139
navigable channels 17, 100, 123ff, **56**,
   135ff
navigation bills 35, 112, 123f
Navy Office 123
Neath, Vale of 44
Neath Abbey Iron Co. 26
Needingworth 148
Needles 136
Neville, Arthur 85
Neville, Jacob 73, 83, 200
Nevin Enclosure 50
New and Complete History . . . of London
   191
New and Universal History . . . of London
   191
Newbury 127
Newcastle 95, 140, 143, 152
Newcastle, Earl of 41
Newcastle Trinity House 137
Newcomen, Robert; & Cockayne,
   Thomas 180
New Forest 54, 65, 201
New History of London 191
Newland, William **19**
New Radnor 152f
Newry 157
Newry Castle 92
Nichols, G. 68
Nimmo, Alexander 114, 137
Nine Year's War: *see*: war: Nine Year's
Nith, River 124
Noble, John; & Keenan, James 73, 83
Noorthouck, John 191
Norden, John 38, 46, 72, 80, 88, 117,
   120, 139, 146, 148, 151, 204,
   205
Norden, John Junior 38
Norfolk **33**, 79, 82, 84, 86, 110
Norfolk, Duke of 27
Norie, John William 136
Norman, Robert 139
Norris, Mount 94
Northallerton 123
Northamptonshire 38, **11**, 50, 63, **33**,
   84, 86, 110, 152
North Cray **7**
Northern Rising 97
North of England Institute of Mining &
   Mechanical Engineers 27
North Vist 48, 68

Northumberland 27, 82, 86, 110
Northumberland, Earl of 38, 48
Northumberland & Durham coalfield:
   see: coalfields: Northumberland &
   Durham
Northumberland Record Office 26
North Wales 73, 84
Norwich 151, **72**, **74**, 157, 178, 196,
   205
Norwich Corporation Sewage &
   Irrigation Committee 178
North Yorkshire Moors **12**
Nottingham 52, 54, 162
Nottinghamshire 84, 86, **102**

Oakley; Daniel Smith Son & **89**
O'Brien, Daniel **97**
O'Connell Bridge **67**
O'Dell Collection 27
Offaly 109, 111
Offa's Dyke 73
official plans: *see*: maps: official
Official Post Office Directory of Glasgow
   166
Ogilby, John 54, 72, 80, 113, 117f, **53**,
   120, 121, 122, 154f
Ogilby, John; & Morgan, William 97,
   154
O'Hagan, James 158
Old Byland **12**
Old Thorndon Hall **38**
Oman, William 51
omnibuses 112, 122
O'Neill, Shane 92
open-field maps: *see*: maps: open-field
Orcades: or, a geographic and hydrographic
   survey of the Orkney and Lewis
   Islands 137
Orders-in-Council 204
Ordnance, Board of 66, 91, 92, 98f,
   131, 164, 167
Ordnance Office, Dublin 27
Ordnance, Office, Southampton 27, **29**,
   49, **50**, **63**, **80**
Ordnance Survey 17, 27, 28, 44, 45,
   48, 58, 66, 72, 73, 77, 79, 80,
   88, 90, 95, 101ff, 122, 129, 133,
   139, 140, 147, **76**, 158ff, 190,
   191, 197, 200f, 203, 204, 205,
   208, 211
Ordnance Survey maps 27, 35, 44f,
   98f, 101ff, 122, 129, 133, 135,
   138, 148, 158ff, 171, 178, 191,
   197, 202, 203, 205
   'Administrative Diagrams' 204
   'Index to Tithe Survey' 203
   manuscript drawings 15, 101f, 200,
      201f
   manuscript drawings of Ireland 27,
      101, 102, 200f, 202
   of England & Wales: 1" 66, 80, 99,
      101ff, 108, 137, 146, 200, 201,
      203
   6" 61, 80, 99, **49**, 101ff, 108, 110,
      112, 158, 164, 178, 198, 200ff,
      203, 204, 207
   12" 164
   25" 54, 58, 99, **50**, 101, 104f, 110,
      112, 157, 164, 178, 183, 184,
      200f, 207
   50" 106
   5' **76**, 158f, 164
   10' 158f, 164
   10.56' 99, 159ff, **79**, **80**

   of Ireland: 1" 66, 103f, 109
   6" 66, 99, 101, 102, 103, 109, 111,
      112, 139, 158, 162, 164, 200f,
      202, 203, 204, 207
   12" 158
   20" 158
   24" 158
   25" 103f, 106, 111, 112, 162,
      204, 207
   5' 158, 162, 164
   10.56' 162f
   of Scotland: 1" 103, 109
   6" 103, 109, 111, 158, 164, 198,
      200ff, 207
   25" 111, 200f, 207
   5' 158
   10.56' 159f
   of Channel Islands: 99
Orford 38, 46, 63, 139
Orford Spit 63, 139, 140, 146f
orientation: *see*: maps: orientation
Orkney Islands 68, 137
Ormonde, Duke of [James Butler] 95
Orridge, A.F. 158
Orwell Haven 92
Ouse, River 71, 123, **58**
Ousefleet **34**
Outhett, John 86
Overton, Henry 157
Overton, Philip 82
Oxford 33, 151, 166, 171, **86**, 172,
   205
Oxford Castle 33
Oxfordshire 79, 80, 82, 84, 86, 201
Oxfordshire County Record Office 26
Oxford University 27, 37, 39, **86**

Pacata Hibernia 92, 95
Packe, Christopher 34, 197
Paddington 125
Palmer, Sutton & Robins **94**
panoramas 151
pantograph 44
paper 17, 18
Paris 90
Paris, Matthew [Mathew] 112, 113,
   123
Parish Area Books 201
parish histories 186
parish plans: *see*: maps: parish
parish records 61, 112, 120
Parkgate harbour 137
park plans: *see*: maps: park
parks 41, 48, 66, **32**, **38**, 79, 88, 116,
   54, 126, 148, 197, 198, **103**,
   200, 202
Parliament 35, 37, 50f, 53, 57, 71,
   112, 114, 120, 121, 123, 125,
   127, 131, 133, 141f, 178, 180,
   197, 203
Parliament, Irish 88
parliamentary deposited plans: *see*:
   maps: parliamentary deposited
Parliamentary Rolls 72
Parliament Street, London **55**
Parochial Assessments Act 190
Parr, Richard **31**
Partington, Charles 171
Paterson, Daniel 118
pathways 48, 67, 116
patronage 20, 32, 202
Peeblesshire 77, 83, 111
Pelham, Henry 85
Pelham, Sir William **42**

Pembrokeshire 86, 108, 110, 135, 152
Penge 48
Pennines 53
Penrith 166
Pepys, Samuel 21
Perambulation of Kent 92, 120
Perceval, Sir Philip 40
Perry, George 166
Perspective Views of all the Ancient Churches 191
Perthshire 85
Peterborough 71, 152
Petermann, Augustus 203
Peter of Savoy 183
petitions, maps in: *see*: maps: [in] petitions
Petre, Sir John 38
Petty, Sir William 40f, 72, 88, 114, 186
Philip, George 122, 203
Phillips, John; & Hutchings, W.F. 86
Phillips, Thomas 92f, 95, 98
Phillips, Sir Thomas 40
'Philpotts' 20
Phoenix Fire Office 164
photographic enlargement 106, 162, **94**
photographic reduction 104, 110, 111, 200
photozincography **50** 110, **80**
physical characteristics of maps: *see*: maps: physical characteristics
picture maps: *see*: maps: picture
Piece, Thomas 205
piers 35, 139, 141
Pierse, Samuel 38
Pigot, James 33
Pinnock, William 171
Pirbright **19**
Pirie, Capt. George **67**
Pite & Habershon 205
place-names 48, 61, 71, 72, 73, 79, 88, 98, 101, 102, 103, 104, 107, 135, 148, 154, 172, 198
plagiarism 21, 72, 79, 80, 113, 117, 118, 122, 127, 133, 134, 135, 136, 137, 146, 152f, 157, 158, 167, 171, 184, 191
plantation plans: *see*: maps: plantation
plantation surveys: *see*: survey: plantation
plates
  amendment 17, 21, 111, 157
  damage 21
  wear 21
Plees, William 68
Plot, Robert 80
Plumstead **15**
Plymouth 77, 91, 99, 100, 137, 141, 171
Plymouth Dock 77, **48**
Poker, Mathew 34, 71
Politica-Politica 152
Polygon **83**
Pont, Timothy 21, 33, 72, 120, 139, 148, 205
Pontefract **51**
Poole 140
Poor Law Commissioners 58, 190
Popinjay, Richard 91, 92, 100, 139, 140
Porcupine Inn 118
Portadown 158
Port Nessock 141

portolan charts: *see*: maps: portolan
Port Patrick 141
ports 35, 123, 126, 140, 146, **91**
Portsmouth 91, 92, 100, 140, 141
Portsmouth Dock 92
Portugal 136
Port Yarrock 141
postal maps: *see*: maps: postal
postal system 114
Post Office 106, 114, 118, 134
Post Office Act 114
Post Office Archives 27
Post Office Directory of Edinburgh **82**
Post Office Management, Committee on 134
post office representation 106, 134
Potter, Joshua **24**
Potter, Peter **98**, 190
Poulter, Richard 139
poverty maps: *see*: maps: poverty
prefatory remarks 20
Preston 95, 101, 103, 108, 157, 158
Prestonpans, Battle of 95
Price, Henry 77, 79, 84
Pride, Thomas; & Luckombe, Philip 67
printing 17, 157
Prior, John 73, 84, 172
Privy Council for Trade, Committee of 126
professional papers 20
projections: *see*: maps: projection
property plans: *see*: maps: property
prospects 34
prospectuses 20, 32, 112, 113, 126, 127
prospectuses, maps in: *see*: maps: [in] prospectuses
provincial maps: *see*: maps: provincial
publication of maps 17, 20, 21, 79, 101ff, 108, 109, 110, 111, 141, 158, 164, 190
Public Health Act 159
public house representation **32**, 92, 102, 106, 118, 121, 125, 135, 136, 179, 186, 190, 205
Public Record Office 25, 26, 28, 51, 61, 201
Public Record Office of Northern Ireland 26f, 28
public utilities 26, 178
public utility plans: *see*: maps: public utility
Purfleet **57**
purpose of maps: *see*: maps: purpose

quarry plans: *see*: maps: quarry
Quartermaster General's Office 91
'Quarter-master's Map' 100
Quarter Session records 112, 116, 120
Quarter Sessions 117
quays 35, 141
Queen's County 63, 73, 77, 83, 85
Queen's Head Inn **20**
Quit-Rent Office 190

Radnor 152f
Radnorshire 86, 178
Radstock Branch of the Somersetshire Coal Canal 127
railways 62, 63, 77, 80, 102, 103, 104, 105, 106, 108, 111, 112, 113, 117, 122, 127ff, **59, 60, 61, 62, 63,** 205
  bills 35, 127

companies 62, 112, 125, 127, 131, 132, 180
  'mania' 113, 129
  maps: *see*: maps: railway
Railway Clearing House 131f
Railway Department of Board of Trade 129, 131
Railway Junction Diagrams 131
Raleigh, Sir Walter 38
Ramsey, Abbot of 123
Ramsgate 140
Rathdowne, Barony of **97**
Rattray 140
Raven, Thomas 33, **13**
Ravenserspurn 139
Ravenser Odd 135
Ravenspurgh 139
Ravenspurn 139
Reading 152
reclamation of land 69f, 200, 201
record offices 25ff, 51, 61, 69
reduction of maps: *see*: maps: reduction
Reformation 57
Regent Street 183
regional maps: *see*: maps: regional
Register House plans 26, 28
rehousing statements 35
Reid, Robert 48, 68
reliability of maps: *see*: maps: reliability
relief representation 42f, 73, 90, 97, 98, 102, 103, 105, 108, 109, 110, 111, **36**
religion maps: *see*: maps: religion
Renfrewshire 77, 83, 85, 111
Rennie, John 123, 127, 140, 141
Report of the Commissioners for Improving the Metropolis 183
Report on the Sanitary Condition of the Labouring Population 204
Report to the Committee of the proposed railway from Leeds to Selby 129
Repository of Arts **92**
Returns and Plans of Iron Bridges 129
review grounds 95, **46**
revisions: *see*: maps: revision
Rhodes, Joshua 41
Ricart, Robert 150
Richardson, Thomas (fl.1762–c.1802) 41
Richardson, Thomas (fl.1786–c.1807) 30, 66
Richardson, Thomas; King, William; & Driver, Abraham & William 54, 201
Richmond, Yorkshire **28**
Richmond, Duke of 41
Richmond Palace 41
Richmond, Royal Manor of 41
rights of way 54, 59, 116f
riot maps: *see*: maps: riot
rivers: *see*: waterways
river bills 35, 112
river plans: *see*: maps: river
roads 33, 36ff, 50, 52ff, 59, 63, 69, 71, 72, 73, **37, 38,** 77, 79, 90, 98, 100, 101ff, 109, **36,** 112ff, 125, 126, 139, 140, 167, 171, **88, 101,** 198, **103,** 201, 204
  book 100, 117, **53, 54,** 120, 121, 122
  closure 116f
  diversion 112, 114, **52,** 116f, 118, **61**
  maps: *see*: maps: road

Roberts, Alfred James 61
Roberts, John 48
Roberts, Thomas **87**
Roberts, William **27**
Robertson, James 87
Rochdale Canal 125
Rochester **7**, 38
Rochester Bridge Estate 38
Rochester Bridge Wardens 38
Rocque, John 32, 41f, **31**, 67f, 73, 79,
    82, 83, 95, 100, **154**, 157, 171,
    194, **103**, 199, 200, 201, 202,
    203
Roe, John **21**
Roecliffe **24**
Rogers, John 33, 91, 92, 179
Rolfe, Edmund **1**
Romney Marsh 34, 42, 71
Roper, J.; & Cole, G. 167
Roscommon 87, 88, 111
Rosehearty 98
Ross, Charles 65, 77, 83, 85, 148,
    171, 202
Rotz, Jean 91
Rowe, Robert 80
Roxburghshire 79, 87
Roy, William 92, 94, 95, 98, 100,
    207
Royal Chase 18
Royal Commission on Coast Erosion
    140
Royal Commission on Historical
    Manuscripts 28
Royal English Atlas 80
Royal Exchange **96**
Royal Forest of the Peak 37, 50
Royal Geographical Society 27, 141
Royal Historical Society 28
Royal Irish Academy 27
Royal Military Canal 25
Royal Society **42**
Royal Society of Arts 21, 73
Royal Standard 204
Royal United Services Institution 25
rundale system 51
runrig maps: *see*: maps: runrig
runrig system 43f, **16** 46, 48, 51
Rutland 84, 86, 202
rutters 135
Rye 141
Rye Road 118, 120, 122

sailing directions 17, 135
sale catalogues, maps in: *see*: maps: [in]
    sale catalogues
Salford 157, **75**, 162
Salmon, Nathaniel 80
Salter's Hall **100**
salt production **37**, 198
Salway, Joseph 114
Sampson, Rev. George Vaughan 85
Sanderson, George 86
Sandwich 140
Sanitary Condition of Stourbridge 178
sanitary maps: *see*: maps: sanitary
Sargeint, George **68**
Sark 68
Savoy, Palace of **92**
Savile Family 38
Saxton, Christopher 38, **12**, 48, 65, 72,
    73, 77, 80, 100, 120, 123, 127,
    152, 202
Saxton, Robert 38
Sayer, Robert 157

scale: *see*: maps: scale
Scalé, Bernard 41f, 157, 199, 201
schedules 17, **17**
school representation 204, 205
scientific records 20
Scilly Isles 108, 146
Scobell, R.W. **94**
Scotland 21, 26f, 33, 43f, 46f, 51, 71,
    72ff, 91ff, 101, 106, 108, 109,
    111, 112, 113f, 118f, 135, 136ff,
    152, 157, 158, 162, 166, 167,
    171, 179, 194, 201, 202, 207
Scott, William 87
Scottish Record Office 26, 27, 28
Seale, Sherrard & Browning 46
Second World War 27
Secondaries' ward plans 191
sections 35, 112, 114, 116, 122, 123,
    125, **59**, 131, **91**, 197
Selby **58**, **60**
Select Committee on Woods and Works
    54
Selkirkshire 83, 87
Seller, John 72, 114, 136, 146
Senior, William 41
Senex, John 73, 82, 118
settlement patterns 46ff, 61, 71, 72,
    73, **36**, **37**, 79, 80, **41**, 90, **42**,
    98, 102ff 117, **54**, 126, 132,
    148ff, 179ff, 197, 206
settlement plans: *see*: maps: settlement
Severn, River 28, 32, 116
sewerage 26, 158ff, 178f, 184
Shakeshaft, William 157
Shakespeare's Birthplace Trust 27
Shalford 184
Shapter, Thomas 205
Sharp, Thomas; Greenwood,
    Christopher; & Fowler, William 87
Sheasby, T. 127
Sheffield 27
Sheffield Central Library 26
Sheppey, Isle of 100
Sherborne, Manor of 201
Sheriff Books 72
Sheriff Court plans 26
Sheriff Court records 26, 112
Sherwood Forest 36, 113
Shetland Islands 68, 139
ship representation 34
Shoreham 141
Shouldam 36
Shrewsbury 157
Shropshire 32, 63, 73, 77, 82, 84, 86
Shuldam, Arthur 41
Sidcup **62**
Sidney, Sir Henry 92
signatures 17, 102, 141
silk industry 194
Singer, Joseph 73, 84
Sketchley, James 166
Skinner, Andrew 77, 85, 120
Skinner, Richard 191
Skinner's Hall **100**
Slade Green **61**
Sligo 85, 111
Sloane, John 73
Sloane, Oliver 73, 83
Smart, H. 132
Smeaton, John **34**, 123, 140
Smith, Charles 65, 80, 118
Smith, Charles & Son 88, 184
Smith, Daniel . . . Son & Oakley **89**
Smith, William 72, 117, 120, 151

Smith, W.H. & Son 133
Smith's New English Atlas 80
Smyth, Hugh 178
Smyth, Payler 71
Snell, Robert 80, 84
Snettisham 123
Snow, Dr John 205
social maps: *see*: maps: social
Society for the Diffusion of Useful
    Knowledge 167
Society of Arts: *see*: Royal Society of
    Arts
Society of Friends 204
soil maps: *see*: maps: soil
solicitors 26, 27
Somerset **38**, **39**, 84, 86, 127, 172
Somerset coalfield: *see*: coalfields:
    Somerset
Somersetshire Coal Canal 126, 127
sources, acknowledgment of 21, 166
sources, from which maps constructed
    21, 57, 58, 65, 72, 79, 80, 101ff,
    108, 109, 110, 111, 113, 122,
    129, 133, 135, 136, 146, 152,
    158, 171, 172f, 191, 194, 202
sources, where maps found 25ff
Southampton 34, **76**, 152, 158, **84**
Southampton Improvement
    Commissioners **76**
Southampton Maps 16
South Mimms Manor 33
Southsea 116
South Vist 68
South Wales 48, 116, 127
South Wales Association for the
    Improvement of Roads 114
Southwark **31**
Southwold **72**
South Yorkshire 80, 82
Spain 91, 92, 94, 95, 98, 135, 139,
    140
specialized urban plans: *see*: maps:
    specialized urban
Speculum Britanniae 80, 152
Speed, John 72, 73, 100, 120, 152f,
    73, 205
Spence, Graeme 141
Spencer, Sir John 38
Spithead 136
Spofforth 48
Spurn Head 65, 72, 135, 139f
St Andrews 151, 154
St Augustine's Abbey 36
St Bartholomew's Hospital 27, 180
St George's Channel 137
St George's Hill **105**
St Helens 158
St John, Church of **101**
St John's Wood 186
St Kilda 68
St Luke and Upper Chelsea 99
St Margaret's Parish **99**
St Marylebone Parish **98**, 190
St Michael, Church of **100**
St Michael le Querne Parish 190
St Michael's Hamlet 26, 158
St Paul's Parish 183
St Rollocks **30**
St Stephen, Church of **100**
St Thomas's Hospital 38
Stafford, Sir Thomas 92, 95
Staffordshire 80, 82, 86, 171
Stamford 54
Standidge, W.; & Co. 61

Stanford, Edward 66, 158, 164, 175, 184, 197, 203, 204
Stanhope, Sir Michael 139
Starcross 140
Starling, J.K. 190
stations 112, 129ff, **62**
statistical maps: *see*: maps: statistical
Statute of Bridges 120
Stead, J.W. 68
steam engines 20, 71, 127, 194, **101**
Steel, David 136
Stenning, Alexander 180
Stephenson, George 25, 127, **59**
Stewart, C.E. **55**
Stirlingshire 85, 111
Stobie, James 85
Stobie, Matthew 77, 79, 83
Stockdale, John 84
Stockton 129
Stockton–Darlington Railway 127
Stokes, Gabriel 73, 83
Stoke Town 77, **48**
Stonehenge 208
Stony Binks shoal 135
Stourbridge 178
Stow, John 117, 191
Stow Uplands 80
Strachey, John 172, 207
Strafford, Earl of 40
Strathbogie Estates 46
Strixton 46
Strype, John 191
Stuarts 18, 92
Stukeley, William 71
subscriptions 20, 32, 121, 165, 190
subways 131
Sudbourne 38, 46
Suffolk **33**, 79, 82, 84, 86
Suffolk Fire Office 148
summary terrier **17**, 46
Sunart, Loch 139
Sun Insurance Office 164
Surrey **6**, **19**, **22**, **27**, **31**, 73, 79, 82, 84, 86, 108, 110, 194, **103**, 201, **105**
survey 17, 20f, 44, 46, 80, 113, 164, 202, 203
    barony 88
    boundary 40, 43, 203
    cadastral 57, 72, 201
    canal 113, 123ff
    costs 21, 158, 162, 164
    county 20f, 72ff, 88, 100
    date of 102ff, 108, 110, 164
    enclosure 50ff
    estate 18, 36ff, 79, 104
    estuary 137
    fair copies 20, **15**
    farm 43, **15**, 202
    field notes and sketches 20, **15**, 45, 51, 164
    'French' school: *see*: 'French' school
    hundred **42**
    hydrographic 27, 98, 135ff
    industrial 194
    insurance 164ff
    instructions 20, 57f, 158f, 190
    instruments 20, 41, 77, 100, 117, 136, 137
    marine 27, 98, 135ff
    method 20, 41, 58, 73, 77, 79, 92, 98, 117, 122, 123, 136, 137, 164, 194, 207
    military 27, 91ff

Ordnance Survey 98f, 101ff, 108, 109, 110, 111, 138, 158ff, 200, 201, 203
    plantation 40f, 72f
    Post Office 114
    pre-improvement 41, 43
    property 36ff, 50f, 57ff, 178ff
    purpose 19
    railway 112f, 127ff
    river 123, 137
    road 73, 113ff
    sanitary 158ff, 178f
    settlement 148ff, 178ff
    specifications 20, 57f, 158f, 178, 190
    speed 20, 21, 79, 102, 103, 111, 129, 200, 201
    technical proficiency 20, 41, 46, 58
    theory and practice 20
    tithe 57ff, 158, 190, 202, 203
    town 66, 150ff
    townland 88
    ward 191
    written 36, 39, 179
Surveyor-General 190
surveyors 20, 32, 73, 158, 164, 202, 203
    Admiralty 139
    board of health 158
    county 72ff, 200
    Crown 36
    district 26
    enclosure 50ff
    estate 36ff, 77, 199f, 203
    grand jury 71
    hydrographic 91, 135ff
    land 36, 40, 137, 140, 154, 179, 198
    marine 91, 135ff
    military 27, 39f, 91ff, **83**
    Ordnance 101ff, 167, 204, 205
    plantation 40f
    Post Office 114
    railway 113, 127ff
    road 113ff
    Royal Navy 27
    settlement 148ff
    tithe 57ff, 129
Surveyorship of the Duchy of Cornwall 38
Sussex 38, 73, 77, 82, 84, 86, 108, 116, 139, 152, 201
Sutherland 87
Swaleness 100
Swansea **77**
Swansea Canal 127
Swansea City Record Office 26
Swansea Local Board of Health 26, **77**
Swinden Brook 123
Swire, William; & Hutchings, W.F. 79, 86, 194
symbolism in maps 19, 21
Symonds, John 179
Symonson, Philip **7**, 37f, 72, 106, 120f, 122, 140

Tallis, John 167
Tannee Parish **97**
Tanshelf 38
Tanworth-in-Arden 36, 46
Tate, Charles **34**
Taunt, Henry 124
Taunton 27
Tayler, Jonathan **93**

Taylor, Alexander 77, 85
Taylor, George; & Skinner, Andrew 77, 85, 120
Taylor, Isaac 41, 73, 82, 84, 127, 157
Teal, Jonathan **23**
Teign, River **65**
telegraph maps: *see*: maps: telegraph
Telford, Thomas 113, 123, 125, 141
Tennant, M. 87
Terbutt, C. 26, 158
terminology in maps 19
terriers 37, **17**, **52**, **97**, 46
Thames, River **6**, **8**, **9**, 99, 123, 124, **57**, 136, 137, 164, 199
'Thames' school 136
thematic maps: *see*: maps: thematic
Thomas, George 139
Thomas, John 95
Thomond, Earl of 98
Thompson & Makins **93**
Thompson, F.P. **99**
Thompson, George 178
Thomson, John 80, 148, 167, 194
Thorndon Hall **38**
Thorney, Lordship of **41**
Thornton, William 191
Thorp Hall **4**
'thumb-nail' maps: *see*: maps: 'thumb-nail'
Thurgood & Martin **95**
Thurles 157
tithe(s) 54, 57ff
    Act 58
    altered apportionments 61f, **29**
    applotments 63
    apportionments 57f, 61f
    Certificate of Capital Value 61
    Certificate of Redemption of Tithe Rent-Charge 62
    Commission 57ff
    Commutation Act 57, 61
    Extraordinary Tithe Redemption Act 61
    files 58, 61
    maps: *see*: maps: tithe
    Redemption Commission 61
    schedules 59, 61
    Survey 44, 129, 158
    surveys: *see*: survey: tithe
titles of maps: *see*: maps: title
Todd, R. **33**
Toddington 152
Tomintoul 44
Toms, William Henry 191
Topographical History of Surrey 37
topographies 28, 80, 88, 126, 127, 166, 167, 207
Topsham 140
Tor Point 140
Torquay 140
Tothill Street **95**
Totternhoe 62
Tovey, Abraham; & Ginver, N. 146
Tower of London 92
town development: *see*: urban development
town maps: *see*: maps: town
town planning 62, 166, 173, 180
town records 25f
Towns Improvement Act 158
Toxteth Park 158
trackways 53, 54, 79, 102, 120, 121
Trafford Wharf Road **91**
Tralee 157

tramroad plans: *see*: maps: tramroad
tramroads 112, 127, 194, 197
tramway plans: *see*: maps: tramway
tramways 35, 112, **55**, 122
transcription errors 17, 18, 21, 61
transport 21, 77, 79, 103, 105, 112ff, 165, 178
transport maps: *see*: maps: transport
Transport Trust Library 27
Treasure, J. 166
Treasury 131
Tress, Richard 190
Tress, Richard; & Chambers, Francis 191
Treswell Family 179
Treswell, Ralph 36, **90**
Treviso, Girolamo da 91
Trinity College 27
Trinity College Library 27
Trinity House 136, 137, 141
trolley vehicles 112
trust records 27, 114
Tudors 18, 91, 92, 94, 97, 117, 135, 150ff, 197
Tuke, John **25**, 80, 194
tunnels 35, 112, 125
Tunstall **25**
turnpike(s) 35, 66f, 73, 101, 102, 103, 105, 114f, 118, 121f, 150
  bills 35, 114
  maps: *see*: maps: turnpike
  trusts 112, 114f, 118, 122
Tweed, River 95, 123
Twickenham 198
Twiss, Colonel 98
Tyne & Wear County Council Archives Department 26
Tyne Improvement Commission 26
Tyne, River 136, 197
Tyrone 77, 85, 88, 103, 109, 111
Tyrone, Earl of 40

Ulster 27, 88, 95, **47**, 98, 135
Ulster plantation 40, 98
Ulster plantation commissioners 40
Universal Magazine 118
universities 27, 62
Upchurch Marshes 46
Upcott, William 28
urban development 48, 54, 61, 62, 63, 66f, **30**, **31**, **32**, 68, 69, 101, 104, 108, 118, 122, **62**, 151ff, 162, 164, 166, 171f, **87**, 183, 184, **88**, 199, 204, 205
Urban, Mr 150

Vallancey, Charles 27, 98
Valuation Office 27, 103, 158, 162, 204
Vaughan, Robert **42**
Vertue, George **92**
vestries 50, 186f
Viceregal Commission on Irish Railways **63**
Victoria, Queen 175, 180
vignettes 31ff, **6**, 167, **100**
von Haschenperg, Stefan: *see*: Haschenperg, Stefan von

Wade, General George 98, 120
waggon ways: *see*: tramroads
Waghenaer, Lucas Janszoon 34, 135f, 140
Wakefield **51**

Walbrook Ward **100**
Wales 36, 43, 48, 50, 54, 61, 73, 79, 100, 101ff, 108, 109, 110, 113, 117, 118, 132, 134, 137f, 141, 152, 162, 171, 190, 197, 201f, 204
Walker, James **60**
Walker, John 36, **10**, 38, **70**, 151
Walker, John & Charles 68, 133
Walk Field **2**
Wallace, Rev. James 68
Wallasey 158f
Wallis, John 141
Waltham Abbey 179
Walton-upon-Thames **105**
Wanstead 41
wars 50
  Civil 92, 100, 123
  Dutch 92
  First World 110, 111
  Irish Civil 190
  Napoleonic 48, 50, 91, 95, 99
  Nine Years' 98
  Second World 27
Warburton, John 80, 82, 207
Ward, Marcus 158
ward: plans: *see*: maps: ward
  Secondaries' plans: *see*: Secondaries' ward plans
Warnford 116
Warwick, *The Town Maps of . . . 1610–1851* 16
Warwick Corporation **78**
Warwick Local Board of Health **78**
Warwickshire 33, 50, 73, 82, 84, 86, 88, **42**, 110, 120, 121, 127, 148
Wash 135, 136
Waterford 85, 116, 140, 157
Waterford, River 140
Waterloo Bridge 183
Waterlow & Sons Ltd **55**
Waterman's Hall **100**
watermarks 17
watermills 20, **4**, **9**, 59, **32**, 69, 77, 102, 105, 118, 194
water supply 26, 35, 151, 178f
waterway maps: *see*: maps: waterway
waterways **34**, 71, 77, 90, 92, 103, 105, 112, 114, 123ff, 133
Watson, Col. David 98
Watson, Justly 141
Watt's Dyke 73
Watts, Thomas **41**
Wavertree 158
Wear, River 197
[River] Wear Commission 26
Web, William 152
Weedon Pinckney **11**
Weekly Dispatch 171
Weldon, Robert 127
Weller, Edward 158
Wells, Samuel 71
Wells-next-the-Sea 140
Wensum, River 159, 178
West, R. 191
West Auckland **59**
West Derby 158
Westheath House Estate **95**
West Horndon **10**
West India Docks 141
West Lexham 36
Westley, William 157, 166
West Lothian 83, 85
West March 95

Westmeath 85, 109, 111
Westminster 51, **31**, 123, 152, **95**, **99**
Westminster Palace 27
Westmorland 82, 86, 110
Weston 11
West Riding of Yorkshire **15**, **18**, **28**, 60
Wexford [City of] 157, 158
Wexford [County of] 63, 77, 85, 109
Whatborough 148
Wheatley Hotel 184
Whitby **53**
White, Martin 68
White & Co. **105**
'White Friers Staires' **8**
White Knight 98
Whitgift **34**
Whithorn 141
Whittle, James 91, **45**, 118, 136
Whitworth, Robert **56**, 126
Wicklow 73, 83, 85, 87, **95**, 109, 111
Wigan Record Office 26
Wight, Isle of 65, 68, 99, 102, 136
Wigtownshire 85, 111
Williamite Trustees 40
Williams, William 46, 73, 82
Williamson, James 77, 85
Williamson, Robert 137
Willis, General 95
Wilson, I. 68
Wilson, John 148
Wiltshire 82, 86, 198, 207
Winchester College 27, 179
Windsor 38, 131, 158
Winter, Thomas 43
Wisbech 71, **41**
Wisbech Castle **41**
Wolds 53
Wolverhampton 171
Wood, Basil 73
Wood, John 82, **85**, 171
Woodlesford **4**
Woodlesford Lock **4**
Wood's Town Atlas **85**, 171
Woolcomb's Island 140
woollen industry 194, **101**
Woolwich Dockyard **66**
Wootton Underwood 27, **68**
Worcester 152
Worcestershire 82, 86, 194
working class statements 35
Wormley 179
Worsley, Manor of 124
Wotton, Sir Edward 39
Wren, Matthew 73, 83
Wrest Park 41
Wright, H.C. **15**
Wyatt, S. 146
Wyld, James 68, 131, 133, 134, 157, 184
Wymondham 41

Yarmouth **72**
Yarranton, Andrew 123
Yates, George 73, 84
Yates, William 73, 82, 84, 127, 171, 179, 197, 200
Yeakell, Thomas 41, 73, 77, 84, 201
Yolland, Capt. William **76**
York **25**, 152
Yorkshire 38, **18**, 48, 50, **23**, 53, **24**, **25**, **28**, 63, 72, 79, 80, 82, 84, 86, 110, 113, **53**, **60**, 139, 158, 166, 171, **93**, 194, 207